INSIDERS' GUIDE® SERIES

# INSIDERS' GUIDE® TO
# DENVER

EIGHTH EDITION

## LINDA CASTRONE AND
## JIM CASTRONE

**INSIDERS'** GUIDE®

GUILFORD, CONNECTICUT
AN IMPRINT OF THE GLOBE PEQUOT PRESS

The prices and rates in this guidebook were confirmed at press time. We recommend, however, that you call establishments before traveling to obtain current information.

To buy books in quantity for corporate use or incentives, call **(800) 962–0973** or e-mail **premiums@GlobePequot.com.**

INSIDERS' GUIDE®

Copyright © 2002, 2004, 2005, 2007 Morris Book Publishing, LLC

A previous edition of this book was published by Falcon Publishing, Inc., in 1999.

Text design by LeAnna Weller Smith
Maps by XNR Productions, Inc. © Morris Book Publishing, LLC

ISSN: 1534-2166
ISBN-13: 978-0-7627-4183-0
ISBN-10: 0-7627-4183-X

Manufactured in the United States of America
Eighth Edition/First Printing

# CONTENTS

# CONTENTS

## Directory of Maps

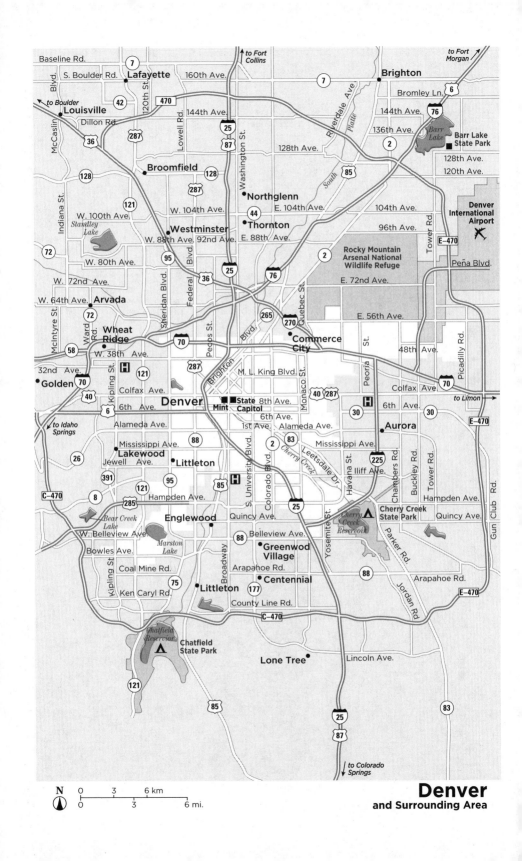

# Denver
and Surrounding Area

# Downtown Denver

Map labels:

CALIFORNIA ST. 700
STOUT ST. 800
CHAMPA ST. 900
CURTIS ST. 1000
ARAPAHOE ST. 1100
LAWRENCE ST. 1200
LARIMER ST. 1300
MARKET ST. 1400
BLAKE ST. 1500
WAZEE ST. 1600
WYNKOOP ST. 1700

287
40
Capitol

LINCOLN ST.
BROADWAY
Denver Pavilions
RTD Light Rail
WELTON ST. 500
Civic Center Park
COURT PL. 300
TREMONT PL. 400
GLENARM PL. 500
Mint
W. 14TH AVE.
Colorado Convention Complex
SPEER BLVD.
Denver Performing Arts Center
13TH ST.
14TH ST.
15TH ST.
16TH ST. MALL
17TH ST.
18TH ST.
19TH ST.
20TH ST.

Coors Field
Tabor Center
Larimer Square
Union Station
CHESTNUT ST.
Cherry Creek
CHOPPER CIR.
ELITCH CIR.
WEWATTA ST.
LITTLE RAVEN ST.
BASSET ST.
Commons Park
Confluence Park
South Platte River
PLATTE ST.
EXIT 212C
EXIT 212AB

Pepsi Center
AURARIA PKWY.
University of Colorado at Denver Auraria Campus
EXIT 210A
25
40 287
EXIT 210B
BRYANT ST.

Six Flags Elitch Gardens
WATER ST.
Downtown Aquarium
Children's Museum
EXIT 211
W. 29TH AVE.
W. 25TH AVE.
W. 23RD AVE.
W. 20TH AVE.
W. 17TH AVE.
CLAY ST.
SPEER BLVD.

INVESCO Field at Mile High

N

0    0.25    0.5 km
0    0.25    0.5 mi.

# PREFACE

Welcome to the Mile High City. Whether you're relocating or just visiting, we're sure you'll love it here. From our sweeping Rocky Mountain vistas to our casual hospitality, Denver is a place rich in history, beauty, and excitement. The *Insiders' Guide to Denver* is designed to help you make the most of your time here.

For starters, chances are good that if you're already in Denver reading this book, the sky will be a startling shade of blue for at least part of the day. The sun shines 300 days a year here, and sunglasses are highly recommended. In fact, bad weather is perhaps the biggest misconception about Denver. Put simply, snowcapped peaks in the Rockies don't mean snow-covered streets in Denver. Sure, we get the occasional blizzard seen on national news, but there's nary a trace after the sun melts it away in a day or so.

Beyond the great climate, Denver is a vibrant, growing city. It's no surprise that Denver was the site of the 1997 Summit of the Eight, which brought together leaders of eight of the world's most economically powerful nations. President Clinton lauded Denver for its thriving economy, warm hospitality, and breathtaking views. Wives of the summit leaders traveled by train to Winter Park Resort to lunch at the mountaintop Sunspot Lodge (you can, too; just check our Ski Country chapter for details). And leaders enjoyed the novelty of Western ways at the famous Fort restaurant in Morrison (check our Restaurants chapter for details). Japan's Prime Minister Ryutaro Hashimoto even donned a new pair of cowboy boots during his trip.

One of the first landmarks many visitors see is Denver International Airport. Beautiful stonework, whimsical art projects, a spectacular tented terminal building, great views of the mountains and the open plains, and a location that provides easy access to Colorado's interstate system are all aspects of Denver's gateway to the rest of the world.

Even die-hard Denver lovers—as we are—find new things to treasure about our city. Our city parks, for instance, are vast expanses of green cut with walking and biking trails and flower beds that are a feast of splendor to stroll amid. If parks are too docile and what you really want is great shopping, you're in luck. Besides the Cherry Creek Shopping Center (which stands as the area's top attraction, surpassing even the Mint, the Coors Brewery, and the Denver museums in tourist draw), Greater Denver has four swanky shopping attractions. Park Meadows, in southeast suburbia (take Interstate 25 south from Denver to the County Line Road exit), opened in August of 1996 to rave reviews and has maintained that positive momentum ever since. FlatIron Crossing opened in 2000 in northwest Denver. Colorado Mills opened in 2002 in the west suburb of Lakewood. And the downtown shopping and entertainment offerings got a much-needed shot in the arm when Denver Pavilions opened in 1998 on the 16th Street Mall. (See our Shopping chapter for more information on all of these venues.)

Denver is also the proud owner of new venues for all its professional sports teams. Coors Field, where Denver's baseball team, the Colorado Rockies, plays, is the oldest of these stadiums, but it still attracts the crowds who have changed the face of Lower Downtown. The glass and steel Pepsi Center, finished in 1999, is the home of the 2001 Stanley Cup champions, the Colorado Avalanche, and Denver's basketball team, the Nuggets. And finally, the Denver Broncos have a new home, INVESCO Field at Mile High. Finished in the fall of 2001, the stadium is worthy of the kind of enthusiasm that makes Denver fans so special.

There are so many things to do in or near downtown these days that boredom is out of the question. Six Flags Elitch Gardens amusement park is located in the once-abandoned Platte Valley area just west of downtown. Brewpubs are a way of life—in or out of baseball season. And Larimer Square (Larimer Street between 14th and 15th Streets downtown) is a year-round destination where visitors can experience Denver's flavor and appreciation for historical buildings and the lore that accompanies them.

Plans are also afoot for more improvements across the metro area. Commons Park (between the South Platte River and Lower Downtown) is the core of urban development in the Platte Valley. It provides plenty of outdoor space to complement the city's crowded streets. Jefferson County continues to add more open space to its mountain parks, and the metropolitan governments continue the expansion of one of the best urban trail systems in the country. If cultural experiences are also your interest, the Denver Art Museum opened the new Frederic C. Hamilton Building in 2006, completing its seven-year, $90.5 million expansion project.

While no book can ever capture everything great about a metropolitan area as diverse as Denver, this one attempts to distill the best of everything into a format that will give newcomers the inside scoop, offer visitors a guide on what to see and experience, and bring even more wisdom to longtime Denverites. So go forth and tour, buy a pair of cowboy boots, picnic in the park, gaze at the mountains from the middle of the city and savor the beauty. When you're done, let us know what you think. Did we leave out your favorite restaurant? Did we neglect to mention some really nifty place to visit, thing to do, or fact worth knowing? Send your comments and suggestions to the following address:

The Globe Pequot Press
Reader Response/Editorial Department
P.O. Box 480
Guilford, CT 06437

Or you may e-mail us at:

editorial@GlobePequot.com

Thanks for your input, and happy travels!

# ACKNOWLEDGMENTS

Two sets of authors preceded us in writing the *Insiders' Guide to Denver*—Bob Ebisch and Laura Caruso, who wrote the original manuscript, then Sally Stich and Jana Miller, who took it through several more editions. By now the book has taken on a life of its own—no longer their work but not entirely ours either. We'd like to thank them for building a strong foundation. Acknowledgments go to Rich Grant, director of the Denver Metro Convention & Visitors Bureau, and Larry Price, former Assistant Managing Editor for Photography at the *Denver Post*.

I'd like to thank my husband, Jim, for teaching me how to share something that has for many years been mine alone. In the process, I also learned that his meticulous editing skills complement my lifelong love for the city in ways that neither of us anticipated.

—Linda Castrone

The first person I want to acknowledge is my wife, Linda, whose consummate professionalism not only allowed us to successfully navigate the land mines of working together, but also taught me the meaning of living with a deadline. I confess to having a favorable bias toward my coauthor, wrought from 30-plus years of marriage. But the truth is that she is a fine journalist, editor, and writer, and working at her side has been a pleasure, an honor, and an education.

I would also like to acknowledge Nicky, who showed loyalty, patience, and ever-present good humor while being my daily canine companion throughout the months of writing this book.

—Jim Castrone

*Denver skyline.* DENVER METRO CONVENTION AND VISITORS BUREAU

# HOW TO USE THIS BOOK

The *Insiders' Guide to Denver* is designed to let you flip easily through the pages to look for something specific or simply find something that catches your eye. For overall subject areas, such as nightlife or shopping, go to the Contents. To find information on specific places, such as the name of a restaurant or a ski resort, consult the Index.

The book is a guide, not a directory. So while we've made sure to include all the leading tourist attractions, restaurants, hotels, and just about every other leading thing in Greater Denver, to a great extent our choices are personal ones. But that's one of the things that makes this guide so valuable. We give honest, knowledgeable Insider-based information on Denver and the surrounding counties of Adams, Arapahoe, Broomfield, Douglas, and Jefferson. Although Boulder is sometimes considered part of the Denver metro area, its offerings are enough to fill a separate book. See our *Insiders' Guide to Boulder and Rocky Mountain National Park*.

Denver, and Colorado's entire Front Range for that matter, is experiencing explosive growth. This has had positive results, such as the blossoming of cultural attractions and job markets. It has negative results, too, such as the impact of a growing population on urban sprawl, increased traffic congestion, and decreased wildlife habitat. But much of what makes people want to move here, or stay here, is intact. The climate is moderate, recreational activities abound, and some of the most beautiful scenery in the country is within a few hours' drive.

As much as this book isn't a directory, neither is it a novel. You don't have to pick it up and read it straight through. Check the Contents and read selectively on a need-to-know or want-to-know basis. Each chapter has its own introduction, so it's clear what's included and how it's organized. However, if you are new to the area, begin by reading through the Area Overview and Getting Here, Getting Around chapters.

This book is meant to be used. Carry it in your backpack, tuck it in the glove box of your car, put one of the kids in charge of carrying it. When you're touring around town and want to know where to stop for lunch, or whether the Denver Zoo is open on Sunday (it is), you'll be glad you have it nearby.

Throughout the book wherever you see an ℹ, you'll find Insiders' Tips, handy hints from those in the know for those who want to be.

Enjoy your stay, whether it be for a few hours or a lifetime.

# AREA OVERVIEW

Let's get one thing straight right away: Denver is not a cow town. Sure, tourism promoters love to emphasize Western lore and you're likely to encounter mounted police on downtown streets, but we don't all wear cowboy hats and keep our horses in the backyard. Some of us do because Denver possesses a strong Western heritage, but we also revel in the city's high-tech economy and upscale, trendy feel.

Denver is today, as it has been for more than 100 years, the largest metropolis between California and Missouri. An expansive self-regard still comes easily to the present inhabitants of Greater Denver, just as it did when the town was being established in the mid-1800s.

The metropolitan area in general is defined by the city and county of Denver and its five suburban counties: Adams, Arapahoe, Broomfield, Douglas, and Jefferson. Boulder County is close by but regarded as having its own identity.

Only about 40 percent of Greater Denver's present citizens were born here. An obvious testimony to their pride—and maybe a little resentment of all the newcomers—is the "Native" bumper sticker visible on cars. The other 60 percent of Greater Denver's residents came here by choice. Some of these may mock the natives' hubris with bumper stickers that are identical except for the disappearance of the "t," but they are no less bullish on the area's attractions and achievements.

Natives and newcomers alike are uneasy about the city's growth, which poses threats to their quality of life with real estate developments that mar views or diminish open spaces. But boosterism runs rampant.

Because of its geographic location near the nation's center, Denver is already a major hub of the railroad, airline, and highway systems. Denver International Airport helped secure the city's potential as a focus of worldwide trade and transportation, playing on its location midway between Munich and Tokyo, Canada and Mexico.

Geography has a lot to do with Denver's historical image of itself at the hinge of the North American continent. No matter where you are in Denver, you have only to look west to see the Rocky Mountains running north and south like a wall dividing west from east. The first slopes of the foothills begin at the edge of Greater Denver. Behind the foothills and front ranges, you can see the gray back ranges rising to the jagged spine of North America, the Continental Divide.

Self-styled since the 1800s as the "Queen City of the Plains," Denver has an urban fabric that extends into the mountains on the west and overlays the first swells of the Great Plains to the east. The mountains are what drew Paleolithic hunters to the sheltering slopes and fertile hunting grounds of the foothills. Between the housing developments of Jefferson County on Denver's southwest fringe, archaeologists have found 10,000-year-old sites where mammoths and camels appear to have been killed by human hunters. Later, modern Indians, principally the Ute, Comanche, Apache, Arapaho, Cheyenne, and Kiowa, gravitated to the area for hunting, trade, and war.

## SETTLING THE LAND

European settlers first came from the south, beginning with Spanish explorers and soldiers in the 1600s. During the next two centuries, a slow movement of mostly agrarian colonists from Mexico and New Mexico gave a distinctly Hispanic culture to the southern part of the state. The city of Pueblo, less than a two-hour drive south of Denver, and all points south were

Mexican territory until the United States grabbed it in the war with Mexico in 1848. As Colorado grew, the ancestors of today's Hispanic citizens generated much of the sweat that built the state's mining, railroads, and agriculture.

Invaders from the east came faster and hit harder. In 1858, little more than 50 years after the first mountain men began trapping furs in the Rockies, a party of prospectors panned gold from the Platte River in what is now the city of Englewood on Denver's southern edge. It wasn't enough to pay each man more than about $10 a day, but it was enough to start the rush.

The history of modern Denver began at the confluence of the South Platte River with tiny Cherry Creek, where cottonwood groves sheltered the camps of Indians and early explorers such as John C. Frémont. By the beginning of 1859, the city of Denver was established at the confluence by friends of James W. Denver, then governor of the Kansas Territory. By the middle of 1859, the cottonwood groves had been axed into oblivion and replaced by some 400 cabins and a lot of bare dirt and mud. Today that area has been revamped into an urban playground where a new breed of pioneer is establishing a creekside neighborhood and where kayakers navigate a fast-running shoot.

## STRIKING GOLD

Gold strikes in the mountains brought not just a growing swarm of fortune seekers from the east but also merchants, industrial entrepreneurs, and other citizens of a real city, including the bad elements in boomtown proportions. Denver had "more brawls, more pistol shots with criminal intent . . . than in any community with equal numbers on Earth," according to Horace Greeley. "Uncle Dick" Wootton, an early merchant, later recalled that "stealing was the only occupation of a considerable portion of the population, who would take anything from a pet calf, or a counterfeit gold dollar, up to a sawmill."

However, as Denver matured to become the capital of the new Colorado Territory in 1867 and capital of the State of Colorado in 1876, it acquired a certain air of refinement. "A shooting affray in the street is as rare as in Liverpool," noted Isabella Bird in 1872, "and one no longer sees men dangling to the lamp posts when one looks out in the morning." Still, she noted, Denver was not a very pretty sight. It was a city that "lay spread out, brown and treeless, upon the brown and treeless plain, which seemed to nourish nothing but wormwood and the Spanish bayonet."

The kind of money needed to polish the city's rough edges was soon to come from Colorado's growing cattle, mining, railroad, steel, banking, and other industries. Journalistic accounts of the time were still filled with news about gambling houses and painted ladies. Yet a new class of aristocrats began decorating Denver's Capitol Hill neighborhood with mansions that have now become tourist destinations. Silver strikes in the mountains in the late 1870s caused another mining boom that poured money into the city until the silver market collapsed in 1893 and threw Denver into a depression. But more gold strikes in the mountains, along with the growth of Colorado's agriculture and manufacturing industries, brought Denver citizens into the 20th century, making them more given to creating parks than cavorting in bawdy houses.

Still, the Queen City of the Plains was more plain than queenly, as one visitor put it. Major credit for making the queen look like a lady generally goes to Mayor Robert Speer, who pursued his dream of a "City Beautiful" during the first two decades of the 20th century by creating parks both in the city and the mountains. He is also credited with laying hundreds of miles of sewers and paved streets, turning Cherry Creek from a garbage dump into the centerpiece of what is today Speer Boulevard, planting thousands of trees, and promoting other projects that culminated in the Denver Civic Center, which was completed nearly two decades after his 1918 death. The Civic Center today is a popular park located

In 1873 British traveler Isabella Bird spent some time in Denver and other areas of Colorado. Her account of her travels, *A Lady's Life in the Rocky Mountains,* is still in print today and easy to find at Denver bookstores and libraries.

Isabella was an intrepid traveler and a keen observer. She came to town after spending a summer in Estes Park, a summer that included a dramatic climb up 14,255-foot-high Longs Peak in what is now Rocky Mountain National Park. The peak had been scaled for the first time only five years before Isabella was hauled up it by a true character named Rocky Mountain Jim. Isabella missed being the first woman to stand on its summit by about three weeks. American writer and orator Anna Dickinson got credit for that.

Isabella was surprised by Denver, which she called a "great, braggart city." Here, as recounted with permission from the biography *Amazing Traveler: Isabella*

*Bird,* is her description of the streets of Denver: "Hunters and trappers in buckskin clothing; men of the Plains with belts and revolvers, in great blue cloaks, relics of the war; horsemen in fur coats and caps and buffalo-hide boots with the hair outside; Broadway dandies in light kid gloves; rich English sporting tourists, clean, comely and supercilious-looking; and hundreds of Indians on their small ponies, the men wearing buckskin suits sewn with beads, and red blankets, with faces painted vermilion, and hair hanging lank and straight, and squaws much bundled up riding astride with furs over their saddles."

Readers interested in learning more about Isabella Bird and her adventures are directed to *A Lady's Life in the Rocky Mountains* by Isabella Bird and *Amazing Traveler: Isabella Bird* by Boulder author Evelyn Kaye (Blue Panda Publications, 1999).

between the magnificent capitol and city and county buildings downtown.

## WAR SPURS GROWTH

Despite the Great Depression, Denver's population grew by more than 50 percent between 1910 and 1940. World War II initiated the area's greatest surge of growth when fear of attack on the nation's coasts transformed the area into a center of military and other government functions. Within a year after Pearl Harbor, major employment bases appeared in

facilities such as the Denver Federal Center, the Rocky Mountain Arsenal, and the Fitzsimons Army Medical Center. Those who came for war-related opportunities stayed on when the war was done, and Greater Denver now contains some 50 percent of Colorado's population.

## OPTIMISM AND DIVERSIFICATION

Since World War II the local economy has had its ups and downs, but Greater Denver has never lost that growth momentum. The latest slump came in 2002 as Denver experienced the same recession felt throughout the country in addition to a bust in the telecommunications industry. Before that, the city's economy had been booming since the oil bust of the 1980s. Even so, optimism is visible in unprecedented spending on transportation infrastructure, including Denver International Airport, a major expansion and installation of light-rail lanes along Interstate 25 (the project is nicknamed T-Rex), and an even more ambitions light-rail project nicknamed FasTracks.

In many ways Denver is still reinventing itself. More than $6 billion was spent on public projects during the 1990s, and another $1.5 billion has been committed to new projects. Among them is a $300 million expansion of the Colorado Convention Center, doubling the size of the building. In 1990 came the opening of Cherry Creek Shopping Center, Greater Denver's prestigious retail mall that boasts the state's first Saks Fifth Avenue and Neiman Marcus stores. Upscale retail got another giant boost in 1996 when Park Meadows opened on the southern edge of town, in 1998 when Denver Pavilions arrived on the downtown scene, in 2000 when FlatIron Crossing opened in northwest Denver, and again in 2002 when Colorado Mills opened in Lakewood. Among the newest additions to Denver retail is NorthField at Stapleton, a 1.2-million-square-foot lifestyle, entertainment, and retail center located just north of Interstate 70 at Quebec Street. Early tenants include Bass Pro Shops, SuperTarget, Circuit City, a Harkins 18-screen theater, and Macy's.

Perhaps nowhere is revitalization more evident than in the area known as the Central Platte Valley, where the city began around the confluence of the South Platte River and Cherry Creek. As the railroads arrived in the 1870s and Denver grew up and outward, the Central Platte Valley became the rail and warehousing district. By the 1980s the Central Platte Valley had become an urban wasteland, with a smattering of businesses in old buildings and a lot of trash-strewn vacant fields criss-crossed by railroad tracks. Now the area is rebounding as the focal point of the new Denver. City planners envision a planned community of green spaces and residential, retail, office, and entertainment developments. Much of the vision is under way, led by the early developments of a few anchor projects. In 1995 the 50,000-seat Coors Field opened on the edge of the Central Platte Valley as home for Denver's major-league baseball team, the Colorado Rockies. Just a half-mile southwest down the valley, Six Flags Elitch Gardens, Denver's premier amusement park, opened its 60 acres of fun in 1995 after a move from the city's far west side, where it had been located since 1890. Across the South Platte River from Six Flags Elitch Gardens is the $67-million Downtown Aquarium, and in 2001 the redevelopment of Denver's Central Platte Valley was kickstarted with the construction of Commons Park, the focal point of a new residential complex.

Lower Downtown, the turn-of-the-20th-century redbrick business and warehousing district along the valley's edge, rebounded ahead of the Central Platte Valley. Since Coors Field opened in 1995, it has become a renovated historic district of restaurants, brewpubs, prestigious offices, condominiums, and lofts around Denver's historic railroad terminal, Union Station. Lower Downtown is particularly hot since the opening of Coors Field. On the north side of Lower Downtown, the area becoming known as the Ballpark neighborhood has seen the opening of hundreds of new housing units and a few dozen restaurants.

*Contrary to popular belief, Denver doesn't have 300 full days of sunshine per year. The state climatologist's office tried to calculate how Greater Denver could live up to the claim and found that 300 days is an accurate figure if you count as a "day of sunshine" those days in which the sun shines for more than 45 minutes.*

## BIG CITY PAINS

Of course, not everything is perfect about Greater Denver.

Tourists strolling amid the stately buildings and luxuriant flower gardens of Denver's Civic Center might well be asked for money by transients who lounge in the shade. Petty crime is as prevalent in Denver as any midsize city. Yet crime in Denver does not distinguish it from other metropolitan areas. In terms of its crime rate, Denver lies between Lubbock, Texas, and Springfield, Massachusetts. Denver is more dangerous than Des Moines, safer than Seattle.

One of Denver's most notorious negatives is what locals call the "brown cloud," the yellow-brown layer of pollution often visible in the air above the city. Denver may be 1 mile above sea level, but it actually lies in a geographic depression. The High Plains rise for 50 miles or so as one travels to the east, and, of course, the mountains rise beyond 14,000 feet to the west.

Summer visitors may wonder, "What brown cloud?" During warm weather, convection carries the pollution up where the winds can carry it away. High-pollution days are most frequently announced during the winter, when temperature inversions trap and concentrate air pollution in the depression. Unfortunately this means that those who buy a house with a wood-burning fireplace may be buying a house with wasted wall space; those nights on which a merry crackling fire would be most comforting often seem to be the same nights when it's against the law to build a fire. More irritating is feeling it in the lungs and eyes. Some of us don't even notice it,

but those with allergies or respiratory conditions can find it distressing. It's ironic, considering that many of Greater Denver's early inhabitants—including Mayor Robert Speer—came here because the clean, dry air was celebrated as a cure for tuberculosis.

Still, those who compare Denver's air pollution to that of Los Angeles are stretching it; Denver rarely violates national clean air standards. Even without air pollution, breathing is a bit more difficult at 1 mile above sea level. This is typically a mild and temporary problem. Only during the first week or so in Denver do some visitors feel headachy and strangely out of sorts. Since Denver is a gateway to the mountains, however, visitors need to take seriously the dangers of acute altitude sickness, a collapse of the body's ability to take in and metabolize oxygen. Those who plan to exert themselves in the mountains need to take a few days to get used to the altitude and drink an abnormally large amount of water; otherwise, they could find themselves beset by abdominal cramps and hyperventilation.

As the population grows, rush-hour traffic jams are worse than natives have ever known. If you're from Chicago or Los Angeles, you may find Denver's traffic jams unimpressive. Former Los Angelenos newly transplanted to Denver can be heard claiming to commute to downtown from homes in the mountains in the time it would take them to drive 1 mile at rush hour in L.A. Most people, however, find Denver traffic tremendously unpleasant and getting worse.

One of the nation's biggest misconceptions about Denver concerns the weather. Nonresidents often have trouble distinguishing Denver from the mountains that are so important to its national image. More than 80 percent of Colorado's population lives along the Front Range, the increasingly interconnected metropolitan areas ranging from Greeley in the north to Pueblo in the south along the base of the mountains. Front Range weather is surprisingly mild. Someone in Chicago or Cleveland may hear of new snow falling on

*When traveling on I-25 through the north side of the metro area, carpool to take advantage of HOV (high-occupancy vehicle) lanes during rush hours. You'll avoid the parking lot Denverites call I-25. Watch the signs carefully, as times and directions change according to traffic patterns.*

6-foot snowpacks in the Rockies, then call a friend in Denver and find out the temperature here is 70 degrees.

Long cold spells do set in periodically from November to February. And Denver does get some whopping snowstorms, more in March than in any other month. Every year at least one storm leaves highways littered with abandoned vehicles. But a few days later, people are out working in their yards. A three-day snowstorm in 2003 turned into a blizzard on March 19, dropping 2 to 3 feet of snow in the metro area and up to 7 feet of snow in the foothills west of Denver. Thousands were trapped in their homes while snowplows worked to open roads and utilities worked to repair downed power lines. Two days later it was 80 degrees, and birds were hopping on dry green lawns. Snow melts particularly fast during the late winter and early spring when Chinook winds come roaring down from the mountains at speeds that have been clocked as high as 143 miles per hour. These warm, dry "snow-eaters" literally suck the moisture out of the snow before it can reach the ground, and they have been known to raise Front Range temperatures by as much as 36 degrees within two hours. They've also been known to tear the roofs off houses, topple trees, and blow semi-trailers right off the interstate.

Mild on average, Greater Denver is the land of weather extremes, one of the reasons why the National Center for Atmospheric Research is just up the road in the city of Boulder. Meteorologists joke that the area is ideal, because they can go golfing in the morning and chase thunderstorms in the afternoon. With Denver's weather extremes, it's easy to understand the common observation: "If you don't like the weather, wait five minutes."

## DENVER SUBURBS

Much of what we've already said about Greater Denver has focused on the city of Denver, but the suburban counties have their own lives and characters. While the city and county of Denver's population grew to 556,835 in 2004, the population of Greater Denver's suburban counties—Arapahoe, Jefferson, Douglas, and Adams—grew to 1,676,983. As Colorado's economy began to attract people and companies again, the suburban counties reaped the lion's share of the growth.

# Jefferson County, West of Denver

Among Greater Denver counties, Jefferson County is second only to the city and county of Denver in population. The county wraps around the western end of the metropolitan area and includes such mountain communities as Evergreen and Conifer and reaches into the Pike National Forest. Only Douglas County rivals Jefferson for scenic beauty. Located nearest the mountains, Jefferson tends to attract residents motivated by quality of life. Colorado's image is one of mountains, and when people immigrate here, those who can afford to locate in or near the mountains generally go that route. Jefferson County has a highly educated population and a high percentage of dual-income families.

Greater Denver's gateway to the mountains, Jefferson County is traversed by streams of skiers and other motorists on Interstate 70 or on U.S. Highway 6 through scenic Clear Creek Canyon, the historic main thoroughfare to the gold and silver meccas of the 1800s. Many of these passersby notice little more of Jefferson County than the city of Golden to the north or the upscale homes of mountain

*If you're a low-altitude person like many new arrivals in Denver, you may wonder why you have a nagging slight headache. Don't worry; it's just the altitude. Drink lots of water and your physiology should be Denverized within a week.*

communities that dot the hills along the route farther into the foothills.

But "Jeffco," in the local slang, is also an urban county in which cities such as Arvada, Edgewater, Westminster, Wheat Ridge, and Lakewood represent a continuum of the urban fabric reaching out from Denver.

Jefferson County is highly industrialized with an emphasis on high technology. Golden, the county seat, claims Greater Denver's highest population percentage of technology Ph.D.s. Up to a third of the students at Golden's Colorado School of Mines stay on in Jefferson County after they graduate. Jefferson County is the regional geotechnology, materials, mining, and energy business cluster.

The U.S. government is the county's largest employer with the mammoth Denver Federal Center in Lakewood, Jefferson County's largest city, and the National Renewable Energy Laboratory in Golden.

# Arapahoe County, East and South of Denver

Back when it was Arapahoe County of the Kansas Territory, it once covered nearly half the present state of Colorado. Now Arapahoe County covers about 800 square miles reaching halfway from Denver to the Kansas border. Arapahoe holds the biggest part of Denver's eastern suburbs and folds under the south side of the city to encompass such south Denver suburbs as Englewood, Greenwood Village, Centennial, and Littleton, the county seat.

Arapahoe contains most of the city of Aurora, and Aurora contains nearly 50 percent of the county's population as well. Aurora is the state's biggest city in area and its third-largest in population. Since World War II Aurora has been heavily influenced by the military. It contains the sites of two former military bases, Fitzsimons Army Medical Center, which is being redeveloped into a new research center and campus for the University of Colorado's

Health Sciences Center, and Lowry Air Force Base, which is almost completely redeveloped into a residential neighborhood. Buckley Air Force Base (the city's largest employer) is still in use on the east. The closing of Lowry in 1994 slapped the city's economy in the face, as did the federal decision in 1995 to close Fitzsimons. Both attracted plenty of development interest, as did the old Stapleton International Airport on Aurora's boundary.

The county's second- and third-largest cities, Englewood and Littleton, south of Denver, also suffered from workforce reductions during the early 1990s at Martin Marietta, now Lockheed Martin. At that decade's dawn, Martin Marietta was Littleton's largest employer, but the city's employment base has become increasingly diversified. Littleton still has something of a small-town feel, but its school system has produced Scholastic Aptitude Test scores that rank in the top echelons of Greater Denver.

Englewood was a prairie when Colorado's first gold discovery occurred there in 1858. By the late 1800s, however, the fruit orchards of Englewood had given that city its modern name from the Old English words for "wooded place." Denver's ladies and gentlemen preferred it for Sunday carriage drives and picnics. Since that time Englewood has developed a strong business community. Today Englewood boasts more jobs and businesses per square mile than any other city in the Rocky Mountains. The small communities of Glendale and Sheridan also are part of Arapahoe County.

# Adams County, Northeast of Denver

Adams County ceded 53 of its approximately 1,200 square miles to the city of Denver so that Denver could build its new airport. But Adams is still Greater Denver's largest county. Lying north of Arapahoe County, Adams County extends as far to the east as Arapahoe but is much wider north to south.

# Greater Denver Vital Statistics

Denver was named for James W. Denver, governor of the Kansas Territory when the city was founded.

Denver became the capital of the new Colorado Territory in 1867 and capital of the State of Colorado in 1876.

**Population:** As of July 2006, the U.S. Census Bureau estimated the city and county of Denver at 556,835, Adams County at 389,857, Arapahoe County at 522,812, Broomfield County at 42,169, Douglas County at 237,963, and Jefferson County at 526,351.

**Location:** The city lies at the base of the Rocky Mountains about a third of the way across Colorado from Wyoming to New Mexico.

**Terrain:** Rocky Mountain foothills on the west, rolling plains on the east.

**Altitude:** A bronze disk imbedded on one of the western steps of the State Capitol building proclaims, ELEVATION 5,280 FEET. The words ONE MILE ABOVE SEA LEVEL are chiseled just above.

**Climate:** Mild. Dry heat in summer makes days bearable and nights pleasantly cool. Snow seldom stays long on the ground during winter. Average maximum temperature in the summer is 85 degrees; minimum is 56. Average maximum winter temperature is 45 degrees; minimum is 18. Average annual rainfall is 11 inches. Average annual snowfall is 60 inches. Average number of days with snow, ice pellets, or hail of 1 inch or more in depth is 18. Clear days: 115. Partly cloudy days: 130. Cloudy days: 120.

Denver government consists of a mayor and a city council. The current mayor is John Hickenlooper.

Adams County is perhaps Greater Denver's most economically diverse county, hosting agriculture, heavy industry, transportation, and high-tech companies. It does have an image as Greater Denver's big-shouldered, blue-collar county, thanks to the spread of warehouses, smokestack industries, and oil refineries that can be seen along I-70 and Interstate 270. At the same time, however, it has its share of communications, biopharmaceutical, and computer software and hardware companies in its eastern urbanized zone. Most of the county's land is used for farming and ranching. The county seat is in Brighton.

Other cities and towns in the county include Northglenn, Thornton, Bennett, Federal Heights, and parts of Arvada and Westminster.

Anyone who looks at a map of Greater Denver will see a large blank space east of Commerce City with a scattering of lakes and the words "Rocky Mountain Arsenal (Restricted Area)." The Rocky Mountain Arsenal was located on 17,000 acres of land 10 miles northeast of downtown Denver during World War II, and the U.S. Army used it to manufacture chemical weapons such as mustard gas, white phosphorus, and napalm. When contaminated groundwater began to cause crop damage to the north in the mid-1950s, cleanup began. More than half the acreage has been cleaned up, with the remainder due to be done by 2011. In the meantime it has become the most impressive wildlife refuge in Greater Denver. A continuous traffic of weekend visitors and weekday school groups take the guided tours on double-decker buses to view eagles, elk, and other wildlife that call the arsenal home.

While dealing gracefully with its past, Adams County is well positioned for its future. Surrounding Denver International Airport, Adams County is a primary beneficiary of economic spin-offs as well as a primary recipient of airport noise. In return for 53 square miles of its land, Adams County was promised economic growth related to development around the airport.

Thanks to residential and commercial development on the county's western side, it now is home to some of the Denver metro area's best golf courses (see our Parks and Recreation chapter for details) and an entertainment complex that rivals any in the area at Church Ranch Road and U.S. Highway 36. More growth is happening between Brighton and DIA that will bring housing, retail, and industrial parks. The county still has a good availability of land and buildings at affordable prices. The county's percentage population growth between 1990 and 2010 has been projected as Greater Denver's second-fastest after Douglas County. Adams County's own airport, Front Range Airport, is just 3 miles from Denver International Airport, having begun operations in 1983. The abundance of air transportation has enhanced basic industries such as metalworking, food processing, and wood products in Adams County's southwestern corner as well as the 120th Avenue corridor of high-technology companies in the county's northwestern corner.

# Douglas County, South of Denver

Flowing through the Pike National Forest southwest of Denver, the South Platte River has some of the most celebrated trout fishing—once called "the St. Peter's Basilica of trout fishing" by *Time* magazine—on Colorado's Front Range. This is Douglas County.

Highlands Ranch—one of Greater Denver's most popular planned communities, offering mountain views and plenty of parks and walkways—is also Douglas County. The population of unincorporated Highlands Ranch is expected to reach 100,000 by the year 2015.

Including the four municipalities of Castle Rock, Lone Tree, Larkspur, and Parker as well as a piece of Littleton, Douglas County is the only metro county that does not share a boundary with the city and county of Denver. It's separated from Denver by a slice of Arapahoe County that wraps under the city's south side.

Douglas County is Greater Denver's southern frontier. It has some impressive planned communities such as Highlands Ranch and Castle Pines, but it's mostly open country. Douglas is the only Greater Denver county in which the vast majority of its population lives in unincorporated communities. It is one of the area's prestigious living zones, with the region's highest median income and home prices. Douglas County is also the region's major bedroom community, with by far the highest ratio of people commuting outside the county to reach their jobs.

As the focus of what local planners call the Denver/Colorado Springs Development Corridor, Douglas also has been Colorado's fastest-growing county with a population that grew 191 percent between 1990 and 2000. That rate had slowed to only 27 percent between 2000 and 2003. But with 29 planned communities and 319 subdivisions covering nearly 18 percent of the county, Douglas anticipates a half-million new residents by the year 2030.

Meanwhile, the county plans to keep as much as 70 percent of its 841 square miles as open space in the form of ranches, greenbelts, and public parks. The county as a whole sometimes seems almost as much a part of Colorado Springs as it is of Denver. The county seat of Castle Rock, so named for the monolith-capped hill that towers above it, is just short of halfway to Colorado Springs, and most of its workers commute to one metropolis or the other.

# GETTING HERE, GETTING AROUND

*If you get lost, look at the mountains.* That's the mantra when it comes to getting around Denver. The mountains to the west can orient even the most turned-around visitor or resident, so take advantage of them as you're navigating your way around.

The second vital feature to remember is that unlike the rest of the metro area, downtown is parallel to Cherry Creek. At times that can make downtown's diagonal street grid feel like a confounding mistake in the midst of streets otherwise neatly laid out in a north-south and east-west fashion.

Denver's first streets were designed to be parallel to Cherry Creek, which cuts the town from northwest to southeast. Later, streets were laid out north-south and east-west. It helps to look at a Denver map to orient yourself. In general, from downtown Denver, Aurora is to the east; the Denver Tech Center, Englewood, and Greenwood Village are to the south; Littleton is southwest; Lakewood, Wheat Ridge, and Golden are to the west; Arvada, Broomfield, and Westminster are to the northwest; and Commerce City, Northglenn, and Thornton are to the north.

"Downtown" refers to the area that is roughly bounded by 13th Avenue on the south, Speer Boulevard (which follows Cherry Creek) on the west, the South Platte River on the north, and Grant Street on the east. Most streets downtown run one way. Seventeenth Street, where most of the banks and big office buildings are located, is in many ways the heart of downtown. The 16th Street Mall is also an important pedestrian thoroughfare, as free shuttle buses run up and down its 1-mile length, connecting the two RTD (Regional Transportation District) bus terminals at Civic Center on Broadway and Market Street, and Union Station. The shuttle buses operate between about 5:00 A.M. and 1:30 A.M. on weekdays, from about 5:30 A.M. to 1:30 A.M. on Saturdays, and from 7:00 A.M. to 1:30 A.M. on Sundays and holidays. Frequency depends on the time of day and ranges from one every ten minutes to almost one a minute during the morning and afternoon rush hours. The 16th Street Mall is closed to auto traffic between Market Street and Broadway. Bikes and in-line skates also aren't allowed.

Somewhere around Market Street, downtown becomes Lower Downtown, or "LoDo" (say "low-dough"). Dana Crawford, who spearheaded the Larimer Street rejuvenation, defines the area narrowly as Larimer and Market Streets west to Union Station, from 20th Street to Cherry Creek. A broader definition extends farther west to the Platte River. Capitol Hill is the name given to the area just east of downtown.

Our Area Overview chapter, which talks about the different counties that make up Greater Denver, should help you orient yourself. For descriptions of neighborhoods see our Relocation chapter.

## LOGISTICS: FINDING AN ADDRESS

In central Denver the streets are laid out on a sort of grid: Broadway runs north-south and serves as the dividing line between east and west addresses. Ellsworth Avenue runs east-west and serves as the dividing line between north and south streets and addresses. Broadway and Ellsworth Avenue are the "zero hundred blocks." As streets travel away from them, address numbers go up.

MAPSCO, 800 Lincoln Street, (303) 623–4299, has every kind of map you'll ever need to find your way around—

GETTING AROUND

**CLOSE-UP**

# Art at the Airport

When Denver International Airport (DIA) was built in the mid-1990s with an enormous construction budget of more than $3.2 billion, the funding for art was equally impressive. That's because Denver, like many other cities, has a percent-for-art ordinance that specifies that an amount equal to 1 percent of the total costs of new city construction be set aside for art at the site. This added up to about $7.5 million worth of art commissions divided among 26 projects.

That sounds like a lot of money and a lot of art—and it is—but DIA is so big that the art still can seem tucked away. It's an airport, not a museum, and nobody would ever mistake the two. Still, a traveler is unlikely to pass through DIA without at least noticing some of the art. The main areas to look for art are in the center and wings of each concourse, along the underground train passages, and throughout the main terminal.

Here are a few of our favorite pieces:

A 30-foot-high fiberglass blue mustang is the first piece of art people see as they come into the airport via Peña Boulevard. Made by well-known New Mexico artist Luis Jiminez, the rearing horse has eyes that shoot out laserlike beams of red light.

Near the carousels in the baggage claim area, check out the two whimsical suitcase gargoyles by Terry Allen. They go by the name *Notre Denver.*

Also in the baggage claim area are two colorful murals painted by Denver artist Leo Tanguma, a Chicano activist-artist who likes to involve the community in creating his murals.

Across the main terminal from Tanguma's murals is Gary Sweeney's *America, Why I Love Her,* two big photo-mural maps of the United States with the artist's small framed snapshots of odd bits of Americana (ever seen the Frog Fantasies Museum in Eureka Springs, Arkansas?) tacked onto the appropriate locations. Sweeney used to work as a baggage handler for Continental Airlines. On Denver's spot on the map, he included a little sign that says: "You are here . . . but your luggage is in Spokane." Needless to say, not everybody was amused, especially when glitches in the automated baggage system caused multiple delays in the airport's opening date in 1995.

On the balustrade at the top of the escalators that connect Level 5 and Level 6 in the main terminal are 28 glossy, vibrant ceramic vases by internationally known ceramicist Betty Woodman.

topographic, recreational, and illustrated. They also stock guidebooks.

## MAIN THOROUGHFARES

Interstate 25 runs north-south through Denver in a line from Cheyenne to Colorado Springs (and farther, of course, in each direction). Just north of downtown, it intersects Interstate 70, which runs east-west through the northern edge of the city and is the major route to the mountains. Interstate 225 cuts diagonally across Aurora northeast to southwest and connects I-70 just west of Peoria Street

Mile High and Rising *by Marcus Akinlana can be seen at Denver International Airport.* THE DENVER POST/ANDY CROSS

Although Woodman has exhibited widely in the United States and Europe, this was her first public commission.

Another favorite piece is the interior garden created by Michael Singer in Concourse C. These mossy ruins are visible from below as you exit the train and from above in the concourse.

Artists have worked on the floors of DIA in several places, including the main terminal and Concourse B, so if you watch where you're walking, you'll see pictographs, fossils, and more inlaid in the terrazzo floor. In the food court areas in Concourse A, you'll notice colorful tile patterns that appear to be abstract—but go up the escalator and take a look from above and you'll see that they form foreshortened figures of people. Barb McKee and Darrell Anderson collaborated on this project.

Finally, on the way out of the airport, you may notice a line of rusted farm implements. It's not that there wasn't time to clean up—this is part of an art project created by Sherry Wiggins and Buster Simpson to acknowledge that agriculture was historically one of the primary uses of the land on which DIA was built.

Curious passersby can get a brochure that identifies and locates the art at DIA in the information booths in the main terminal and in Concourses A and C.

with I-25 near the Denver Tech Center.

The so-called Denver Beltway is comprised of three separate highways (with a fourth segment planned) that form a loop around the city. The Northwest Parkway toll road opened in late 2003, and it cuts across the north between U.S. Highway 36 at Broomfield and E-470 at north I-25. From there the E-470 toll road extends east to Interstate 76, where it turns south, passes by Denver International Airport (take the Peña Boulevard exit to reach DIA from here), and joins C-470 at south I-25 near Park Meadows. C-470, the only section that doesn't charge a toll, rounds the south and west sections of the metro area, from I–25 at the Arapahoe County/Douglas County border, west past Littleton, then north to I–70. The final segment is intended to connect C–470 at I–70 with the Northwest Parkway to complete the loop. This last piece is the subject of a hotly contested debate in the northwest communities of Golden and Arvada; plans remain in place but are under vigorous discussion.

Other major thoroughfares are Sixth Avenue (U.S. Highway 6), which joins up with I–70 at Golden; Santa Fe Drive (U.S. Highway 85), a north-south route that can be a good alternative to I–25; and Broadway. Colfax Avenue (Highway 40) is an east-west route, but, like Broadway, it has a lot of traffic and can be a slow way to get from one side of town to another. Speer Boulevard runs parallel to Cherry Creek and connects downtown with the Cherry Creek shopping area.

Rush hour comes early in Denver. Assuming all goes well, the highways have cleared by 9:00 A.M., but the evening rush hour starts as early as 3:30 P.M. The T-Rex project has been the most congested area, but the project has moved along rapidly and has a scheduled completion date of September 2006.

There are HOV (high-occupancy vehicle) lanes to encourage carpooling on several of Denver's major commuter routes, including South Santa Fe Drive, eastbound US 36, and I–25 north of downtown. Watch for them and use them; they'll save you 15 to 20 minutes of stop-and-go in rush hours. To use these lanes, you must have at least two occupants per vehicle.

Denver's notorious "brown cloud" has prompted much hand-wringing about auto pollution. The pollution is worse in winter when temperature inversions clamp down on the city. A program called Clean Air Colorado monitors air quality between November and April of each year and declares voluntary "no drive" days when things look particularly bad. (On these high-pollution days, wood burning is banned.) News programs regularly broadcast the status, or you can call the Air-Quality Advisory Line, (303) 758-4848.

Parking is tight but not impossible downtown and much cheaper than in other big cities. Options for drivers are on-street meters and parking lots. Bring coins and small bills; you'll need to spend anywhere from $6.00 to $15.00 for an afternoon shopping or touring spree.

## T-REX TRANSPORTATION EXPANSION PROJECT

If you're visiting or new to Denver, you might hear newscasters talking about T-Rex. They're not talking about the dinosaur, but rather a $1.67 billion project that began in summer 2001 to provide new light-rail transit and 17 miles of highway improvement.

The project is concentrated in the southeast corridor of I–25 and I–225, one of the most heavily used sections of road in the state. This area, home to the Denver Tech Center, is also one of the fastest growing residential areas in the state and the country.

When completed in 2006, there will be four lanes in each direction on I–25 from Logan Street in Denver to I–225, five lanes from I–225 to the C–470/E–470 interchange, and three lanes in each direction on I–225 from Parker Road in Aurora to the I–25 interchange. Additionally the project includes reconstruction of interchanges and bridges as well as improved pedestrian and bicycle access. On the light-rail side, the project provides approximately 19 miles of double-track light-rail with 13 stations (12 with parking) along the way.

When the project first began, lane closures, exit ramp detours, and construction wreaked havoc on the area. As the project nears completion, however, the final pieces cause minimal disturbance, and the completed sections have succeeded spectacularly in opening up highway traffic flow in this heavily traveled part of the metro area. Completion is scheduled for September 2006.

FasTracks is a 12-year plan that will add 119 miles of new light-rail lines, 18 new miles of express bus service, 21,000 new parking spaces at rail and bus stations, and expanded bus service throughout Denver. It will cost $4.7 billion and will finish in 2016. Construction will begin in 2008. It's partly funded by a 0.4 percent sales tax increase approved by voters that began in 2005.

*Ski traffic on I-70 has become a major problem, one that is predicted to worsen as the population grows. Prepare for the worst when day skiing: A trip from Denver to Breckenridge that used to take an hour and a half can take up to three hours during peak times.*

## PUBLIC TRANSPORTATION

**Regional Transportation District**
**1600 Blake Street**
**(303) 299-6000**
**www.rtd-denver.com**
The Regional Transportation District (RTD) runs buses throughout the city and suburbs as well as a light-rail leg in the downtown area.

Light Rail—Light rail runs north-south along a central corridor (the Metro Area Connection, or MAC) from 30th Avenue and Downing Street through the Five Points neighborhood, downtown Denver, the Auraria campus, and then south along Santa Fe Drive to Mineral Avenue in Littleton and includes 18 stations on the C and D lines, and connects with bus routes at the I-25/Broadway station. Four new lines began service in October 2006 that run south from downtown Denver along I-25 to Lincoln Avenue and east along I-225 to South Parker Road, adding 12 new stations. Feeder buses serve all stations, providing rapid transit for residents of Aurora, Englewood, Greenwood Village, Lone Tree, and Parker. Fares range from $1.50 to $3.75 each way, depending on how far you travel on the train. Seniors 65 and over, people with disabilities, Medicare recipients, and students ages 6 to 19 pay roughly half price.

**Buses**—RTD runs local, express, and regional bus service. Local buses operate on many routes downtown and cost $1.50. Express routes travel longer distances without as many stops; the basic fare is $2.75. Regional routes run to Boulder and other outlying areas; the fare is $3.75. The regional buses are comfortably upholstered, with reclining seats and air-conditioning. In all cases, exact change is required. Tokens, ticket books, and monthly passes are available at supermarkets, and many discounts apply (for senior citizens, students, and the disabled). For schedule and route information, call (303) 299-6000, visit www.rtd-denver.com, or stop in at the Market Street Station at 16th and Market Streets.

RTD's Downtown Express service benefits commuters who live north of downtown. Two-way bus lanes run along the middle of I-25 from 84th Street to the downtown Market Street Station on an extension of the 16th Street Mall that runs past Union Station. Carpools of two or more persons (in addition to buses) are also allowed to use the lanes.

For information about public transportation to and from the airport, see the Airports section later in this chapter. RTD also provides transportation to professional football and baseball games; check our Spectator Sports chapter or call (303) 299-6000 for details.

## TAXIS

Generally you don't just wave down a cruising taxi on a Greater Denver street, although it's possible downtown; you usually call ahead. In fact, it's a good idea to call 30 minutes ahead of time, especially on weekend nights. The taxi companies that serve Greater Denver may take you out of the city if you wish, but it gets expensive. All taxi services provide rides to and from Denver International Airport for around $45.

All the taxi companies in Denver

charge the same amount: $2.00 entry fee and $2.00 a mile: Metro Taxi, (303) 333-3333; Yellow Cab, (303) 777-7777; Freedom Cab, (303) 444-4444.

## LEAVING TOWN: PLANES, TRAINS, AND BUSES

# Airports

**Denver International Airport**
**8500 Peña Boulevard**
**(303) 342-2000**
**www.flydenver.com**
Is there anybody out there who hasn't heard about Denver International Airport and can't recite at least one joke about the baggage system or what DIA stands for? Its postponed opening dates (four, before it opened on February 28, 1995), distance from downtown (24 miles), and escalating price tag ($4.9 billion is a modest estimate) generated no respect from the rest of the nation. Denverites, however, have fondly grown proud of it, and many have learned to love it as it has become the nation's 6th and the world's 11th busiest airport. DIA is larger than Dallas–Fort Worth Airport and Chicago's O'Hare Airport combined, extending across an area of 53 square miles. It is the first major U.S. airport to be built from the ground up in more than 20 years. DIA's six runways can land three aircraft at once using state-of-the-art radar, an improvement over Stapleton International Airport, which closed for business when DIA opened.

DIA is situated to the north and east of Denver and is accessed via Peña Boulevard. Peña Boulevard can be reached via exit 284 off I-70. Travelers from the north can get to the airport by taking 104th Avenue to Tower Road and then driving south to Peña Boulevard, or by taking the Northwest Parkway or E-470 toll roads to the Peña Boulevard exit.

Charges for short-term parking run from $2.00 an hour up to a 24-hour maximum of $18.00. Long-term parking costs between $5.00 and $9.00 a day.

You could let RTD do the driving. SkyRide operates seven major routes to DIA. Call or visit the Web site for routes. One-way fare for the suburban routes is $10.00; from downtown, $8.00; and from Stapleton, $6.00. SkyRide passengers can park at Stapleton for free. For SkyRide information call RTD at (303) 299-6000.

DIA is a handsome airport, with a dramatic tented roof of Teflon-coated fiberglass fashioned into 34 peaks symbolizing the Rocky Mountains. From a distance the roof also looks like an encampment of tepees, a nod to the site's historical usage as American Indians' migratory land. Inside, many surfaces are brushed steel, and $7.5 million worth of commissioned art adorns the floors, walls, and ceilings (see our Close-up in this chapter for a more complete description of the art).

DIA has three concourses and a main terminal, all of which are connected by underground trains. There is also a pedestrian bridge between Concourse A and the main terminal that provides a good view of the airfield.

Travelers should appreciate DIA's retail shops and restaurants, which, by the terms of their concession contracts, are prevented from charging more than 10 percent above what comparable prices are elsewhere in Denver.

Ground transportation from DIA into Greater Denver is plentiful. Taxis can be hailed outside the baggage claim area and cost around $45 to downtown, more if you're going farther (see the Taxis section in this chapter). Shuttle buses are provided by many major hotels, so check with yours. Otherwise, there are more than 350 "commuter" services operating out of DIA. Call (303) 342-4059 and you will be connected with the one right for you. You must have a destination in order to get a price quote, but DIA to downtown will cost around $20 to $25. Out of Colorado, you can call (800) AIR-2-DEN to make arrangements ahead of time.

Pick any rental car service, and it is available at DIA. Rental car counters are near baggage claim, and there are signs

*Denver International Airport.* THE DENVER POST/CRAIG F. WALKER

leading you to them. Rental agents recommend making arrangements before you arrive, as many agencies run out of cars during peak times.

**Advantage Rent-A-Car, (800) 777-5500**
**Alamo Rent A Car, (800) GO ALAMO**
**Avis Rent A Car, (800) 331-1212**
**Budget Rent A Car, (800) 527-0700**
**Dollar Rent A Car, (800) 800-4000**
**Enterprise Rent-A-Car,**
    **(800) RENT A CAR**
**Hertz Rent A Car, (800) 654-3131**
**National Car Rental, (800) 227-7368**
**Payless Car Rental, (800) PAY LESS**
**Thrifty Car Rental, (800) 367-2277**

**Colorado Springs Airport**
**7770 Drennan Road, Colorado Springs**
**(719) 550-1972**
**www.flycos.com**
This small airport is about 90 miles south of Denver. The best thing to do is to check with your travel agent. Shuttle and van service is available to a variety of locations in the Denver area starting at $13 per person.

**Centennial Airport**
**7800 South Peoria Street, Englewood**
**(303) 790-0598**
**www.centennial-airport.com**
This suburban airport southeast of Denver is among the busiest general aviation airports in the country. It features three lighted runways, no landing fees, and an instrument-landing system for bad weather. Two full-service fixed-base operators are on hand for fueling. Ground transportation is limited to taxis and crew cars for corporate pilots.

## Trains

**Union Station**
**1701 Wynkoop Street**
**(303) 534-2812**
**www.denverunionstation.org**

Like many cities in the West and Midwest, Denver has a Union Station that dates from the 19th century and used to be much busier than it is now. Among the east-west trains that still run through Denver is the famous *California Zephyr,* which travels an amazingly scenic route across the Continental Divide and through Glenwood Canyon on its way to Salt Lake City and, eventually, Oakland, California. In the winter a ski train makes the round-trip to Winter Park (see our Ski Country chapter for details). Union Station is in Lower Downtown at Wynkoop and 17th Streets. For Amtrak information call (800) USA-RAIL. For recorded information about Amtrak departures and arrivals in Denver, call the Denver Amtrak ticket office, (303) 534-2812.

## Buses

**Greyhound Bus Terminal**
**1055 19th Street**
**(303) 293-6555, (800) 231-2222**
**www.greyhound.com**
The Denver terminus for Greyhound and other private bus lines is at 20th and Curtis Streets, only a few blocks away from RTD's Market Street Station. Generally RTD provides bus service to points less than an hour away, such as Boulder and Longmont. (See the section on Public Transportation in this chapter.) Longer trips, including trips to Fort Collins and the mountains, originate at the 20th and Curtis station. Because both stations are downtown, make sure you know whether you will need the RTD Market Street Station or the Greyhound station. For Greyhound fare and schedule information, call one of the numbers listed here. As seems to always be the case with big-city bus terminals, this one is not in the nicest part of town. There's no reason to avoid it; just be alert.

# ACCOMMODATIONS

Greater Denver is a community of travelers: those who traveled here to live, those who travel here for vacations, and, increasingly, those who travel here on business. It's a popular spot for conventions, and it's one of those places where the residents seldom have any trouble convincing people from other states to come and visit.

The appetites of travelers for good accommodations are well matched by more than 16,000 hotel and motel rooms in the Denver area. Whether your tastes tend toward the magnificent or the humble, you'll find plenty of choices.

In its infancy stage is the new 1,100-room Hyatt Hotel at the Convention Center. Completed in 2006, it serves the throngs that meet at the downtown center.

One good general source of hotel information is the Colorado Tourism office. It has a free vacation guide you can get by visiting the Web site at www.colorado.com.

Lodging prices in the mountain resorts show amazing bargains in the off-seasons of spring and fall, but Denver hotels, tending to be less vacation- and more commerce-oriented, don't show that much variation year-round. As commercial hotels, however, they do tend to give much better rates on weekends than during the week, a boon for the working person who wants a weekend getaway.

The average room rate is not what you'll pay all the time, of course. Most hotels have a wide range of rates on any specific day, and, in addition to good weekend rates, most offer special package deals. Romantic weekend packages are popular with hotels, often lumping together such things as tickets and a limousine ride to a show, carriage rides, or dinner at a local fine restaurant.

At the more moderately priced downtown hotels, you might want to check what kind of conventions they have going.

Nothing is more disruptive to a vacation than lying down for a good night's sleep only to discover there are 500 high-school debaters at a regional competition in the same hotel, and it sounds like they are all in the room next door.

The two biggest sources of hotel bookings are business, including conventions, and tourism. Business travelers stay in the greatest numbers at hotels in downtown Denver, the Denver Tech Center to the southeast, and near the airport. Tourists will generally stay anywhere they can get a good price, but downtown is the preferred location for seeing the sights of Denver.

If you're interested in seeing Rocky Mountain National Park and want Denver to be part of your trip, choose from the many lodgings in Denver's northwest quadrant. The near-east side of Denver is the most convenient place to stay if you're visiting the Denver Museum of Nature and Science, Colorado's sixth most popular attraction. Lodgings on the west side of Denver provide the best access to Golden, home of the Coors Brewery. The west side also allows for fast access to downtown and makes for a speedy mountain getaway via Interstate 70. Sporting events are another big attraction, and the downtown or the near-west side are prime lodging locations for ready access to the Colorado Rockies at Coors Field or the Denver Broncos at INVESCO Field at Mile High.

Big news for Denver is that hotels are finally going up in the vicinity of Denver International Airport. In fact, one Insider says it looks like someone waters the soil along Peña Boulevard at night since on any given day you can see new construction popping up. The first hotel opened in January of 1996—a Fairfield Inn by Marriott, part of an eventual $1 billion Denver International Business Center constructed along Tower Road between 64th and 72nd Avenues, just a few miles from the terminal.

According to the Denver Metro Convention and Visitors Bureau, the number of tourists to Denver who stayed overnight grew slightly in 2004 after suffering a steep decline in 2003. About 7.9 million visitors came to Denver in 2004, a little more than a 1 percent increase. And that doesn't count business travelers. Add another 2 million business travelers, and Greater Denver hosted 9.9 million people in 2004. All of that adds up to some big money. In 2004 those 9.9 million overnight visitors spent more than $2.3 billion dollars, making tourism the second-largest industry in the city, after manufacturing. Statewide, there were 22.3 million pleasure travelers in 2004.

Though we get more tourists in the summer, skiers are bigger spenders. On the other hand, skiers do most of their spending in the mountains, tending to hop the first rental car or resort shuttle they can catch out of town. Besides visiting the Web site listed earlier for the Colorado Tourism office, visitors interested in hitting the slopes can call a central reservations number at every major resort for help with prices and availability. See our Ski Country chapter. Also consult the yellow pages of the Denver phone book.

Hotels in the southeastern part of Greater Denver, especially around the Denver Tech Center area, seem far from Denver International Airport northeast of the city. But they're actually closer in terms of time and traffic than many more central areas thanks to Interstate 225, which runs up the east side of the metro area to connect with I-70. Hotels in that area are also closer than it would seem to the mountains via I-70, thanks to C-470 and E-470, the completed southwest and eastern quadrants of Denver's beltway.

A lot of hotels have free continental breakfasts, free transportation, free newspapers delivered to your door, free attached parking, and free or discounted access to nearby athletic clubs. In most of our listings, we haven't detailed all the freebies, so make a point of asking when you check in.

All hotels, bed-and-breakfasts, and hostels in this chapter accept credit cards.

To save yourself confusion and possible grief, be aware that many Englewood addresses are not in Englewood. They actually are in unincorporated parts of Arapahoe County (which includes Englewood) and therefore have an Englewood mailing address. We've noted this in each such listing.

## HOTELS
### PRICE CODE

Our listings rate hotels according to a three-symbol price key, representing average room cost per night during the week for a double occupancy.

| | |
|---|---|
| $ | **less than $100** |
| $$ | **$101 to $150** |
| $$$ | **more than $150** |

# Denver

**Adam's Mark Denver Hotel**　　$$$
**1550 Court Place**
**(303) 893-3333, (800) 444-2326**
**www.adamsmark.com**
A complete 1997 renovation of the Adam's Mark expanded this downtown property to 1,225 rooms and 92 suites and placed it among the 25 largest hotels in the nation. The Concorde Club is the concierge level of the hotel, occupying the top two floors and offering upgraded guest amenities. The Club offers a continental breakfast, early evening cocktails with complimentary hors d'ouevres, and evening desserts and coffee, as well as a stunning panoramic view of the city. Every room in the hotel is equipped with work space, and the phones have speed dial, speaker action, dataports, and complimentary high-speed Internet service. The hotel has more than 133,000 square feet of meeting space, three restaurants, two bars and a nightclub with live entertainment nightly, a florist, a gift shop, a business center, a beauty salon, and a

# Ancient Secrets of the Brown Palace Hotel

The Navarre Building, 1727 Tremont Place, across the street from the Brown Palace, was built in 1890 as the Brinker Collegiate Institution, the first coeducational college west of the Missouri River. Nine years later it was converted into the Hotel Richelieu, the city's most elegant gambling house and brothel. In its basement you can still see rails disappearing into the wall where rail carts once traveled a tunnel beneath Tremont Place, delivering fine foods from the Brown Palace kitchens. Legend has it that these carts also delivered Brown Palace patrons too discreet to be seen aboveground entering and leaving the Hotel Richelieu.

barbershop. There's also a fitness center with a steam room, exercise equipment, an outdoor heated pool, and a sundeck. It's on the 16th Street Mall a block away from the Denver Civic Center, four blocks from the Colorado Convention Center, and a few blocks from the Denver Pavilions shopping center.

**Brown Palace Hotel** $$$
**321 17th Street**
**(303) 297-3111, (800) 321-2599**
**www.brownpalace.com**
This is Denver's most famous hotel, and deservedly so. If you want a central downtown location, prestige accommodations, and a historic experience all in one, you can't do better than the Brown Palace. The list of celebs and potentates who have stayed here since Henry C. Brown opened the doors in 1892 includes every U.S. president since Teddy Roosevelt except for Jimmy Carter; the Beatles and Elvis Presley; British royalty; kings from Sweden and Romania; Japan's emperor; and entertainment industry names ranging from Lionel Barrymore to Bruce Willis. Flo Ziegfield wanted to stay here, but they wouldn't let him bring his dog in so he stormed off in a huff.

When the Brown Palace opened, it represented the state of the Victorian art in Italian Renaissance hotel design, with a sunlit eight-story atrium lobby and tiers of balconies above white onyx walls. Today its 241 rooms feature all the modern conveniences required by business and pleasure travelers alike. A five-year $14 million restoration includes remodeled staterooms and suites on the top two floors. The hotel offers more than 13,000 square feet of meeting space; an elegant dining room; an award-winning restaurant, the Palace Arms (described in our Restaurants chapter); a tavern; a lounge; a new full-service spa; and, once again, a central location at the head of 17th Street.

**The Burnsley Hotel** $$
**1000 Grant Street**
**(303) 830-1000, (800) 231-3915**
**www.burnsley.com**
Equipped for and specializing in the extended stay, the Burnsley also compares with the finest Denver hotels in its offerings for even the one-night visitor. All the rooms are apartment-style suites, and each tastefully furnished unit has a fully equipped kitchen, separate living room, dining area, and bedroom with king-size bed. The Burnsley also has an on-site self-serve business center, an outdoor pool, and complimentary parking. If you'd prefer not to cook in your kitchen, there's the Burnsley Dining Room and Lounge, offering contemporary American Cuisine, live piano music in the lounge on Monday through Saturday, and live jazz on Thursday through Saturday.

# Denver's Most Famous Hotel

Quite simply, the Brown Palace—known locally as "The Brown"—is Denver's most famous hotel. Opened on August 12, 1892, it has conducted business every day since—never even stopping to catch its breath during one of its many renovations.

It was the brainchild of Henry Brown, a real estate mogul from Ohio who came to Denver in 1860 and purchased acres of land, including the triangular plot at the corner of Broadway, Tremont, and 17th Street, where the hotel stands today. (Not surprisingly, the hotel is also triangular.)

Brown decided Denver needed a grand hotel, and, sparing no expense, he hired Denver architect Frank Edbrooke, who'd also designed the State Capitol. Edbrooke designed the hotel in the Italian Renaissance style. The grand exterior was matched by an equally grand interior. In fact, the lobby boasted the country's first atrium with balconies rising eight floors aboveground. Cast-iron railings with ornate grillwork panels surround each floor. (Two of the grillwork panels are upside down—no one knows if this was an accident or intentional.)

The hotel opened in 1892 with 400 guest rooms that rented for between $1.00 and $4.00 a night. It had no restaurants (today there are four), but it did have at least 18 stores (today there are two gift shops, a flower shop, and an art gallery).

The Brown has always had its own water supply, using artesian wells that provide water to every faucet in the hotel. The hotel also produces all its own baked goods in a carousel oven that is one of only three in the world. The Brown's melba toast, served in the restaurants, is considered one of its specialties.

Over the years The Brown has housed its share of famous guests. President Dwight Eisenhower not only stayed here, he also left a dent in the fireplace molding when his erratic golf ball hit the wall. The Beatles stayed in 1964, and the hotel received a slew of applications from young girls to be housekeepers. Even the singer once-again-known-as Prince spent a few days at The Brown. He requested that the bed be stripped to the frame so that he could place his own water-filled pad on it.

**Cherry Creek Hotel**　　　**$$**
**1475 South Colorado Boulevard**
**(303) 757-8797**
**www.cherrycreekhotel.com**
Just north of Interstate 25 on Colorado Boulevard, this hotel offers fast access to downtown and the Denver Tech Center, and it's also in a commercial area with a lot of restaurants and movie theaters an easy walk away. Besides 245 rooms, it has a cafe and lounge on the lobby level and an indoor pool. Used for banquets, the Skyline Ballroom on the top floor has commanding views of the Front Range.

**Comfort Inn Downtown**　　　**$**
**401 17th Street**
**(303) 296-0400**
**www.comfortinn.com**
You can see the big yellow letters "Comfort Inn" high on the side of this 231-room downtown hotel. Although it's an economy

Naturally, a hotel of this caliber has had its share of unusual situations. At one time, pets were allowed in the hotel. One of the first canine visitors was a fox terrier from Philadelphia who'd inherited $50,000 from his owner and on the advice of his veterinarian came to the Rocky Mountains to cure his consumption. The pooch and the daughter of his master, as well as a nursemaid, took a seven-room suite for an indefinite period.

Another wealthy visitor arranged for his dog to be fed on hotel china with silver domes. The pampered canine did, however, have to eat on the sidewalk since his visit came after dogs were prohibited from sleeping in the hotel. Where'd this pup take naps? In a rented limo outside the hotel.

The hotel is still the palace that Henry Brown envisioned. But it doesn't necessarily mean those without deep pockets can't enjoy it. For many locals, taking afternoon tea in the lobby is urbanely sophisticated. Tea and an individual platter of sandwiches and sweets runs $20.00 to $24.50.

If you don't want to drop a dime, you can still enjoy The Brown. Free tours are offered every Wednesday and Saturday at 2:00 P.M. Depending on whether it's occupied or not, the Presidential Suite

*The Brown Palace, known as "The Brown."*
THE DENVER POST

where Eisenhower stayed is on the tour. Even if you don't get to see that room, the tour offers a great anecdotal history of the hotel and a chance to see exactly which two cast-iron panels are upside down. (You can try to figure it out yourself, but chances are you'll fail.)

hotel, it's connected by a skywalk across Tremont Place to the Brown Palace Hotel, one of Denver's luxury inns. That means the Comfort Inn can offer as amenities the restaurants, lounges, meeting spaces, and elegant lobby of the Brown Palace.

The Comfort Inn is near the head of 17th Street, where the State Capitol and Civic Center and Denver Art Museum are a short walk away, and where you can hop one of the free shuttles on the 16th

Street Mall to Larimer Square and Lower Downtown.

**Comfort Inn & Suites
Denver–Northeast** $
**4685 Quebec Street
(303) 388-8100
www.denver.com/comfort-inn/**
This Comfort Inn offers 138 rooms near the former Stapleton International Airport. At 18 miles from DIA, it is still convenient

when DIA hotels fill up. It offers a complimentary continental buffet breakfast.

### Courtyard by Marriott–Denver Airport $$
6901 Tower Road
(303) 371-0300
www.marriott.com

Billing itself as one of the closest hotels to DIA, this Courtyard property has 202 rooms and features a full-service restaurant and bar. One important distinction for all-night travelers: Room service ends at 10:00 P.M., so late-night dinner is out.

### Courtyard by Marriott–Denver Downtown $$
934 16th Street
(303) 571-1114
www.marriott.com

Located on Denver's downtown 16th Street Mall, this Courtyard gets extra points for its proximity to just about everything. Its 177 rooms are at least one story above the pedestrian mall, which makes for excellent people-watching. It's just a few blocks away from the theaters and convention center, and by taking advantage of the free shuttles, guests have easy access to the government buildings on one end of the mall and the raucous ballpark neighborhood on the other. Amenities include an indoor pool, 4,000 square feet of meeting rooms, and a comfortable restaurant at street level. The only drawback—guests must pay for on-site parking.

### Courtyard by Marriott–Stapleton $$
7415 East 41st Avenue
(303) 333-3303
www.marriott.com

Aside from the trademark gazebo by the indoor pool in the courtyard, the Courtyards by Marriott are the basic upscale hotels for the discerning business traveler. Positioned off I-70 on Denver's northeast side, it is 1 mile from the old Stapleton International Airport and 17 miles from DIA. It offers 134 rooms, 12 suites, 1,274 square feet of meeting space, and free on-site parking.

### Denver Marriott City Center $$
1701 California Street
(303) 297-1300
www.marriott.com

Marriott's flagship hotel in the city, the Denver Marriott City Center lies in the thick of downtown activities. Within a block of 17th Street, less than two blocks from the 16th Street Mall, and less than four blocks from the Colorado Convention Center, it has prestige accommodations in 601 rooms and 14 suites. The fitness center has an indoor pool, exercise room, whirlpool, and sauna. The hotel has a large meeting facility, with more than 25,000 square feet of space.

### Denver Marriott Tech Center $$$
4900 South Syracuse Street
(303) 779-1100
www.marriott.com

On the edge of the city of Denver's farthest southeast corner, and right off I-25, this hotel is well named for its access to the Denver Tech Center area. There are good views of the mountains here. Recreational facilities include a workout room, indoor pool, whirlpool, and massage and tanning beds. The hotel has 658 rooms, more than 42,000 square feet of meeting space, two restaurants, and a deli. Guests may also use the nearby outdoor pool, sauna, steam room, and racquetball and handball courts.

### Doubletree Hotel Denver $$$
3203 Quebec Street
(303) 321-3333
www.doubletree.com

One of the finer "airport hotels," the Doubletree is just off I-70 near the old Stapleton International Airport and offers ready access to DIA as well (via free shuttle). It has an outdoor hot tub, an indoor pool, and exercise equipment for the guests in its 561 rooms. As with other large hotels, it's a major meeting venue with 32,000 square feet of conference space, a 10,000-square-foot ballroom, two restaurants, two lounges, a deli bar, and a renovated fitness center.

**Drury Inn Denver East**     $
4400 Peoria Street
(303) 373-1983
www.druryhotels.com
A well-situated inn for the price-conscious traveler, the Drury Inn is off I-70 between the old Stapleton International Airport and DIA. A free breakfast bar and evening cocktails and snacks are available in the lobby daily. This hotel has a heated indoor-outdoor pool and meeting rooms.

**Embassy Suites Aurora**     $$
4444 North Havana Street
(303) 375-0400
www.embassysuites.com
Amid construction of a new generation of airport hotels at DIA, this property closer to old Stapleton offers fine accommodations. Located 12 miles west of DIA, it is near I-70 for connections west and close to I-225 for connections south. It has 210 suites, 10,000 square feet of meeting and banquet space, a restaurant and lounge, indoor pool, steam room, sauna, whirlpool, exercise equipment, outdoor sundeck, grand ballroom, 12 executive meeting suites, complimentary cooked-to-order breakfast in the atrium, and complimentary cocktails and nonalcoholic beverages for two hours every evening.

**Embassy Suites Denver Southeast**     $$
7525 East Hampden Avenue
(303) 696-6644
www.embassysuites.com
Of the Embassy Suites hotels in Greater Denver, this one is nearest the intersection of Hampden Avenue and I-25—just 2 miles from the Denver Tech Center with fast access to downtown as well. Each of its 206 suites has a living room as well as a bedroom, and guests can enjoy exercise facilities, an indoor pool, banquet facilities, and free cooked-to-order breakfast in the atrium.

**Embassy Suites Downtown**     $$$
1881 Curtis Street
(303) 297-8888
www.embassysuites.com

This fine, big beauty of a hotel is Embassy Suites' downtown flagship. It's a little more than two blocks from the 16th Street Mall and all its attractions. It's also close to the pubs, shops, and galleries of Lower Downtown. The hotel has 337 suites with one or two bedrooms and a living room and also has an outdoor swimming pool.

A highlight of the hotel is its Athletic Club at Denver Place. It costs $10 extra for hotel guests, but it's a 65,000-square-foot, three-tier facility with an indoor swimming pool; racquetball, squash, and basketball courts; what the hotel claims is the longest indoor running track in Denver; cardiovascular equipment and circuit training area; aerobic and conditioning classes; and a masseuse. There's also a deli and a restaurant at the hotel.

**Fairfield Inn by Marriott–Cherry Creek**   $
1680 South Colorado Boulevard
(303) 691-2223
www.marriott.com
Just a block north off I-25 on Colorado Boulevard, the Fairfield Inn by Marriott is midway between downtown Denver and the Denver Tech Center. Three miles to the north and west is Cherry Creek. The hotel has undergone a $3.5 million renovation of its 134 guest rooms and 36 suites, which feature new bedding and Marriott lighting. Other amenities include free high-speed Internet access, free cable TV and HBO, a complimentary continental breakfast, and a newly equipped exercise room.

**Fairfield Inn by Marriott–DIA**     $
6851 Tower Road
(303) 576-9640
www.marriott.com
Oh joyous day for the business traveler! This was the first DIA hotel to open. It was

*Many of the hotels near Denver International Airport offer a convenient low-cost shuttle to and from. Check with the reservation desk for details.*

a modest beginning to the ongoing hotel development around DIA, with 161 rooms and a free continental breakfast but no restaurant (although you can dine at the Courtyard by Marriott next door).

Midday and evening meals are available in the form of microwavable vending-machine fare. For relaxation, it has a heated pool and Jacuzzi, and each room has a whirlpool bathtub. It also has meeting rooms for 120 (three rooms for 40 people) and van transportation to and from the airport.

**Four Points Denver–Cherry Creek**     **$$**
**600 South Colorado Boulevard**
**(303) 757-3341**
**www.starwoodhotels.com**
Although located on a busy boulevard, this inn has one of Denver's nicer locations on the Cherry Creek greenbelt and near the Cherry Creek shopping-arts-dining area. It's something of a business-traveler hotel, emphasizing desks in each of the 210 rooms and a business center that can help with such things as laptop computers and faxes, and aid in preparing presentations for the 12,000 square feet of meeting/social space. It has a heated outdoor pool, restaurant, gift and sundry store, and beauty shop as well as a complimentary 24-hour health club.

**Four Points by Sheraton**
**Denver Southeast**     **$$$**
**6363 Hampden Avenue**
**(303) 758-7000**
**www.starwoodhotels.com**
The Four Points by Sheraton Denver Southeast is about halfway between downtown Denver and the Denver Tech Center. It's a big place, with 475 rooms, and nearly 16,000 square feet of meeting space. Inside the hotel there are two restaurants and a sports bar, indoor and outdoor pools, a hydrotherapy pool, and an exercise room. You've got the Wellshire Municipal Golf Course a little more than a mile west and a lot of theaters and restaurants within a couple of miles.

**Grand Hyatt Denver**     **$$$**
**1750 Welton Street**
**(303) 295-1234**
**www.granddenver.hyatt.com**
Looking down from high-rises on the northeastern end of Capitol Hill, the eye is immediately attracted to a large outdoor jogging track and tennis court next to a pool on one of the rooftops in downtown Denver. That's a part of the Grand Hyatt Denver, which offers guests a "Colorado theme," including a vast Colorado sandstone fireplace in the lobby, a restaurant called 1876, and 25 deluxe suites. In all, the Grand Hyatt has 511 rooms, 57,000 square feet of meeting space, the previously mentioned rooftop recreational facilities, and one of Denver's best hotel health clubs.

**Holiday Inn Denver–Central**     **$$**
**4849 Bannock Street**
**(303) 292-9500**
**www.ichotelsgroup.com**
You'll see this Holiday Inn on the west side of I-25 as you drive just north of I-25's intersection with I-70. That intersection is not the most scenic place in the area, but you can't find a better location for immediate access to all four points of the city compass. In addition to 200 rooms and 6 two-bedroom suites, the hotel has an outdoor heated pool, a full-service dining room, a deli, and a tavern, Teddy's, that got Channel 7's nod as one of the top seven clubs in Colorado (see our Nightlife chapter).

**Holiday Inn Denver–City Center**     **$$**
**1450 Glenarm Place**
**(303) 573-1450**
**www.ichotelsgroup.com**
This downtown Denver hotel is centrally situated 1½ blocks from the 16th Street Mall and an equal distance from the U.S. Mint. Holiday Inn's city-center prestige hotel, it's a 21-story high-rise with 371 rooms, a restaurant, lounge, banquet capabilities, conference rooms for up to 400 people, and an outdoor, rooftop pool open in season. Staff members speak English, French, German, Italian, Portuguese, and Spanish.

### Holiday Inn–Denver International
**Airport** $$
**15500 East 40th Avenue**
**(303) 371-9494**
**www.ichotelsgroup.com**
The closest Holiday Inn to DIA has 255
rooms, 3 suites, 2 restaurants, a cocktail
lounge, and 70,000 square feet of meeting
space and public areas. Located north of
the Chambers Avenue exit from I-70, almost
in the city of Aurora, it also has an indoor
pool, whirlpool, sauna, and fitness room.

### Holiday Inn Select–Denver/
**Cherry Creek** $$
**455 South Colorado Boulevard**
**(303) 388-5561**
**www.ichotelsgroup.com**
This hotel is within walking distance of the
Cherry Creek Shopping Center (about a
mile away). It was completely redecorated
in 1997 and now houses 281 rooms, a
restaurant, meeting space for 1,000 with
conference and banquet rooms, an attractive indoor pool and hot tub with skylights, and a poolside lounge.

### Hotel Monaco $$$
**1717 Champa Street**
**(303) 296-1717, (800) 397-5380**
**www.monaco-denver.com**
Offering guests a "world of hip, high style
luxury," Hotel Monaco came on the scene
in October 1998 in the renovated 1917 Railway Exchange and 1937 Moderne Title
buildings. Similar to properties in San Francisco, Seattle, Chicago, and Salt Lake City,
Hotel Monaco offers 189 rooms decked in
plush interiors designed to create a residential feeling. Included are two phone
lines with dataports and CD players. Four-
teen of the 32 suites contain whirlpool
spas. On-site exercise facilities and an
Aveda Lifestyle Spa pamper guests.

### Hotel Teatro $$
**1100 14th Street**
**(303) 228-1100**
**www.hotelteatro.com**
Teatro has made grandeur out of the
historic Tramway Tower built in 1911.

*Can't travel without your beloved pet?*
*No problem at the Hotel Monaco, (303)*
*296-1717. Or if you need a temporary*
*pet, the hotel will provide a pet goldfish*
*during your stay.*

The downtown property caters to the
luxury business and upscale leisure markets with 111 rooms featuring Asian and
European appointments, two phone lines,
fax, copier, and scanner. The hotel also
houses two restaurants by well-known
local chef Kevin Taylor as well as a private
wine cellar. Meeting space is limited but
does include an executive boardroom
with a mountain view and fireplace. A fitness center and 24-hour room service are
available. There is complimentary Cadillac
Escalade service for guests to downtown
locations.

### Howard Johnson Lodge West $
**4765 Federal Boulevard**
**(303) 433-8441**
**www.hojo.com**
Off I-70 at Federal Boulevard, Howard
Johnson Lodge West is next to Rocky
Mountain Park and Lake, an easy walk
from Regis College, and 1.5 miles from
Lakeside Amusement Park. Close to the
business areas around I-25 and on the
near-west side convenient to downtown,
this Howard Johnson has an outdoor
pool, restaurant, and cocktail lounge.

### Hyatt Regency Denver
**at Colorado Convention Center** $$$
**650 15th Street**
**(303) 436-1234**
**denverregency.hyatt.com**
When it opened in 2006, this fancy 37-
floor Hyatt was downtown Denver's first
new high-rise in more than two decades.
It also signified a new chapter in the life of
the city's convention business, providing
1,100 hotel rooms and another 60,000
square feet of meeting and banquet space
across the street from Denver's new con-
vention center. With 72 suites, several of

which have 3,000 square feet of space and/or outside patio decks, the Hyatt can meet almost any guest's needs. It consists of two towers that sit side by side, with the Peaks Lounge topping the shortest of the two. Its 27th-floor windows provide one of the best panoramic views of the city, but the view doesn't come cheap. Expect to pay $10 to $12 apiece for cocktails. The ground-floor Strata Bar often has live entertainment. Breakfast, lunch, and dinner are served at the Altitude restaurant. For snacks around the clock, visit Perks coffee bar and gift shop. Also on-site: a full-service health club and spa and a 24-hour business lounge.

### Hyatt Regency Tech Center    $$$
**7800 East Tufts Avenue**
**(303) 779-1234**
**www.techcenter.hyatt.com**
The Tech Center Hyatt is an outstanding visual landmark in this part of the Tech Center because it's surrounded by a lot of open ground and because, of course, it's a Hyatt. The landscape is so open around it, you have great views of the Rockies even if you're standing in the parking lot. A majestic facility with 451 rooms and 12 suites, it's designed to give you the sense of being inside a large old Colorado train station. But it doesn't look old at all, and its grand ballroom, four banquet rooms, and 20 meeting rooms (totaling 30,000 square feet) make it a favorite meeting place for the business/convention crowd. A rooftop restaurant and lounge makes for scenic dining, and relaxation opportunities include an indoor pool, dry sauna, sundeck, hot tub, and exercise room.

### La Quinta Inn–Denver Cherry Creek   $
**1975 South Colorado Boulevard**
**(303) 758-8886**
**www.lq.com**
It's nice to find an inexpensive but pleasant place to stay in the central business location of I-25 at South Colorado Boulevard, midway between downtown Denver and the Denver Tech Center. La Quinta Inn–Denver Cherry Creek is such a place,

with the dependable La Quinta features of quiet, comfortable rooms, free high-speed Internet access, an outdoor heated pool, a continental breakfast, and a guest laundry facility. This particular area of Colorado Boulevard also has a lot of midrange and chain restaurants to choose from.

### La Quinta Inn–Denver Downtown    $
**3500 Park Avenue West**
**(303) 458-1222**
**www.lq.com**
Just north of downtown Denver, La Quinta Inn–Denver Downtown is a three-story, 106-room hotel with an outdoor swimming pool and a renovated lobby. A continental breakfast is offered. It's close by Coors Field and Six Flags Elitch Gardens amusement park, and convenient to downtown, the west side, and the sports complexes of INVESCO Field at Mile High and the Pepsi Center.

### La Quinta Inn & Suites–DIA    $
**6801 Tower Road**
**(303) 371-0888**
**www.lq.com**
For those early-morning departures (or late-night arrivals), visitors and locals alike find this La Quinta a convenient place to stay. It has 169 rooms and a 24-hour fitness center that includes an indoor pool. Guests receive a free continental breakfast.

### Loews Denver Hotel    $$$
**4150 East Mississippi Avenue**
**(303) 782-9300**
**www.loewshotels.com**
There's enough elegant Italian styling to make your head swim at this 11-story hotel near the intersection of Colorado Boulevard and Mississippi Avenue. Inside the lobby, library, 5,000 square feet of meeting rooms, and 183 guest rooms, all you see is custom furnishings, marble, murals, frescoes, and continental antiques. The Tuscany Restaurant exclusively has Italian wines. Guests interested in exercise can take advantage of the aerobic center, which has equipment such as exercise bikes and rowing machines.

## Magnolia Hotel　　$$$
**818 17th Street**
**(303) 607–9000, (888) 915–1110**
**www.magnoliahoteldenver.com**

One of downtown Denver's newer hotels, opened in 1995, is a 244-room (117 of them suites) hotel resulting from a $20 million renovation of one of 17th Street's oldest buildings, the American National Bank Building at 17th and Stout Streets. Many of the rooms have big windows overlooking 17th Street, while others look into an interior atrium with a rock garden and waterfall beneath skylights. The hotel does not serve meals, but provides room service from a nearby restaurant. The Magnolia also includes a health club, free continental breakfast, and the 3,000-square-foot Magnolia Club room, filled with wonderful couches and chairs, periodicals, and an intimate atmosphere.

## Oxford Hotel　　$$$
**1600 17th Street**
**(303) 628–5400**
**www.theoxfordhotel.com**

The 80-room Oxford Hotel is in the heart of Lower Downtown's recently renovated redbrick district, a block from Union Station and a block from the Wynkoop Brewing Company's restaurant, bar, cabaret, and billiard parlor, across the street from an antiques shop and adjacent to an art gallery. The Oxford was built a year before the Brown Palace Hotel and was designed by the same architect, and it was once the preeminent lodging for travelers arriving in Denver by rail. It's not as beautiful as the Brown Palace, but the surroundings are more historic. The Cruise Room bar contained in the hotel is a popular nightspot, and the Oxford is within easy walking distance to other nightspots in Lower Downtown and Larimer Square. And it's just three blocks away from Coors Field, home of the Colorado Rockies. McCormick's Fish House and Bar, also in the hotel, is one of Denver's best places to eat (see our Restaurants chapter). Next door on the other side of the art gallery is the Oxford Club, a very nice health club

with barbering and styling available upstairs at the Oxford Salon & Spa.

## Quality Inn　　$
**3975 Peoria Way**
**(303) 371–5640**
**www.choicehotels.com**

This is one of the hotels that benefits from proximity to DIA. Located on I-70, west of the intersection with I-225, it's also convenient to the Denver Coliseum and the city of Aurora. It's a typical moderately priced business-traveler hotel. The 112 rooms are attractive but basic affairs with small work tables. Complimentary airport shuttle is available. It has a free continental breakfast and a guest laundry facility.

## Radisson Hotel Denver–Stapleton Plaza　　$$
**3333 Quebec Street**
**(303) 321–3500**
**www.radisson.com**

The hotel's 300 guest rooms are arrayed around a striking 11-story atrium lobby. Boardrooms are available on each floor, and the hotel has a 20,000-square-foot conference center, a business-services center, a restaurant, and a lounge. The health club has fitness consultants, aerobics classes, racquetball courts, a year-round heated outdoor pool, a whirlpool, a steam room/sauna, and very nice exercise equipment.

## Ramada Inn Downtown　　$$
**1150 East Colfax Avenue**
**(303) 831–7700**
**www.ramadadenverdowntown.com**

---

*A few years ago urban archaeologists went probing to find an underground tunnel that supposedly used to exist between Union Station and the Oxford Hotel. They didn't find the tunnel, but according to local legend, Teddy Roosevelt's aides once used it to whisk him from Union Station to the hotel when they decided he'd had too many spirits to be seen by the public.*

East Colfax is not the most scenic street in Denver, but you're in the Capitol Hill area here, and you're about halfway between the city center and the Colfax–University Avenue area. There are some fine restaurants within a few blocks, not to mention the attractions of the Denver Botanic Gardens and City Park, with the Denver Zoo and Denver Museum of Nature and Science. The Ramada has 143 rooms at very reasonable prices and a heated outdoor pool with a hot tub.

### Ramada Limited & Suites DIA     $
**7020 Tower Road**
**(303) 373-1600**
**www.ramada.com**
This Ramada is best known for being airport accessible. Along with 102 rooms that come equipped with two phone lines, a dataport, and a computer-fax hookup, the hotel offers an indoor pool and spa, a business center, and a complimentary airport shuttle.

### Red Lion Hotel–Denver Central     $
**4040 Quebec Street**
**(303) 321-6666**
**www.redlion.com**
Among one of many hotels near Stapleton, the Red Lion now serves the airport and the west side of Denver. It's just off I-70, so there's also fast access to downtown Denver and points west. Previously a Holiday Inn, the hotel underwent a $10 million renovation of its public space. It now boasts 297 guest rooms, 2 ballrooms, a restaurant and lounge, and 15,000 square feet of meeting space.

### Red Lion Hotel–Denver Downtown     $
**1975 Bryant Street**
**(303) 433-8331**
**www.redlion.com**

---

> **i**    *As long as you're downtown, location doesn't matter all that much, thanks to free shuttle buses that run frequently along the 16th Street Mall.*

---

One of the most convenient hotels to Denver sporting events, this 13-story circular tower has 171 rooms. And nearby INVESCO Field at Mile High is right across I-25 from downtown. The restaurant and lounge is on the 14th floor, with great views of the area, including downtown. The hotel also has an outdoor pool, exercise facilities, and more than 1,200 square feet of meeting space.

### Renaissance Denver Hotel     $$$
**3801 Quebec Street**
**(303) 399-7500**
**www.marriott.com**
Formerly the Stouffer Concourse Hotel and now owned by Marriott, this is another hotel that has in the past focused on business from Stapleton International Airport. Now it continues to offer high-end accommodations to air travelers from the new airport as well as people doing business in the north and east sides of Greater Denver. Just south of I-70, it has great connections to downtown Denver and the west. It has 400 guest rooms, two Club Floors with enhanced facilities and service, a restaurant, a health club with spas and indoor and outdoor pools, and more than 25,500 square feet of meeting space. The DIA shuttle is complimentary.

### Residence Inn Denver City Center     $$-$$$
**1725 Champa Street**
**(303) 296-3444**
**www.marriott.com**
Hospitality-mogul Walter Isenberg opened this all-suite hotel in 2006, with 14 floors, 229 suites, and 760 square feet of meeting space. Suites range from studios to two-bedrooms and come with full kitchens, flat-screen televisions, and wireless Internet. Amenities include a small fitness center, an eighth-floor patio with hot tub, and complimentary breakfast buffet and cocktails. The hotel's biggest selling point is its location—within walking distance of the 16th Street pedestrian mall, the 17th Street financial district, the State Capitol, and Coors Field and the Pepsi Center.

**Residence Inn by Marriott–
Denver Downtown**     **$$$**
**2777 North Zuni Street**
**(303) 458-5318**
**www.marriott.com**
Residence Inns are equipped as extended-stay accommodations, with per-night prices dropping substantially if you're there more than a week. Each of the 159 suites has a fully equipped kitchen and living room area. Either one-bed studio suites or two-bed, loft-style penthouse suites are available. This inn lies just off Speer Boulevard across the Central Platte Valley and I-25 from downtown Denver. It has a heated outdoor swimming pool, a hot tub, and an exercise room. There's a central dining room with complimentary breakfast, and they'll do your grocery shopping for you for free (you just pay for the groceries). It offers 900 square feet of meeting space, plus great access to Six Flags Elitch Gardens and downtown.

**Studio Suites Stapleton**     **$**
**4950 Quebec Street**
**(303) 320-0260**
**www.daysinn.com**
Just north of the old Stapleton International Airport, this former Days Inn is also a good bet for travelers coming into Denver International Airport because I-70 whizzes right past the hotel. DIA is 13 miles away. It has 193 rooms and an outdoor pool.

**Warwick Hotel**     **$$$**
**1776 Grant Street**
**(303) 861-2000**
**www.warwick.denver.com**
The accommodations shine in this tony hotel on Capitol Hill. All of the 219 rooms have recently undergone major renovation. The hotel features a number of romantic and night-on-the-town weekend packages. The open-air, rooftop pool is nice, as is the 24-hour health club.

**Westin Tabor Center**     **$$$**
**1672 Lawrence Street**
**(303) 572-9100**
**www.westin.com**
Although the alphabet places this downtown hotel at the bottom of our list, it really deserves to be near the top, if not the first on the list. All downtown hotels can claim a central location, but the Westin is truly central to the best shopping, entertainment, and nightlife of downtown Denver. It's on the 16th Street Mall, at the Tabor Center shopping complex, and it's a short walk away from the historic buildings, wonderful shops, and fine dining of Larimer Square and Lower Downtown. The hotel itself is palatial, with 430 rooms, a great restaurant and lounge, and enough ballroom and meeting space (more than 24,000 square feet, including a 200-seat auditorium) to make it one of the city's preferred gathering spots. The lobby lounge is a great place for people-watching. There's a health club, racquetball courts, an indoor/outdoor pool with a channel that allows you to swim between them, a sauna, and a nice hot tub on the western sundeck by the outdoor pool. The swanky Palm restaurant, across the street from the hotel, is the place to power lunch.

# Adams County

**Comfort Inn Central**     **$$**
**401 East 58th Avenue, Denver**
**(303) 297-1717**
**www.choicehotels.com**
Although Denver is the mailing address, the Quality Inn is actually in a patch of unincorporated Adams County. That's a relatively unimportant distinction, though, because it's on I-25 north of I-70 and well connected to Denver and its environs. It's also adjacent to the Merchandise Mart, a prime business venue. It was recently renovated and has 161 rooms, a restaurant, a lounge, a balcony on every room above the second floor, an outdoor heated pool, a beauty/barber shop, and a post office. It also offers ATM service and an exercise facility.

**La Quinta Inn–Northglenn**    $
345 West 120th Avenue, Westminster
(303) 252-9800
www.laquinta.com

When you stay this far north on I-25, you're putting yourself in a position convenient not just to Greater Denver, but to the northern attractions as well: Weld County, Fort Collins, Cheyenne, Rocky Mountain National Park via U.S. Highway 36, Big Thompson Canyon via U.S. Highway 34 out of Loveland, etc. Still, the Northglenn La Quinta is near commercial areas and companies, such as the headquarters of Gerry Baby Products.

The 130 rooms are basic but tidy and attractive, and you can opt for a "King Plus" room with a king-size bed, recliner chair, and two telephones. All the rooms offer free high-speed Internet access. This is the only La Quinta in Greater Denver with privileges at a nearby health club, and it also has a heated outdoor pool, free continental breakfast, and guest laundry facility. Nearby restaurants include the Village Inn and Perkins.

**Radisson North Denver**    $$
**Graystone Castle**
83 East 120th Avenue, Thornton
(303) 451-1002
www.radisson.com

You can't miss this place because it is, in fact, a gray stone castle. The medieval theme is carried out in some of the interior decoration, but it's a modern hotel with close to 9,000 square feet of meeting space and 133 rooms. Enjoy controlled access to the Concierge/Business Class level on the fifth floor, a restaurant, a pub lounge, an indoor heated swimming pool, a hot tub, a sauna, and an exercise room.

# Arapahoe County

**AmeriSuites Denver Airport**    $$
16250 East 40th Avenue, Aurora
(303) 371-0700

**AmeriSuites Park Meadows**
9030 East Westview Road, Lone Tree
(303) 662-8500

**AmeriSuites Tech Center**
8300 East Crescent Parkway, Englewood
(303) 804-0700
www.amerisuites.com

Corporate travelers may be familiar with the consistent accommodations and little extras of AmeriSuites, recently acquired by Hyatt, that help make doing business easier. All three properties are identical and feature 128 suites with refrigerator, microwave, coffeemaker, iron and ironing board, VHS, and dataports for computers (some with two phone lines). There also is a business center with computers, Internet access, copiers, and fax machines. For amenities you'll find an indoor pool and fitness center, and you'll be served a continental breakfast.

**Courtyard by Marriott–
Denver Tech Center**    $$
6565 South Boston Street,
Greenwood Village
(303) 721-0300
www.marriott.com

The Courtyard by Marriott is in Greenwood Village's southeastern tip, near the intersection of I-25 and Arapahoe Road. This Courtyard bills itself as "the hotel designed by business travelers," and that's appropriate for its setting in the Denver Tech Center area. The hotel has 143 large rooms, most with king-size or double beds, and suites with a closed-out bedroom and living room area. The hotel offers 1,304 square feet of meeting space, a minigym, indoor pool and Jacuzzi, and, of course, the courtyard with gazebo and barbecue grills. The Courtyard Cafe serves breakfast buffets, and the hotel also has a lounge bar open Sunday through Thursday. Free shuttle rides are offered within a 5-mile radius.

**Crystal Inn–Denver Airport**    $$
3300 North Ouray Street, Aurora
(303) 340-3800
www.crystalinns.com

Opened in 1997 to serve DIA, the Crystal Inn houses 157 rooms, 17 of which are suites with a living area, refrigerator, and microwave; some have Jacuzzis. Amenities include 3,500 square feet of meeting space, an indoor pool and Jacuzzi, laundry facilities, and a fitness area. Breakfast is served daily, and there is free shuttle service to DIA.

### Denver Marriott South $$
**10345 Park Meadows Drive, Littleton**
**(303) 925-0004**
**www.marriott.com**
Opened in February 2003, this 279-room hotel is just 1 mile from Park Meadows Mall and is near such business hubs as the Park Ridge Corporate Center, the Meridian and Inverness office parks, and the Denver Tech Center. Its decor is inspired by the Arts and Crafts architecture popularized at the turn of the 20th century, and its main floor is anchored by a two-sided stone fireplace. Guests find themselves in what the hotel calls "rooms that work," three of which are suites. They come equipped for business with a desk, ergonomic chair, two-line phones with voice mail, and high-speed Internet access. The hotel also has 12,000 square feet of meeting space, an 8,230-square-foot ballroom, and a 24-hour fitness center.

### Doubletree Hotel Denver Southeast $$
**13696 East Iliff Place, Aurora**
**(303) 337-2800**
**www.doubletree.com**
On I-225 in Aurora, the Doubletree Southeast has the best of that side of town and fast connections south toward the Denver Tech Center and north to the airport. The hotel has recently completed a major renovation of the entire property. It offers 248 rooms, each with two double beds or a king-size bed. The hotel also features Fitzgerald's Restaurant, serving breakfast, lunch, and dinner.

### Embassy Suites Denver Tech Center $$$
**10250 East Costilla Avenue, Centennial**
**(303) 792-0433**
**www.embassysuites.hilton.com**

Another property in unincorporated Arapahoe County, this hotel is close to the Denver Tech Center, Inverness Business Park, and I-25. It has 246 two-room suites that each include a separate living room with a sofa bed and a table. Free transportation is provided within a 6-mile radius. The restaurant has Southwestern and traditional cuisine, and you can work your meal off at the fitness center, indoor pool, and whirlpool or at a nearby full-service health club.

### Hampton Inn Denver/Aurora $
**1500 South Abilene Street, Aurora**
**(303) 369-8400**
**www.hamptoninn.hilton.com**
Serving a central location in the city of Aurora, this hotel is also located along I-225 for fast access north to Denver International Airport and south to the Denver Tech Center and Colorado Springs. The hotel has 132 rooms with coffeemakers, ironing boards, and irons. The hotel also provides a free continental breakfast buffet, a pass to a local health club, and meeting space for 60 people.

### Hampton Inn Denver/Southeast $
**9231 East Arapahoe Road**
**Greenwood Village**
**(303) 792-9999**
**www.hamptoninn.hilton.com**
The Hampton Inn Denver/Southeast is in the hotel cluster on the southeastern tip of Greenwood Village, adjacent to the intersection of Arapahoe Road and I-25, south of the Denver Tech Center. The hotel has 150 rooms, an outdoor swimming pool, workout facilities, in-room coffee service, ironing boards and irons in all rooms, and a free continental buffet breakfast. It offers great access to the Park Meadows shopping center.

### Holiday Inn Denver South/ Centennial Airport $
**7770 South Peoria Street, Englewood**
**(303) 790-7770**
**www.ichotelsgroup.com**
Located in unincorporated Arapahoe

County, this Holiday Inn is conveniently situated at the Centennial Airport, near the Denver Tech Center and Inverness Business Park and on the way to Colorado Springs. It's close to C-470 around the southwest side of Greater Denver and has good connections to Denver International Airport via I-25, I-225, and I-70. This hotel has 120 guest rooms, 45 of which are suites with separate bedrooms and living rooms. It has a cafe and lounge, an outdoor pool, a health club with sauna, and six flexible meeting rooms.

### The Inverness Hotel and Golf Club $$$
**200 Inverness Drive West, Englewood**
**(303) 799-5800, (800) 832-9053**
**www.invernesshotel.com**
It's not in Englewood but in unincorporated Arapahoe County just west of Centennial Airport. At the intersection of I-25 and County Line Road, one of I-25's last major intersections before it heads south through Douglas County to Colorado Springs, the hotel is centrally located in the "Piedmont Megalopolis," as some are beginning to call the increasingly interconnected Front Range urban landscape. Absolutely stunning from the outside, the Inverness Hotel's high-tech, high-style exterior fits the state-of-the-art conference facilities inside, with 42 meeting rooms (60,000 square feet total) including auditoriums, conference rooms, boardrooms, and breakout rooms with sophisticated audiovisual accommodations built in and aided by audiovisual specialists in a central control room. The hotel's meeting space is certified by the International Association of Conference Centers, and it hosts more than 750 meetings per year.

You don't have to attend a conference to enjoy the adjoining Inverness Golf Course, but you do have to be a hotel guest. The hotel has its own pro shop as well as a billiards room, three lighted tennis courts, indoor and outdoor pools, saunas, indoor and outdoor whirlpool baths, and a health club with aerobics studio, exercise circuit, and exercise equipment. Guests in

the 302 rooms can also enjoy four fine restaurants, including the award-winning, four-diamond Swan restaurant.

### La Quinta Inn–Aurora $
**1011 South Abilene Street, Aurora**
**(303) 337-0206**
**www.lq.com**
Aurora Regional Medical Center is right across I-225 from this centrally located hotel, and I-225 provides quick access north to the airport and south to the Denver Tech Center, Douglas County, and points south. It has a heated outdoor pool and laundry facilities and includes a free continental breakfast and free cable TV. There are plenty of nearby restaurants. Its 121 rooms are basic but tidy and attractive, and you can opt for a "King Plus" room with a king-size bed, recliner chair, and two telephones, one of which is a dataport phone, accessible to computer. Pets weighing 40 pounds or less are welcome.

### Quality Suites–Tech Center South $$
**7374 South Clinton Street, Englewood**
**(303) 858-0700**
**www.choicehotels.com**
The Quality Suites–Tech Center South is well positioned for travel. Besides its 78 guest suites, restaurant, lounge, and banquet facilities, this hotel has an indoor-outdoor pool, sauna, and hot tub.

### Residence Inn by Marriott–Denver South Tech Center $$$
**6565 South Yosemite Street, Englewood**
**(303) 740-7177**
**www.marriott.com**
This 128-suite hotel is actually on the border of unincorporated Arapahoe County and Greenwood Village in the Denver Tech Center area. That needs to be said for the benefit of those who want to find this tasteful extended-stay hotel in the Tech Center area. Even the "studio suites" include a fully equipped kitchen. Set in a neighborhood environment, the hotel has an outdoor swimming pool, heated spa, and complimentary passes to a nearby fitness club. There also is a fair amount of

strip mall shopping, including coffee and bagel shops, nearby.

## Sheraton Denver Tech Center $$$
**7007 South Clinton Street, Englewood**
**(303) 799-6200**
**www.starwoodhotels.com**
No, it's not in Englewood. It's just off I-25 at the far southeastern tip of Greenwood Village between the Denver Tech Center and Centennial Airport, near Park Meadows. It's a good place to stay if your Denver visit includes business or pleasure in Castle Rock or Colorado Springs. It also has great access to shopping at the Castle Rock Factory Outlet stores. Like other big hotels in this burgeoning part of town, it has great views of the mountains, especially from the club levels on the 9th and 10th floors, where you have concierge service, complimentary complete breakfast in the morning, and cocktails and hors d'oeuvres in the evening. Formerly a Radisson, the hotel has undergone a multimillion-dollar renovation, including all of its 263 rooms and its business center. The conference center meeting space totals 12,000 square feet. The hotel has a restaurant, lounge, exercise facility, outdoor heated pool, and whirlpool.

# Jefferson County

## Denver Days Inn & Suites West $
**15059 West Colfax Avenue, Golden**
**(303) 277-0200**
**www.daysinn.com**
Another cost-conscious alternative on the west side, this Days Inn sits at a major node of the west side's transportation web. You can go straight west to Golden, hop on I-70 west or east, or jog south to catch U.S. Highway 6 for a fast (unless its morning rush time) no-stoplight run to downtown Denver. The hotel has 157 newly renovated rooms, a restaurant, heated outdoor swimming pool, hot tub, and sauna and exercise area.

## Denver Marriott West $$
**1717 Denver West Boulevard, Golden**
**(303) 279-9100**
**www.marriott.com**
One of the first places people mention when asked about fine accommodations on the far-west side, Denver Marriott West is set in the Denver West Office Park just off I-70 in Golden. Guests in its 305 rooms are 20 minutes from downtown Denver. Only 10 minutes on I-70 west and you'll be in the mountains. It has an indoor and outdoor pool, exercise equipment, saunas, restaurant, lounge, and 9,600 square feet of meeting space. Pets are welcome.

## Denver West Inn $
**7150 West Colfax Avenue, Lakewood**
**(303) 238-1251**
**www.denverwestinn.com**
This is a nice, inexpensive hotel for business and vacation travelers. Just off of two major east-west thoroughfares, West Colfax Avenue and US 6, and less than 5 miles east of I-70, it's a good location for access to both downtown Denver and the mountains. There's an on-site laundry, a seasonal outdoor pool, and free coffee 24 hours a day in the lobby. That's about it for amenities, but the 122 rooms were totally remodeled in the summer of 1997.

## Doubletree Hotel Denver North $
**8773 Yates Drive, Westminster**
**(303) 427-4000**
**www.doubletreehilton.com**
Perched on a nice Rocky Mountain vantage point just north of US 36, this is a good hotel for those seeking ready access both to Greater Denver and Boulder County to the northwest. In addition to its 180 rooms, including "Jacuzzi suites," it has 8,400 square feet of meeting space, a restaurant, a lounge, and a very nice whirlpool, sauna, indoor swimming pool, and exercise room.

**Hampton Inn Denver–Southwest**    **$**
**3605 South Wadsworth Boulevard**
**Lakewood**
**(303) 989–6900**
**www.hamptoninn.hilton.com**
South of U.S. Highway 285, on the southern tip of Lakewood where it borders unincorporated Jefferson County, the Hampton Inn Denver–Southwest is convenient to the mountains and to the big employers of southwest and western Jefferson County, such as the Denver Federal Center, Martin Marietta, Qwest, Coors, and Manville. It has 150 rooms, an outdoor swimming pool, free continental breakfast, meeting rooms, neighborhood surroundings, and the Foothills Golf Course nearby.

**Hilltop Inn**    **$$**
**9009 Jeffco Airport Avenue, Broomfield**
**(303) 469–3900**
**www.guest-house.com/hilltop.html**
The Hilltop Inn could almost be listed in our Bed-and-Breakfast Inns section, with its quiet country-inn ambience, its complimentary breakfast, and its "great room" with fireplace and collection of books. Then again, it has amenities similar to those found in a hotel, such as satellite TV, T1 Internet access, a laundry room, conference and meeting rooms, an on-site catering and special-events coordinator, and a corporate atmosphere. One might describe it as a "corporate B&B," although it's not just for the business crowd. The great room and patio are good places for wedding-related events as well as corporate cocktail parties. Each separate suite has its own private entrance and fireplace, kitchenette, private bath, and king-size bed. Some have whirlpool baths and separate sitting rooms.

**La Quinta Inn–Golden**    **$**
**3301 Youngfield Service Road, Golden**
**(303) 279–5565**
**www.lq.com**
This is a great location for access to the mountains on I-70 west or to the business and tourist attractions of Jefferson County. Practically out its front door,

32nd Avenue winds west past the Adolph Coors Co. brewery to the city of Golden. On the other side of I-70, an extensive shopping center has nearly everything you might need, including a Starbucks. The hotel has 129 rooms on three floors and a heated outdoor pool. Pets are welcome.

**La Quinta Inn–Westminster Mall**    **$**
**8701 Turnpike Drive, Westminster**
**(303) 425–9099**
**www.lq.com**
Just south of US 36, east of Sheridan Avenue, this hotel puts you in an intermediate location between Denver and Boulder. And Sheridan, of all the north-south thoroughfares on the west side, is one of the fastest moving, so that means a decent connection with I-70 to the south. The hotel has 130 rooms, a heated outdoor pool, continental breakfast, and guest laundry facilities. Rooms are basic but tidy and attractive, and you can opt for a "King Plus" room with a king-size bed, recliner chair, and two telephones, one of which is a dataport phone, accessible to computer. Pets are welcome.

**Omni Interlocken Resort**    **$$$**
**500 Interlocken Boulevard, Broomfield**
**(303) 438–6600**
**www.omnihotels.com**
This 390-room four-diamond resort opened in 1999, providing luxury accommodations in a rather unlikely spot along the four-lane turnpike between Boulder and Denver. Over the years the surrounding area has grown up to meet it, and by 2006 its corporate neighbors in the Interlocken Business Park included Vail Resorts, Sun Microsystems, Level 3, and Corporate Express. The hotel boasts a 27-hole golf course, a full-service spa, an outdoor pavilion suitable for weddings and other large gatherings, a business center, a 9,000-square-foot ballroom, a conference concierge to oversee meetings and conferences, and free evening champagne in the lobby. High rollers who prefer to arrive in their own planes can land at

nearby Jefferson County Airport and catch a shuttle to the Omni. The Tap Room offers microbrews, foosball, and pool tables. The Meritage restaurant is open for breakfast, lunch, and dinner, with classically trained chef Will Chenowith directing the menu. The restaurant is gaining an extracurricular reputation as the place for monthly Iron Chef competitions in which local chefs compete against each other for bragging rights and the chance to compete again. Tickets to the prix fixe meal sell out quickly, so advance reservations are recommended.

### Sheraton Denver West Hotel & Conference Center $$
**360 Union Boulevard, Lakewood**
**(303) 987-2000**
**www.starwoodhotels.com**
Aimed at the business traveler, with a full-service business center and 18,000 square feet of meeting space in 16 meeting rooms, this 242-room hotel is also one of the nicest places to stay on your vacation. Right off US 6, it's a great staging point for trips to the mountains; it's also in a thriving business and commercial area of western Greater Denver. The Sheraton has a restaurant and lounge and an in-house health club, weight room, indoor pool, and sauna. If you want to go whole hog, the oversize rooms on the concierge floor have whirlpool tubs and other amenities.

### Table Mountain Inn $$
**1310 Washington Avenue, Golden**
**(303) 277-9898**
**www.tablemountaininn.com**
The Table Mountain Inn shares an important characteristic with the Westin Tabor Center in our Denver listings: The alphabet places it at the bottom, but it ranks at the top for the county. First of all, it's very charming with its Santa Fe–style architecture and interiors. Second, its Southwestern-cuisine restaurant is not just a hotel restaurant but a west-side treasure that people drive to from nearby cities just to enjoy. Third, it's right on the main street of downtown Golden in the

midst of the neighborly, small-town atmosphere. It's within walking distance of the Coors Brewery and the Colorado School of Mines to boot. In 1999 the hotel expanded from 32 rooms to 74 and added a new parking area and weight room.

### Westin Westminster $$$
**10600 Westminster Boulevard, Westminster**
**(303) 410-5000**
**www.starwoodhotels.com/westin**
This four-star hotel has 369 guest rooms, 30,000 square feet of meeting rooms, another 30,000 square feet of outdoor space that can be used for functions, and an elegant restaurant called O's. The adjacent O Room is a comfortable spot for an evening cocktail and is known for its fresh oyster and seafood bar. An even bigger selling point is the Westin's location along the Boulder-Denver turnpike. It is situated across the boulevard from Westminster's western playground, the Promenade. Guests are within walking distance of a three-rink ice arena, a bowling alley, a dozen restaurants, a 24-screen theater, the unique Butterfly Pavilion, and the upscale Westminster Recreation Center. Holistic health-guru Deepak Chopra also is building a new Chopra Center and Spa nearby.

## BED-AND-BREAKFAST INNS

There are some who don't care for the bed-and-breakfast experience; they want a modern room, a pool, a restaurant, a gift shop, and a lobby. But others enjoy the charm, personal touch, intimacy, and often historic surroundings of a bed-and-breakfast inn. Greater Denver has inns that compare with the best anywhere.

In the use of our price-key symbols ($, $$, or $$$), representing double occupancy during the week, we've tried to represent the average price of accommodations for each bed-and-breakfast inn, but remember that the inns often have a limited number of rooms and have widely varying price ranges.

All the bed-and-breakfasts in our listing are located in downtown Denver. All of them accept credit cards, and none of them accept pets. None of them will turn away people with children, but in some cases, as indicated, children may be difficult to accommodate due to limits on the number of people allowed in rooms or the inability to add an extra bed to rooms.

### Capitol Hill Mansion $$$
**1207 Pennsylvania Street**
**(303) 839-5221, (800) 839-9329**
**www.capitolhillmansion.com**

All the fineries you expect from a bed-and-breakfast inn can be found in this mansion of ruby sandstone, along with all the sense of place and history you expect in the historic inn experience. The mansion is on the National Register of Historic Places, having been built in 1891 as one of the last great mansions raised before the silver crash put a temporary damper on local development. It's in an area near the State Capitol, surrounded by ornate historic structures built when Capitol Hill was known as "snob knob." The exterior is a turreted, balconied affair with a grand curved porch. The interior lives up to even the most aristocratic expectations, with crafted, patterned plaster and golden oak paneling opening to a dramatic sweeping staircase with stained- and beveled-glass windows. The public parlors are inviting, and each room is individually decorated with such touches as brass beds, claw-foot tubs, private balconies, curved-glass windows, high ceilings, fireplaces, and oak floors. There is also a solarium and a hand-painted mural. Soothing music, soft lighting, and jetted tubs are among the other attractions. There are eight guest rooms in all, each with a private bath, some with whirlpools. Be sure to visit the Web site for photos of each.

### Castle Marne $$$
**1572 Race Street**
**(303) 331-0621, (800) 926-2763**
**www.castlemarne.com**

Victorian architecture with an eccentric flair is the charm of this bed-and-breakfast on Denver's near-east side, 20 blocks from downtown and an easier and more scenic walk from the Denver Zoo, the Denver Museum of Nature and Science, and the Denver Botanic Gardens. Built in 1889, Castle Marne really looks like a small castle. Its designer was the eclectic architect William Lang, who also designed Denver's famous "Unsinkable" Molly Brown House, now a major landmark and tourist attraction. Castle Marne is striking on the outside, stunning on the inside.

Some of the nine guest rooms have their own Jacuzzi tubs for two. Three of the rooms have private balconies with hot tubs for two. All have furnishings chosen to bring together authentic period antiques, family heirlooms, and exacting reproductions to create a mood of tranquil and elegant charm. You can find that same mood in the parlor, a serene retreat of high ceilings and glowing dark woods, and the cherry-paneled dining room. The castle's big visual treasure is what they call their Peacock Window, a circular stained-glass beauty partway up the grand staircase. The castle also has a gift shop, a game room, a Victorian garden, an airy veranda, and a guest office for the business traveler, including computer. Generally only well-behaved children older than age 10 are allowed. Although that is the only restriction on children at Castle Marne, most rooms are subject to a maximum occupancy of two persons per room.

### Holiday Chalet $$
**1820 East Colfax Avenue**
**(303) 437-8245, (800) 626-4497**
**www.holidaychalet.net**

Though each of the 10 rooms has its own kitchen, Holiday Chalet serves a continental breakfast. This Victorian-charm hotel is a restored three-story brownstone mansion built in 1896 for a prominent Denver jeweler. The present owners represent the third generation of the same family that has served guests here. It's situated for easy walking to the Denver Zoo, the Denver

Museum of Nature and Science, and the Denver Botanic Gardens. It's about 10 blocks from downtown.

### Lumber Baron Inn & Gardens    $$$
**2555 West 37th Avenue**
**(303) 477-8205**
**www.lumberbaron.com**
One of Denver's newer bed-and-breakfast inns, the Lumber Baron was refurbished and opened for business in the summer of 1994. But it goes way back before that, being an 1890s brick mansion built by John Mouat, a Scottish immigrant who ran a major mill-work and construction supply company. He put six different kinds of wood into his house's fancy woodwork. The first two floors have 12-foot ceilings, there's a 2,000-square-foot ballroom on the third floor, and there is space for banquets and event rental. The Lumber Baron has five suites, all of them with Jacuzzis for two. All the suites, as with the entire house and grounds, are pure Victorian elegance. The inn is also known for its Murder Mystery Dinners. A full breakfast is part of the package.

### Queen Anne Bed & Breakfast Inn    $$
**2147 Tremont Place**
**(303) 296-6666**
**www.queenannebnb.com**
The Queen Anne Bed & Breakfast Inn is in a restored area on the edge of downtown—the Clements Historic District, Denver's oldest continuously occupied residential neighborhood. The Queen Anne itself consists of two adjacent Victorian buildings in the Queen Anne style of architecture, of 1879 and 1886 vintage, both of which are on the National Register of Historic Places. They give you a list of guidebook editors to write to, and that's because they know they're a good bet for a favorable review, with their elegantly restored interiors, period furnishings, eager service, and 14 quaintly homey rooms featuring individual baths, writing desks, piped-in chamber music at your control, and fresh flowers. This inn has been rated one of the best of Denver by *Westword* and among the seven most

romantic destinations in Colorado by a local television station. Coors Field is about a 15-minute walk away, which hasn't hurt the bed-and-breakfast's business.

## HOSTELS

Hostels are for the truly cost-conscious traveler who is not looking for frills or even a bathroom in the room. If you're traveling on a budget and love an offbeat atmosphere and what might seem like bohemian accommodations to the folks at the Westin and the Hyatt, there's nothing like that special camaraderie that prevails in the hostel environment.

They used to call these "youth hostels" because older folks tended to think they were OK for kids but déclassé for adults, or that they were just plain dives for the down-and-out. Now, in a more enlightened era, we know that all ages can enjoy the hostel experience. OK, hostels sometimes look like flophouses from the outside, and they're sometimes in seedier parts of town. Then again, some of them are unexpectedly attractive. One thing for sure is they tend to be close to the center of town, with prices that allow you to stay for a week on what would be one night's price at a reasonably fancy hotel. Our price key, explained at the beginning of the chapter, doesn't really tell you how cheap they are, because prices for the following hostels can be less than $10 per night. Denver has several choice venues for the hosteler.

You can get the full scoop on hostels in the Denver area and the rest of the United States by calling American Youth Hostels–Hostelling International at (202) 783-6161. There's also a Boulder number, (303) 442-1166, that's good for Rocky Mountains hostels. We've listed below the downtown Denver possibilities.

The hostels listed all accept major credit cards but no personal checks. There are no age restrictions on occupants, except that people younger than age 18 cannot check in without a parent or guardian.

## Denver International Youth Hostel    $
### 630 East 16th Avenue
### (303) 832-9996

The Denver International Hostel is just 6 blocks east of Broadway and the edge of downtown. It's all dormitories, meaning you share bedrooms with other people, but the dormitories are separated into men's and women's sections. How many people share a room? It depends on the night. Bathrooms are down the hall. They have showers, a kitchen you can use, a common room with a TV, library, and stereo, balconies, storage, and sports equipment. You have to check in between 8:00 and 10:00 A.M. or between 5:00 and 10:30 P.M., when the office is open. There's no curfew; you get keys to come and go when you please.

## Hostel of the Rockies    $
### 1530 Downing Street
### (303) 861-7777
### www.innkeeperrockies.com

One of the newest hostels in the area, this one offers rooms with 4 beds (50 beds in all), as well as four private rooms. Each dorm-style room has its own bath and shower and kitchen. Every room also has TV with HBO. The location is great, with easy bus access and dozens of restaurants within 1 mile. They also offer bikes for rent, Internet access, and tours to mountain locations.

## Melbourne Hotel & Hostel    $
### 607 22nd Street
### (303) 292-6386

An old hotel, the Melbourne is within easy walking distance of the Greyhound bus terminal and the Amtrak train station. Rooms have sinks and beds. Bathrooms are off the hall. The 16 hostel rooms are dormitories, meaning you share a room with three to five people. Wine and beer are allowed, but no hard liquor. The Melbourne is Denver's most child-accommodating hostel. It has four family rooms, each of which has a double bed plus a set of bunk beds.

# RESTAURANTS

Dining out, like shopping, is an area in which Greater Denver excels. Lots of hot young chefs are busy in the kitchens here, enough so that their food has collectively earned the name "Rocky Mountain cuisine."

What this means is an emphasis on game and other local products, like trout and lamb. (Colorado has the country's fourth-largest population of lamb and is the country's largest processor of lamb.) Southwestern influences abound; many of the new chefs are liberal in their use of chiles, cilantro, tomatillos, and black beans.

Of course, there's plenty of old-fashioned Rocky Mountain cuisine, too. A number of restaurants pride themselves on what they're able to do with buffalo meat. Buffalo, along with other game such as elk and pheasant, has long been on the menu at Denver's oldest restaurant, the Buckhorn Exchange. Leaner than beef, buffalo is enjoying a resurgence of popularity nationwide, and Colorado restaurateurs, such as Sam Arnold of the Fort, are leading the way. Strong-stomached Denver diners may want to sample Rocky Mountain oysters, which are—how shall we put it?—the testicles of the male buffalo or cow, sautéed or breaded and deep-fried. Believe us, not everyone eats the stuff.

Getting fresh seafood used to be a problem in Denver, but no more. Pacific Coast fish such as salmon and river fish such as trout are widely available and consistently good. Maine lobster isn't hard to find either, and fans of clams and oysters on the half shell can find them at several restaurants that have them flown in daily. Fresh sushi is also easy to find.

As for ethnicity, Greater Denver counts among its blessings several Ethiopian eateries and top-notch Vietnamese, Japanese, Korean, Mexican, Peruvian, and Brazilian restaurants. There are also plenty of California-influenced bistros, especially in the Cherry Creek area. Most serve pastas, burgers, and pizzas, many made in on-site wood-burning ovens.

In this section we've left out chain restaurants such as Chili's and Pizza Hut, not because we have anything against them, but on the assumption that readers already know what to expect at these places. Locally owned chains that operate only within the Greater Denver area are included, as visitors couldn't be expected to know their fare. A national chain may have slipped into the listings here and there, either inadvertently because we didn't know it was one of many, or because to omit it would leave a particular geographic area underrepresented. In the case of exceptional merit, we've bent our rules on chains.

As you can imagine, no one book could ever describe all of Greater Denver's restaurants. We've picked out the best and the brightest, as is our mandate throughout this guide. Some are special-occasion places, others are neighborhood joints. Some are widely known local institutions, others much less so. We also tried to be clear about whether it's the food, the ambience, the crowd, the service, or all of the above that makes a place worth a visit. Obviously we don't expect everyone to agree with all our choices, and restaurants are notoriously mutable creatures, apt to get better or worse or go out of business without warning. Hours and days of operation change, too, so we suggest you call before you go. Also, while some restaurants serve continuously, others close between lunch and dinner, so if it's a midafternoon bite that you're after, definitely call first.

For dining out with children, take a look at our Kidstuff chapter, where we have described restaurants that cater to kids or places where the entertainment is at least as much of a draw as the food. If you're looking to combine eating with music, or if you're more in the mood for a bar than a restaurant, check our Nightlife chapter.

We've listed restaurants alphabetically by category, based on our experience that Denverites, like most Westerners, are more inclined to drive to a destination than to pick a restaurant on the basis of what's within walking distance. At the end of each listing, however, we've given an indication of location. Downtown restaurants are all within walking (or free shuttle bus) distance of downtown hotels. Restaurants we've described as being central are usually more than a half-mile walk from downtown. Each restaurant is in Denver unless otherwise noted.

Listing by category has its own set of problems, of course. In Denver it seems that every third restaurant has at least a few Mexican-inspired items on the menu, and steak houses and seafood restaurants usually cross over into each other's territory. We placed restaurants by their specialty, but if you read the descriptions themselves, you'll get a better sense of what else each offers.

Denver is a very casual city and the suburbs even more so. It's possible to eat a $100 dinner in shorts and sandals and not feel like the waiter is looking down at you. But Denverites generally do dress up for a nice meal, especially at trendy bistros. In general, price is a good guide to how formal a restaurant is: the more expensive, the more dressed-up the clientele. Consider location, too. At virtually all the restaurants we've listed in West Denver, a person who shows up dressed to the nines is going to feel very much out of place. Another rule of thumb is that restaurants that don't take any credit cards tend to be the most casual and located in neighborhoods that aren't the most fashionable. (This isn't necessarily true of coffeehouses and bakeries, however.)

To help you find the restaurants, we've added the general location within the city or suburbs in parentheses at the end of each listing.

## FOOD OF ALL KINDS

Most of the restaurants listed in this chapter accept major credit cards; we have specified those that do not.

Unless we've noted otherwise, all restaurants are open for lunch and dinner. Many downtown restaurants serve lunch on weekdays only.

Most Greater Denver restaurants accept local (but rarely out-of-state) checks. Occasionally a check-guarantee card is required, and, of course, there are some restaurants that don't take checks at all. Policies change, so call first if this is important to you.

Also, the nonsmoking movement is strong along Colorado's Front Range (especially in Boulder), and a growing number of restaurants are totally non-smoking. Once again, if this is an issue for you, it's best to call ahead. Or you can check the online database of smoke-free dining at www.gaspforair.org.

Remember that lunch at an expensive place is likely to be quite a bit less costly than dinner, although the price difference varies from restaurant to restaurant. Happy dining!

## PRICE CODE

To give an idea of price, we've used the following symbols. These price codes are based on the average price of two entrees, excluding alcohol, dessert, tax, and tip.

| $ | less than $16 |
| $$ | $17 to $26 |
| $$$ | $27 to $34 |
| $$$$ | $35 and higher |

## AFRICAN

**The Ethiopian Restaurant**          $-$$
**2816 East Colfax Avenue**
**(303) 322-5939**
The small, homey Ethiopian Restaurant has a warm pink dining room and serves lunch and dinner daily at reasonable prices. This is a nonsmoking establish-

ment, and it serves Ethiopian honey wine. No credit cards. (Central/East)

### Mataam Fez Moroccan Restaurant $$$$
**4609 East Colfax Avenue**
**(303) 399-9282**
**www.mataamfez.com**

A meal at Mataam Fez is more than a meal, it's an experience. A five-course Moroccan feast is served in sumptuous tented surroundings with entertainment on the weekends. Patrons dine using their fingers, while sitting on the floor with their shoes off. This nonsmoking restaurant is open for dinner only. There is also a location in Boulder. (Central)

### Queen of Sheba Ethiopian Restaurant $
**7225 East Colfax Avenue**
**at Quebec Street**
**(303) 399-9442**

This is a small, casual spot that offers smiling service. Prices at Queen of Sheba are rock bottom. A favorite with meat eaters is the shish kebab. Smoking is not allowed, and beer and wine are the only alcohol served. Queen of Sheba serves lunch and dinner and is closed on Monday. (Central/East)

## AMERICAN

### Avenue Grill $$-$$$
**630 East 17th Avenue**
**(303) 861-2820**
**www.avenuegrill.com**

Denver's young movers and shakers gather at the long bar here and do business at the banquettes with their cellular phones. This is not a place to hide out in a dark corner, as there are none. So what's to eat? Salads, sandwiches, burgers, a few Southwestern dishes, a tasty cioppino, and some killer desserts. It's a great people-watching spot on Denver's "restaurant row." Lunch and dinner are served daily, except Sunday when it's open for dinner only. (Central)

### Bang! $$
**3472 West 32nd Avenue**
**(303) 455-1117**

This popular Highland spot seats about 30 inside and 16 outside on its patio. It can be noisy and crowded, but that's part of the charm. Down-home specialties include meat loaf and catfish, and there are less traditional offerings as well. Beer and wine are served. Dinner only Tuesday through Saturday. (Northwest)

### Bayou Bob's $
**1635 Glenarm Place**
**(303) 573-6828**

Itching for some jambalaya, red beans and rice, a po'boy sandwich, shrimp gumbo, or fried catfish? Bayou Bob's is one of the few places in town that serves authentic Louisiana Cajun food. Open Monday and Tuesday 11:00 A.M. to 9:00 P.M., Wednesday through Saturday 11:00 A.M. to 10:00 P.M., and Sunday 11:00 A.M. to 9:00 P.M. (Downtown)

### The Broker $$$-$$$$
**821 17th Street**
**(303) 292-5065**
**www.thebrokerrestaurant.com**

The downtown Broker is situated in what was once a bank—some tables are in the old vault. It serves classic and contemporary American entrees and is known for its steaks, ice-cold peeled shrimp, good wine lists, and excellent desserts. This downtown restaurant is a popular place for a business lunch and is open for dinner seven days a week 5:10 to 10:00 P.M. and for lunch weekdays only 11:00 A.M. to 2:00 P.M. This is one of the rare Denver dining spots where the attire tends to be somewhat dressy, though it's not required. (Downtown)

### Café Star $$-$$$
**3201 East Colfax Avenue**
**(303) 320-8635**

Chef Rebecca Weitzman has quickly turned this relatively new spot into the place to go for just about any reason—a

*Denver has always been a town whose inhabitants enjoy dining out. In fact restaurants are often filled all week long. If a restaurant takes reservations, make them. Otherwise count on long wait lists or plan to dine very early or late.*

fine meal, a quick cocktail, or shared appetizers. Our good friend Lisa recommends the pot pies, especially the ones with lobster in them. Café Star is open for lunch and dinner but closed on Monday and Tuesday. (Central)

### The Cherry Cricket     $–$$
**2641 East Second Avenue**
**(303) 322-7666**
**www.cherrycricket.com**
The Cherry Cricket is known for its famously juicy burgers and its extensive roster of microbrews. The salads are substantial, fresh, and quite good. This is a loud neighborhood joint that goes crazy on St. Patrick's Day. It's open for lunch and dinner daily. (Cherry Creek)

### Croc's Mexican Grill     $$
**1630 Market Street**
**(303) 436-1144**
**www.crocsmexicangrill.com**
A high-energy restaurant with brick walls, a big bar, and a 20-foot-long fake crocodile suspended from the ceiling, Croc's serves mainly Mexican food at reasonable prices. There are also burgers, seafood, and a wall-to-wall happy hour. Lunch and dinner are served daily in addition to a weekend brunch of Mexican omelets, huevos rancheros, and breakfast burritos. (Downtown)

### Dixons Downtown Grill     $–$$
**1610 16th Street**
**(303) 573-6100**
**www.grdeating.com/dixons/**
Dixons is the place to go when everyone is hungry for something different. You'll find steaks, seafood, a chili plate, South-

western fare, pastas, burgers, and more. The atmosphere is relaxed, with large booths and an oak bar area. Popular items include the penne pasta with sausage, the peppercorn steak, and the herb-baked salmon. Dixons is owned by the same folks who own Goodfriends on East Colfax Avenue and Racine's on Bannock. It's open for breakfast, lunch, and dinner Monday through Friday and brunch and dinner on weekends. (Downtown)

### El Rancho Restaurant & Mountain Lodge     $$$
**El Rancho exit 252 off Interstate 70,**
**El Rancho**
**(303) 526-0661**
**www.historicelrancho.com**
A restaurant and lodge about 18 miles west of Denver near Genesee, El Rancho has a rustic atmosphere and seven fireplaces. The main dining room has a view of the Rocky Mountains and serves such regional specialties as prime rib and trout. The cinnamon rolls are locally famous. Open since 1948, El Rancho serves lunch, dinner, and a Sunday breakfast buffet. Live entertainment is offered on some weekend nights. The outdoor patio with its great views makes a meal special. The eight lodges are fun for a weekend getaway or for out-of-town visitors. (West suburbs)

### Giggling Grizzly     $–$$
**1320 20th Street**
**(303) 297-8300**
**www.giggling-grizzly.com**
From the big grizzly (yes, giggling) painted outside, you can tell this will be a fun place. It's really more of a bar than a restaurant, but you can get burgers, sandwiches, and the like. The crowd tends to be young, the music rockin' and on the loud end. Giggling Grizzly does a robust business, especially during Rockies games. It's a good place to sample LoDo fever and, well, drink lots of alcohol. The Grizzly serves dinner nightly. (Downtown)

**Goodfriends** $
3100 East Colfax Avenue
(303) 399-1751
www.grdeating.com/goodfriends/
The name says it all. Here's an easygoing place to get together with friends and enjoy sandwiches, burgers, or Southwestern food, with virtually everything on the menu prepared in low-fat fashion upon request (not a bad idea, given the generous portions and heavy hand with such things as cheese). The menu also includes scads of vegetarian choices. Lunch and dinner are served daily; brunch and dinner on Saturday and Sunday. (Central/East)

**Govnr's Park** $
672 Logan Street
(303) 831-8605
www.govnrspark.com
Named for its proximity to the governor's mansion across the street, this is a popular spot with the Friday-night crowd looking for the relaxed after-work scene. Once a dry cleaners, Govnr's Park is now a big, boisterous neighborhood restaurant and tavern with a massive beer list and sandwiches, burgers, and tavern dishes on the menu. The front patio, shaded by a large awning, is especially nice for an informal Sunday brunch. Lunch and dinner are served every day. Half of Govnr's is a pool room that draws a mainly twenty-something crowd. (Central)

**Gunther Toody's** $
4500 East Alameda Avenue, Glendale
(303) 399-1959

9220 East Arapahoe Road, Englewood
(303) 799-1958

7355 Ralston Road, Arvada
(303) 422-1954
8266 West Bowles Avenue, Littleton
(303) 932-1957

301 West 104th Street, Northglenn
(303) 453-1956
www.gunthertoodys.com
"Howdy Doody. . . . Gunther Toody's, this is Sandra Dee, what's shakin' bacon?"

That's the way the phone gets answered when you call one of these local spots. You'll feel like you're in a scene in the movie *Grease* at this '50s-concept diner with gum-chewing waiters and waitresses. The food is classic American fare, and the milk shakes will bring out the kid in you. We highly recommend it for children. Breakfast, lunch, and dinner are served every day. (East, Southeast, West, and North suburbs)

**LoDo's Bar & Grill** $$
1946 Market Street
(303) 293-8555

**LoDo's Highlands Ranch**
8545 South Quebec Street, Highlands Ranch
(303) 346-2930
www.lodosbarandgrill.com
The rooftop deck of the downtown location near the home-plate entrance to Coors Field lets you drink in the view while enjoying your meal. Meanwhile, the new Highlands Ranch south location offers a rooftop deck with stunning views of the Denver skyline and the mountains, including Pikes Peak. Both locations have big-screen TVs for watching sports, 24 beers on tap, and eats that include fish and chips, shrimp, fajitas, pasta, sandwiches, and salads. Lunch and dinner are served daily at both locations. (Downtown, South central suburbs)

**Marlowe's** $$$
511 16th Street
(303) 595-3700
www.marlowesdenver.com
The epitome of Denver's singles scene in the 1980s, Marlowe's remains a popular gathering spot for lunch, dinner, or after work. The restaurant serves steaks, chops, seafood, salads, pasta, and fresh Maine lobster. Marlowe's features an extensive martini list as well as daily happy hour specials. Located across from Denver Pavilions, it boasts a nice patio on the 16th Street Mall with prime people-watching. Lunch and dinner are served daily. (Downtown)

## Mel's Bar & Grill $$$$
**235 Fillmore Street**
**(303) 333-3979**
**www.melsbarandgrill.com**
Mediterranean fare and an upscale yet comfortable atmosphere are on the menu at Mel's. A prime Cherry Creek location, good wine list, and creative beef, chicken, and pasta choices make this a popular spot. The cozy bar draws folks in their 30s to 50s. Live jazz is performed most nights. Lunch and dinner daily except Sunday, which is dinner only. (Cherry Creek)

## Mercury Cafe $-$$
**2199 California Street**
**(303) 294-9281**
In addition to hosting one of the best and most eclectic performing arts series in town, the funky, friendly Mercury Cafe serves breakfast and lunch Saturday and Sunday and dinner Tuesday through Sunday, with an emphasis on natural foods. The food is as varied as the entertainment lineup; a meal here might include tofu enchiladas, steaks, salmon, or sandwiches. Closed Monday, and they do not accept credit cards. (Downtown/Central)

## Mustard's Last Stand II $
**2081 South University Boulevard**
**(303) 722-7936**
You can't get more American than hot dogs, french fries, and root beer floats, all of which this plain little joint does to perfection. Its location near the University of Denver guarantees a steady clientele, but older folks sneak over for the Polish sausage, too. The original Mustard's Last Stand is at 1719 Broadway (at Arapahoe Avenue) in Boulder, (303) 444-5841. It's open daily; credit cards not accepted. (South central)

## My Brother's Bar $
**2376 15th Street**
**(303) 455-9991**
The entrance to this corner tavern looks less than inviting, but everyone is welcome. A mixed crowd gathers here for burgers (a tasty vegetarian version is available) and beers. The pleasantly shaded patio out back is a hidden delight. It's a good place to keep in mind when you're hungry late at night, as they serve past midnight. It's closed on Sunday. (Downtown/Platte River area)

## Nine75 $$$
**975 Lincoln Street**
**(303) 975-1975**
This Golden Triangle hot spot is hard to forget, and not just because the name is actually the address and the phone number. It's located in a chichi high-rise across the street from Denver's premiere jazz club and attracts movers and shakers well into the evening. Those fans line up for big dishes to share with friends and for small dishes to mix and match. Among my friend Lisa's favorites are the creamed spinach, baked mac and cheese, crabmeat California rolls (which look more like Napoleons), and, for dessert, a plateful of cotton candy. The owners call it comfort food with a twist. Open for lunch Monday through Thursday and dinner Monday through Saturday. (Central)

## Painted Bench $$
**400 East 20th Avenue**
**(303) 863-7473**
**www.paintedbenchdenver.com**
Located in a row of once-dilapidated storefronts, the Painted Bench is a key player in the gentrification process of an urban area now known as Uptown. Its antique bar is a reminder that the place has history. Its bistro-style food is succulent enough to pull in diners from across the metro area. Open Monday through Friday for lunch and dinner, Saturday for dinner only; closed Sunday. Reservations are recommended. (Uptown)

## Palace Arms $$$$
**321 17th Avenue,**
**at the Brown Palace Hotel**
**(303) 297-3111**
**www.brownpalace.com**
The poshest of the Brown Palace's four restaurants, the Palace Arms is one of the

very few places in Denver where gentlemen are required to wear jackets and ties. The setting and service are superb, holdovers from a more formal era. The room is decorated with antiques dating from the 18th century, including a pair of dueling pistols said to have belonged to Napoleon. The fare is contemporary regional cuisine, and the award-winning wine list features close to 1,000 varieties. Reservations are strongly recommended. Lunch and dinner served Monday through Friday, dinner only on Saturday; closed Sunday. (Downtown)

### The Palm $$$$
**1201 16th Street**
**(303) 825-7256**
**www.thepalm.com**

This is the place for the gigantic-martini power lunch. The Westin at Tabor Center provides the backdrop for this top-notch restaurant, where Denver's business set devours thick slabs of dry-aged beef as heartily as talk of mergers and acquisitions. Lobsters are so big they once needed their own apartment. Caricatures of Denver's noted and notorious hang on the wall. Everything is a la carte, so bring your American Express. Lunch and dinner Monday through Friday; dinner only on weekends. Reservations are recommended. (Downtown)

### Paramount Cafe $
**519 16th Street**
**(303) 893-2000**
**www.paramountcafe.com**

A favorite for people-watching, the Paramount's outdoor seating area extends into the 16th Street Mall. This casual lunch or dinner spot serves burgers, sandwiches, and Tex-Mex food at low prices in a setting reminiscent of a '50s diner. Happy hour after work is a lively scene. Lunch and dinner are served daily. (Downtown)

### Pearl Street Grill $-$$
**1477 South Pearl Street**
**(303) 778-6475**
**www.pearlstreetgrilldenver.com**

A big friendly bar and restaurant with a particularly nice outdoor patio, the Pearl Street Grill has soups, salads, sandwiches, burgers, etc., along with a large selection of beers on tap. It serves lunch and dinner every day and offers brunch on Sunday. No reservations are taken. (South central)

### Potager $$$
**1109 Ogden Street**
**(303) 832-5788**

Every so often you come across a restaurant you can't wait to tell your friends about. Potager is one of them. It's everything a great restaurant should be: intimate, friendly, and unpretentious. And the food, sublime. Potager opened in 1997 in the heart of Capitol Hill and draws raves from everyone who discovers this elegant yet cozy neighborhood spot. Chef Teri Basoli is creative and bold in her choices. She specializes in fresh, seasonal food and changes the menu monthly. The decor is stark yet soft, with natural wood and nearly bare walls. Dinner is served Tuesday through Saturday. (Central)

### Racine's $-$$
**650 Sherman Street**
**(303) 595-0418**
**www.grdeating.com/racines/**

Racine's is a large, laid-back place that is fun for breakfast, weekend brunch, lunch, dinner, or anything in between. The menu has something for everyone, from sandwiches to pastas to a selection of Mexican entrees. An in-house bakery makes carrot cake, muffins, and Racine's locally famous brownies (in addition to the usual chocolate with or without nuts, flavors include

*In 1944 Louis Ballast grilled a slice of cheese onto a hamburger at his Denver drive-in restaurant and patented the invention as "the Cheeseburger." Other claimants can take up their case with the Denver Metro Convention & Visitors Bureau, which stands by this bit of trivia.*

white chocolate, peanut butter, and German chocolate)—all ready to be packaged up and taken home. (Central)

### Reiver's $$
**1085 South Gaylord Street**
**(303) 733-8856**

A popular watering hole in the Washington Park neighborhood, Reiver's is best known for its burgers and casual atmosphere. The delicious shepherd's pie is packed with potatoes. After your meal, stroll around the neighborhood and window-shop. Reservations are accepted, except on Friday evening. Lunch and dinner are served every day. It's also a great place for a casual Sunday brunch. (South central)

### Rialto Cafe $$$$
**934 16th Street**
**(303) 893-2233**
**www.rialtocafe.com**

Housed in the former Joslins department store building, this great-looking restaurant features dark woods, a pressed-tin ceiling, and motifs from the '20s and '30s. The food is New American cuisine, served by a well-trained and attentive staff. Friday and Saturday evenings are good for martinis. Breakfast, lunch, and dinner served daily. (Downtown)

### Ristorante Amore $$$
**2355 East Third Avenue**
**(303) 321-2066**
**www.amoredenver.com**

This popular small Cherry Creek eatery serves northern Italian cuisine and luscious desserts. Reservations are recommended at this nonsmoking restaurant. It's open for lunch Monday through Friday, dinner seven days a week, and brunch on Sunday. (Cherry Creek)

### Rocky Mountain Diner $-$$
**800 18th Street, at Stout Street**
**(303) 293-8383**
**www.rockymountaindiner.com**

A retro-Western diner with handsome green-leather booths, the Rocky Mountain Diner serves big portions of meat loaf, chicken-fried steak, and pot roast with mashed potatoes and vegetables. Save room for the white-chocolate banana-cream pie. Lunch and dinner are served daily. (Downtown)

### Ship Tavern $$$
**321 17th Street,**
**at the Brown Palace Hotel**
**(303) 297-3111**
**www.brownpalace.com**

In the Brown Palace Hotel (but accessible through its own entrance off Tremont Place), the Ship Tavern is modeled after a classic English pub and is crammed with replicas of actual ships from America's clipper period. The food is classic, too: prime rib, Rocky Mountain trout, chicken, lamb, and sandwiches. Lunch and dinner served daily. (Downtown)

### Steuben's $$$
**523 East 17th Avenue**
**(303) 830-1001**
**www.steubens.com**

In 2005, this little building on East 17th Avenue was a rundown auto shop in an emerging neighborhood. Two years later it is one of the hottest addresses in town. A trace of the old garage decor lingers in the renovated space, although there's nothing rundown about it now. Don't expect diner prices for dishes that mix nostalgia—tomato soup, deviled eggs, iceberg wedge with blue cheese dressing, milkshakes, grilled cheese, butterscotch pudding—with new takes on regional specialties—cayenne etouffe, king crab, Maine lobster roll, baked little neck clams. Steuben's is the second Denver restaurant from Josh and Jen Wolkon and chef Matt Selby. Their first was Vesta Dipping Grill in Lodo. Open for lunch, dinner, brunch, and cocktails 11:00 A.M. to 11:00 P.M. Monday through Thursday, 11:00 A.M. to midnight Friday, 9:00 A.M. to midnight Saturday, and 9:00 A.M. to 11:00 P.M. Sunday. (Uptown)

**Strings** $$$
**1700 Humboldt Street**
**(303) 831-7310**
**www.stringsrestaurant.com**
Diners rate this classy spot as one of
Denver's best. They like its distinctively
eclectic California-Italian menu of pasta,
seafood, warm salads, and grilled dishes;
they appreciate the artistic presentation;
they enjoy its extensive wine list; and they
like its friendly owner, Noel Cunningham.
The place is a perfect example of the
vibrant spirit that typifies Denver, where
the casual and the elegant mingle. Strings
underwent a renovation in 1998 that
included a face-lift and changes to the
menu. Lunch and dinner are served week-
days, dinner only Saturday and Sunday.
Reservations are recommended. (Central)

**Trinity Grille** $$$
**1801 Broadway**
**(303) 293-2288**
**www.trinitygrille.com**
A popular spot for lunching lawyers, the
Trinity Grille is brisk and shiny with pol-
ished wood, brass railings, and a black-
and-white tile floor. Steaks, soups,
sandwiches, fish, and homemade pasta
dishes are the mainstay of the menu. The
crab cakes, in particular, are highly recommended. It's closed Sunday and serves
lunch and dinner weekdays year-round.
(Downtown)

**Vesta Dipping Grill** $$$-$$$$
**1822 Blake Street**
**(303) 296-1970**
**www.vestagrill.com**
Kudos to owners Josh and Jen Wolkon's
great concept in relaxed yet upscale din-
ing. Vesta Dipping Grill is housed in a
stunning space in a renovated warehouse,
with exposed brick walls, high-backed
booths, and funky lighting. So stunning, in
fact, that the American Institute of Archi-
tects saw fit to single it out among Col-
orado restaurants. Vesta is a creative and
welcome addition to the familiar brew-

pubs around Coors Field. Start off with a
variety of appetizers (the melt-in-your-
mouth sesame-crusted tuna roll in a
kickin' wasabi cream sauce is a personal
favorite). Then choose a skewer dinner or
a traditional "knife and fork" entree, such
as a great-tasting pork tenderloin cubano
served with black forest ham, saffron rice,
and roasted-pepper pickle relish. The "dip-
ping" comes in the form of your choice of
3 homemade sauces per entree (a total of
34 in all) that give the meal spice, pizazz,
and variety; sharing is definitely in at the
Dipping Grill. Dinner is served nightly;
Thursdays feature live jazz. Reservations
are recommended. (Central)

**Wazee Lounge & Supper Club** $
**1600 15th Street**
**(303) 623-9518**
**www.wazeesupperclub.com**
It's back to the '40s, or some other
unspecified prior decade, at this laid-back
pizza-and-burgers joint. A Lower Down-
town favorite for years, it's hard to say just
what makes this place so neat. The
diverse crowd? The bohemian ambience?
The pizza? Regardless, it remains popular
year after year. Lunch and dinner served
daily. (Downtown)

# ASIAN

**Ba Le Sandwich** $
**1044 South Federal Boulevard**
**(303) 922-2129**
*Denver Post* restaurant critics love Ba Le
for a number of reasons. First, it's located
in the heart of the largest Asian neighbor-
hood, which means its diners know what
they're looking for. Second, it specializes
in the classic Banh Mi sandwich, a South-
east Asian/Fresh staple made of French
bread, pork pâté, carrots, cabbage, and
chili. Third, prices are reasonable—just
$2.50 for the sandwich, which is best
when washed down with a sugarcane
soda. (South central)

## BD's Mongolian Barbecue $$$
1620 Wazee Street
(303) 571-1824
www.bdsmongolianbarbeque.com

Once you choose your meats, vegetables, and sauce, the cook stir-fries it while you watch. BD's is a no-frills way to dine when you're tired of all the upscale joints around town. Lunch and dinner daily. (Downtown)

## Domo Restaurant $$$
1365 Osage Street
(303) 595-3666
www.domorestaurant.com

No sushi. No upscale see-and-be-seen surroundings. Domo is all about an authentic Japanese country food experience. Teriyaki meats and fish, for example, are flavored like the real thing, not layered in gooey sauce. Lunch and dinner Thursday through Saturday. Reservations are required. (Central)

## Imperial Chinese Restaurant & Lounge $$
431 South Broadway
(303) 698-2800
www.imperialchinese.com

Imperial does indeed live up to its name, with opulent decor that resembles the set of *The Last Emperor.* And better, the food matches the quality decor. The restaurant specializes in seafood, but don't pass up the sesame chicken or, if you're in the mood for the royal treatment, the fabulous Peking duck. Reservations are accepted for parties of four or more only. Lunch and dinner are served daily. (Central)

## J's Noodles $
945-E South Federal Boulevard
(303) 922-5495

Many of Greater Denver's best and most authentic Asian restaurants are located along South Federal Boulevard. For many aficionados of Thai food, this plain storefront restaurant tops the list for its combination of outstanding Thai food and low prices. Try a noodle bowl at lunch or a curry for dinner. J's Noodles is open Tuesday through Sunday. (Southwest)

## Little Ollie's Asian Cafe $$
2364 East Third Avenue
(303) 316-8888

Voted "Best Chinese Restaurant" in 2002 in the local weekly *Westword,* Little Ollie's puts a new twist on old favorites, with dishes such as stir-fried lobster and steamed sea bass. You might get a personal greeting at the door from owner Charlie Huang. And with a patio that's open year-round (heated in winter), you can always indulge in some sidewalk dining. Lunch and dinner are served daily, with daily lunch specials offered as well. (Cherry Creek)

## Mori Sushi Bar & Tokyo Cuisine $$-$$$
2019 Market Street
(303) 298-1864

Just a baseball's throw from Coors Field on the corner of Market Street and 20th Avenue, Mori Sushi offers a great selection of sushi, noodle dishes (the seafood udon noodles are a personal favorite), and other Japanese specialties in a pleasant setting that includes a small aquarium. The restaurant is popular with downtown workers at lunch. At dinner the menu expands into what seems like a book, but rest assured, you're unlikely to make a bad choice. Lunch and dinner are served daily except Sunday, when it's closed. (Downtown)

## New Orient $$
10203 East Iliff Avenue, Aurora
(303) 751-1288

A small, simply decorated restaurant, New Orient serves Vietnamese, Chinese, and "Amerasian" cuisine, updating traditional recipes with creative touches. What this means is that you can have roast-duck soup and pineapple-paprika shrimp for lunch with cappuccino mud torte for dessert. Seafood is a specialty at this non-smoking restaurant. Reservations are recommended on the weekend. It's closed on Monday. (Southeast)

## New Saigon $$
630 South Federal Boulevard
(303) 936-4954
www.newsaigon.com

Yet another Federal Boulevard restaurant, New Saigon is a perennial winner in *Westword*'s "Best Vietnamese Restaurant" category. One of Denver's first Vietnamese restaurants, it's been in business more than 10 years. Despite tons of competition, its loyal fans can't be lured away from the spicy beef and the acclaimed fish dishes. New Saigon offers great food in slightly more upscale surroundings than its Federal Boulevard counterparts. Lunch and dinner are served daily. (Southwest)

**P.F. Chang's China Bistro**          **$$**
**1415 15th Street**
**(303) 260-7222**

**8315 South Park Meadows Center Drive**
**Littleton**
**(303) 790-7744**

**1 West Flatlrons Circle, Broomfield**
**(720) 887-6200**
**www.pfchangs.com**
Don't expect the usual sweet-and-sour chicken at Chang's. In fact, don't expect the usual Chinese fare at all; Chang's does it with a stylish twist. From crab wontons to mouth-melting flourless chocolate cake, P.F. Chang's serves flavorful meals to the LoDo crowd. And the decor speaks LoDo's elegant language: exposed brick, polished woods, and ornate sculptures. Our only gripe: Entrees can be a bit sweet. Enlist the excellent waitstaff to help ensure the best combination of items. Appetizers are a must. Our favorites: shrimp dumplings and lettuce cups stuffed with chicken. And don't forget the garlic snap peas—a P.F. Chang signature side dish. Lunch and dinner daily. Also a Park Meadows location and a FlatIron Crossing location. (Downtown, South, Northwest suburbs)

**Parallel Seventeen**          **$$**
**1600 East 17th Avenue**
**(303) 399-0988**
**www.parallelseventeen.com**
For small plates served in a small, cosmopolitan space, Parallel Seventeen is unparalleled. The food is fancy even though the prices aren't, and most cocktails on the large drink menu come with lychee fruit garnishes. Family recipes have been modernized, and the owners urge their guests to eat family style. Try the sticky Vietnamese barbequed ribs or the calamari fried with lemons and limes and served with mango on a bed of greens. Open for lunch on weekdays and dinner seven days a week. (Uptown)

**Sonoda's**          **$$$**
**1620 Market Street**
**(303) 595-9500**

**550 Broadway**
**(303) 991-1000**

**Park Meadows Shopping Center**
**Littleton**
**(303) 708-8800**
**3108 South Parker Road, Aurora**
**(303) 337-3800**
**www.sonodassushi.com**
Proprietor Kenny Sonoda calls his casual restaurant a "Japanese seafood house and sushi bar," and, indeed, the menu features changing seafood specials depending on what's fresh and available. Local restaurant critics are fond of the sushi, which wins praise for freshness. The sushi lunch offers six to eight types, including a tuna roll. All the locations receive good reviews for freshness and flavor. Sonoda's serves lunch and dinner daily. (Central, South, and Southeast)

**Sushi Den**          **$$$**
**1487 South Pearl Street**
**(303) 777-0826**
**www.sushiden.net/**
A chic, modern restaurant that just happens to be a sushi bar, Sushi Den does a superb job with cooked fish, too. The standout is the steamed fresh fish in a bamboo basket. The sushi bar is a visual feast, and the dining room is modern with lots of black, granite, and concrete. Presentation here is artful, from decor to plate. Dinner is served nightly, but lunch is served only on weekdays. (South central)

## Thai Bistro $$
5924 South Kipling Street, Littleton
(720) 981-7600
www.thaibistro.net/

Thai Bistro offers a wide array of menu choices that range from pad thai to curries to Thai tapioca, all excellent picks. The menus are user-friendly, and the servers will help guide you through the choices. Chef Noi Phromthong focuses on balancing sweet and sour, spicy and mild. Lunch and dinner are served Monday through Saturday. (Littleton)

## T-Wa Inn $$
555 South Federal Boulevard
(303) 922-2378

The T-Wa Inn was Denver's first Vietnamese restaurant. It has a huge menu that emphasizes seafood—a point driven home by the foyer's aquarium filled with giant silver arrow wanna fish (for decoration only). The Asian decor is exotic without being overwhelming. Dinner offers a variety of vegetarian and meat dishes. Should you desire Vietnamese coffee, it will be French-pressed for you right at the table. Lunch and dinner served every day. (Southwest)

## Tommy's Thai $
3410 East Colfax Avenue
(303) 377-4244

Tommy's has been a staple among Capitol Hill diners for years, but its popularity is growing along with the gentrification of seedy Colfax Avenue. Once a narrow one-room joint, Tommy's has been remodeled and expanded into a hip place for young and old. Although Chinese food is served, the best items on the menu are the Thai dishes. Those of note include the hot and creamy tom kha gai soup, fried tofu wedges, pork shumi dumplings, spring

rolls, and, for the traditionalist, phad Thai with Thai iced coffee. (Central)

## Yoisho Restaurant $
7236 East Colfax Avenue
(303) 322-6265

A tiny Japanese restaurant with a devoted following, Yoisho has a simple menu with mostly fried Japanese dishes (no sushi here) and notable gyoza dumplings. There's no smoking and no alcohol. Yoisho serves lunch and dinner every day. (East)

# BAKERIES

## Devil's Food $
1024 South Gaylord Street
(303) 733-7448
www.devilsfoodbakery.com

Devil's Food started as a Washington Park bakery whose motto was "Open Bright and Surly." Then came the breakfast and lunch crowds, and the late-night weekend group that wanted to cap their evenings with wine and tarts. The luscious homemade baked goods are present throughout the day, either over the counter for walk-ins or in the funky restaurant next door. Servers are as artistic as the atmosphere, and we've been told the owners are as mellow as their day is long. Open weekends until midnight, but closed Monday. (East Denver)

## Omonia Bakery $
2813 East Colfax Avenue
(303) 394-9333

This authentic Greek bakery will satisfy a craving for baklava, koularakia, kataifi, or galataboureko. A napoleon is available, too, and, of course, there's strong coffee to go with whatever sweet your heart desires. It's open daily until 9:00 P.M. and doesn't accept credit cards. (Central)

## Rheinlander Bakery $
5721 Olde Wadsworth Boulevard
Arvada
(303) 467-1810
www.rheinlanderbakery.com

---

*Some of Denver's most unusual restaurants can be found in the small one-to-five-shop shopping centers in Denver's older neighborhoods.*

*Devil's Food started as a Washington Park bakery and now serves breakfast, lunch, and after-dinner treats.* ELLEN CASTRONE

Authentic German rye bread tops the list at this charming family-run old-world bakery in Arvada's historic Olde Town district. Coffee cakes, Danish pastries, European-style tortes, and cookies are available, too. It's open seven days a week: 7:00 A.M. to 7:00 P.M. Monday through Saturday and 9:00 A.M. to 4:00 P.M. Sunday. Credit cards are not accepted. (Western suburbs)

### Rosales Mexican Bakery $
**2636 West 32nd Avenue**
**(303) 458–8420**
This family-operated bakery features 80 varieties of authentic Mexican pastries and bread baked fresh daily as well as a selection of imported Mexican items. Rosales serves carnitas, tortas, and tamales daily. It's open daily from 6:00 A.M. to 10:00 P.M. (West Denver)

## BARBECUE

### Brothers BBQ $
**6499 Leetsdale Drive**
**(303) 322–3289**

**105 Wadsworth Boulevard, Unit E, Lakewood**
**(303) 232–3422**

**2589A South Lewis Way, Lakewood**
**(303) 989–9595**

**565 U.S. Highway 287, Broomfield**
**(303) 635–2424**

**9069 Arapahoe Road, Greenwood Village**
**(303) 799–9777**

**568 Washington Street**
**(720) 570–4227**
**www.brothers-bbq.com**
Brothers BBQ dishes up award-winning slow-smoked ribs either vinegary Memphis-style or sweet and smoky Kansas City–style. You might also try their smoky barbecued chicken or pulled-pork sandwich. Any choice is sure to be a good one. Most folks are amazed to discover that these American delicacies are being dished up by two Brits, the O'Brien brothers. Open for lunch and dinner daily, take-out is a good option as well. Call ahead for pickup. (North, Southeast, South Central, Central, Southwest)

### M&D's Cafe and Fish Palace $
**2004 East 28th Avenue**
**(303) 296–1760**
Owners Mack and Daisy Shead brought the family barbecue recipe with them when they migrated from Texas. Now their place is one of the few that appear on all "Best of" lists. The decor is plain, but the sweet-hot BBQ is authentic, as are the cornmeal-battered and fried whiting and catfish. To round out a meal, add a side of collard greens, corn bread, and some sweet-potato pie. (Central)

### Sam Taylor's Bar-B-Q $
**435 South Cherry Street, Glendale**
**(303) 388–9300**
**www.samtaylorsbbq.com**

## Breakfast Burritos

Spend a few days in Denver and you should notice a fast food like none other, the hearty hold-in-one-hand breakfast burrito. Find it at vendors' stands throughout downtown and along major thoroughfares, or in neighborhood restaurants. The favorites of a *Denver Post* taste panel came from Little Anita's, 1050 West Colfax Avenue; Cafe Mexico, 3815 West 72nd Avenue, Westminster; The Burrito Co., 1290 South Santa Fe Drive; and Bow-Ree-Toe De-Lite, 5050 South Federal Boulevard.

Is Sam Taylor's smoky-sweet and spicy barbecue the best in town? Lots of folks say it is. For years Taylor's restaurant was located on the links at City Park Golf Course, but, due to differences with the landlords at the city of Denver, it moved to a new location. The atmosphere is still ultracasual family style, with picnic tables on the patio. The amazing melt-in-your-mouth barbecue is served daily for lunch and dinner. (Central/East)

### Winston Hill's Ribs & Stuff        $
### 5090 East Arapahoe Road, Centennial
### (303) 843-6475
For decades Daddy Bruce Randolph was the revered king of barbecue, but after his death in 1994, relatives have vied for the honor. Winston Hill is a cousin, and he's also a football player. He uses Daddy's Arkansas-based recipes and serves them to the world's smallest crowd (about eight can squeeze into the restaurant at any one time). The larger audience comes to the "rib shack" for takeout. Closed Sunday. (Southeast)

### Wolfe's Barbeque        $
### 333 East Colfax Avenue
### (303) 831-1500
### www.wolfesbbq.samsbiz.com
Here's hope for committed vegetarians: In addition to Wolfe's scrumptious traditional barbecued meats, you can get smoked, grilled tofu and vegetarian baked beans at this eatery a block from the State Capitol. For the carnivores, the barbecue is first-rate. Wolfe's serves lunch and dinner Monday through Friday only. (Central)

## BREAKFAST

### Benny's Restaurante and Tequila Bar  $
### 301 East Seventh Avenue
### (303) 894-0788
### www.bennysrestaurant.com
Benny's is actually a full-service Mexican joint with as much history as flavor in its food. But we've listed it under breakfasts because it serves the best breakfast burrito known to humankind. Fat and filled with eggs, potatoes, and a choice of menudo, sausage, or meat, it's served smothered in green chili with tender chunks of pork. It's no diet plate, mind you, but great comfort food. And while you wait you can munch chips and salsa (also among the best in Denver). There are other breakfast items, all with Benny's Mexican flair. For lunch or dinner, choose from a variety of combos and a la carte items. If you go on the weekend, plan on slurping a few margaritas while you wait an hour for a table. Lunch and dinner served daily; breakfast is served Saturday and Sunday. (Central)

### Delectable Egg        $
### 1642 Market Street
### (303) 572-8146

200 Quebec Street
(720) 859-9933

1005 West 120th Avenue, Westminster
(303) 451-7227

1625 Court Place
(303) 892-5720
www.delectableegg.com

Traditional breakfast choices including omelets, eggs Benedict, waffles, French toast, and pancakes fill customers at this spot. Similar to the Egg Shell, Delectable Egg is housed in an old warehouse, which makes it look a little like greasy-diner-gone-chic (although the food isn't unusually greasy). Otherwise, Delectable Egg is standard, but good, breakfast stuff. Breakfast and lunch daily. (Downtown, Northeast, East)  .

**Dozens**                                   **$**
**236 West 13th Avenue**
**(303) 572-0066**

Want a breakfast that will stay with you, but don't want to ingest too much grease? Dozens is the place. Located in a quaint renovated house on the outskirts of downtown, it serves a traditional American breakfast of wonderful omelets, griddle combinations, waffles, and pancakes. Homemade baked goods are served, too. Dozens bustles weekdays with the business crowd and on weekends with the more relaxed coffee-drinking, paper-reading crowd. It serves breakfast and lunch daily. (Central)

**Egg Shell Cafe**                           **$**
**1520 Blake Street**
**(303) 623-7555**

Homemade soups, desserts, and an extensive breakfast menu provide something for everyone. And it's in a great downtown location across from the farmers' market (summer weekends). Platter-size pancakes, omelets of every combination, and even some breakfast pasta make the Egg Shell good. The atmosphere is just right to wake you up: busy and often loud. Breakfast and lunch daily. (Downtown)

**Ellyngton's**
**321 17th Street**                          **$$$**
**at the Brown Palace Hotel**
**(303) 297-3111**
**www.brownpalace.com**

Best known for its lavish champagne brunch (with Dom Perignon, if you've got the bucks for it), the classy and urbane Ellyngton's also serves a tasteful breakfast and lunch, but no dinner. Sunday brunch is an extravagant buffet with impressive displays of food. (Downtown)

**Hot Cakes Diner**                          **$**
**1400 East 18th Avenue**
**(303) 832-4351**

If you're in the mood for pancakes (or any other home-cooked breakfast for that matter), head to Hot Cakes, a favorite of uptown residents and employees from the surrounding hospitals. The cakes are so big that one is enough, and they come in a mind-boggling range of flavors. The lunch menu is just as appealing, as is the environment. The walls are filled with original works of art, and the waitstaff is young, friendly, and appealingly funky. Open daily 6:00 A.M. to 2:00 P.M. (Uptown)

**Le Peep Restaurant**                       **$**
**3030 East 2nd Avenue**
**(303) 394-2040**

**1699 South Colorado Boulevard**
**(303) 759-3388**

**2456 South Parker Road**
**(303) 369-5404**

**1875 York Street**
**(303) 399-7320**
**www.lepeep.com**

There's a small selection of sandwiches, but Le Peep is all about breakfast.

---

*Some LoDo establishments, especially brewpubs and sports bars, have special hours and offerings during game days at Coors Field. Call specific locales for details.*

---

Omelets, pancakes, French toast—you get the picture. There's nothing gourmet here, but it's tasty. Coffee drinkers will like the self-serve pot left on the table. Breakfast and lunch daily. (Cherry Creek, South, Southeast, East)

## BREWPUBS

**Breckenridge Brewery**     **$$-$$$**
**2220 Blake Street**
**(303) 297-3644**
**www.breckbrew.com**
The emphasis here is on the microbrewed beers and ales, but no one need go hungry with a menu that includes hearty pub fare—burgers, chicken sandwiches, salads, soups—for lunch and dinner daily. Close to Coors Field, it's a great place for an after-game brew. (Downtown)

**Rock Bottom Brewery**     **$$**
**1001 16th Street**
**(303) 534-7616**
**www.rockbottom.com**
A huge brewpub with outdoor seating on the 16th Street Mall, the Rock Bottom is related to the Walnut Brewery in Boulder. It's popular from lunchtime well into the evening, and the extensive menu includes salads, pastas, barbecued meats, and sandwiches. It's an all-around favorite with locals, whether the action is on the patio or around the impressive bar. Open daily. (Downtown)

**Sports Column**     **$-$$**
**1930 Blake Street**
**(303) 296-1930**
**www.denversportscolumn.com**

*The Seattle-style coffee shop is still popular in Denver, as in other big cities. Many of Denver's are great spots to take a break, experience a local neighborhood, and have a light meal. Most serve bagels, scones, desserts, and other treats as well as light sandwiches.*

This traditional sports bar hops during all Colorado Rockies, Colorado Avalanche, Denver Broncos, and Denver Nuggets games. The menu is fairly extensive for a sports bar and includes variations on burgers, sandwiches, pastas, salads, appetizers, and burritos. And they serve late: until 1:00 A.M. daily. Happy hour caters to the after-work crowd from 4:00 to 7:00 P.M. Enjoy lunch or dinner daily with good views of several big-screen televisions. A nice summertime feature is the rooftop deck with views of the city lights. (Downtown)

**Wynkoop Brewing Company**     **$-$$**
**1634 18th Street at Wynkoop Street**
**(303) 297-2700**
**www.wynkoop.com**
Housed in the historic J. S. Brown Mercantile Building, the Wynkoop led the way in the resurgence of Lower Downtown. Hizzoner John Hickenlooper opened Denver's first brewpub in 1988 before he became mayor. It serves a variety of handcrafted ales and pub fare, such as pot pies with quinoa crust, at reasonable prices for lunch and dinner. The main dining area is noisy, crowded, and often smoky—not necessarily a reason to stay away, we're just warning you. Upstairs is a classic pool hall that hops with the 20 to 30 set. Reservations are accepted for large groups only. Sunday lunch starts at 11:00 A.M., and lunch and dinner are served daily. (Downtown)

## COFFEE

**Common Grounds**     **$**
**3484 West 32nd Avenue**
**(303) 458-5248**

**1601 17th Street**
**(303) 296-9248**
A coffeehouse in the European tradition, Common Grounds doubles as a community center for the west Highlands neighborhood and has a second location in LoDo. Lots of free reading material, board games, and a piano for would-be Liberaces make this a place to stop and sit a

spell. Pastries, cakes, muffins, and bagels are available. Sign of the times: This coffeehouse prohibits smoking. It's open seven days a week until 11:00 P.M. (West Denver, Downtown)

**Paris on the Platte**             $
**1553 Platte Street**
**(303) 455-2451**
Popular with neighborhood artists, some of whom exhibit their paintings here, Paris on the Platte is connected to a used bookstore. If coffee isn't enough, sandwiches, salads, and soups are available as well as pastries and bagels. It's open till 1:00 A.M. Sunday through Thursday and 3:00 A.M. Friday and Saturday. (Downtown/Platte River)

**St. Mark's Coffeehouse**             $
**2019 East 17th Avenue**
**(303) 322-8384**
**www.stmarkscoffeehouse.com**
The bohemian alternative to the much more crowded Market on Larimer Street, St. Mark's serves coffee, cappuccino, and baked goods from 6:30 A.M. to 11:00 P.M. on weekdays and 7:30 A.M. to 11:00 P.M. on Saturday. Patrons sit outside for people-watching or inside on folding chairs and former church pews. It's open daily. Checks and credit cards are not accepted.

**Stella's Coffeehouse**             $
**1476 South Pearl Street**
**(303) 777-1031**
**www.stellascoffeehaus.com**
Stella's is almost certainly the only Denver coffeehouse with a branch in Amsterdam—the owner's family runs a cafe by the same name in that European city. Stella's has lots of outdoor seating and scrumptious baked goods and desserts. It also serves a light lunch. The adjoining Amsterdam Room has live entertainment on weekends and can be booked for private meetings and parties. No smoking is allowed, a custom we suspect doesn't hold true for the trans-Atlantic Stella's. It's open seven days a week until midnight and until 11:00 P.M. on Sunday. (South central)

## CONTINENTAL

**Briarwood Inn**             $$$$
**1630 Eighth Street, Golden**
**(303) 279-3121**
**www.thebriarwoodinn.com**
The Briarwood Inn isn't that far from downtown and not far at all for those who live in Denver's western suburbs, but it's a world away from the hustle-bustle. A romantic getaway, the formal, old-fashioned Briarwood Inn is Victorian in its decor and continental in its cuisine. Dinner is served Saturday and Sunday, and lunch is served on weekdays. It's especially nice for a sumptuous Sunday brunch or when it's decorated for the winter holidays. Reservations are required. (West suburbs)

**The Burnsley Hotel**             $$$
**1000 Grant Street**
**(303) 830-1000**
**www.burnsley.com**
The intimate dining room at this small Capitol Hill hotel is extravagantly wallpapered and almost fussily furnished. This is the place to go when you don't want to run into everyone you know and would rather sink into a banquette and sip a martini than schmooze. Live jazz bands play Thursday through Saturday evenings. The food is Americanized continental cuisine of lamb, chicken, and seafood, with frequently changing specials. It serves breakfast, lunch, and dinner daily. (Central)

**Chinook Tavern**             $$$
**265 Detroit Street**
**(303) 394-0044**
**www.chinooktavern.com**
There's always a hot new place in Cherry Creek, and in the spring and summer of 1995 it was the Chinook Tavern. But unlike many Cherry Creek spots that fold after their 15 minutes of fame, this one has lasted. The menu is German-influenced, but the translation is a very contemporary one, and the warm decor avoids any Bavarian cliches. Single diners love the community table. The grilled fish dishes are flavored with delicious sauces. Lunch

and dinner are served Monday through Saturday. (Cherry Creek)

### The Manor House $$$
**1 Manor House Road, Littleton**
**(303) 973-8064**
**www.themanorhouserestaurant.com**
In a beautiful setting perched atop Ken Caryl Ranch, the Manor House serves Colorado continental cuisine, including roast duck, lamb chops, steaks, and prime rib on weekends. Salmon is a specialty. The 1914 Southern-style mansion was the original manor home for Ken Caryl Ranch. Dinner only is served Tuesday through Sunday. Reservations are requested. (Southwest)

### Wellshire Inn $$$-$$$$
**3333 South Colorado Boulevard**
**(303) 759-3333**
**www.levyrestaurants.com**
Housed in an English Tudor mansion on the grounds of the Wellshire Municipal Golf Course, the Wellshire Inn is richly decorated with 100+-year-old tapestries, stained glass, and handsome wood paneling. The Wellshire serves sophisticated continental fare, including rack of lamb and salmon. There are nightly specials. Lunch, dinner, and Sunday brunch are served. The eggs Benedict is the specialty, but the French toast with vanilla ice cream melted into the batter could tempt you away from the standard. (Southeast)

## DELICATESSENS

### The Bagel Deli $-$$
**6439 East Hampden Avenue**
**at Monaco Street**
**(303) 756-6667**
**www.thebageldeli.com**
A big, family, and kosher-style restaurant and deli that serves breakfast, lunch, and dinner, The Bagel Deli has been in business in Denver since 1967. Never mind nouvelle; come here when you want chopped liver, Dr. Brown's sodas, gefilte fish, knishes, blintzes, and oversize deli sandwiches including, of course, corned

beef on rye. Open for lunch and early dinner every day until 6:30 or 7:30 P.M., depending on the crowd. (Southeast)

### Economy Greek Foods $
**717 Lipan Street**
**(303) 861-3001**
A Denver institution since 1901, the Economy stocks hard-to-find varieties of imported feta cheese and olives as well as other Greek and Mediterranean specialties. It's open weekdays for breakfast and lunch, featuring gyros and other deli items. (Central)

### The Market $
**1445 Larimer Street**
**(303) 534-5140**
Come to The Market for great food and desserts or just a cup of coffee and amazing people-watching. It's all here, from gourmet pasta to killer cakes, from black-leather-clad bikers to CEOs. You can make a meal out of the gourmet offerings, which include made-to-order deli sandwiches and a changing variety of soups and salads. It's not really a restaurant, so we've included it in this category. The baked goods, top-of-the-line chocolates, and shelves of imported food items make this as much a shopping destination as a dining spot, and the espresso bar is always busy. Bring a cup of cappuccino and a plate of biscotti out to a table on the sidewalk and watch the world go by. It's open seven days a week. (Downtown)

### New York Deli News $
**7105 East Hampden Avenue**
**(303) 759-4741**
Similar in offerings, prices, and easygoing style to The Bagel Deli, New York Deli News also serves breakfast, lunch, and dinner daily. You'll enjoy great pumpernickel bread, pastrami, bagels, corned beef (all flown in from New York), and—loosen your belt—genuine New York–style cheesecake. (Southeast)

### The Spicy Pickle $
**988 Lincoln Street**
**(303) 860-0730**

**745 South Colorado Boulevard**
(303) 321-8353
www.spicypickle.com
This "upscale dive," as it's been called,
serves up some of the freshest and most
innovative sandwiches in town, with
homemade mayo spreads and a choice of
19 toppings. The bread is Italian artisan
style and is a great starting point for
either sub or panini. The meats are all top
quality, and every sandwich is accompanied by the spicy house-made pickle.
Order at the counter, and your sandwich
will be brought to your inside or outside
table. Lunch and an early dinner are
offered daily (open until 6:00 or 7:00 P.M.
depending on the day). (Central)

**Zaidy's Deli** $$
121 Adams Street
(303) 333-5336

**15th and Lawrence Streets**
(303) 893-3600
www.zaidysdeli.com
Zaidy's may very well be the closest thing to
an authentic New York Jewish deli as can be
found in Greater Denver. This is a prime
source for breakfast and a lunch of potato
latkes, smoked fish, and matzo ball soup just
like your grandmother used to make. The
Cherry Creek store is open from 6:30 A.M. to
5:00 P.M. Monday through Friday, 7:30 A.M. to
4:00 P.M. Saturday and Sunday. At the down-
town store the hours are 6:30 A.M. to 3:00
P.M. every day. (Cherry Creek, Downtown)

## FRENCH

**Le Central** $$
112 East Eighth Avenue
(303) 863-8094
www.lecentral.com
Le Central styles itself as "the affordable
French restaurant" and does a good job of
living up to that claim without skimping
on quality. The restaurant is a charming
series of low-ceilinged rooms; the food is
country French. Lunch and dinner are
served daily in addition to brunch on Saturday and Sunday. (Central)

**Aix** $$$
719 East 17th Avenue
(303) 831-1296
www.restaurantaix.com
This little place may not look like much
from the outside, but inside it is filled with
the smells of Provence. The menu is ever
changing and often features venison,
quail, and other game dishes. It serves
dinner Tuesday through Saturday and one
of the best (and most unusual) Sunday
brunches in town. Closed Monday.
(Uptown)

## GREEK

**Yanni's** $$
2223 South Monaco Parkway
(303) 692-0404
This is a classic Greek family-run taverna,
with a blue-and-white interior and outdoor tables with umbrellas. The menu
leans heavily on traditional, hearty dishes
such as moussaka and pastitsio. Everything here is fresh, including the homemade bread. Knock back a shot of ouzo
and let the feasting begin! Lunch is served
Monday through Saturday, dinner nightly.
(Southeast)

## ICE CREAM

**All For the Better** $
3501 South Clarkson Street, Englewood
(303) 781-0230
This is a sweet, old-fashioned ice-cream
parlor that also serves soup and sandwiches. The ice cream is homemade, and
flavors vary daily. It's across the street
from Swedish Medical Center, and it's
open during lunch and dinner hours Monday through Saturday. No credit cards.
(Southeast)

**Liks** $
2039 East 13th Avenue
(303) 321-2370
www.liksicecream.com
Take a number and get in line for this well-

known Denver spot. Formerly known as Lickety Split, this old-fashioned ice-cream parlor is the place to go for a fabulously indulgent sundae. The homemade ice creams come in such tempting flavors as Almond Roca and Cheesman Park (a strawberry-cheesecake concoction named for the park a few blocks away). Don't fret if they're out of your favorite flavor; they'll put it on the request list and call you when it's available. It's open seven days a week and doesn't accept credit cards. (Central)

## INDIAN

| India House | $$$ |
|---|---|

**1514 Blake Street**
**(303) 595-0680**
**www.indiahouse.us/index.html**
Downtown's only Indian restaurant is refined in its decor and in its wide range of tandoori dishes, which include two kinds of Cornish game hens and quail in addition to the more standard chicken. The lunch buffet is an especially good value, with a choice of entrees and as many as 22 items in all. Vegetarians will appreciate the many meatless dishes. Lunch and dinner are served daily. (Downtown)

| India's | $$-$$$ |
|---|---|

**3333 South Tamarac Drive**
**(303) 755-4284**
India's is a feast for the senses, with its tantalizing aromas, colorful cloth hangings, and hypnotic Indian music. Located in a strip shopping mall just behind Tamarac Square, India's is Denver's oldest Indian restaurant and one of the finest you are ever likely to encounter. The curries are hot and spicy, and the tandoori dishes are very popular. Reservations are recommended. Dinner is served nightly, lunch Monday through Saturday. (Southeast)

| Jewel of India | $$ |
|---|---|

**10343 North Federal Boulevard,**
**Westminster**
**(303) 469-7779**
**www.jewelofindia.com**
Suburban Westminster may seem an unlikely place for one of the area's finest Indian restaurants, as may Jewel of India's location in a shopping center anchored by King Soopers. But once inside the narrow door, the truth becomes evident. Jujhar Singh has managed to transform the storefront into a little slice of India, complete with lamb, chicken, seafood, and vegetarian dishes, all of which come with homemade naan. If you're unfamiliar with the dishes, try the Thalis, which includes a little bit of everything to serve one or two people. Singh was raised in Punjab, India, and uses family recipes from the region. His Jewel of India serves lunch buffets and full-service dinners seven days a week. (Northwest suburbs)

## ITALIAN

| Bambino's Ristorante | $$$ |
|---|---|

**1135 Bannock Street**
**(303) 221-7215**
**www.bambinosdenver.com**
The Caninos have been feeding Denver Italian food for generations, but Bambino's may be their fanciest place yet. With an uptown urbanity and down-home cooking, it feels like a perfect spot for Carmella and Tony Soprano to steal away for some time away from the mob. Open for lunch Monday through Friday and dinner Monday through Saturday. Closed Sunday. (Central)

| Barolo Grill | $$$ |
|---|---|

**3030 East Sixth Avenue**
**(303) 393-1040**
Since its opening in 1992, Barolo has consistently ranked as one of the hottest of the city's hot spots. The food in this chic restaurant could be called "Cal-Ital," combining as it does northern Italian recipes with California ingredients. Barolo does

several good fish dishes with great sauces. Wines are an especially good value. It serves dinner only, Tuesday through Saturday; reservations are strongly recommended. (Central)

**Bravo! Ristorante**                    $$$
**1550 Court Place, in Adam's Mark Hotel**
**(303) 626-2581**
**www.adamsmark.com**
It's not every day diners are treated to show tunes and opera pieces by their waitstaff. At Bravo! that's the norm. The staff are professional singers, so it's quite a treat. The dining room is large and spacious, and the cuisine is as memorable as the singing. The menu ranges from antipasto platter and bruschetta to ravioli, scaloppini piccata, and pizza. Lunch is served weekdays only, and dinner is served daily. (Downtown)

**Carmine's on Penn**                    $$
**92 South Pennsylvania Street**
**(303) 777-6443**
**www.carminesonpenn.citysearch.com**
Make a reservation; this place is way too popular to expect a table during the civilized dinner hour without one. And for good reason. Piles of homemade pasta form the bed for spicy and flavorful sauces. The portions are enough to feed two, plus lunch the next day. The wine list is adequate, if not expansive. The atmosphere bustles with an eclectic neighborhood scene. Carmine's is fast becoming a Denver institution. Dinner only, Tuesday through Sunday. (Central)

**Cherry Tomato**                    $$
**4645 East 23rd Avenue**
**(303) 377-1914**
The Cherry Tomato is another Insiders' favorite, best known as a neighborhood restaurant for Park Hill dwellers. Its Italian entrees are as filling as they are delicious, so come with an empty stomach. Among the specialties is Pasta Felese, made with chicken, artichoke hearts, and sun-dried tomatoes in a white-wine cream sauce. The place fills up fast and doesn't take

reservations for parties of fewer than six. You can call ahead when you're leaving home to be put on the waiting list. Open for dinner only, Tuesday through Sunday; closed Monday. (East Denver)

**Cinzetti's Italian Market**                    $$$
**281 West 104th Avenue, Northglenn**
**(303) 451-7300**
**www.cinzettis.com**
Cinzetti's (pronounced Chin-ZEH-tees) is a "concept" restaurant that either works for you or it doesn't. It's designed around a central marketplace with food lines that resemble buffets, each serving something different—pastas, pizzas, fish and meats, and desserts, for example. All diners pay a flat rate at the door and can sample anything that strikes their fancies. The food is surprisingly tasty for mass-produced buffet fare, and wine and soft drinks are included in the price. Open daily for lunch and dinner. (North suburbs)

**Dino's**                    $$
**10040 West Colfax Avenue, Lakewood**
**(303) 238-7393**
*Denver Post* restaurant critics rave about this landmark Italian restaurant in Lakewood, an early suburb west of downtown Denver. Homemade pasta, sausage, meatballs, lasagna, and spumoni are among the standouts on the menu. Lots of regulars come for the authentic Italian food; on Sunday they come right after church for a traditional family dinner. (Southwest)

**Il Fornaio**                    $$$
**1631 Wazee Street**
**(303) 573-5050**

**1 West FlatIron Circle, Broomfield**
**(720) 887-1400**

**8000 East Belleview Avenue,**
**Greenwood Village**
**(303) 221-8400**
**www.ilfornaio.com**
A deliciously elegant LoDo spot, with branches at FlatIron Crossing in Broomfield and Greenwood Village, Il Fornaio is a California-based restaurant whose spe-

cialty is its breads and baked goods (*il fornaio* means "the baker"). Meals can be quite good, too, though not always up to par with the prices and surroundings. Ask the server what's good and fresh to make the best selection. Lunch and dinner daily. (Downtown, Northwest suburbs, South)

**Luca d'Italia**                    **$$$**
**711 Grant Street**
**(303) 832-6600**
Chef Frank Bonanno was a Denver legend before he opened this Tuscan place around the corner from his Mizuna restaurant. He quickly created buzz with the wild-boar ragu, the trio of rabbit (a confit of leg, tenderloin, and braised meat with leeks), and the classic Italian bread pudding (panzanella). (Central)

**Maggiano's Little Italy**      **$$$$**
**510 16th Street, Denver Pavilions**
**(303) 260-7707**

**7401 South Clinton Street** •
**Denver Tech Center**
**(303) 858-1405**
**www.maggianos.com**
Dark woods, brass, and red-checkered tablecloths give the feel of 1940s Little Italy at this family-style restaurant. Both places are friendly, and the large food portions are served with gusto. Salads are simple but fresh and crisp. Lunch and dinner daily. (Downtown, South)

**Pagliacci's**                     **$$$**
**1440 West 33rd Avenue**
**(303) 458-0530**
Family-run for more than 50 years, Pagliacci's is another West Denver institution. The neon clown on the roof is famously

visible from Interstate 25 but not from the restaurant itself, which has a handsome, grottolike interior. If you can't stay for a meal, you can get the famous minestrone to go. The food is excellent and sure to please for family dining or for romantic dates in one of the many red booths. It serves dinner only and is closed Monday. (West Denver)

**Panzano**                         **$$$**
**909 17th Street**
**(303) 296-3525**
Housed in the Hotel Monaco Denver, Panzano is a trip into calming dark woods and earth tones. Chef Elise Wiggins is among Denver's finest, spending time in Central America and Puerto Rico before settling in Denver. Two open kitchens fill the air with scents of baked goods. Reservations, especially at the bustling noontime, are recommended. Breakfast, lunch, and dinner served weekdays, brunch and dinner served Saturday and Sunday. (Downtown)

**Pasta's**                         **$$$**
**9126 West Bowles Avenue, Littleton**
**(303) 933-2829**
Pasta's is a big, friendly, family-run southern Italian restaurant that specializes in big portions and solicitous service. The staff will treat you like a relative as you enjoy their pasta, chicken, veal, and seafood entrees. Pasta's serves lunch and dinner daily, except Sunday when it's dinner only. (Southwest)

# LATIN

**Cafe Brazil**                     **$$$**
**4408 Lowell Boulevard**
**(303) 480-1877**
Cafe Brazil is a tiny, intimate restaurant in what used to be an old-world Italian neighborhood but has become more ethnically mixed. Try the feijoada completa, Brazil's national dish. It combines black beans, meat, fruit, and rice in a most delicious way. Cafe Brazil is open for dinner

only and is closed Sunday and Monday. Reservations are recommended. (West Denver)

**Cuba Cuba** $$
**1173 Delaware Street**
**(303) 605-2822**
**www.cubacubacafe.com**
Two tiny historic homes were joined together to make room for this Latin American restaurant in the Golden Triangle. You'll enter one and find yourself in the bar. Cross over into the other and you're in the dining room. The food is zesty and heavy on pork (Lechon Asado—or roasted pork, onions, and garlic—is its signature dish). Salads and coconut-lime rice make good vegetarian alternatives, and if cocktails are your thing, try the mojitos. They're among Denver's best. Open weekdays for lunch and Monday through Saturday for dinner. (Central)

**Sabor Latino** $-$$
**4340 West 35th Avenue**
**(303) 455-8664**
A charming place in an interesting neighborhood, Sabor Latino serves South American and Mexican cuisine. The restaurant recently went upscale, at least in its new, expanded digs. But the food is still the same, and still good. Specialties of the house include Colombian tamales and South American empanadas, baked or fried. A nice selection of Chilean wines is available. It serves lunch and dinner Monday through Friday and dinner only on Saturday; closed on Sunday. Reservations accepted for parties of eight or more only. (West Denver)

**Samba Room** $$$$
**1460 Larimer Street**
**(720) 956-1701**
**www.sambaroom.net**
Situated in LoDo, the Samba Room anchors historic Larimer Square, and does it to a hip Latin beat. The after-work crowd favors the comfy bar, and lunch and dinner guests enjoy entrees with Latin American influences. House specialties range from mango barbecued ribs to fried yucca, and afterward, the banana split comes with a fried banana. Reservations are accepted. Samba Room is open Monday through Wednesday 11:00 A.M. to 11:00 P.M.; Thursday through Saturday 11:00 A.M. to midnight; Sunday 11:00 A.M. to 10:00 P.M. (Downtown)

## MEXICAN/SOUTHWESTERN

**The Blue Bonnet Cafe** $
**457 South Broadway**
**(303) 778-0147**
This Mexican joint was "discovered" by Denver yuppies in the 1980s and remains popular—prepare to wait a while for a table. There's nothing fancy here, but there's lots of it with great big margaritas to wash it all down. The refried beans are a standout. Lunch and dinner are served daily. (Central)

**El Noa Noa** $
**722 Santa Fe Drive**
**(303) 623-9968**
El Noa Noa is located in an authentic Mexican-American neighborhood that is the site each year of a Cinco de Mayo parade and street festival. In good weather you can enjoy the large patio with wrought-iron chairs and a fountain. El Noa Noa dishes out tasty enchiladas, burritos, tacos, and rellenos. Lunch and dinner are served daily. (Central)

**El Taco de Mexico** $
**714 Santa Fe Drive**
**(303) 623-3926**
This simple restaurant holds its own, despite stiff competition from larger and better-known El Noa Noa next door. Dining here is ultracasual with a few tables and bar seating. It's open for breakfast, lunch, and dinner daily. Credit cards not accepted. (Central)

### Jack-n-Grill                     $–$$
**2524 Federal Boulevard**
**(303) 964–9544**
New Mexican dishes have made this cemented hole-in-the-wall's reputation. It serves a mean green chili, vaquero tacos moistened with barbecue sauce, and seven-pound burritos so big they'll take your picture if you finish one. (Northwest)

### Julia Blackbird's New Mexican Cafe  $$
**3434 West 32nd Avenue**
**(303) 433–2688**
This little jewel in the charming Highland area is quickly gaining in reputation, and the weekend lines prove it. The menu is true to its New Mexican roots with blue-corn tortillas, hearty posole, light and delicious sopapillas, and pine nut chocolate cake. Brunch is served Saturday and Sunday. Lunch and dinner are served Tuesday through Saturday. (Northwest)

### La Estrellita                     $
**7617 West 88th Avenue, Arvada**
**(303) 422–3700**

**45 North Main Street, Brighton**
**(303) 654–9900**
**www.salsalaest.com**
There are three Mexican restaurants owned and operated by the Montoya family; the other is in Boulder. The award-winning green chili is available hot, medium, mild, or vegetarian. Buy it by the quart for takeout. The atmosphere is casual. Breakfast is served all day. It's open seven days for all meals. (West, North)

### La Loma Restaurant                $–$$
**2527 West 26th Avenue**
**(303) 433–8300**
**www.lalomarestaurant.com**
In the up-and-coming Diamond Hill neighborhood just west of I-25 at Speer Boulevard, La Loma is rather incongruously housed in an 1887 Victorian home that's been renovated into a sprawling restaurant with a series of dining rooms. The restaurant is known for its big margaritas

and authentic food. Lunch and dinner are served every day. (West Denver)

### Las Delicias                     $–$$
**439 East 19th Avenue**
**(303) 839–5675**

**51 Del Norte**
**(303) 430–0422**

**19553 Main Street, Parker**
**(303) 840–0325**

**4301 East Kentucky Avenue, Glendale**
**(303) 692–0912**
This family-run restaurant has four locations, and loyal customers still can't get enough of their Michoacán-style carnitas and fajitas, carne adobada, taquitos, carne asada, and steak ranchero. It offers great breakfasts in addition to lunch and dinner every day. (Central, North, Downtown, South)

### Mexico City Lounge & Cafe          $
**2115 Larimer Street**
**(303) 296–0563**
Denverites make a big fuss about authenticity when discussing the comparative merits of restaurants. No argument here: This is the real thing. The green chile and burritos are favorites, and breakfast is a real eye-opener. If you're a fan of menudo, this is the place to go. It's closed Monday, but serves breakfast and lunch on the other days. No credit cards. (Downtown)

### Morrison Inn                      $–$$
**301 Bear Creek Avenue, Morrison**
**(303) 697–6650**
This is a fun, Americanized restaurant in an 1885 building in the heart of the foothills town of Morrison. It's known for its custom-made (not premixed) margaritas and for being a beginning—or ending—spot for mountain bikers and hikers. The fare is standard Mexican served for lunch and dinner daily. (West suburbs)

### Playa de Oro                      $
**3555 West 38th Avenue**
**(303) 433–5777**
Playa de Oro is known for its crispy,

golden brown chile rellenos—poblano chiles stuffed with Monterey Jack. They also serve a wide array of other Mexican dishes for breakfast, lunch, and dinner Monday through Saturday and breakfast and lunch on Sunday. Prices are incredibly low to very reasonable. (Northwest)

### Rosa Linda's Mexican Cafe $
### 2005 West 33rd Avenue
### (303) 455-0608
You say you want a neighborhood restaurant? Check out this one. Run by the Aquirre family since 1985, Rosa Linda's is a small, plain place with great burritos, enchiladas, and soft chile rellenos. It wins awards for its shredded beef burritos, chile rellenos, and other specialties. There are a few tables on the sidewalk. Open Monday through Saturday for lunch and dinner. (West Denver)

### Table Mountain Inn &
### Restaurant $$-$$$
### 1310 Washington Avenue, Golden
### (303) 277-9898
### www.tablemountaininn.com
Enter this adobe-style inn for a variety of Southwestern dishes. Here you'll find such dinner specialties as prime rib of buffalo, cowboy chops, and grilled salmon. For lunch, choose among buffalo burgers, chicken, salads, and daily specials—all spiced and prepared with Southwest flair. Breakfast, lunch, and dinner served daily; brunch is available Saturday and Sunday. (Western suburbs)

### Taqueria Patzcuaro $
### 2616 West 32nd Avenue
### (303) 455-4389
An ultracasual restaurant in a Spanish-speaking neighborhood, Taqueria Patzcuaro draws fans of its green chile and soft tacos from all over the city. The neighborhood around Taqueria is alive with Mexican music. Lunch and dinner are served daily. There's no alcohol, and credit cards are not accepted. (West Denver)

## MIDDLE EASTERN

### Jerusalem Restaurant $
### 1890 East Evans Avenue
### (303) 777-8828
### www.jerusalemrestaurant.com
A tiny eight-table restaurant that does a bustling take-out business, Jerusalem is popular with students from the University of Denver campus nearby. Everything is good here, including the kebabs, hummus, baba ghanouj, and phyllo pastries. Students cramming for an exam no doubt also appreciate the fact that Jerusalem is virtually always open, from 9:00 A.M. to 4:00 A.M. Sunday through Thursday and 24 hours Friday and Saturday. The space crunch is eased in the summer by the outdoor patio. Alcohol is not served. (South central)

### Pita Jungle $-$$
### 2017 South University Boulevard
### (720) 570-1900
Pita Jungle makes its own pita bread, and it serves as a deserving base for the outstanding hummus and shawarma served in this eatery. Lunch and dinner are served daily. (South central)

## PIZZA

### Beau Jo's Pizza $-$$
### 2710 South Colorado Boulevard
### (303) 758-1519

### 7805 Wadsworth Boulevard, Arvada
### (303) 420-8376
### www.beaujos.com
The original Beau Jo's is still in Idaho Springs and is a beloved stopping point on the way home from skiing for Denverites who crave thick-crusted pizza loaded with toppings. While diners wait for the pizza (good things take time), they can draw on napkins and pin them on the wall along with the thousands of others. Finally, Beau Jo's opened up branches in southeast Denver and Arvada. They are open for lunch and dinner daily. (Southeast, West suburbs)

With a few notable exceptions, Denver's independent and unique restaurants tend to be located in the central city. Suburbs, while they offer good dining, are home to more chain restaurants and familiar family spots.

**Bonnie Brae Tavern**  $-$$
740 South University Boulevard
(303) 777-2262
www.menusfirst.com/denver/bonniebrae
The crowds! The noise! The pizza! This astoundingly popular neighborhood pizza joint founded in 1934 is locally famous and always busy, busy, busy. It's a fun place, but don't come here if you're in a hurry. Bonnie Brae serves lunch and dinner daily except Monday. Takeout is available. (South central)

**Cafe Colore**  $-$$
1512 Larimer Street
(303) 534-6844
www.cafecoloredenver.com
The Rocky Mountain offshoot of a small New Jersey chain, Cafe Colore has a menu that's built around a clever gimmick: Pizzas come with sauces of red, green, or white, the three colors of the Italian flag. Other Italian entrees, plus calzones, are available. Smoking is allowed on the patio, which is where you'll want to be anyway in good weather. Cafe Colore has an upscale cousin in Cherry Creek, Cucina Colore, at 3041 East Third Avenue, (303) 393-6917. Both locations are open seven days for lunch and dinner. (Downtown, Cherry Creek)

**Legends of Cherry Creek**  $
201 Milwaukee Street
(303) 320-6300
This casual New York–style pizzeria in the heart of Cherry Creek North has many fans, and the double-crusted spinach pizza with black olives is especially well-thought-of. The lasagna would make Mom proud. Takeout is available. Lunch and dinner are served daily. (Cherry Creek)

**Parisi**  $
4401 Tennyson Street
(303) 561-0234
Parisi is a combination grocery, Italian deli, and pizza place—and they excel in all areas. Simone Parisi, who grew up in Florence, makes pizza in the true Italian tradition, meaning you order a *rustica* or *margherita*, not pepperoni and mushroom. The crust is medium-thick, the tomato sauce chunky, and the mozzarella fresh. Sandwiches and pastas are equally fresh and delicious. Enjoy your meal in the recently renovated building or have your feast packed to go. You can also find authentic Italian groceries on the shelves in the shop. Open Monday through Saturday 11:00 A.M. to 9:00 P.M. (Northwest)

**Pasquini's Pizzeria**  $
1310 South Broadway
(303) 744-0917

1336 East 17th Avenue
(303) 863-8252

816 Main Street, Louisville
(303) 673-9400
www.pasquinis.com
A nifty little pizzeria with an artsy interior and mosaic-topped tables, Pasquini's serves New York–style thin crust, sauce-less bianca, and thick-crust Sicilian-style pizzas and individual pizzettas with interesting toppings. Also on the menu are calzones and subs. The original Pasquini's is nestled amid the antiques stores on South Broadway at Louisiana Avenue. Lunch and dinner are served daily except Sunday, which is dinner only. Takeout and delivery are available. (South central, Uptown, Northwest suburbs)

**Proto's Pizzeria Napoletana**  $
2401 15th Street
(720) 855-9400
www.protospizza.com
Owners Pam Proto and Rayme Rossello developed their pizza tastes while on an extended trip to Italy. They then came back to their home in Longmont and started selling the thin-crusted pies lay-

ered with fresh ingredients. They now own four restaurants, including one in Denver's Central Platte Valley. (The others are at 600 South Airport Road in Longmont; at 489 North U.S. Highway 287 in Lafayette; and at 4670 Broadway in Boulder.) Their places are hip and on the expensive side, but legions of fans say they're the best in town. (Central) ·

# SEAFOOD

### Fresh Fish Company          $$$
7800 East Hampden Avenue
(303) 740-9556

The aquatic theme extends to the decor at this big restaurant, which consists of walls of beautiful tropical aquariums. Mesquite grilling is a specialty here, and the Sunday brunch, with all-you-can-eat crab legs and shrimp, is very popular. On Sunday night there's a lobster bake, with discounts on the lobster. Lunch is served Monday through Friday, dinner nightly. (Southeast)

### Hemingway's Key West Grille     $$
1052 South Gaylord Street
(303) 722-7456
www.hemingways-denver.com

A sometimes hit-or-miss dining experience in the past, Hemingway's is now a clear hit under chef Randy Pyren's reign. The fish is fresh and well prepared, the atmosphere low-key and somewhat nautical, and the prices reasonable. There's a happy hour Monday through Friday with even better prices on seafood appetizers. (Central)

### Jax Fishhouse          $$-$$$
1539 17th Street
(303) 292-5767
www.rhumbarestaurant.com/jax

Jax won't slip a skimpy slice of fish on your plate. Here you'll get a hearty slab of fresh fish, well seasoned and served with a nice variety of side dishes. The raw oysters, stone crab claws, and crawfish are all delicious and succulent. Non-fish eaters can opt for a burger or steak, but fish is truly the dish. The place is hopping, too, so don't expect to be seated right away. Just take your time and enjoy the buildup. Jax serves dinner only, every night. (Downtown)

### McCormick's Fish House & Bar     $$$
1659 Wazee Street
(303) 825-1107
www.theoxfordhotel.com

In McCormick's elegant dining room can be found some of the freshest fish in Denver. If oysters are in season, this is one of the few places in town to get them. And for one of the best deals around, try the happy hour bar menu from 3:00 to 6:00 P.M. or 9:00 to 11:00 P.M. This is a great deal and a good choice for pre- and post-theater meals (the Denver Performing Arts Complex is just a few blocks away). Private dining rooms are available; call for information. Lunch and dinner are served daily. (Downtown)

### 240 Union          $$-$$$
240 Union Boulevard at Sixth Avenue
Lakewood
(303) 989-3562

The menu changes seasonally at this creative restaurant, which specializes in seafood. Pastas and pizzas round out the offerings. Co-owner and executive chef Matthew Franklin did a stint at the original Rattlesnake Club, Denver's most innovative restaurant during the 1980s. 240 Union sports blue skylights and wooden dividers that represent "the city meeting the foothills." There's a nice enclosed patio and a wall-to-wall open grill. It serves dinner nightly and lunch on weekdays. (West suburbs)

# STEAKS

### Aurora Summit          $$$$
2700 South Havana Street, Aurora
(303) 751-2112
www.aurorasummit.com

A classic steak house with a dark, woodsy, masculine ambience, Aurora Summit serves only the finest grade of USDA prime, aged, corn-fed beef. In the tradition of steak houses, the menu also includes seafood entrees. In the large front lounge, there's a piano bar Monday through Saturday nights and a small dance floor. Aurora Summit serves dinner seven days a week. Reservations are preferred. (Southeast)

## The Buckhorn Exchange $$$$
**1000 Osage Street**
**(303) 534-9505**
**www.buckhorn.com**

The Buckhorn Exchange was the first Denver restaurant to be granted a liquor license. It was founded in 1893 by "Shorty Scout" Zietz, who, along with his family, amassed an astounding collection of animal trophies, including moose, elk, buffalo, and bear. More than 500 stuffed animals and birds are displayed—it's sort of like dining in a natural history museum. The menu, accordingly, runs to traditional Western fare: beef, barbecued pork ribs, and game meats. For something more unusual, try the rattlesnake or alligator tail appetizers. Vegetarian alert: You may feel a little squeamish here, but if you can put up with the dead heads on the wall, call ahead and the restaurant will put together a vegetarian plate just for you. Dinner entrees are expensive but lunch is quite reasonable. Thursday through Saturday nights feature folk and cowboy music in the saloon upstairs. It's probably more popular with tourists than locals, but there's no other place like it. Reservations are recommended for dinner, which is served daily. Lunch is served Monday through Friday only. (Central)

## The Denver ChopHouse & Brewery $$$
**1735 19th Street**
**(303) 296-0800**
**www.rockbottomrestaurantsinc.com**

The Denver ChopHouse is housed in the old Union Pacific Railroad warehouse, a block away from Coors Field. Its outdoor barbecue area, with its patio and rolling roof, is a big draw. The decor is rich with dark wood and high booths. The food is inventive; try the portobello mushrooms dipped in Worcestershire and garlic, then grilled. Lunch and dinner are served daily. Reservations are suggested for weekends. (Downtown)

## Elway's $$$
**2500 East First Avenue**
**(303) 399-5353**

Bronco quarterback John Elway is a Denver legend, and after a few short years in business, so is his restaurant. In addition to good steaks and sides, cold martinis, and a great location alongside the tony Cherry Creek Shopping Center, Elway's often serves up celebrities who got hungry while shopping at Neiman Marcus and decided to drop in for a bite. It's open for lunch on weekdays and for dinner seven days a week. (Cherry Creek)

## The Fort $$$$
**19192 Route 8, Morrison**
**(303) 697-4771**
**www.thefort.com**

The Fort combines Wild West flair with classy fare; where else do waiters dressed in leather vests and beads open bottles of champagne with a tomahawk? Located in the foothills, with a panoramic view of the plains below, the restaurant is a full-size adobe replica of Bent's Fort, Colorado's first fur-trading post. Owners Sam Arnold and Holly Arnold Kinney were among the first restaurateurs to feature buffalo meat on the menu; other unusual entrees include elk, quail, rattlesnake, and Rocky Mountain oysters (rolled in seasoned flour and deep-fried). More traditional preparations of trout and steak are available, and for those who wish to sample a little bit of everything, there's a game plate. As we said about the Buckhorn Exchange, there's no place else like it. Reservations are recommended. The Fort serves dinner nightly. (West suburbs)

## Morton's The Steakhouse $$$$
**1710 Wynkoop Street**
**(303) 825-3353**

**Denver Crescent Town Center**
**8480 East Belleview Avenue**
**Greenwood Village**
**(303) 409-1177**
www.mortons.com
With locations in Lower Downtown across from Union Station and at the Denver Tech Center, Morton's is a classic, classy steak house. It is always mentioned when people talk about where to get great steaks. Only USDA prime served here. If surf and turf is what you're after, Morton's flies live lobster in from Maine daily. It serves dinner nightly; reservations are recommended. (Downtown, South)

**Ruth's Chris Steak House**     $$$-$$$$
**1445 Market Street**
**(303) 446-2233**
www.ruthschris.com
Ruth's Chris is a steak-lover's steak house

(only prime served here). The atmosphere is relaxed with plenty of dark wood, and the booths are big and private. The 20-ounce T-bone is the biggest; the 8-ounce filet the smallest. Also available are lobster, veal, chicken, and halibut. Dinner is served nightly, and reservations are recommended. (Downtown)

**Sullivan's Steakhouse**     $$$$
**1745 Wazee Street**
**(303) 295-2664**
www.sullivansteakhouse.com
The interior of this LoDo favorite is as dark and rich as a medium-well steak. Live music from the bar drifts throughout as diners enjoy one of Denver's best steak dinners with all the trimmings. Open daily for dinner; reservations recommended; valet parking available. (Downtown)

# NIGHTLIFE 🍸

Visitors who haven't strolled Denver streets for a few years will notice something remarkably different about downtown these days: The city hops until the wee hours. As recently as the early 1990s, downtown Denver businesses were scheming ways to keep people in the city after dark. Today parking rates are at a premium (when you can find a spot), and waiting for a restaurant table is part of the experience. But don't let that dissuade you from venturing downtown; it's an experience not to be missed.

Downtown rocks on weekends, as do bars, restaurants, dance clubs, and movie theaters all over town. When the sun goes down, this town is once again exciting, eclectic, and electrifying.

In this chapter we survey Denver's nightlife, stopping in at a few of our favorite bars, brewpubs, live music venues, comedy clubs, and movie houses. This isn't meant to be a comprehensive listing; for that kind of inclusiveness, the best place to turn is *Westword*, Denver's free weekly paper. The Friday editions of the *Denver Post* and *Rocky Mountain News* carry weekend entertainment listings, as does the *Daily Camera* with Boulder's happenings. The newspaper *Out Front* is a good source of information about gay and lesbian nightlife. The paper is free and widely distributed in most coffee and sandwich shops.

Because people interpret "nightlife" so broadly—it includes everything from a coffeehouse with live poetry readings to an outdoor rock concert at a stadium—there is some inevitable overlap with other chapters. A brewpub such as the Wynkoop serves dinner but also draws a late-night billiards crowd. Martini and wine bars house the chic set (get to the Cruise Room early for a sought-after booth).

Theater and dance performances and concerts, such as those at the Denver Performing Arts Complex, are covered in our Arts chapter. We direct your attention to such popular in-town music venues as the Paramount Theatre, the Ogden Theatre, and the Swallow Hill Music Association.

Unlike concert halls, where advance ticketing is recommended, most of the live music venues described in this chapter serve food and drink and can be visited on a drop-in basis, although this is no hard-and-fast rule. Finally you'll find family attractions that don't shut down at dusk, such as Six Flags Elitch Gardens, described in our Tours and Attractions chapter.

Keep in mind, too, that today's hot spot could be tomorrow's Siberia. No guidebook could ever hope to keep up with the strange twists of taste that make one place worth lining up for and another worth taking pains to avoid. And, of course, music and dance clubs change their format and hours frequently. Some clubs rotate nightly, offering, for example, hip-hop on Monday, electronic music on Tuesday, karaoke on Wednesday, and DJs on Thursday. If you're looking for a specific kind of music, it's always best to call ahead.

The drinking age for any kind of alcoholic beverage is 21. Closing time at bars and nightclubs is generally 2:00 A.M., but most restaurants stop serving food at 11:00 P.M or even earlier.

Colorado is not a state that takes drunk driving lightly. Penalties for driving under the influence or driving while impaired are severe. If you've had too much to drink, any restaurant or bar will call a taxi for you. If you're headed up to Central City and Black Hawk for an

*If a listing in this chapter has an asterisk (\*) after its name, that means it's described in further detail in our Restaurants chapter.*

evening of gambling (see the end of this chapter), we strongly recommend that you avail yourself of one of the shuttle services rather than driving your own car.

# BARS AND OTHER GATHERING SPOTS

**Bannock Street Garage**
**1015 Bannock Street**
**(303) 246-8275**
This Golden Triangle watering hole is out of the way and sparkling, but its patrons still think of it as a dive bar. That may be because the walls are filled with motorcycle parts and logos, and the regulars tend to ride—and/or love—fast bikes.

**Brown Palace**
**321 17th Street**
**(303) 297-3111**
**www.brownpalace.com**
The grande dame of Denver hotels, the Brown Palace has three dining rooms, including Ellyngton's* and the formal Palace Arms*, where gentlemen diners are requested to wear jackets and ties. The Ship Tavern* is the most casual (though not necessarily the least expensive) of the trio and a good place to stop in for a drink or a bite to eat. It's more restaurant than bar, but with its dark wood and nautical decor, it has the feel of an English pub. The walls and ceiling are hung with models of actual ships from America's clipper period. The Ship Tavern can be entered through the Brown Palace Hotel lobby, at 321 17th Street, or from the street at Tremont Place.

Churchill Bar is tucked unobtrusively into a corner of the lobby, which makes it an excellent place to slip away for a snifter of cognac, a cigar, or a quiet conversation. Its menu includes more than 60 cigars, single-malt scotches, small-batch bourbons, and other temptations. Thanks to a fancy ventilation system, even nonsmokers can enjoy the ambience. Lunch and hors d'oeuvres can also be ordered.

**The Buckhorn Exchange***
**1000 Osage Street**
**(303) 534-9505**
**www.buckhorn.com**
The upstairs bar at the Buckhorn Exchange has been a Denver institution for more than 100 years—Colorado's first liquor license is posted on the wall. The hand-carved, white-oak bar dates from 1857 and was brought over from Germany. The Buckhorn is also famous for its vast collection of animal heads mounted on the walls. Expect a daily happy hour from 4:00 to 6:00 P.M. and live entertainment at 7:30 P.M. Wednesday through Saturday.

**Cruise Room**
**1600 17th Street**
**(303) 628-5400**
The restored Oxford Hotel, a block away from Union Station, boasts a restaurant and bar complex that's among the city's best. The intimately sized Cruise Room was modeled after a lounge on the *Queen Mary* and has a wonderful art deco interior that dates from the lifting of Prohibition in 1933. A favorite with visiting authors, the Cruise Room is a great place for a late-night drink, especially if your taste runs to martinis. The bar doesn't have live music, but the jukebox is well stocked with jazz and Big Band music. Be forewarned: It can be tough to get a seat on the weekend unless you arrive early and stake out your spot.

**Fadó Irish Pub**
**1735 19th Street**
**(303) 297-0066**
**www.fadoirishpub.com**
A welcome departure from the LoDo brewpub scene, Fadó brings Ireland to Denver. Most of this authentic Irish pub really is authentic—built in Ireland and brought to Denver piece by piece. Relax in one of nearly a dozen cozy nooks, or be in the middle of the crowd that surrounds the large central bar. There's a full Irish menu, too, with appetizers served

until midnight. On Monday and Wednesday nights, Irish bands provide the entertainment.

### Gabor's
### 1223 East 13th Avenue
### (303) 832-3108

Capitol Hill residents know Gabor's as a comfortable neighborhood bar with cheap beer and funky jukebox music. It attracts the young and artistic, serves a killer hamburger, and spices things up with daily drink specials.

### McCormick's Fish House and Bar*
### 1659 Wazee Street
### (303) 825-1107

The roomy corner bar at McCormick's attracts a big crowd after 5:00 P.M. for Guinness Stout on tap and other libations. If you decide to stay for dinner, some of the freshest fish in town can be had in McCormick's main dining room just across the hallway. Check out their well-priced happy hour appetizers after work and late night.

### Paris Wine Bar
### 1553 Platte Street
### (303) 217-5805

The Central Platte Valley is filling with brownstones and pricey apartments, so what better place for the locals to relax than a warm, narrow womb of a bar? Wine lovers have a wide variety to choose from, and those in need of a light snack can order desserts or bread and cheese platters. DJs and live bands often shoehorn themselves into a corner of the bar, transforming what can be a quiet retreat into a rocking venue.

*If you like the nightlife but aren't into the skimpy miniskirt crowd, try Fadó Irish Pub at 19th and Wynkoop. You'll find cozy spots for conversation and enjoy the authentic decor, much of which was shipped over from Ireland.*

### Sancho's Broken Arrow
### 741 East Colfax Avenue
### (303) 832-5288
### www.quixotes.com/sancho.htm

Sancho's is best described as a dive bar, but it's a very hip one devoted to the Grateful Dead and its fans. The decor, the music, the bands, and the crowd are as tie-dyed as they come. Sancho's is located across the street from the Fillmore Auditorium and on Monday night books jam bands. It's one of four clubs owned by nightlife entrepreneurs Jay, Philip, and Aric-Dante Bianchi.

## LIVE MUSIC

### Bender's 13th Avenue Tavern
### 314 East 13th Avenue
### (303) 861-7070
### www.benderstavern.com

The building at this location has been lots of things, but none of the businesses have been as successful as Bender's. It's known for the mural that covers its eastern exterior, and also for the odd assortment of bands that climb onto its stage. Offerings include rock, punk, rockabilly, and alt country. Or, as one regular described it, "everything but jazz."

### Bluebird Theater
### 3317 East Colfax Avenue
### (303) 322-2308
### www.nipp.com

For a diverse range of musical acts in a gritty neighborhood, try the Bluebird. Located on Denver's infamous East Colfax Avenue, the Bluebird opened as a movie house in 1913 and has since had several incarnations (including a stint as a porn house). Local bands as well as up-and-coming acts share the marquee. There's a balcony for the under-21 set, 550 seats on the main level, and several tables arranged to accommodate the evening's musical attraction (arrive early to secure a table).

*This mural should help you locate Bender's 13th Avenue Tavern, a happening night spot with an odd assortment of live music.*
ELLEN CASTRONE

A dance floor sometimes serves as a mosh pit, depending on the act. Hours and ticket prices vary depending on who's playing.

## Dazzle
### 930 Lincoln Street
### (303) 839-5100
### www.dazzlejazz.com

Dazzle has become one of Denver's most respected jazz venues. Its location, along Lincoln Street in the Golden Triangle neighborhood, appeals to locals who are tired of fighting for parking in trendy LoDo. The stage appeals to mature jazz musicians who make their living seeking out the fans who, in turn, work hard to seek out the music they love. The crowd is mature, too—in their 30s to 50s—and the restaurant and bar menus reflect their tastes. Expect martinis and smooth sounds here.

## Dulcinea's 100th Monkey
### 717 East Colfax Avenue
### (303) 832-3601
### www.quixotes.com

Care for a dive bar with jazz? While Dulcinea's skimps on the atmosphere, it more than makes up for it with the music. The owners book wonderful jazz and funk bands Tuesday through Saturday, and on Sunday Dulcinea's features a reggae DJ. It's located next door to Sancho's Broken Arrow, another of the Bianchi brothers' ventures, and is a block away from the Fillmore Auditorium.

## El Chapultepec
### 1962 Market Street
### (303) 295-9126

Once on the edge of gentrified Denver, El Chapultepec used to be a slightly danger-ous place to drink beer, eat a burrito, and listen to jazz. It now finds itself in the rising shadow of Coors Field and encroached upon by brewpubs, art galleries, and designer tile shops. So far, the essential attraction—sizzling jazz—has remained the same. The "'pec" is a landmark that often attracts touring musicians, who jam with other jazz greats on its tiny bandstand after leaving the stage at larger venues. El Chapultepec is open every night; there's no cover charge, and they don't take reservations.

## Funky Buddha
### 776 Lincoln Street
### (303) 832-5075
### www.funkybuddha.com

*Denver Post* critic Ricardo Baca calls Funky Buddha "a happy-hour favorite," with cheap drinks from 4:00 to 8:00 P.M.

*If you like listening to music outside on cool Denver evenings, check out the summer live-music offerings in our Annual Events and Festivals chapter and in Denver's local newspapers. Notable events include Hot Sounds at the Pavil-ions, held at the Denver Pavilions.*

weeknights and an hors d'oeuvres menu that includes stuffed mushrooms, hummus, red pepper dip, and lamb skewers. Denvercitysearch.com describes it as "La La Land without all the famous folk." With no dancing but DJ music on the weekends, this chic urban bar is a hip place to meet and greet, located just south of downtown in the Golden Triangle neighborhood.

## Jazz@Jack's
**500 16th Street, #320**
**(303) 433-1000**
**www.jazzatjacks.com**
Since 1984 Stephen and Dave Watts have been playing their own blend of smooth and fusion jazz in a band called Dotsero. For many of those years, they played at their own club in the Central Platte Valley. In 2006 they moved their Jazz@Jack's venue to the heart of Denver's downtown, on the third floor of the Denver Pavilions complex. Dotsero shares the stage with a broad range of guest artists and comedians. The room with a view can also be rented for private occasions.

## Lannie's Clocktower Cabaret
**1601 Arapahoe Street, lower level**
**(303) 293-0075**
**www.lannies.com**
This is an old-style nightclub but with the hippest acts in town. Singer Lannie Garrett spent several decades performing at other people's clubs before starting her own in downtown's historic Daniels & Fisher tower, and everything about the place is special. The underground room is intimate and romantic. When Lannie is on stage, expect anything from swing to torch songs, Hollywood tunes, disco hits, and the over-ripe country and western routine of her alter ego, Patsy DeCline. On other nights she fills the stage with burlesque, drag, R&B, soul, and traveling artists of all types. The kitchen is open until midnight, serving appetizers and desserts.

## Ogden Theatre
**935 East Colfax Avenue**
**(303) 830-2525**
**www.nipp.com**
Another of Denver's famed former movie houses, the Ogden attracts a wide range of acts, from the likes of Offspring to the more sedate Jackson Browne. The Ogden often has the best ticket in town, aside from major concert venues. Hours and ticket prices vary.

## Purple Martini
**1020 15th Street, Tabor Center**
**(800) 780-8218**

**Belleview Promenade Center**
**Interstate 25 and Belleview,**
**Greenwood Village**
**www.purplemartini.com**
In the mood for an exotic martini? The Purple Martini offers 80 different kinds as well as live jazz Wednesday, Thursday, and Saturday. Acid jazz is played the other nights (although not live). Look for a 20- to 30-something crowd dressed in "business casual." Half-off happy hour is from 4:00 to 6:30 P.M.

## Sing Sing
**1735 19th Street**
**(303) 291-0880**
**www.rockbottomrestaurantsinc.com/RockBottomWeb/ss/denver.asp**
Located beneath the ChopHouse, Sing Sing offers dueling pianos in a sometimes-wild late-night setting and a chance to sing your heart out. This is definitely a more mainstream crowd that enjoys the likes of Billy Joel tunes. It's also not for the frail, as the improvisational songs can lean toward the raunchy. Food includes Old Chicago pizza and calzones. Sing Sing opens at 7:00 P.M. Tuesday through Thursday, 6:00 P.M. Friday and Saturday. Arrive early for best seating.

## Trios Enoteca
**1730 Wynkoop Street**
**(303) 293-2887**
**www.triosenoteca.com**
The popularity of Trios Enoteca waxes and

wanes with the whims of trendy bar life, but it's still a great (if pricey) place to order from more than 300 wines or 25 different martinis. The cigar room draws the 30- and 40-something crowds. Live music is performed five nights a week, usually jazz and always loud. The decor is elegant, light woods with comfortable couches and high-backed chairs. A light menu is served. Closed Sunday and Monday.

## DANCING

**The Church**
**1160 Lincoln Street**
**(303) 832-3528**
**www.coclubs.com/church/churchMain.html**
Take an old cathedral and transform it into a dance club, complete with stained-glass windows and an elevated altar area, and you've got one of Denver's hottest clubs. The Church attracts dancers of all ages (of course, the weekends tend toward the younger set) mainly because it is large enough to offer a variety of music styles; we recommend it for ages 18 to 25. The weekends offer different music in different rooms. There is a sushi bar, a wine bar, and a cigar bar. Thursday is 18+ night, and there's no cover before 10:00 P.M. Friday and Saturday.

**the hi-dive**
**7 South Broadway**
**(720) 570-4500**
**www.hi-dive.com**
For live music try the hi-dive for hip new bands, record-release parties, and DJs. Plan on occasional cover charges.

**Jackson's Hole**
**1520 20th Street**
**(303) 298-7625**
A great place to drink while you listen to Top 40, hip-hop, and alternative music, Jackson's Hole attracts a youngish crowd—ages 21 to 30. There's a $5.00 cover after 9:30 P.M. (women get in free until 11:00 P.M.). It's open Friday and Saturday.

*While locals and visitors still flock to LoDo nightclubs, hipsters prefer these grittier scenes: the warehouse district, on Larimer Street but centered around 27th and 29th Streets; upper downtown, between 20th and 22nd Streets on California, Welton, Stout, and Champa Streets; and Broadway and Lincoln Streets as they intersect 11th Street.*

**La Rumba**
**99 West Ninth Avenue**
**(303) 572-8006**
Catch the Latin, salsa, and swing craze at this neighborhood spot. The 14-piece salsa band is popular, as are the salsa and swing lessons offered prior to dancing at 9:30 P.M. Thursday and Saturday. The decor is fun with comfy couches for resting between steps. The dress is classy. Cover is $5.00 to $7.00.

**Market 41**
**1941 Market Street**
**(303) 292-5641**
Market 41 attracts a dancing crowd, somewhere in the age range of 21 to 50. Open Wednesday through Saturday only, it offers different kinds of music on different nights. Call ahead to see who's playing

**Polly Esther's**
**2301 Blake Street**
**(303) 382-1976**
**www.pollyesthers.com**
A dance card wouldn't be complete without a trip into the '70s and '80s. Luckily Polly Esther's features the groovy mirrored ball, '70s-garb scene (not required, but a good option) upstairs and '80s music downstairs. Cover runs up to $8.00.

**Ziggies Saloon**
**4923 West 38th Avenue**
**(303) 455-9930**
**www.ziggiessaloon.com**
Denver's oldest blues club, Ziggies offers live music nightly and a dance floor for those who rock. On Sunday afternoon

there's a no-cover-charge open-stage acoustic jam 4:00 to 8:00 P.M., followed by a blues jam 8:30 P.M. to 12:30 A.M.

## ROADHOUSES

**Buffalo Rose Saloon**
**1119 Washington Street, Golden**
**(303) 278-6800**
Buffalo Rose Saloon was established in 1851. It presents a variety of musical acts, from well-known rock groups to folk singers, Wednesday through Saturday nights. Cover charge for lesser-known acts is around $3.00. Otherwise, tickets are available from TicketMaster, (303) 830-TIXS. Buffalo Rose serves a full menu until 10:00 P.M. and a late-night menu until closing.

**Herman's Hideaway**
**1578 South Broadway**
**(303) 777-5840**
**www.hermanshideaway.com**
Herman's Hideaway is a live-music show-case with a large dance floor. The entertainment can vary from rock to Cajun. As you might expect of a roadhouse, the decor is casual and the atmosphere laid-back. The crowd is 20s to 40s. Advance ticketing is advisable for special bookings of nationally known acts; call Herman's or TicketMaster, (303) 830-TIXS.

**Little Bear**
**28075 Highway 74**
**(Main Street), Evergreen**
**(303) 674-9991**
**www.littlebearsaloon.com**

*A few restaurants that are equally good spots for a predinner or late-night drink and a nosh are Marlowe's\* at 16th Street and Glenarm Place, (303) 595-3700; Paramount Cafe\*, next door to Marlowe's at 519 16th Street, (303) 893-2000; and Avenue Grill\*, 630 East 17th Avenue, (303) 861-2820, the choice of Denver's uptown movers and shakers.*

Even folks from the plains brave the narrow mountain roads to make the scene at Little Bear. Neither the route nor the rollicking roadhouse atmosphere is for the timid, but it's a fine place to listen to national and local rock, folk, and blues musicians. Advance tickets for special bookings are available at TicketMaster, (303) 830-TIXS. Pizza and burgers are served from 11:00 A.M., and it's open every day. There's a $3.00 to $5.00 cover charge on the weekends.

## COUNTRY-AND-WESTERN NIGHTCLUBS

**Grizzly Rose Saloon & Dance Emporium**
**5450 North Valley Highway**
**(303) 295-2353 (hotline)**
**(303) 295-1330 (concert line)**
**www.grizzlyrose.com**
Grizzly Rose was voted the nation's No. 1 country music dance hall by the Country Music Association, and it's where the big names come to play when they're in town. With a 5,000-square-foot dance floor and headliners such as Willie Nelson, Merle Haggard, and Toby Keith, it's not hard to see why Grizzly Rose is the undisputed favorite in the live-music C&W category. Advance ticketing is recommended for national acts; call Grizzly Rose or Ticket-Master, (303) 830-TIXS. When no concert is scheduled, Tuesday and Wednesday are no-cover nights. Sunday night is family night, when all ages are welcome.

**Stampede Mesquite Grill & Steakhouse**
**2430 South Havana Street, Aurora**
**(303) 337-6909**
Stampede Mesquite is a club with a giant racetrack dance floor, line dancing and lessons, a yuppie clientele, and an antique bar. Call ahead for reservations at the restaurant, which is on a second-floor balcony overlooking the nightclub and offers well-priced dinner specials.

**Teddy's Restaurant and Lounge**
**4849 Bannock Street**
**(303) 292-9500**

*Denver skyline at night.* DENVER METRO CONVENTION AND VISITORS BUREAU

Teddy's Restaurant and Lounge, located in the Denver North Holiday Inn near the intersection of Interstates 70 and 25, has a different musical format every night. Ladies pay no cover and gents pay $5.00 on Sunday and Wednesday for merengue, cumbia, and Latin rock. Other nights include country, disco, oldies, or Top 40. Happy hour with free hors d'oeuvres runs from 5:00 to 7:00 P.M. Teddy's is a full-service restaurant serving breakfast, lunch, and dinner.

## BREWPUBS, SPORTS BARS, AND POOL HALLS

**Blake Street Tavern**
**2401 Blake Street**
**(303) 675-0505**
**www.flyingdogales.com**
One of the first brewpubs in the Rocky

Mountain region, Flying Dog Brewery originated in Aspen in 1991. When demand outgrew capacity, operations were moved in 1994 to Denver, where Flying Dog currently produces and ships more than 400,000 cases of seven different brews. The tavern in front of their brewery now serves microbrews as well as a menu of salads, pizzas, calzones, and sandwiches plus pool tables and music. Just 4 short blocks from Coors Field, it's a good choice for Rockies fans.

**Breckenridge Brewery***
**2220 Blake Street**
**(303) 297-3644**
**www.breckbrew.com**
The Breckenridge Brewery, opened in 1992, makes the same beers and ales as its Summit County cousin. Pub fare is served, and there's beer drinking and bil-

liards late into the evening (and early into the morning). Tuesday evenings are set aside for a blues jam, and there's live music on weekends on the patio, weather permitting. There is no cover charge.

**Rock Bottom Brewery***
**1001 16th Street**
**(303) 534-7616**
Yet another brewpub and pool hall, the huge, sunny Rock Bottom Brewery is popular with the young lawyers and bankers who work on 17th Street. Try the Red Rocks Red Ale—the popular brew here. The large patio affords some of the best people-watching on the 16th Street Mall. The food's pretty good, too. And, of course, you can shop at the in-house boutique for T-shirts and the like.

**Shakespeare's**
**2375 15th Street**
**(303) 433-6000**
**www.usmenuguide.com/shakespeares.html**
This restaurant, bar, and pool hall opened in 1995 and has been packing 'em in ever since. Shakespeare's offers 19 pool, 2 snooker, and 4 billiard tables. A full menu is available, and all ages are welcome.

**Sports Column***
**1930 Blake Street**
**(303) 296-1930**
**www.denversportscolumn.com**
Billing itself as "major league excitement," Sports Column joins the ranks of Lower Downtown sports bars. It has the requisite pool tables, foosball, and food. It also features five big-screen TVs and plenty of video games.

**Wynkoop Brewing Company***
**1634 18th Street**
**(303) 297-2700**
**www.wynkoop.com**
After 5:00 P.M. is a busy time for the Wynkoop Brewing Company, Denver's first brewpub. Opened in 1988 by John Hickenlooper, now Denver's mayor, the Wynkoop offers comedy downstairs, dining on the first floor, and pool upstairs,

all in the historic circa 1899 J. S. Brown Mercantile Building. Regulars like the Railyard Ale. Wynkoop also brews its own root beer. The billiards room has 25 pool tables, dart lanes, and shuffleboard as well as a full-service bar. Cue rentals and lessons are available; call for more information. Comedy in the basement is offered Thursday through Saturday for $18 and a one-drink minimum.

## ALL-AGES NIGHTLIFE

**Mercury Cafe***
**2199 California Street**
**(303) 294-9281**
**www.mercurycafe.com**
The reincarnation of a legendary Denver nightclub of the '70s and early '80s, Mercury Cafe offers everything from swing dancing and Big Band music to performance art, comedy, theater, and lectures. Mercury serves dinner Tuesday through Sunday from 5:30 to 11:00 P.M. and brunch on weekends from 9:00 A.M. to 3:00 P.M., with an emphasis on natural foods. Credit cards are not accepted.

**Rock Island**
**1614 15th Street**
**(303) 572-7625**
**www.rockislandclub.com**
Rock Island was cool before LoDo was hot. Opened in 1985, it has always attracted a younger crowd that not only likes to dance to alternative music but also believes that black is the best color of clothing. One of Rock Island's great attractions is that each Saturday it offers a 16-and-older night for the younger crowd. Cover charge varies with performers, and anyone younger than age 18 must clear out by 11:30 P.M.

## COMEDY CLUBS

**Comedy Works**
**1226 15th Street**
**(303) 595-3637**
**www.comedyworks.com**

Roseanne (formerly Barr and Arnold) is among the many comics who made appearances early in their careers at Comedy Works. Tuesday night is new talent night; Wednesday through Sunday nights are for established performers. Ticket prices vary, but $18 is about the upper limit unless a headliner is on the bill, which could cost up to $40. Reservations are recommended, and it's for ages 21 and older only.

**Impulse Theater**
**1634 18th Street**
**(302) 297-2111**
**www.impulsetheater.com**
This show originally called Comedy Sports opened in 1987 and is billed as Denver's longest-running comedy show. It occupies the lower level of the Wynkoop Brewing Company with performances Thursday, Friday, and Saturday. Don't expect stand-up. This place does skits, scenes, and ensemble comedy similar to *Saturday Night Live.* And customers feel like they're attending a sporting event since they decide which "team" is funniest. Reservations are recommended. Tickets cost $18.

**Wits End Comedy Club**
**8861 Harlan Street, Westminster**
**(303) 430-4242**
**www.witsendcomedyclub.com**
Wits End Comedy Club offers the comic hijinks of local, national, and international jokemeisters. The humor tends toward the clean side, but you still have to be age 21 or older to attend. There are no nonsmoking performances, though there is a non-smoking section on Friday and Saturday nights. Tickets run $8.00 to $10.00.

# MOVIES

Denver offers an extensive array of neighborhood theaters, most like those in any other town. The theaters listed below will give you a more unusual experience.

**Film on the Rocks**
**Red Rocks Amphitheatre**
**I-70 West to Morrison exit, Morrison**
**(866) 464-2626**
**www.redrocksonline.com**
This summer series pairs performances by local bands with screenings of great movies such as *Willy Wonka and the Chocolate Factory,* with opening act The Flobots and headliner Buckner Funken Jazz. The outdoor setting makes it a magical movie experience. Tickets are $8.00 in advance and $10.00 at the door—a bargain for both music and a movie. Bring something soft to sit on and rain gear, just in case.

**Landmark Esquire**
**590 Downing Street**
**(303) 352-1992**
**www.landmarktheatres.com**
Home of limited-release films, the Esquire is a favorite of urban moviegoers looking for a more old-fashioned experience. It's located in Denver's Capitol Hill neighborhood, so parking is in short supply.

**Landmark Mayan**
**First Avenue and Broadway**
**(303) 352-1992**
**www.landmarktheaters.com**
Denver's finest art-movie house is the Mayan. This 1930s-era theater is decorated on every inch of its wall and ceiling surface with wonderful Mayan figures and other designs. Everything is classy here: the decor, the audience, the films, even the espresso and pastries served in the second-floor cafe. There's one large screen on the main level and two smaller ones above. The Landmark Chez Artiste Cinema, at 2800 South Colorado Boulevard, and the Esquire Theater, at 590 Downing Street, are owned by the same company. Discounted multiple admission tickets are available and can be used at all three locations. Be sure to buy popcorn at any of these theaters: They use real butter!

**Starz FilmCenter**
**900 Auraria Parkway**
**(303) 820-3456**
**www.starzfilmcenter.com**

The Starz FilmCenter is home to the Denver Film Society and the University of Colorado at Denver and Health Sciences Center's College of Arts & Media film education program, in addition to offering a broad selection of films that appeal to viewers with discretion. It also is host to the Starz Denver International Film Festival. The center books indie films as well as classics, foreign films as well as wide-release films that slip in and out of commercial theaters too quickly. The Starz FilmCenter is located in the old Tivoli Brewery building, which was saved during the construction of UC-D's Auraria campus. The theater is newer than most art houses, which means the seats are more comfortable and the sound system is stronger.

## GAMBLING

Since gambling was legalized in 1991, casinos have replaced nearly every retail shop, restaurant, snack shop, and business in the historic mining towns of Central City and Black Hawk, a little more than 30 miles from downtown Denver.

To get there, take U.S. Highway 6 west through Clear Creek Canyon to Highway 119 and follow the signs, or take I-70 westbound to the Central City exit 243 and head north. Parking is at a premium and difficult to find close in, but the good news is that it's validated as long as you gamble. Better yet, let someone else do the driving. If you're just visiting, ask at your hotel about transportation, or check the yellow pages under "Buses—Charter and Rental" for the names of companies that offer round-trip bus and shuttle service to Central City and Black Hawk. A few shuttle services you might look into are the Coach U.S.A./Ace Express, (303) 421-2780, and the People's Choice, (303) 289-2222.

Once you get there, one casino is

pretty much the same as the next. The biggest decision is whether to stay in Black Hawk, which is right on Highway 119, or turn in on the spur road and travel 1 mile farther to Central City. Shuttle buses connect the two, but if you're only up for the evening, you probably won't want to spend your time going back and forth. If you'd like to mix your gambling with a little history, head into Central City. It's been tarted-up a lot since its mining days, but you can still get a sense of what it used to be like.

Limited-stakes gambling is the rule here, with $5.00 being the maximum bet. Only poker, blackjack, and lots of one-armed bandits are allowed at the nearly 40 parlors that operate between 8:00 A.M. and 2:00 A.M.

For a complete listing of casinos and accommodations, visit www.blackhawk colorado.com and www.centralcitycolorado .com. The *Colorado Gambler,* a free newspaper, is also a good guide. It's widely available in the gambling towns and often in Denver, especially at hotels.

**Ameristar Black Hawk**
**111 Richman Street, Black Hawk**
**(866) MORE FUN (toll free)**
**www.ameristarcasinos.com**
National powerhouse Ameristar bought this casino in 2004 and promptly remodeled until it was the state's largest gambling complex. It boasts 15 blackjack and 10 poker tables, as well as slot machines, live entertainment, and one of the area's best casino buffets. Other food options include a steak house, a grill, a pizza joint, and a coffee shop. A 300-room hotel is under construction, with an expected completion date of 2007.

**Canyon Casino**
**131 Main Street, Black Hawk**
**(303) 777-1111**
**www.canyoncasino.com**
Canyon Casino is more of a Las Vegas–style casino and is well supplied with slot machines. As for entertainment in addition to gambling, well, this ain't

Vegas by a long shot, so you won't find any here.

**Fortune Valley Hotel and Casino**
**321 Gregory Street, Central City**
**(303) 582-0800, (800) 924-6646**
**www.fortunevalleycasino.com**
This is one of Colorado's largest combination hotel–casinos, with 117 rooms. Look for live entertainment, live casino action, slots, and a restaurant that serves barbecue.

**The Gilpin Hotel and Casino**
**111 Main Street, Black Hawk**
**(303) 582-1133**
**www.thegilpincasino.com**

The Gilpin Hotel has poker tables, something not all the casinos can claim. Its Mineshaft Bar long predates gambling—it has been a local hangout for more than 100 years.

**Isle of Capri**
**401 Main Street, Black Hawk**
**(800) THE ISLE (toll free)**
**www.isleofcapricasino.com**
The Isle of Capri has a high profile in Black Hawk, with 238 rooms and minisuites, two restaurants and two grills, and live entertainment. Gambling is possible between 8:00 A.M. and 3:00 A.M. at slot machines and 14 tables.

# SHONG ⊞

What a difference a decade makes. Within the past five years, Denver's shopping scene has gone from ho-hum to Holy Cow! It has always been possible to find good merchandise, of course, but since 1996 shopping malls have been sprouting up all over the metro area. The Denver Metro Convention & Visitors Bureau now calls it the "shopping capital of the Rocky Mountain West." In addition to half a dozen large malls, Denver has a growing number of smaller "lifestyle" centers, as well as a respectable number of locally owned "only in Colorado" businesses.

Until 1996 Cherry Creek Shopping Center was the area's largest, and faithful fans still consider it a sentimental favorite. The mall attracts 16 million visitors a year and is in the top 1 percent of all shopping centers in the United States in sales per square foot. In fact, the Cherry Creek mall always makes the area's list of top 10 attractions, often outdrawing the U.S. Mint, Coors Brewery, and the Denver museums.

In 1996 Park Meadows opened in Littleton, bringing with it the area's first Nordstrom, Restoration Hardware, and Crate and Barrel stores. In 2001 it moved ahead of Cherry Creek in terms of sales dollars, and each year it is listed among the nation's elite shopping centers. It continues to grow, adding tentacles of big-box and off-price stores such as the Great Indoors, Home Depot, and Designer Shoe Warehouse. Shoppers on the metro area's south side find its location convenient.

In 2000 FlatIron Crossing opened in Broomfield with 1.2 million square feet of indoor shopping and another 240,000 square feet of streetscaped outdoor shopping in the FlatIron Crossing Village. It was billed as the region's first fully integrated indoor-outdoor shopping environment and is located off the Boulder Turnpike, equally convenient to shoppers on the west and north sides of the metro area.

And in 2002 Colorado Mills opened in Lakewood, filling another void by bringing together high-end manufacturers and retail outlet stores. The mall has since struggled to find its niche, but its biggest draws include Last Call from Neiman Marcus, Off 5th Saks Fifth Avenue, and Off Broadway Shoes. Shoppers from the metro area's downtown and west side find this location convenient.

As is the case with many other cities, large department stores left Denver's core in the 1970s and 1980s as malls were built in outlying areas. Smaller specialty stores continue to operate in Larimer Square, a historically rich area with interesting boutiques and restaurants. Galleries, restaurants, and sports bars ring it, and Tabor Center, a minimall at the lower end of 16th Street, houses more specialty stores. But in 1998 Denver Pavilions opened a larger venue on the downtown 16th Street Mall, offering 350,000 square feet of entertainment, restaurants, and retail. It houses larger chain stores such as Ann Taylor and Talbot's and provides the downtown workforce with a place to buy everyday essentials such as nylons and greeting cards.

In this chapter we've focused on three major shopping areas that have a great concentration and variety of stores: Cherry Creek North; Downtown, LoDo, and Larimer Square; and South Broadway. The Cherry Creek and Larimer Square areas are small enough to walk around in, and that's how we've written those sections, with directions from one place to the next. South Broadway is more spread out—we survey the shops from north to south, but you'll want to travel by car or bus rather than on foot to cover the whole span.

To finish off your introduction to Denver shopping, we've included a roundup of where to go for arts and crafts, books, clothes, food and gourmet cooking supplies, furniture, gifts, and outlet and bargain stores.

Most stores are open daily and accept credit cards, but call ahead to be sure.

But first, the basics—department and grocery stores. Major department stores with more than one location in Greater Denver include Macy's, Dillard's, and JCPenney. For Western wear, Rockmont, Miller Stockman, and Sheplers have locations throughout the metro area. Sports Authority, Recreational Equipment Inc. (REI), Eastern Mountain Sports (EMS), Dick's, BassPro Shops, and Cabela's stores supply Denverites with gear for camping, hiking, biking, rafting, and other outdoor activities.

A top source for consumer electronics, including stereos, televisions, VCRs, and cellular phones, is Ultimate Electronics. There are several stores throughout the metro area. You'll find the Denver location at 1370 South Colorado Boulevard.

The big supermarket chains include King Soopers, Safeway, and Albertsons. For natural foods, visit any of the several Wild Oats, Whole Foods, Sunflower, or Vitamin Cottage markets.

## MAJOR SHOPPING AREAS
# Cherry Creek North

The neighborhood directly to the north of the mall, Cherry Creek North, is a delightful mélange of interesting shops, galleries, clothing designers, cafes, and restaurants.

At the corner of Detroit Street and Second Avenue is **Room & Board,** a contemporary furniture store that consistently ranks high in local "Best of" polls. Just across the street at 221 Detroit Street is **DjUNA,** a locally owned vintage-inspired furniture store. If you're looking for something to hang above the sofa, **Saks Galleries,** 3019 East Second Avenue, specializes in 19th- and 20th-century representational art.

**Pismo Contemporary Art Glass,** 2770 East Second Avenue, stocks an unmatched selection of art glass by Coloradans Brian Maytum, Kit Karbler, and internationally known glass artist Dale Chihuly in its luxurious gallery. More art glass can be found at **International Villa,** 239 Detroit Street, named one of America's Top 100 Galleries. A great source for funky clothing and inexpensive jewelry for men and women is **Eccentricity,** 290 Fillmore Street.

**Gallery M,** 2830 East Third Avenue, features contemporary fine art, photography, and sculpture by both national and international artists. **Show of Hands,** 210 Clayton Street, on the other hand, showcases American crafts in clay, metal, wood, and fiber as well as stocking wall art and paintings.

Among the designer labels carried at **Lawrence Covell,** 225 Steele Street, are Helmut Lang, Kiton, and Luciano Barbera. This upscale men's and women's store is known for its first-class service.

Kids' stuff can be found at **The Wizard's Chest,** 230 Fillmore Street, which in addition to children's toys carries grown-up games and an attic full of costumes and masks. **Kazoo & Company,** 2930 East Second Avenue, has educational games and toys.

Gardeners will love the **Smith & Hawken** store at 268 Detroit Street. Shop for high-quality gardening tools, workwear, containers, plants, and garden furniture.

**Hermitage Antiquarian Bookshop,** 290 Fillmore Street, is a pleasant spot with neat library stacks of first editions and other rare and/or old books.

# Downtown, LoDo, and Larimer Square

Downtown Denver's main shopping thoroughfare, 16th Street, was transformed into a tree-lined pedestrian mall in 1980 and now boasts 25,000 flowers in the summer. Free shuttle buses run the length of the mall as often as every 90 seconds, connecting Lower Downtown with the Civic Center area. Many of the stores along 16th Street are touristy, but it's worth strolling the mile-long stretch to see what's here. With **TJMaxx** and **Ross,** the corner of 16th and California Streets has become a mini off-price mecca in downtown. Restaurants along the mall often have outdoor seating—great for people-watching—and there are shaded benches for those who've brought their own lunch or their laptops. The entire mall offers free wi-fi service to all outdoor visitors. If you haven't planned ahead, buy a to-go lunch from a street vendor or fast-food restaurant.

More traditional shopping takes place at the glass-enclosed **Tabor Center,** which extends along 16th Street from Arapahoe to Larimer. Once a shining star in the downtown shopping scene, Tabor Center has struggled in recent years. It is undergoing a renovation that is expected to reenergize the center. Among the goals of the renovation is a desire to simplify navigation into and through the shopping center.

The heart of Larimer Square is Larimer Street between 15th and 14th Streets. From Tabor Center, walk 1 block south through the cluster of stores and restaurants called **Writer Square,** and on the other side you'll find yourself standing on the spot where Denver got its start in 1858. Denver's first bank, bookstore, photographer, and dry-goods store were located on this block. The original buildings were made of wood and were destroyed in a fire in 1863; the brick structures that now line the street were erected for the most part in the 1870s to 1890s, and the entire area was renovated in the mid-1970s. Interested visitors can pick up a walking-tour brochure and information on the individual buildings at the kiosk on the east side of the street.

Larimer Square has a nice mix of shops and restaurants, including **Cry Baby Ranch,** which has Western furnishings and pricey trinkets. **The Market** has an exhaustive selection of gourmet goodies as well as coffee, deli, and bakery items to take out or eat on the premises. **Z Gallerie,** on the corner of 15th and Larimer Streets, has contemporary home furnishings and accessories. Also on the block: **John Atencio** jewelry; **HUB** euro streetwear; **UROK** euro clothing, bags, and accessories for women; and **Ted Turner's Montana Grill.**

**American Costume,** 1526 Blake Street, has more than 10,000 costumes in stock.

Whether you're looking for something off-beat for Halloween or are slated to play Santa at the office party, they'll suit you up. At this point you're just a few blocks from the **Tattered Cover Book Store** at 16th and Wynkoop Streets.

As you move into LoDo, check out **Bouquets,** 1525 15th Street, for the most unusual flowers and flower arrangements in town. It was voted Denver's top florist in 2003 by *5280* magazine.

Stop at **Rockmont Ranch Wear,** at 1626 Wazee Street, for a look back in time as well as an opportunity to buy authentic Western clothing. Rockmont founders invented the snap-front Western shirt, and for more than 60 years have been generating duds for rodeo cowboys, Hollywood stars, and cityslickers alike. The building, open Monday through Saturday, includes a museum and a retail store.

The 1700 block of Wazee Street was once the heart of Denver's contemporary art district, and it still is, in a sense, although closures and additions have shifted the emphasis away from the avant-garde. We write more about that in our The Arts chapter.

A bit farther uptown, collectors of Native-American crafts head for the **Mudhead Gallery** in the Hyatt Regency Hotel, 555 17th Street.

**The Native American Trading Company,** a fine source for pots, textiles, and Edward S. Curtis photogravures, is across from the **Denver Art Museum** at 1301 Bannock Street.

On the upper, southern edge of downtown is one of Denver's most venerable stores. **Sports Authority** is at 10th Avenue and Broadway, in a wildly extravagant building known as the Sports Castle. This seven-level store, originally built as a car dealership, stocks everything, including tents, cameras, bicycles, and tennis shoes. Originally known as Gart Sports, it now has dozens of other locations throughout the state (find them at www.sportsauthority.com) but none so architecturally distinctive as this one.

# South Broadway

South Broadway is an antiques lover's paradise. In fact, the area between Arizona and Iowa Streets is dubbed "Antiques Row." There are a few furniture stores tucked in as well. Your best bet is to just make your way south on Broadway (it's one way north of the Interstate 25 interchange). Below are a few shops to look out for; more are listed in our Antiques category.

**Manos Folk Art,** 422 Broadway, has a broad selection of mirrors, Mexican milagros, Peruvian folk art, masks, and wood furniture.

**Mecca Modern Interior,** 21 South Broadway, is the avant-garde kid on the block, with furniture and accessories that are recognizable modern classics.

**Sheptons Antiques,** 389 South Broadway, also has an international selection of furniture and salvaged architectural elements, including carved-wood doors and portions of wrought-iron fences.

**The Antique Guild,** 1298 South Broadway, consolidates the wares of many dealers under one roof.

A few blocks farther south is **Hooked on Glass,** 1407 South Broadway, which specializes in Depression-era glass and other collectibles.

## SHOPPING MALLS

**Aspen Grove Lifestyle Center**
**7301 South Santa Fe Drive, Littleton**
**(303) 794-0640**
**www.shopaspengrove.com**
Built in 2001, Aspen Grove was one of metro Denver's first "lifestyle centers," or outdoor shopping centers that allow for more than just mall shopping. It draws clients from throughout the area, but its primary customers come from Littleton and southwest Denver. Its stores include Chico's, Talbot's, Children's Place, Pier 1, and Williams Sonoma. Dining choices include Buca di Beppo, Kyoto Asian Fusion, Ted's Montana Grill, and Panera Bread Co.

**Belmar**
**Wadsworth Boulevard and Alameda Avenue, Lakewood**
**(303) 742-1520**
**www.belmarcolorado.com**
Until 2004 Villa Italia Shopping Mall held most of Lakewood's stores. Then it was replaced by Belmar, creating a new downtown for this first-tier Denver suburb. The new Belmar is still coming into its own, but fans already know it for the summer farmers' market, fall Italian festival, and winter holiday celebrations. They also know it as home to the area's newest Whole Foods Market, as well as chain stores and local restaurants strewn out along a network of new streets. Condos, row houses, and detached homes are being built on the site and will bring with them new residents who will amble down to the movie theater or Lucky Strike bowling alley. Until then, shoppers from throughout the metro area drive in to taste the development that has gained national attention for its scope, creativity, and future potential. In addition to national chains that are represented in most malls, Belmar boasts a Coldwater Creek that has a full-service spa, two dentists, five electronics and wireless phone stores, banks, bars and restaurants that serve American, Asian, Italian, and Mexican food, as well as one fine-dining restaurant called Home.

**Cherry Creek Shopping Center**
**3000 East First Avenue**
**(303) 388-3900**
**www.cherrycreekmall.com**
Anchored by Saks Fifth Avenue, Neiman Marcus, and Macy's, the Cherry Creek Shopping Center also has high-end specialty stores such as Louis Vuitton, Abercrombie & Fitch, Banana Republic, and Ann Taylor. Even the restroom is above average: Clad in marble, with automatic fixtures, it was written up in *Time* magazine! There is a dining area with quick food and several upscale restaurants, such as Kona Grill. Retail tenants include Tiffany & Co., Williams Sonoma, Tommy Bahama's, and Anthropologie.

*Downtown's Denver Pavilions.* DENVER METRO CONVENTION AND VISITORS BUREAU

Another attraction is an elaborate play area for kids, with seating for adults, near the mall entrance to Macy's. The area features super-size, colorful breakfast-food items for the kids to crawl on. Kids can't resist sliding down the bacon into an egg yolk. The attraction is so popular that mini playgroups have formed for regular visits.

### Colorado Mills
**14500 West Colfax Avenue, Lakewood**
**(303) 384-3000**
**www.coloradomills.com**
Colorado Mills is one of the newest malls in the metro area, and its format reflects our economic times. The stores in this snazzy center are all one-of-a-kind outlets, offering reduced prices on merchandise from such retailers as Ann Taylor, Last Call, Neiman Marcus, Tommy Hilfiger, Off 5th Saks Fifth Avenue, Borders Books and Music, Bath & Body Works, SKECHERS, Levi's, Kenneth Cole, Eddie Bauer, Chico's, and Nine West. Off Broadway Shoes is big enough to satisfy any shoe lover, carrying designs that range from sane to gotta-have-it crazy.

Located off Interstate 70 on the west side of the metro area, Colorado Mills is a convenient stop for travelers on their way to and from the mountains, and residents from all parts of town find it worth the drive for the unique selection and bargain prices. The mall has a standard food court and a 16-screen theater complex. Mall hours are 10:00 A.M. to 9:30 P.M. Monday through Saturday and 11:00 A.M. to 7:00 P.M. Sunday.

### Denver Pavilions
**On the 16th Street Mall between**
**Tremont and Welton Streets**
**(303) 260-6000**
**www.denverpavilions.com**
The Pavilions doesn't fit into traditional mall or shopping area categories because it offers more than retail. Pavilions bills itself as the new wave of retail, restaurant, and entertainment. You can browse Banana Republic, indulge in something decadent at the Corner Bakery, then take in a flick at the United Artist theater (all high-backed stadium seating).

Denver Pavilions boasts several large attractions, including Maggiano's Little Italy, a Virgin Records Megastore, Barnes & Noble, and Hard Rock Café, along with more familiar shops such as Bath and

# Indoor-outdoor Flatlron Crossing

FlatIron Crossing opened with a splash in August 2000 and continues to attract both stores and shoppers. Touted as reflecting the outdoor lifestyle of Coloradans, the center combines a 1.2-million-square-foot interior mall with a 240,000-square-foot outdoor, street-scaped shopping area. A 14-screen AMC theater anchors the southwestern corner.

The idea was to create more than just another shopping experience. According to Westcor Partners, the center's developer, the goal was to create a place that people think of as both a community showplace and a great place to spend a Saturday afternoon. With its 30 acres of green space and parks, access to local trail systems, and two parklike areas with lush landscapes and streams and fountains, FlatIron Crossing may do just that.

Inside the mall, natural materials and abundant sunlight were essential design elements. The interior makes generous use of wood beams, iron, patterned stone, and Colorado limestone. Some windows allow high-morning sun, while others are set to capture the glow of late afternoons.

The center's largest tenants are Nordstrom, Macy's, and Dillard's. The interior stores tend to be highly recognizable national chains like Eddie Bauer, Banana Republic, Fossil, and Pottery Barn, while smaller and, in some cases, local stores such as DjUNA populate the Village. All told, there are more than 200 specialty retailers and restaurants located throughout the mall's far-flung properties. In an effort to bring more people out of the mall and into the Village, the center hosts farmers' markets and Thursday-evening street fairs.

FlatIron Crossing launched the FlatIron Crossing Music & Art Foundation to help restore endangered music and arts programs in Colorado schools and communities. Guided by board members from the local arts and education communities, the foundation will benefit from many activities at FlatIron Crossing over the years as well as raise funds through community, business, and government sources.

Located off U.S. Highway 36, the center is conveniently situated along the growing Denver-Boulder corridor and draws residents of both cities.

Body Works, Gap, and Victoria's Secret. A 30,000-square-foot NikeTown opened in 1999 (one of only 15 in the United States).

Mall crawlers used to the confines of suburban malls will be surprised at the Pavilions' open-air setting. But with a yearly average of 300 days of sunshine, outdoor shopping is rarely a problem in Denver. During summer months the Pavil-

ions offers a free Hot Sounds concert series on Thursday nights.

**FlatIron Crossing
U.S. Highway 36 at Interlocken or
FlatIron Circle exits
(720) 887-9900
www.flatironcrossing.com**
FlatIron Crossing is an indoor-outdoor cen-

ter with 1.5 million square feet of shopping. It is anchored by Nordstrom, Macy's, and Dillard's. Its 170 specialty retailers include well-known names like Gap and Ann Taylor as well as lesser-known shops in the Village. The center is located amid 30 acres of green space and parklike settings and offers access to local trails as well.

**Northfield Stapleton**
**8340 East 49th Avenue**
**(303) 375-5464**
**www.northfieldstapleton.com**
Northfield is one of Denver's newest outdoor-lifestyles centers, opening in 2006 with Harkins Theatre, Colorado's only Bass Pro Shop, Circuit City, SuperTarget, and Macy's as anchors. Another 50 tenants fill out the Main Street segment, with 25 more to follow. Restaurants include Bar Louie, La Sandia, and Ling & Louie's Asian Bar & Grill. In addition to providing one of the region's roomiest parking lots, the center is located at what may be the best crossroad for out-of-state visitors. I-70 (which runs from Kansas to Utah) and Interstate 270 (which veers north to Nebraska) intersect near the center's southwest corner.

**Park Meadows**
**8401 Park Meadows Center Drive**
**Littleton**
**(303) 792-2999**
**www.parkmeadows.com**
Park Meadows is anchored by Nordstrom, Dillard's, and Macy's. The dining hall is huge, and the restaurants are on the swanky side. Park Meadows grows ever-larger each year with the addition of retail around its perimeter. It's a great mix of low-, mid-, and high-end retail.

**Southwest Plaza**
**Wadsworth Boulevard and West Bowles Avenue, Littleton**
**(303) 973-5300**
**www.southwestplaza.com**
Once Denver's largest mall, Southwest Plaza serves Jefferson County's booming population. It has almost every type of clothing, food, music, and shoe store. There are even a couple of furniture and accessories stores, a movie theater, and a Target.

**The Streets at Southglenn**
**South University Boulevard and East Arapahoe Road, Centennial**
**(303) 795-0834**
**www.southglenn.com**
Like many other aging indoor shopping malls, Southglenn Mall is in the process of being reinvented as an outdoor lifestyle center. The existing mall was demolished in June 2006, although anchor tenants Sears and Macy's will remain open during the transformation. Once the new center is completed in 2008, city officials and tenants hope the 70-acre site will become a focal point for community events and festivals as well as providing destination shopping. Although tenants weren't announced at publication time, Southglenn spokesmen promised a gourmet natural foods market, a movie theater, European bistros, sidewalk cafes, and unique men's and women's clothing stores.

**Thornton Town Center Mall**
**10001 Grant Street (off Interstate 25 at 104th Avenue East), Thornton**
**(303) 252-0007**
This fairly small mall (25 stores) is anchored by a Super Walmart. There's also a Home Depot and a theater complex.

**Town Center at Aurora**
**Off Interstate 225 at Alameda Avenue and Sable Street, Aurora**
**(303) 344-4120**
**www.simon.com/find_mall**
This center has the look and feel of a fairly typical suburban mall. Anchored by Macy's and JCPenney, it offers recognizable stores like the Disney Store and Old Navy, as well as 125 smaller, more boutique-type shops.

# Park Meadows Draws Shoppers from Afar

When Park Meadows opened in August 1996, it was hailed as a shopping center unlike any ever built. In fact, it was described as a retail "resort." Whether or not shoppers feel like they're on vacation is uncertain, but what is known is that Park Meadows has attracted visitors as if it were a vacation spot. In its first year, 13 million people came to check out Greater Denver's largest shopping center—all 1.5 million square feet of it.

With three top-drawer anchors—Colorado's first Nordstrom, Denver's first Dillard's, and Colorado's largest Macy's—Park Meadows is a shopping mecca for a seven-state region. Park Meadows is fast becoming one of the area's must-see

*Park Meadows was designed to have the look and feel of a rustic ski lodge.*
PARK MEADOWS

places, although it's not exactly in the hub of activity, as is Cherry Creek Shopping Center. Rather, it was built in Douglas County, the area's fastest-growing county, in an area not previously known for great shopping opportunities.

What makes it different from other shopping centers is its "feel." While most malls are conglomerates of stores, Park Meadows was designed to feel like a mountain ski lodge (a very, very busy one!). Massive natural wood-beam cathedral ceilings soar above the second level, the shopping center is bathed in natural light, and large stone fireplaces are located throughout. Shoppers can rest in overstuffed leather chairs and couches. Hahn Company, the developer of Park Meadows, also commissioned eight Colorado artists to create $2 million worth of artwork.

The shopping center is home to 160 stores, many of which were new to Colorado when they opened, including Crate and Barrel, Restoration Hardware, and Nordstrom. While the obligatory dining area is located right near the center, Park Meadows also houses "better" restaurants, including California Café, Red Robin, and P.F. Chang's China Bistro. Even the United Artists Movie Theater here is a little bigger and a little glitzier. In addition to the multiscreen movie theater, there are four virtual-reality experiences, including "Virtual Hanglider."

**Westminster Mall**
**Sheridan Boulevard and 88th Avenue**
**Westminster**
**(303) 428-5634**
**www.shopwestminstermall.com**
Westminster Mall has four anchor stores, Dillard's, Macy's, JCPenney, and Sears. With more than 140 stores, Westminster draws from all over the state, especially folks from the mountain communities. Though more than 20 years old, the mall was renovated in 2000–2001, so it's up-to-date.

## ANTIQUES

The South Broadway area has the greatest concentration of antiques stores in the Greater Denver area. In addition to the stores we mention by name below, you're sure to find more, especially continuing farther south on Broadway. And if you're willing to travel out of Denver 30 to 40 minutes, you might want to check out the town of Niwot and its 2-block main street filled with antiques shops. Auctions are sometimes held on Sunday. To get to Niwot, take Interstate 25 north to Highway 52 west to connect with Highway 119. Niwot is about 1 mile north of the intersection of Highways 52 and 119.

The town of Lyons, which lies at the mouth of St. Vrain Canyon on the way to Estes Park, about 45 minutes from downtown Denver, is another great antiques-lover's mecca. Antiques stores dot both sides of the old-fashioned Main Street. You'll find a few that specialize in Western memorabilia. To get there from central Denver, take I-25 north to the Highway 66 exit, then go west about 17 miles.

Closer to town, check out the following shops.

**Antique Mall of Lakewood**
**9635 West Colfax Avenue, Lakewood**
**(303) 238-6940**
**www.mountainstatescollector.com**
This "mall" has about 150 dealers on three floors under one roof. In addition to a cafe, there's also a dealer who specializes

in books—both old books and reference books about antiques.

**Architectural Antiques**
**2669 Larimer Street**
**(303) 297-9722**
**www.aasalvageco.com**
This high-end antiques store features an amazing array of architectural finds dating back hundreds of years. Among the categories of goods carried are ecclesiastical artifacts from churches and cathedrals across the country, doors and windows (including stained glass) and hardware, vintage lighting, and outdoor ornamentation.

**Decade**
**56 South Broadway**
**(303) 733-2288**
Voted "Best Store Anywhere on Broadway" in 2001 by the readers and editors of *West-word,* this little shop mixes vintage and new. They have a constantly changing array of furniture that spans the decades and a good selection of home accessories as well. They also have a small clothing boutique in the back that offers mostly new men's and women's clothing, jewelry, and such. The shop tends to carry more vintage options in the fall than earlier in the year.

## ARTS AND CRAFTS

For arts and crafts, make Cherry Creek North your first stop (see Major Shopping Areas at the beginning of this chapter). Additional sources include the following.

**Akente Express**
**919 Park Avenue West**
**(303) 297-8817**
Akente Express is an African-American heritage shop that stocks original fabrics from Africa, handmade clothing, jewelry, artwork, sculpture, and all-natural, alcohol-free essential oils.

**The Clay Pigeon**
**601 Ogden Street**
**(303) 832-5538**
**www.claypigeon.com**

The Clay Pigeon is Denver's oldest gallery specializing in handmade works of clay, including both stoneware and porcelain. This is a great place to buy unusual serving pieces and wedding gifts.

### Jackalope
**12450 South Parker Road, Parker**
**(303) 805-7687**
**www.jackalope.com**
"Everything under the sun" is their motto, and that pretty much holds true here. A Santa Fe and Albuquerque favorite for years, Jackalope now brings its extensive array of furniture, pottery, glassware, fabrics, tableware, and much more to the Denver area. Items arrive weekly, if not daily, from such destinations as Mexico, China, India, and Vietnam. And prices tend to be reasonable.

### Old Santa Fe Pottery
**2485 South Santa Fe Drive**
**(303) 871-9434**
**www.oldsantafepottery.com**
Old Santa Fe Pottery houses two rows of shops filled with Oaxacan wood carvings, painted Talavera ceramics, furniture, rugs, and all sorts of pottery. You'll enjoy a pretty central courtyard reminiscent of a Mexican village.

## BARGAIN SHOPPING

Denver has its share of off-price retailers, including Loehmann's, 9555 East County Line Road, (303) 708-9966, which sells primarily name-brand women's clothing at low prices. Beyond that, there are several great consignment and near-new stores, such as the following.

### Gumballs
**5787 South Gallup Street, Littleton**
**(303) 795-6557**
Tired of paying top dollar for kids' blue jeans? Gumballs often has a rack of them priced around a dollar. But that's not all; go here to find a lot of gently used children's clothing.

### The Snob Shop
**2804 East Sixth Avenue**
**(303) 355-6939**
**www.thesnobshopdenver.com**
This one's been around for a while and is known for its discriminating selection of clothing for men, women, and children plus shoes and accessories. Check it out for anything from casual to dressy.

### Twice as Haute
**600 Downing Street**
**(303) 753-6003**
**www.twiceashaute.com**
This consignment shop deals only in women's clothing. As its name implies, it features labels such as Carole Little, Donna Karan, Armani, and the like. It has a broad selection of dresses for special occasions.

## BOOKS

The behemoth Tattered Cover Book Store dominates Greater Denver's literary scene, but Denver's readers are avid enough to support more than one general-interest bookstore. Large chains such as Waldenbooks and B. Dalton Bookseller have branches in many regional shopping malls, and Barnes & Noble Booksellers is found all over town. Another good all-around bookstore, the Book Rack, has four locations, 1930 South Havana Street in Aurora, 2313 South Dawson Way in Aurora, 2382 South Colorado Boulevard in Denver, and in Lakewood at 1535 South Kipling Parkway.

## Specialty Bookstores

### The Bookies
**4315 East Mississippi Avenue, Glendale**
**(303) 759-1117**
Though The Bookies is primarily known for its great children's selection, it also carries most best-seller titles, too. Better yet, every book is sold at a discount—at least 15 percent off. (The discount does not apply to educational and teacher resource books.)

### Cultural Legacy Bookstore
**3633 West 32nd Avenue**
**(303) 964-9049**
**www.culturallegacy.com**
Cultural Legacy Bookstore is the only bookstore in Colorado to specialize in Chicano and Latino literature, with Spanish, English, and bilingual books and magazines for children and adults. Ask about book signings and other special events.

### Gallagher Collection
**1498 South Broadway**
**(303) 756-5821**
**www.gallagherbooks.com**
Located on Denver's famed antiques row, Gallagher Collection is a member of the Rocky Mountain Antiquarian Booksellers Association. The shop features rare and out-of-print books, books and posters on WWI and WWII, fine binding, and other specialty items.

### Murder by the Book
**1574 South Pearl Street**
**(303) 871-9401**
**www.murderbythebook.com**
Murder by the Book, a cozy store in a former home, specializes in new and used mystery novels and crime fiction. If your kids love mysteries, check out the children's selections.

### Neighborhood Bookstore
**8021 Broadway, Littleton**
**(303) 730-3682**
The Neighborhood Bookstore is your basic general-use bookstore. You'll find mostly modern, currently popular titles in just about every genre. About 20 percent of the titles are new; the rest are used books. Ask about their trade-in system for used books.

### Reel Books Audio Bookstore
**1580 Blake Street**
**(303) 629-5528**
**www.reelbooks.com**
Reel Books has thousands of books on tape, for adults and children, to buy or rent. Whether you want mysteries, self-help, the classics, or biographies, chances are you can find it on tape here. On-line purchases are 20 percent off and support the Columbia Lighthouse for the Blind.

### Tattered Cover Cherry Creek
**Colfax Avenue and Elizabeth Street in the Historic Lowenstein Theater**
**(303) 322-7727**

### Tattered Cover LoDo
**1628 16th Street**
**(303) 436-1070**

### Tattered Cover Highlands Ranch
**9315 Dorchester Street, Highlands Ranch**
**(303) 470-7050**
**www.tatteredcover.com**
The Tattered Cover is truly one of the country's finest independent bookstores—and for book lovers, one of Denver's finest attractions. Built on the philosophy of comfort and personal service, the store provides readers and browsers a place to while away an afternoon (or full day) amid shelf after shelf of books, cozy corners, and overstuffed chairs and couches.

Opened more than 35 years ago, the original Cherry Creek store expanded a number of times before moving into the renovated Lowenstein Theater, on the corner of Colfax Avenue and Elizabeth Street, in 2006. A few years ago, a second location opened in historic LoDo, just blocks from Coors Field. In 2004 a third location sprang up in suburban Highlands Ranch, a 21,754-square-foot addition to the suburban neighborhood. Tattered Cover now houses more than half a million books—150,000 titles—in its three locations.

In addition to this expansive book selection, all locations offer a coffee shop, newsstand, and extensive calendar of signings and literary events. You can sign up for the online mailing list to receive an online newsletter and announcements of special events and promotions. And if you're looking for a book group, you can call the Book Clubs Information Line at (303) 322-1965.

## CLOTHING

See our Major Shopping Areas section earlier in this chapter for a good overall roundup of clothing stores. Here are some more options to consider.

**Andrisen Morton Co.**
**210 and 270 St. Paul Street**
**(303) 321-0404**
**www.avers.com**
Andrisen Morton is for men and women who want elegant designer clothes with fancy prices. With such brands as Armani, Escada, Dolce and Gabbana, and YSL, it carries clothes you won't see everywhere else, and the sales staff helps customers put together perfect outfits.

**Barbara & Company**
**7777 East Hampden Avenue**
**(303) 751-2618**
Funky yet classic clothes in beige, white, black, and brown make up the mainstay of Barbara & Company's clothing. If you're unable to put things together, let the knowledgeable staff outfit you from head to toe. But plan to pay high prices for the clothes and accessories.

**Iris Fields**
**1099 South Gaylord Street**
**(303) 777-0516**
At Iris Fields you'll find women's clothing that is unusual but comfortable, affordable but not cheap. Better yet, you won't see everyone else in the same outfit. The store specializes in outfitting businesswomen age 30 and older in contemporary fashions.

## FOOD AND GOURMET COOKING SUPPLIES

Don't forget The Market at Larimer Square. But keep in mind these other spots as well.

**Boyer's Coffee Company**
**7295 North Washington Street**
**(800) 452-5282, (303) 289-3345**
**www.boyerscoffee.com**
Boyer's, a Denver-based coffee roaster and packager, offers its coffee and related items at lower-than-supermarket prices. Its warehouse store is open to the public 6:30 A.M. to 4:00 P.M. weekdays and 9:00 A.M. to 3:00 P.M. Saturdays.

**European Mart**
**5225 Leetsdale Drive**
**(303) 321-7144**
When you're in the mood for Hungarian salami or hearty sausage, the European Mart is the place to stop. Filled with eastern European delicacies—meats, fish, candies, cookies—this shop is the real thing. The Russian owners are helpful and eager to please, and the food is great.

**Stephany's Chocolates**
**6770 West 52nd Avenue, Arvada**
**(303) 421-7229**
Stephany's Chocolates, with several locations, are a Colorado tradition and a popular gift for visitors to take home. The Denver Mints—get it?—are a big seller. Stephany's has stores in Denver Pavilions, Park Meadows, and Cherry Creek Shopping Center as well as DIA and Westminster Mall.

**Sur La Table**
**Cherry Creek Shopping Center**
**(303) 780-7800**
**www.surlatable.com**
This upscale cooking store (one of many throughout the country) sells appliances, cookware, tableware, and specialty foods. It's a kitchen lover's delight.

## FURNITURE

A number of furniture warehouses are along the west side of I-25 (take the 58th Avenue exit and go south). Quality and prices vary, but it's worth stopping to at least comparison shop. We've also mentioned a few furniture stores in our Major

Shopping Areas section. You might also consider the following.

### Decor Southwest
**151 West Mineral Avenue, #103, Littleton**
**(720) 222-2660**
**www.decorsouthwest.com**
Decor Southwest specializes in hand-crafted Southwestern furniture, accessories, and lighting. Prices range from medium to high, and if you don't see what you want, just ask. They do custom work.

### Howard Lorton Galleries
**12 East 12th Avenue**
**(303) 831-1212**
**www.howardlorton.com**
If you're into traditional, classic, expensive furniture, Howard Lorton is one of Denver's premier galleries. Open since 1927, this four-story shop offers top-of-the-line furniture, lamps, carpeting, and draperies.

### Kacey Fine Furniture
**1201 Auraria Parkway**
**(303) 571-5123**

**311 East County Line Road, Littleton**
**(720) 283-0900**

**11000 South Parker Road, Parker**
**(720) 214-6700**

**11305 West Sixth Avenue, Lakewood**
**(303) 233-8888**
**www.kacey.com**
Although Kacey Fine Furniture is in several locations (there's even one in Frisco), the main store on Auraria Parkway is the largest, with floor after floor of everything from leather couches to traditional bedroom sets to funky coffee tables. Kacey has a great selection and reasonable prices. Better yet, every year on the owner's birthday, she offers a discount equal to her age. She's currently in her early 50s.

### Lakewood Furniture
**8425 West Colfax Avenue, Lakewood**
**(303) 233-5811**
Lakewood Furniture features unfinished furniture in a variety of styles, including Mexican, country, Shaker, Russian, and

barn-wood. If you don't see what you want, they'll build it for you.

### Whitney's of Greenwood Village
**5910 South University Boulevard**
**Greenwood Village**
**(303) 794-0990**
Whitney's features 500 furniture manufacturers from around the world. From traditional to contemporary furniture and accessories, Whitney's also offers a staff of interior designers who can help with a room or a whole house.

## GIFTS

In a sense, this category exists for stores we couldn't fit anyplace else because at this point in the chapter, we've listed dozens of places to buy gifts—from gourmet food stores to arts and crafts cooperatives. But here are three more of our favorites that you won't want to miss.

### For Heaven's Sake
**4383 Tennyson Street**
**(303) 964-9339**
**www.forheavensake.com**
This New Age gift and book shop in the Highlands Square area offers a wide array of products such as candles, crystals, books, music, and the increasingly popular "lucky bamboo." The store also sponsors in-house events and classes, including a monthly Psychic Fair, which features palm and tarot readings among other events.

### Made in Colorado
**(303) 838-7343**
**www.madeincolorado.com**
Gifts, collectibles, and foods from 250 Colorado regional artisans and craftspeople are featured in this Internet-only store. The works encompass the artistic, the whimsical, the edible, the decorative, the readable, the touchable. Its "unusual" gift collection includes a gold-panning kit—everything you need to strike it rich in the hills.

**Thistle & Shamrock**
**8101 East Belleview Avenue, Littleton**
**(720) 482-1488**
**www.thistle-shamrock.com**
Thistle & Shamrock features Scottish and Irish imports, including kilts, jewelry, fine china, music, and assorted collectibles. Look for Beleek china and Edinburgh crystal. As you shop, enjoy lovely Scottish or Irish music in the background.

## OUTLETS

**The Outlets at Castle Rock**
**Exit 184, Meadow Parkway**
**(off I-25 South), Castle Rock**
**(303) 688-4494**
**www.outletsatcastlerock.com**
The largest outlet mall in the Front Range, Castle Rock has 110 stores—everything from designer clothes to electronics. Open seven days a week, the outlet has an easy and convenient layout and a central food court with the usual fast-food offerings.

**The Outlets at Loveland**
**I-25 North to exit 257B, Loveland**
**(970) 663-1717**
**www.outletsatloveland.com**
With 82 stores, The Outlets at Loveland includes a Mikasa factory store and a Bose (stereo equipment). There's the standard offering of clothes and kitchenware, with savings up to 70 percent off everyday prices. Though there is no food court on-site, several restaurants are within walking distance.

**Silverthorne Factory Stores**
**I-70 West to exit 205, Silverthorne**
**(970) 468-5780**
**www.silverthornefactorystores.com**
Started as a fashion and active outerwear outlet, Silverthorne has 80 stores that now include kitchenware and shoe sellers. It offers 30 to 70 percent off regular prices and is surrounded by restaurants in this small mountain town.

# TOURS AND ATTRACTIONS

In this chapter we've rounded up our favorite museums, gardens, and historic houses. What Greater Denver has to offer in this category may surprise newcomers: The Museum of Nature and Science is the fifth largest of its kind in the country, and the newly expanded Denver Art Museum is the largest such institution between Kansas City and the West Coast. Denver's Zoo and its Botanic Gardens are both highly respected, and the city is full of special-interest museums devoted to such diverse subjects as firefighters, railroads, African Americans in the West, dolls, and the English painter J. M. W. Turner. Among the most popular tourist attractions in the area are the tours at the United States Mint in Denver and Coors Brewery in Golden.

We've organized this chapter by category: museums, historic houses and other historic sites, parks and gardens, and tours. Readers with a particular interest in the arts may also want to check our The Arts chapter, as community art centers and galleries are listed there. At the end of the chapter, we suggest ways to combine visits to different sites that are near each other or that tie in thematically (for example, if you want to spend a day immersing yourself in Western history).

Hours and admission prices are subject to change. Also, be aware that some Greater Denver attractions either have shorter hours or are closed during winter. Please call before planning a visit.

## MUSEUMS

**The Black American West Museum and Heritage Center**
**3091 California Street**
**(303) 292-2566**
**www.blackamericanwest.org**

The Black American West Museum is a small but fascinating place that sets a lot of records straight and provides a long-buried picture of the role played by black Americans on the frontier. For example, few people know that the first black mayor of a major American city was Francisco Reyes, owner of the San Fernando Valley until he sold it in the 1790s and became the mayor of Los Angeles. The 1950 Van Heflin movie *Tomahawk* featured white actor Jack Okie playing explorer Jim Beckwourth, who discovered Beckwourth Pass through the Sierras. The movie's only problem: Beckwourth was black, as were up to one-third of all cowboys in the early West. The museum is housed in the former home of Dr. Justina L. Ford, Colorado's first licensed African-American female doctor. It is closed Monday and Tuesday and open only from 10:00 A.M. to 2:00 P.M. Wednesday through Friday, 10:00 A.M. to 5:00 P.M. Saturday, and 1:00 to 5:00 P.M. Sunday.

**Buffalo Bill Grave and Museum**
**987 ½ Lookout Mountain Road, Golden**
**(303) 526-0747**
**www.buffalobill.org**
Dramatically located on top of Lookout Mountain, this fascinating museum is filled with memorabilia honoring the famous frontier scout, showman, and Pony Express rider William F. Cody, colloquially known as Buffalo Bill. Included are gun collections, costumes, and posters from the Wild West show and a collection of dime novels. The grave site affords an expansive view of the plains to the east and mountains to the west. A kids' corral offers young visitors interactive opportunities. The museum is open 9:00 A.M. to 5:00 P.M. daily from May through October; 9:00 A.M. to 4:00 P.M. Tuesday through Sunday the rest of the

*Colorado History Museum.* DENVER METRO CONVENTION AND VISITORS BUREAU

year. Admission is $3.00 adults, $2.00 seniors, $1.00 children ages 6 to 15, free for children age 5 and younger.

### Colorado History Museum
### 1300 Broadway
### (303) 866-3682
### www.coloradohistory.org

The Colorado History Museum offers permanent and changing exhibitions about state history. Special exhibits have included everything from the story of Colorado's Hispano residents to the tale of Cheyenne Dog Soldiers who fought at the historic Sand Creek massacre. As part of what is called the Civic Center Cultural Complex, the history museum, the library, and the art museum collaborate on programs and share resources. The museum has an outstanding collection of William Henry Jackson photos and a comprehensive research library that is free and open to the public Tuesday through Saturday from 10:00 A.M. to 4:30 P.M. The museum is open 10:00 A.M. to 5:00 P.M. Monday through Saturday and noon to 5:00 P.M. on Sunday. Admission is $7.00 adults, $6.00 seniors age 65 and older and students with ID, $5.00 kids age 6 to 12, free for children younger than age 6.

### Colorado Railroad Museum
### 17155 West 44th Avenue, Golden
### (303) 279-4591, (800) 365-6263
### www.crrm.org

One of our personal favorites, this museum houses more than 70 historic locomotives and cars as well as additional exhibits in a 15-acre outdoor setting. Don't miss the D&RG Engine No. 346, the oldest operating locomotive in Colorado. The museum is open daily from 9:00 A.M. to 5:00 P.M. (until 6:00 P.M. June through August). Admission is $8.00 for adults, $7.00 for seniors older than age 60, $5.00 for kids younger than age 16. Family admission is $18 (two parents and children younger than age 16). To get to the museum, take exit 265 off Interstate 70 West and follow the signs.

**The Denver Art Museum**
**100 West 14th Avenue Parkway**
**(720) 865-5000 (recorded information)**
**www.denverartmuseum.org**
The Denver Art Museum is the largest art museum between Kansas City and the West Coast and is especially noted for its superb collections of Native American, pre-Columbian, and Spanish colonial art. Its seven floors also house impressive displays of American, Asian, and contemporary art and galleries devoted to design, graphics, and architecture. See our The Arts chapter for more details.

**Denver Firefighters Museum**
**1326 Tremont Place**
**(303) 892-1436**
**www.denverfirefightersmuseum.org**
Housed in old Station No. 1, which was built in 1909, the museum has a collection of original hand-drawn firefighting equipment, two engines from the 1920s, and various antique firefighting memorabilia, including helmets, uniforms, and trophies. The museum is open from 10:00 A.M. to 4:00 P.M. Monday through Saturday. Admission is $4.00 for adults, $3.00 for seniors, and $2.00 for children age 14 and younger.

**Denver Museum of Miniatures,**
**Dolls and Toys**
**Pearce-McAllister Cottage**
**1880 Gaylord Street**
**(303) 322-1053**
**www.dmmdt.com**
The two-story Pearce-McAllister Cottage, built in 1899, is of interest for its architecture, original decor, and changing displays of vintage dolls, dollhouses, toys, and miniatures. The museum offers year-round workshops for adults and kids on doll-making, toys, and arts and crafts in miniature. There are three free days in the summer sponsored by the Scientific and Cultural Facilities District; call to find out when. A small gift shop sells toys, dolls, and dollhouse furniture. The museum is open 10:00 A.M. to 4:00 P.M. Tuesday through Saturday and 1:00 to 4:00 P.M. Sunday (closed major holidays). Admission

is $5.00 for adults and $4.00 for senior citizens and kids ages 5 to 16 and includes a tour of both the cottage and museum. A group discount rate is available.

**The Denver Museum of Nature**
**and Science**
**2001 Colorado Boulevard (in City Park,**
**at Colorado Boulevard and Montview)**
**(303) 322-7009**
**(303) 370-8257 (hearing-impaired TDD)**
**(800) 925-2250**
**www.dmns.org**
The Denver Museum of Nature and Science is the largest cultural attraction in the Rocky Mountain region, with an average of 1.5 million visitors annually. In addition to more than 90 dioramas depicting animals from around the world, the museum's permanent exhibitions include a Hall of Life devoted to studying the human body and a fine gem and mineral collection that includes examples of Colorado gold and the largest rhodochrosite gem in the world. Other highlights include the Hall of Ancient Peoples, which deals with early man and early civilizations. Don't forget to take a look at the redesigned Egyptian Mummies exhibit. The museum also houses an award-winning dinosaur exhibit, the $7.7 million Prehistoric Journey. It includes walk-through "enviroramas" complete with controlled lighting and temperatures, sounds, vegetation, and even bugs!

In June 2003 the museum opened the $50 million, 24,000-square-foot Space Odyssey. Designed to provide an immersion experience in the wonders of space, it provides interactive opportunities to learn about areas of the cosmos. Visitors can feel what it's like to dock a space shuttle, fly into deep space, and walk on the surface of Mars. The Gates Planetarium, renovated to be completely digital in 2003, enables visitors to leave Earth's surface and fly through the solar system. It's one of the country's first all-digital planetariums and is equipped with surround sound. Although Space Odyssey is free to those who buy admission to the museum, the planetarium shows are extra. Between 9:00 A.M. and 5:00 P.M. daily, they're an extra $5.00 for adults and $4.00 for children and seniors. Friday through Sunday between 4:00 and 8:00 P.M., tickets may be purchased for the planetarium shows only, for $8.00 adults, $6.00 children and seniors. Call for schedules, as they change seasonally.

Watch for special exhibitions, which in the past have included artistic and archaeological blockbusters such as *Ramses II* and *Body Worlds 2,* and entertaining fare such as *Star Trek: Federation Science.*

The museum is open 9:00 A.M. to 5:00 P.M. daily. Admission is $10.00 for adults and $6.00 for seniors age 60 and older and children age 3 to 18. Admission to the IMAX is $8.00 for adults and $6.00 for seniors and children age 3 to 18. Call the recorded information lines listed above for show details. Combination museum and IMAX theater tickets are available; call or ask at the museum for more information. Also, some special exhibitions require an additional charge and advance reservations. The museum has a cafeteria-style restaurant and the T-Rex cafeteria.

## Downtown Aquarium
**700 Water Street (in the Platte River Valley just west of downtown)**
**(303) 561–4450, (888) 561–4450**
**www.aquariumrestaurants.com**
Denver's most unusual attraction isn't exactly a museum, but it fits well under the category of other top-notch local and tourist spots in this chapter. Opened in the summer of 1999, this long-awaited addition to the Central Platte Valley provided a unique experience in the arid west (far from the undersea land of coastal areas). Ocean Journey was a world-class aquarium offering the wonders of water on two journeys: from the Continental Divide to the Sea of Cortez and from an Indonesian rain forest to the depths of the Pacific. Located across the Platte River from Six Flags Elitch Gardens, its $93 million price tag ensured hours of interactive fun. The 17-acre complex was purchased in 2003 by

Landry's Restaurants and reopened in 2005 as an entertainment and dining complex. Downtown Aquarium's hours are 10:00 A.M. to 10:00 P.M. Sunday through Thursday, 10:00 A.M. to 11:00 P.M. Friday and Saturday. Tickets range from $10.00 to $13.95 for adults, $7.00 to $8.00 for children. Parking is extra, as are meals.

## Forney Transportation Museum
**4303 Brighton Boulevard**
**(303) 297–1113**
**www.forneymuseum.com**
This longtime Denver favorite moved to its new location near the Denver Coliseum in 1999, but its exhibits remained the same. The Forney Museum displays all kinds of old vehicles, including a number of one-of-a-kinds. Of special interest are the world's largest steam locomotive, Prince Aly Khan's Rolls Royce Phantom I, and an original McCormick reaper. The museum is open 9:00 A.M. to 5:00 P.M. Monday through Saturday and closed on Sunday. It's closed on Christmas, Thanksgiving, and New Year's Day. Admission prices are $7.00 adults, $6.00 seniors, $4.50 youths age 11 to 15, $3.50 children age 5 to 10.

## Fort Vasquez
**13412 U.S. Highway 85, Platteville**
**(970) 785–2832**
**www.coloradohistory.org**
Forty miles downstream from Denver on the South Platte River lies Fort Vasquez, a reconstructed 1830s fur-trading post operated as a museum by the Colorado Historical Society. The museum features exhibits and dioramas depicting the trading era. In summer "mountain men" entertain visitors with reenactments of Old West trading days. A buffalo tepee will interest youngsters. Admission is free; hours are 9:30 A.M. to 4:30 P.M. Monday through Saturday year-round, and Sunday hours are 1:00 to 4:30 P.M.

## Mizel Museum
**400 South Kearney Street**
**(303) 394–9993**
**www.mizelmuseum.org**

The Rocky Mountain region's only museum of Judaica was established in 1982. Special programs, workshops, speakers, seminars, and films are designed to complement the museum's changing exhibitions, whether drawn from its own collection or borrowed from such prestigious institutions as the Israel Museum and the Smithsonian Institution. In 2001 it merged with the Mizel Family Cultural Arts Center and moved to the campus of the Jewish Community Center. Call for details about programs, hours, and fees.

## Museo de las Americas
**861 Santa Fe Drive**
**(303) 571-4401**
**www.museo.org**
This is the first museum in the Rocky Mountain region dedicated to Latin-American art, history, and culture. The Museo de las Americas showcases art from all the Americas, including the Caribbean, in changing exhibitions. (See our The Arts chapter for more information.)

## Museum of Outdoor Arts
**1000 Englewood Parkway, No. 200-230, Englewood**
**(303) 806-0444**
**www.moaonline.org**
More than 50 outdoor sculptures comprise this "museum without walls" in the 400-acre Greenwood Plaza Business Park in the Denver Tech Center area. The museum is a collection of buildings, plazas, and sculptures that combine into an artistic setting. (See our The Arts chapter for more information.)

## Rocky Mountain Quilt Museum
**1111 Washington Avenue, Golden**
**(303) 277-0377**
**www.rmqm.org**
As much a resource center for quilters as a museum, the tiny Rocky Mountain Quilt Museum has more than 300 old and new quilts in its collection. Exhibits change five times a year. Quilts and other needlework are offered for sale at the museum, which also conducts classes and outreach pro-

grams. The museum is open 10:00 A.M. to 4:00 P.M. Monday through Saturday. Admission is $5.00 for adults, $4.00 for seniors, and $3.00 for kids.

## Wildlife Experience
**10035 South Peoria Street, Parker**
**(720) 488-3300**
**www.wildlifeexperience.org**
The $50 million Wildlife Experience opened in 2002 about 10 miles south of downtown Denver and 1 mile east of Interstate 25. It's the brainchild of RE/MAX cofounders Dave and Gail Liniger, in which art and natural history are combined. They describe the museum as "where art and education lead to greater appreciation of animals in their natural habitats."

The 101,000-square-foot facility has space for oil paintings, metal sculptures, traveling exhibits, art and photo galleries, and a 315-seat IWERKS theater for wildlife movies. The museum also contains a cafe, a gift shop, and both indoor and outdoor facilities big enough for special parties and meetings. Hours are 9:00 A.M. to 5:00 P.M. Tuesday through Sunday, closed Thanksgiving and Christmas. Admission is $7.95 for adults, $6.95 for seniors older than age 65, $4.95 for kids age 5 to 12, free for kids younger than age 5. IWERKS tickets are the same price, or they can be purchased at a discount in combination with museum admission. To reach Wildlife Experience, travel south on I-25, take E-470 east, then exit at Peoria and follow it south to Lincoln Avenue.

## Wings Over the Rockies Air and Space Museum
**7711 East Academy Boulevard**
**(303) 360-5360**
**www.wingsmuseum.org**
Perhaps the last remnant of Lowry Air Force Base in east Denver, this air and space museum on the site of the decommissioned base houses a wide range of aircraft and space memorabilia. Its permanent collection includes a B-18 Bolo, an RF-84K Thundercraft parasite, a B-1A Lancer, and an Apollo control module. It's

open 10:00 A.M. to 5:00 P.M. Monday through Saturday, noon to 5:00 P.M. Sunday. Admission is $7.00 for adults age 13 and older, $6.00 for seniors, and $5.00 for children age 6 to 12.

## HISTORIC HOUSES AND OTHER HISTORIC SITES

### Byers-Evans House
**1310 Bannock Street**
**(303) 620-4933**
**www.coloradohistory.org**
John Evans was Colorado's second territorial governor. William Byers founded the *Rocky Mountain News.* Both men and their families were prominent during Denver's early years, and their names appear on avenues and mountain peaks. This house, built by Byers in 1883 and sold to Evans's son in 1889, has been restored to the 1912–1924 period. The house is open from 11:00 A.M. to 3:00 P.M. Tuesday through Sunday. Admission is $3.00 adults, $2.50 seniors, $1.50 children age 6 to 16, younger than age 6 free. Combination tickets including entrance to the Colorado History Museum (a block and a half away) are available.

### Colorado Governor's Mansion
**400 East Eighth Avenue**
**(303) 837-8350**
**(303) 866-3682 (tours)**
Completed in 1907, the governor's mansion was originally the private residence of the Walter Scott Cheesman family. In 1927 the house was sold to the Boettcher family, and in 1960 the Boettcher Foundation gave the property to the state to use as the governor's mansion. The Colonial Revival structure contains artwork from all around the world and a Waterford chandelier that once hung in the White House. The mansion can be visited on Tuesday afternoon between 1:00 and 3:00 P.M. June through August. Tours leave every 10 minutes. The mansion is open to the public for a week during December, when it's decorated for Christmas. Call for dates, as they vary every year.

### Colorado State Capitol
**Broadway and Colfax Avenue**
**(303) 866-2604**
**colorado.gov/dpa/doit/archives/cap/first.htm**
The Colorado State Capitol stands exactly 1 mile above sea level. On the 13th step there's a carving stating the elevation as 5,280 feet, but a small brass plaque on the 18th step corrects the carving and proclaims itself the true mile-high marker. Inside the capitol building, free tours lasting about 45 minutes are given weekdays from 9:15 A.M. to 2:30 P.M. Monday through Friday. Due to heightened security, there is no public access to the gold-plated dome.

Although the gold on the outside of the dome tends to receive more attention from the casual passersby, the real precious mineral is on the inside of the building, where rose-colored Colorado onyx was used as wainscoting. The onyx came from a small quarry in Beulah, Colorado, and has never been mined elsewhere.

### Cussler Museum
**14959 West 69th Avenue, Arvada**
**(303) 420-2795**
**www.cusslermuseum.com**
Author Clive Cussler lived in metro Denver during his early years, and, as his popularity grew, he diverted some of his financial proceeds into an extensive vintage automobile collection. Among the rarest are the foreign cars—a 1929 Isotta Fraschini and a 1936 Avions Voisins, for example. Cussler found ways to write many of the vehicles into his Dirk Pitt novels, and he often posed with them for the book jacket photos. Today the collection is tended by his daughter, and it's open to the public during the summer months. Hours are 10:00 A.M. to 7:00 P.M. Monday and Tuesday. Admission is $7.00 for adults, $5.00 for seniors, and $3.00 for children younger than age 12.

### Fairmount Cemetery
**430 South Quebec Street**
**(303) 399-0692**

*Visitors at the Capitol rotunda.* DENVER METRO CONVENTION AND VISITORS BUREAU

This 320-acre privately owned cemetery dates from 1890 and is the final resting place for many former mayors, socialites, gunfighters, madams, and Civil War veterans. An infamous "resident" is Col. John M. Chivington, responsible for the massacre of defenseless Indians at Sand Creek in 1864. The grounds contain more than 50 types of trees, and tours are given periodically by the Denver Botanic Gardens for those interested in this aspect of the cemetery. Self-guided tours are possible anytime (a guidebook can be purchased at the site), and free guided tours are available.

### Four Mile Historic Park
### 715 South Forest Street
### (303) 399-1859
### www.fourmilehistoricpark.org

Designated a Denver Landmark in 1968, Four Mile Historic Park commemorates the site of a former stage stop and contains the oldest home still standing in Denver. In addition to the 1859 log home, visitors can tour the living-history farmstead and, on nice days, have a picnic here. Special-events days are held about six times a year and include horse-drawn wagon rides and demonstrations of blacksmithing, butter churning, and other chores. There are reenactments of Civil War events during the spring and summer as well as a heritage program and evening concerts. Hours are noon to 4:00 P.M. Wednesday through Friday, 10:00 A.M. to 4:00 P.M. weekends. Admission is $3.50 adults, $2.00 seniors and students age 6 to 15, free for children younger than age 6. Additional fees may apply to special events and concerts. Winter hours are Saturday and Sunday noon to 4:00 P.M.

### Lakewood Heritage Center
### 797 South Wadsworth Boulevard
### Lakewood
### (303) 987-7850
### www.lakewood.org

A historic site and museum with several structures, including an 1880s farmhouse and a 1920s schoolhouse, Lakewood Heritage Center also has a barn gallery with changing exhibits. The visitor center has a permanent exhibit on May Bonfils, daughter of one of the founders of the *Denver Post,* and exhibits of work by local artists that change monthly. Admission, which includes a tour, is $3.00 adults, $2.00 children, free for kids younger than age 3. Hours are 10:00 A.M. to 4:00 P.M. Monday through Friday and noon to 4:00 P.M. Saturday (last tour leaves at 3:00 P.M.). Ask about special children's programs. Groups of five or more should make reservations.

### Littleton Historical Museum
### 6028 South Gallup Street, Littleton
### (303) 795-3950
### www.littletongov.org/museum/

This living-history museum consists of a reconstructed 1860s homestead and a turn-of-the-20th-century farm that re-creates pioneer life. Among the original buildings on the 14-acre site are a 1910 ice house, a sheep and goat shelter originally built as a settler's cabin in the 1860s, an 1890s farmhouse, and the first schoolhouse in Littleton. The main museum underwent a three-year, $8.5 million expansion and reopened in 2006 with expanded galleries and workshops and a lecture hall and research center. Outdoors, costumed staff and volunteers care for the chickens and livestock and go about the business of tending a 19th-century farm. They're not too busy to stop and explain things to visitors, however. Admission is free (large groups are charged a small fee and should call first). The museum is open 8:00 A.M. to 5:00 P.M. Tuesday through Friday, 10:00 A.M. to 5:00 P.M. on Saturday, and 1:00 to 5:00 P.M. on Sunday; it's closed on Monday and major holidays.

### Molly Brown House Museum
### 1340 Pennsylvania Street
### (303) 832-4092
### www.mollybrown.org

Only Baby Doe Tabor can match Molly Brown for name recognition among turn-of-the-20th-century Denver women. Each has had her life memorialized in song:

Baby Doe, in the opera *The Ballad of Baby Doe,* and Molly Brown, in the Broadway musical *The Unsinkable Molly Brown.* Molly was one of early Denver's more flamboyant characters and achieved true heroine status for her actions during the sinking of the *Titanic,* which she survived. Her Victorian home has been restored and furnished in period style with many personal mementos and possessions.

Museum officials suggest arriving early as they do not take reservations. The museum is open in summer from 10:00 A.M. to 3:30 P.M. Monday through Saturday and noon to 3:30 P.M. on Sunday. Winter hours are 10:00 A.M. to 3:30 P.M. Tuesday through Saturday, noon to 3:30 P.M. on Sunday. The museum is closed on all major holidays. Admission is $6.50 adults, $5.00 seniors, $3.00 kids age 6 to 12, free for children younger than age 6. A number of special dinners, teas, readings, and workshops are scheduled throughout the year; call for more information.

### Riverside Cemetery
**5201 Brighton Boulevard**
**Commerce City**
**(303) 293-2466**
Denver's oldest cemetery, founded in 1876, contains the graves of three Civil War medal-of-honor winners; Augusta Tabor, the first wife of turn-of-the-20th-century silver baron Horace Tabor; and Colorado's first black ballplayer, Oliver E. Marcel. Visitors can pick up a booklet and map for $2.00 during office hours, 8:30 A.M. to 4:30 P.M. Monday through Thursday and 10:00 A.M. to 4:30 P.M. Friday. The office is closed weekends. The cemetery is on Brighton Boulevard about 2 miles north of I-70.

## PARKS AND GARDENS

### Denver Botanic Gardens
**1005 York Street**
**(720) 865-3500**
**www.botanicgardens.org**
One of Greater Denver's most lovely refuges, the Botanic Gardens encompasses 23 acres and includes an herb garden and other specialty gardens. The one-acre rock alpine garden is considered one of the finest in the country. Our personal favorite is the lovely Japanese Shofu-en (Garden of Pine Wind) designed by America's foremost Japanese landscaper, Koichi Kawana. It is complete with an authentic teahouse. Local residents look to the water-saving xeriscape demonstration garden and the home demonstration garden for ideas they can put into use in their own yards.

A tropical conservatory and pavilion houses orchids, bromeliads, and other warmth-loving species. Outdoor concerts are held here in the summer; come early and bring a picnic dinner. Schedules are available at the gate in early spring, but they sell out quickly.

The Botanic Gardens are open May through September (summer hours) from 9:00 A.M to 8:00 P.M. Saturday through Tuesday, and from 9:00 A.M. to 5:00 P.M. Wednesday through Friday. Winter hours (October 1 through April 30) are 9:00 A.M. to 5:00 P.M. seven days a week. Summer admission is $8.50 adults, $5.50 seniors, $5.00 students with ID and kids ages 4 to 15, free for children younger than age 4. Winter admission rates are $1.00 less.

### The Denver Zoo
**City Park, East 23rd Avenue**
**and Steele Street**
**(303) 376-4800**
**www.denverzoo.org**
Easily combined with a trip to the Museum of Nature and Science, the Denver Zoo has the usual complement of lions and tigers and (polar) bears as well as monkeys and birds, in a mix of enclosed and open habitat areas. Perhaps the most famous creatures to come from the Denver Zoo are Klondike and Snow, the adorable polar bear siblings who made national news while being nursed to health by zoo officials. Klondike and Snow have since moved on to another home.

The $10 million Tropical Discovery exhibit is designed to re-create a rain forest habitat inside a glass-enclosed pyramid. More than 700 animal species live here, nearly double what the zoo had previously. There is a separate nursery area where new arrivals needing human help get their first taste of what it's like to be in the public eye. Primate Panorama, a five-acre, all-natural habitat, is always a crowd-pleaser. For those who can't or don't feel like walking the zoo, a fun train circles the major outdoor exhibits frequently throughout the day. The zoo unveiled a new exhibit, Predator Ridge, and a new main entrance complex in June 2004.

The zoo is open daily, including all holidays, from 9:00 A.M. to 6:00 P.M. in summer, 10:00 A.M. to 5:00 P.M. in winter. Tropical Discovery and Bird World have slightly shortened hours. Admission is $11.00 adults ($9.00 in winter), $9.00 seniors, $7.00 children age 4 to 12, free for children age 3 and younger. About seven free days for Colorado residents are scheduled throughout the year; call for exact dates.

**Lakeside Amusement Park**
**4601 Sheridan Boulevard**
**(I-70 and Sheridan)**
**(303) 477-1621**
**www.lakesideamusementpark.com**
An all-ages amusement park, Lakeside has a merry-go-round, a Ferris wheel, a roller coaster, and other exciting rides. One of the best things to do at Lakeside is to ride the train around the lake after dark. The park is open from May through Labor Day weekend. In May the park is open on weekends only. It is open seven days a week June through Labor Day. Kids younger than age 8 are welcome in the kiddie playland from 1:00 to 10:00 P.M. on weekdays, but the major rides don't begin operating until 6:00 P.M. weekdays and noon on weekends. Gate admission is $2.00 a person. An unlimited ride ticket costs $12.75 a person weekdays; $17.75 Saturday, Sunday, and holidays. Individual ride coupons can also be purchased. Prices are the same for adults and children.

*The Denver Zoo features ever-growing Komodo dragons, the massive man-eating reptiles, sure to enchant visitors.*

**Six Flags Elitch Gardens**
**Interstate 25 and Speer Boulevard**
**(exit 212A)**
**(303) 595-4386**
**www.sixflags.com/parks/elitchgardens**
For more than 100 years, Elitch Gardens was a west Denver tradition. Opened in May 1890 as Elitch Zoological Gardens by John and Mary Elitch, it boasted three thrilling roller coasters: the Wildcat, the wooden Twister, and the Sidewinder.

In 1995 Elitch Gardens reopened in a larger, 68-acre location in the Central Platte River Valley just off the Speer Boulevard exit from I-25. (At night, all lit up, it's a beautiful and memorable sight for anyone driving through Denver on the interstate.) In 1998 the park was sold and renamed Six Flags Elitch Gardens. A rebuilt 100-foot-high Twister II is one of the top attractions. There are 49 major rides in all, including several added in the past few years: The Flying Coaster (billed as the cure for the common coaster), an indescribable face-down ride that feels like you're literally flying through the air; The Half-Pipe, a 100-foot-tall ride on a 40-foot-long snowboard; and the new Edge ride at the Island Kingdom Water Park, a four-story near-vertical waterslide. For tamer pursuits there's a 300-foot-high observation tower with a panoramic view. The 1925 carousel made the move downtown.

In general, Elitch's is open daily from 10:00 A.M. until 10:00 P.M. from Memorial Day through Labor Day. There are shortened hours for the few weekends before and after Memorial and Labor Days; call for times. Buying tickets online is the easiest and least expensive way to go because they're discounted and you can print them out at your computer. Adult admission at the gate is $44.99, online it's $34.99 (adult admission is required for anyone more than 48 inches tall).

## CLOSE-UP

# Six Flags Elitch Gardens
# Thrills Downtown Visitors

There are those who say the beloved original Elitch Gardens, situated in an established Denver neighborhood covered by an emerald canopy of trees, can never be topped by the new park sandwiched between skyscrapers and INVESCO Field at Mile High.

Apparently they haven't ridden the 22-story, free-falling Tower of Doom.

"It's the best," according to one teenager spotted at the park. "When you ride it, everything inside you disappears—like everything drops to the bottom and it's gone."

The expansion is all part of a bigger, better Elitch's that began in 1994 when the park closed its doors after 104 years as a west Denver institution. The closing was mourned by longtime Denverites as the end of a treasured institution. The park reopened in 1995 in the city's Central Platte Valley, in the shadow of Coors Field and Denver's skyline. In 1998 Elitch's was sold to Six Flags.

Elitch's started in 1890 when John and

Mary Elitch turned a small apple orchard into picnic areas and ball fields open to the public. It later boasted Denver's first zoo. In 1891 the Elitch Theatre opened its first season and for 96 years hosted such luminaries as Sarah Bernhardt, Cecil B. DeMille, Grace Kelly, and Edward G. Robinson. In 1925 the treasured carousel with 67 hand-carved horses and chariots was installed. The restored carousel is a focal point of the new park.

Over the years, Elitch's became known for its signature gardens, a sprawling collection of impressive flowers, trees, and shrubs. It will take many years before the "gardens" in the new Elitch Gardens come anywhere close to the impressive foliage tenderly raised at the old site. Meantime, efforts have been made to capture some of the nostalgia of the old Elitch's. A Victorian-style promenade with colorful storefronts and restaurants harkens to the old Elitch days. The Trocadero Theater, built in honor of Elitch's famed Trocadero Ballroom at the old

Restricted admission tickets for people shorter than 48 inches are $32.49 at the front gate, $22.49 online. Season passes are available online for $79.99.

## TOURS

**Coors Brewery**
**13th Avenue and Ford Street, Golden**
**(303) 277–BEER (2337)**
**www.coors.com**

Colorado is the second-largest producer of beer in the United States, and most of it comes from the Coors Brewery in Golden, the world's largest single-site brewing facility. The free tour and tasting ranks as one of Greater Denver's top tourist attractions; more than 10 million people have taken the 35- to 40-minute tour. Tours run every 20 to 30 minutes from 10:00 A.M. to 4:00 P.M. Monday through Saturday and end with free beer sampling. All ages are welcome; children

park, seats 700 and features live shows.

Despite a greater emphasis on high-quality rides, visitors still might find Elitch's minuscule compared to such mega-theme parks as Disney World, Paramount's King's Island, and Cedar Point (both in Ohio) or any of the other Six Flags operations. But it seems to be winning converts in Colorado and surrounding states.

Although the park opens weekends in May, Memorial Day is the official launch of the season. It was the perfect time for Sidney, Montana, resident Colton Martini to test his queasiness quotient. A ride on Twister II was fun, but his sights were set elsewhere.

"That didn't take my stomach like I thought it would, but I think that will," he said, pointing toward scream-inducing Mind Eraser. The $10 million twisted steel coaster ride consists of two 16-passenger trains suspended over 2,172 feet of steel track. Secured by space-age harnesses, riders ascend a 100-foot hill before blasting almost straight down the other side to enter a breathtaking corkscrew that hurls the train upside down—twice. In all, Mind Eraser is two minutes of dives, rollovers, and spins. The screams are hair-raising the entire time.

*Six Flags Elitch Gardens amusement park.*
DENVER METRO CONVENTION AND VISITORS BUREAU

"That was a total rush," exclaimed Andrew Sartorio, of Denver. "Total adrenaline the whole way."

age 18 and younger must be accompanied by an adult.

**United States Mint**
**320 West Colfax Avenue**
**(303) 405–4761**
**www.usmint.gov**
One of Denver's most popular tourist attractions, the Mint produces 15 billion · coins each year. Free tours are conducted weekdays from 8:00 A.M. to 3:00 P.M. Reservations are required for the 15-minute

tours, and the Mint strongly suggests that you make them online, since walk-up reservations are first-come, first-served and may not always be available. Go to the Web site listed above, click on "Make A Reservation," and follow the instructions. The tours leave every 15 to 20 minutes from the Cherokee Street entrance. Expect a long line during the summer. Children younger than age 14 must be accompanied by an adult. Wheelchairs are OK but cameras are not. No photos can be taken inside the building. Hours for coin sales are the same as tour hours. The Mint is closed on all legal holidays and for one week in summer, usually in late June, for inventory.

## SUGGESTED OUTINGS

### One-day family outing . . .
Visit the Denver Museum of Nature and Science and the Denver Zoo. Take in a show at the IMAX theater. Then, if you have time, the Denver Museum of Miniatures, Dolls and Toys isn't far away.

### Within walking distance downtown . . .
The Denver Art Museum, the Museum of Western Art, the Colorado History Museum, the U.S. Mint, the Colorado State Capitol, the Molly Brown House, the Firefighters Museum, and the Byers-Evans House are all within walking distance of one another downtown. Don't try to see all these sights in one day, but pick the ones that interest you most; plot a route and save the rest for another afternoon.

### For art lovers . . .
The Denver Art Museum and the Western Art Museum can be visited in one day if you don't try to see the whole art museum. If you're at the Denver Art Museum at lunchtime, eat in its cafe.

### Trains and automobiles . . .
Greater Denver has three museums of special interest in this category: the Forney Transportation Museum, the Colorado Railroad Museum, and the Denver Firefighters Museum. With a car, all could be visited in one day.

### One-day outing in Golden . . .
Start with a tour of the Coors Brewery (or end here if you're afraid the free beer samples will make you too sleepy to enjoy what comes next). Then drive up to the Buffalo Bill Grave and Museum and the nearby Mother Cabrini Shrine, which honors the first American saint (see our Worship chapter for more information). For lunch take a picnic to Red Rocks Park if the weather's nice, or pick a spot in downtown Golden. In the afternoon visit the Colorado Railroad Museum or, for the more artistically inclined, the Foothills Art Center, a small community arts center at 809 15th Street, (303) 279–3922. (We fully describe the art center in our The Arts chapter.) You may also want to visit the Rocky Mountain Quilt Museum, 1111 Washington Avenue, (303) 277–0377.

### History buffs . . .
Don't miss the Black American West Museum. A visit there combines well with a visit to the Colorado History Museum.

### Ethnic heritage tour (half-day) . . .
Divide your time between the Black American West Museum and the Museo de las Americas. Afterward stop for lunch at one of the authentic Mexican restaurants along Santa Fe Drive. Try El Noa Noa or El Taco de Mexico (see our Restaurants chapter for full descriptions of these eateries).

### Art and garden tour . . .
Spend half the day at the Denver Art Museum, the rest at the Denver Botanic Gardens.

### Fauna and flora . . .
Spend half the day at the Denver Zoo, the rest at the Denver Botanic Gardens.

### Walking tours . . .
A booklet of six downtown walking tours collectively called the Mile High Trail is available at the Greater Denver Chamber of Commerce, 1445 Market Street, (303) 534–8500, or log on to www.denver chamber.org. The information booth at Larimer Square can provide historical and architectural information about buildings in the 1400 block of Larimer Street. The Denver Metro Convention and Visitors

Bureau conducts free walking tours of Denver; call (303) 892–1112 for details. The city of Denver home page on the Web offers several walking and driving tours that you can download and print, including tours of the downtown Civic Center area and Fairmount Cemetery (the oldest cemetery in the city). Go to www.denver gov.org/aboutdenver/today_walking_civic center.asp.

**Public art tour . . .**
A brochure identifying public art throughout the city is available at the Denver Visitors Information Center, 918 16th Street, (303) 892–1112. The brochure contains a suggested walking tour and driving tour. Don't miss the outdoor murals on the 15th Street viaduct and Barbara Jo Revelle's vast tile mural of photographic images of people from Colorado's history.

# KIDSTUFF

**W**e think of Denver as kids' country. Greater Denver offers a multitude of activities for the younger set—but we admit we like the outings, too. Best of all, Denver's laid-back attitude says kids are welcome just about anywhere—assuming they aren't totally unrestrained, of course.

One of the first places guests to Greater Denver should look for fun is outdoors: Take them out to play with Mother Nature. It doesn't matter what trail or mountainside you take them to; short hikes or climbs for smaller kids are found in the same places where adults and older kids go to get serious. There's an abundance of trails and natural beauty close to Denver. Go to a local bookstore and pick up a copy of *Best Hikes With Children in Colorado* by Maureen Kielty for good directions to a lot of kid hikes on the edge of the metro area. When hiking, make sure to protect yourself and your kids by using sunscreen and taking water bottles.

Mother Nature is only one of the kid-friendly attractions around Greater Denver. Check the other chapters of this book for ideas, especially Tours and Attractions, Spectator Sports, Annual Events and Festivals, Parks and Recreation, and Day Trips.

What follows is limited to a reasonable number of unique attractions aimed at the younger set, but there are others too numerous to mention. Take the kids fishing at any of the many reservoirs and rivers along the Front Range and in the nearby mountains. Go horseback riding at any of the stables around Greater Denver. Walk or ride bicycles on trails, usually along creeks, rivers, canals, and lakeshores that thread the greenbelts of the metro area.

Call nearby public libraries about story hours and other child-oriented activities. Call city and county departments of parks and recreation in your area to see about kid activities ranging from soccer and baseball to art classes. Local recreation centers are listed in our Parks and Recreation chapter.

One of your best local resources to kid activities is *Parent Pages*. This annual directory is a comprehensive family resource guide and has just about everything a parent would want to know about the area; it's a good place to go for entertainment as well. It's produced by *Colorado Parent* magazine, (303) 320-1000, a free monthly publication that can be found at 800 locations ranging from bookstores and libraries to doctors' offices and daycare centers.

## WET 'N' WILD

There are swimming pools all over metro Denver, and some of them go the extra mile to be kid-friendly.

### Carpenter Recreation Center
**11151 Colorado Boulevard, Thornton**
**(303) 255-7800**
The Carpenter Recreation Center is a fantastic indoor 15,000-square-foot aquatics center, which includes artificially generated waves, lap swimming, a raindrop play area with waterfall and Jacuzzi, a lazy river, and a waterslide. Admission ranges from $4.00 to $6.50.

### The Golden Community Center
**1470 10th Street, Golden**
**(303) 384-8100**
The Golden Community Center has an indoor pool that kids will love, with a raindrop play area, waterslide, and hot tub as well as a lap pool and leisure pool. Admission ranges from $1.75 to $5.00.

### Water World
**88th Avenue and Pecos Street**
**Federal Heights**
**(303) 427-7873**
**www.waterworldcolorado.com**

Greater Denver's biggest outdoor water park, Water World offers more than 64 acres of aquatic fun. Float down a circular series of chutes and pools on an inner tube. Ride a huge rubber raft down a torrent. Sit on a plastic sled that plunges almost straight down and builds up enough speed to aquaplane across the pool at the bottom. Or try the newest attraction, the Zoomerang. Water World has it all. The park also added a Journey to the Center of the Earth ride, in which you cruise through caves where moving dinosaurs menace you. From late May to the end of summer, Water World operates from 10:00 A.M. to 6:00 P.M. every day. Admission is $28.95 for adults and $23.95 for kids age 4 to 12. If you're age 60 and older or age 3 and younger, it's free. Check the Web site for promotional discounts.

**Westminster City Park Recreation Center**
**10455 Sheridan Boulevard**
**Westminster**
**(303) 460-9690**
This indoor facility has a large children's pool with a tile beach sloping gently at one end, a fountain, and a slide just for kids. The main pool for lap swimmers bulges out at one side under a waterfall. You can go behind the waterfall and look through windows to get an underwater view of the next pool, one floor above and dedicated entirely to swinging out on and dropping from a rope fastened at the ceiling three stories up. Above the rope-swing pool is the beginning of a waterslide that ends with a splash in the main pool. Admission is $3.75 to $5.25.

# EATING OUT

Kids are welcome at just about any restaurant in town. Still, we've listed those that have true kid appeal.

**Casa Bonita**
**6715 West Colfax Avenue, Lakewood**
**(303) 232-5115**

Rising from the JCRS Shopping Center in Lakewood, the distinctive steeple of Casa Bonita has become a Greater Denver landmark. Although this is a perfectly good Mexican restaurant with American dishes, too, people come here more for the play than for the food. It's like eating in a cave with huge chambers and a complex labyrinth of tunnels and hidden nooks. Strolling mariachis and cliff divers entertain while you eat. Kids love Black Bart's cave, a series of creepy scares in tunnels sized for kids. There's a video arcade and other entertainment. The crowning glory is the 30-foot waterfall, where divers plunge into a pool below while performances at the top of the waterfall involve cowboy gunfights and explorers tangling with a gorilla. Every performance ends with somebody falling 30 feet into the pool. It's a popular place for kid birthday parties and for parents who want to kick back while their kids run wild. Hours are 11:00 A.M. to 9:30 P.M. Sunday through Thursday, 11:00 A.M. to 10:00 P.M. Friday and Saturday.

**Gunther Toody's**
**4500 East Alameda Avenue, Glendale**
**(303) 399-1959**

**9220 East Arapahoe Road, Englewood**
**(303) 799-1958**

**7355 Ralston Road, Arvada**
**(303) 422-1954**

**8266 West Bowles, Littleton**
**(303) 932-1957**

**301 West 104th Avenue, Northglenn**
**(303) 453-1956**
The staff at Gunther Toody's dress like characters from *Grease* at this 1950s-concept restaurant, and they usually do such a good job of acting their sassy, gum-chewing parts that there must be a Gunther Toody's acting school somewhere. The only games are a few classic pinball machines, and it's not exclusively a kid restaurant. But that's why we're mentioning it here, because it deserves wider recognition as a great, non-arcade dining place for kids and their families.

## Original Pancake House
**5900 South University Boulevard**
**Englewood**
**(303) 795-0573**
Go to this breakfast and lunch place at 9:00 A.M. on Saturday or Sunday and you'll see a mess of families—so many you can easily plan on an hour's wait. But it's worth it. The variety of pancakes and waffles is mind-boggling, and kids love the huge apple pancake, which is the house specialty.

## Piccolo's
**3563 South Monaco Parkway**
**(303) 757-5166**

**1744 East Evans Avenue**
**(303) 722-4955**

**7585 South University Boulevard,**
**Centennial**
**(303) 797-0686**
This neighborhood restaurant is packed with families, not only because their Italian and Mexican food is good, but also because they know kids' eyes are often bigger than their stomachs. To that end, they offer half-portions of any pasta dish—even quarter-portions if your child so desires.

## Trail Dust Steak House
**7101 South Clinton Street, Centennial**
**(303) 790-2420**

**9101 Benton Street, Westminster**
**(303) 427-1446**
Kids love the two-story slide that empties onto the hardwood dance floor at the Trail Dust Steak Houses, and they'll howl when a waitperson cuts off someone's tie. The steaks are good, as are all the fixin's. Once the band begins to play, Mom and Dad can enjoy a little country dancing.

# PLANES, TRAINS, AND BOATS

## Colorado Railroad Museum
**17155 West 44th Avenue, Golden**
**(303) 279-4591**
**www.crrm.org**

A lot of Western city parks used to have trains that kids could climb around on, but now they're mostly surrounded by fences to keep the kids out. None of that nonsense here! The Colorado Railroad Museum is described in our Tours and Attractions chapter, but at 12.5 acres, with more than 50 pieces of "rolling stock," it's so fantastic for kids that it bears repeating. Kids can climb up and walk through the antique railway cars, climb into the cupolas of the cabooses to look out the windows, and climb up on the big engine right outside the museum building and pull the rope and ring the awesome bell. You have to be a bit older to appreciate most of the two floors of memorabilia inside the museum building, but kids love the enormous model train set up in the basement, which you can run by plugging in a quarter. Several times a year the museum fires up and runs the state's oldest railway engine. The first week of December, Santa Claus parks inside a caboose and receives children between the hours of 10:00 A.M. and 4:00 P.M. Admission is $8.00 for adults, $5.00 for kids younger than age 16 accompanied by a parent, $7.00 for people older than age 60, and $18.00 for a family, which the museum defines as two adults and children younger than age 16. Hours are 9:00 A.M. to 6:00 P.M. every day of the week in June, July, and August, and 9:00 A.M. to 5:00 P.M. the rest of the year.

## Pikes Peak Cog Railway
**U.S. Highway 24 West from Colorado Springs to the Manitou exit, west on Manitou Avenue, and left onto Ruxton Avenue, Colorado Springs**
**(719) 685-5401**
**www.cograilway.com**
Adults become kids again during this delightful experience. We cover this in greater detail in our Day Trips chapter, yet this is one of the greatest kid activities on the Front Range: a 3½-hour trip to the top of Pikes Peak on the highest cog railway in the world. All this presumes, of course, that your kids are of an age and

temperament to tolerate the long ride. Reservations are required. The train costs $29.00 to $31.00 for adults, $16.00 to $16.50 for kids age 3 to 12. Check the Web site for seasonal promotions.

### Platte Valley Trolley
**2785 North Speer Boulevard**
**(303) 458-6255**
**www.denvertrolley.org**
To get to the trolley, park at the Children's Museum of Denver (see our listing in this chapter) and walk from the museum east to the Platte River. This turn-of-the-20th-century streetcar tour is for all ages. Small tykes may recognize its near-exact resemblance to the streetcar on the *Mister Rogers' Neighborhood* TV show. Kids 6 years of age and younger may prefer the half-hour tour to the hour tour. You'll enjoy a narrated tour along the Platte River, with bits of history and expositions on present and future features of this area such as INVESCO Field at Mile High and Golda Meir's former residence. The hour tour goes up Lakewood Gulch, along the tracks where the interurban trolley used to run from Denver to Golden.

Admission for the half-hour tour is $3.00 for adults and $2.00 for kids and seniors; tours operate 12:30 to 3:30 P.M. Wednesday through Sunday Memorial Day to Labor Day. The hour tour costs $6.00 for adults, $4.00 for seniors, and kids; tours leave at 11:30 A.M. Wednesday through Sunday Memorial Day to Labor Day. April 1 to Memorial Day and Labor Day to October 31, tours operate Friday through Sunday.

### Venice on the Creek
**Creek Front Plaza, at Larimer Street and Speer Boulevard**
**(303) 893-0750**
**www.greenwayfoundation.org**
One of Denver's newest attractions, Venice on the Creek is a great way to see Lower Downtown from the vantage point of a boat—or punt, in this case. A punt is a flat-bottomed boat, similar to a gondola. You can take a 10-block ride downstream

and back up while hearing the history of Cherry Creek and the history of punts. Reservations are strongly recommended since the boats sometimes sell out their seats as much as two weeks in advance. Take a few steps down to the pedestrian path and follow it 1 block to Market Street where you'll embark. The punts operate from 5:00 to 10:00 P.M. Thursday through Sunday, with candlelight rides starting at 8:30 P.M. June through August. Boats leave every 10 to 15 minutes for the 60- to 70-minute round-trip. Pricing is by the bench, with each punt having three benches, so you can purchase a whole bench for two people or a whole bench for one person if you want room to spread out. For the full trip adults pay $30, seniors and children age 3 to 12 pay $25. Half-trip or one-way-trip (approximately 35 minutes) prices are $20 for adults, $15 for seniors and children age 3 to 12. You can also rent a private boat for up to six people for $75 for the full trip or $50 for the half trip. Children younger than age 3 ride for free on all trips. All children must wear life jackets, which are provided by your guide. Candlelight rides are offered by reservation only.

### Wings Over the Rockies
**7711 East Academy Parkway**
**(303) 360-5360**
**www.wingsmuseum.org**
The closing of Lowry Air Force Base in the fall of 1994 was accompanied by the opening a few months later of what is now one of Greater Denver's greatest museums. Wings Over the Rockies does for aviation what the Colorado Railroad Museum does for the railroads: puts the biggest and best of the historic hardware on very impressive display for the public. With the exception of the Space Station Module, you can't actually go inside the displays, but up-close and gargantuan, they have a tremendous, visceral impact. Among the three dozen aircraft on display in the museum are big bombers, racy fighter jets, and helicopters—a scan of aviation history. You've got civilian and

military aircraft, models, simulations, photographs, and space-related objects so visitors can experience scientific discovery. It's all contained in the vast interior of Lowry's Hangar 1. Since it's all indoors, it's particularly nice on a winter day when outside activities are curtailed. This excepts the B-52 bomber on display outside. There are also a variety of historic aviation artifacts and a museum store. Admission is free to museum members, and for others it costs $7.00 for adults, $6.00 for children age 6 to 12 and seniors older than age 60, and it's free for kids age 5 and younger. Wings Over the Rockies is open from 10:00 A.M. to 5:00 P.M. Monday through Saturday and noon to 5:00 P.M. on Sunday.

From Interstate 225 take Sixth Avenue west to Lowry Boulevard, turn left at the dead end, and proceed until you see the hangars. It's the first one to the west. Or you can take Alameda Street west to Fairmount Cemetery and turn right onto Fairmount Drive. Straight ahead you'll see the two hangars, and it's the first one to the east.

## NIGHTLIFE FOR THE YOUNGER CROWD

**Club 22**
**Northglenn Recreation Center, 11801 Community Center Drive, Northglenn**
**(303) 450-8800**
Club 22 stands for "2 old for a sitter and 2 young to drive." This is a safe and supervised nightspot for adolescents of middle-school age. Parents check their kids in, and the kids don't leave until the parents check them out. In between, there's music and dancing, swimming, and other activities, such as volleyball and wallyball in the Rec Center's athletic facilities. There are contests, food and beverage concessions, and always some sort of special event, such as a movie or an entertainer or demonstrator. Admission is $4.00. Club 22 takes place on the first and third Saturday of each month from 7:00 to 10:30 P.M.

**Rec and Rock and Kids Night Out**
**Goodson Recreation Center**
**6315 South University Boulevard**
**Littleton**
**(303) 798-2476**
The Rec and Rock and Kids Night Out program features safe and supervised weekend nightlife for adolescents age 9 to 14. They've turned out to be popular programs and take place during the school year.

You'll typically find games, dancing, and music with a live DJ; activities such as basketball, dodgeball, wallyball, and volleyball; concessions for pizza and soft drinks; movies, contests, and special guests. There is one adult counselor for every 25 kids, a uniformed policeman on hand at all times, and parental check-in and checkout. Call the rec center for admission fees. Hours are 7:00 to 11:00 P.M.

## THE PLANT AND ANIMAL KINGDOMS

**Butterfly Pavilion & Insect Center**
**6252 West 104th Avenue, Westminster**
**(303) 469-5441**
**www.butterflies.org**
If your child loves butterflies, this place is a perfect destination. More than 1,200 butterflies live in a 7,200-square-foot tropical forest. At the emergence viewing area, you can watch the last two stages of metamorphosis as butterflies emerge from their chrysalids. Outside is a butterfly garden, with flowers designed to attract butterflies. The Pavilion is open daily from 9:00 A.M. to 5:00 P.M., 9:00 A.M. to 6:00 P.M. Memorial Day to Labor Day. Admission ranges from $4.95 to $7.95; kids age 2 and younger are admitted free. The Butterfly Pavilion now has an outreach program. Call for details.

**Denver Botanic Gardens**
**1005 York Street**
**(720) 865-3500**
**www.botanicgardens.org**
Kids of all ages enjoy these lovely gardens

*Prehistoric Journey at The Denver Museum of Nature and Science.* DENVER METRO CONVENTION AND VISITORS BUREAU

and the tropical conservatory. We've described the gardens in detail in our Tours and Attractions chapter. Most likely, however, children will be more interested in the changing menu of year-round kid activities, such as the Pumpkin Fest and the summer evening concerts listed in our Annual Events and Festivals chapter. It's also a pretty place to run around, with a couple of grassy knolls that small kids love to climb on and roll down. It's a nice place for a picnic, like being out in the country when you're in the city. Admission is $7.50 for adults and $5.00 for children and students with an ID. The gardens are open from 9:00 A.M to 8:00 P.M. Saturday through Tuesday and 9:00 A.M. to 5:00 P.M Wednesday, Thursday, and Friday. Winter hours (mid-September through April) are 9:00 A.M. to 5:00 P.M. daily.

**The Denver Museum of Nature and Science**
**2001 Colorado Boulevard**
**(in City Park, at Colorado Boulevard and Montview Street)**
**(303) 322-7009**
**www.dmns.org**
See our Tours and Attractions chapter for more details on this museum, but don't forget it's one of the greatest places around for kids. When you walk under the claws of the huge *Tyrannosaurus rex* skeleton as you enter the front door, you know you've

ℹ

*The Tattered Cover Book Stores devote lots of shelf space to children's books. There are also little tables and chairs where kids can sit and read or look at pictures.*

# A Day in the Park

For many Denverites the way to spend a perfect day with the kids is at one of Denver's wonderful parks. Thanks to the vision of Mayor Robert Speer (after whom Speer Boulevard is named), Denver has a system of parks and greenways that is the largest in the nation.

The story goes that Speer attended the 1893 Chicago Exposition where he gathered ideas for turning Denver into a beautiful city of open spaces intended for public use. Elected mayor in 1904, he formulated a "City Beautiful Plan," establishing a tree-lined parkway system and central Denver parks that form the framework for the city's open space (Civic Center Park, Washington Park, City Park, and Alamo Placita Park). Denver's first park, however, opened in 1968. Mestizo-Curtis Park (originally called Curtis Park after postmaster Samuel Curtis) was developed at 31st and Curtis Streets, and it is still a vital part of this north Denver neighborhood.

Today, more than a century after Speer was elected, the city and county of Denver has 281 urban parks, 125 miles of hiking and biking paths, 100 miles of parkways, and 20,000 acres of mountain parks. And that only includes those areas administered by the city of Denver. Go to the suburbs and you'll find many more.

Though all the parks are soothing oases, the following are particularly beloved by kids.

### Belleview Park
**5001 South Inca Street, Englewood**
Belleview is simply one of the most fun family parks around. Often called Airplane Park, it has two playgrounds filled with space-related jungle gyms, slides, and swings. It also has a miniature train that takes visitors around the park and a petting zoo with cows, pigs, goats, and rabbits. If that's not quite enough, a clear shallow stream runs through the park, and it's perfect for wading.

### Cheesman Park
**East 12th Avenue and Humboldt Street**
Cheesman Park has some terrific play-

entered a place of wonder. Sure, kids have to be older to appreciate a lot of things here, but the exhibits of dinosaurs and Pleistocene megafauna, such as the two saber-toothed tigers attacking the giant sloth, are sure winners. So are the many dioramas showing different kinds of fauna in exquisitely crafted natural settings that blend so flawlessly into painted backdrops that you really feel like you're on a mountaintop with an eagle family or at the seashore with the sea lions. A number of the woodland backdrops have elves painted into them or elf figurines hiding in the foreground foliage or under rocks or

logs. A real challenge is trying to find them. The IMAX theater with its four-story-high screen is a treat some Denverites enjoy taking their kids to frequently. The museum also has some great children's educational programs, although they fill up frighteningly fast once their scheduling becomes public knowledge. Admission to the museum is $10.00 for adults and $6.00 for children age 3 to 18, students with an ID, and seniors. IMAX tickets are $8.00 for adults and $6.00 for children age 3 to 18, students with an ID, and seniors. The museum is open from 9:00 A.M. to 5:00 P.M. daily.

ground equipment (not to mention a pretty spectacular view of the mountains). Kids love the castle structure for climbing and hiding, and the jungle gym is one of the best around. Most striking is the Cheesman Park Pavilion, a Parthenon-like structure perfect for running around in or watching the sunset.

## City Park
### 17th Avenue and Colorado Boulevard
This park just east of downtown is full of possibilities, not the least of which are visits to the Denver Zoo and the Denver Museum of Natural History. A lake in the park offers paddleboating. A rose garden close to the museum provides a great picnic site. Need more activity? The park has a public golf course and tennis courts. And in the summer, it's easy to find a free concert in the bandshell near the lake.

## Cushing Park
### 795 West Eastman Street, Englewood
This is the site of one of Denver's first gold discoveries. Not surprisingly, its playground is reminiscent of the Old West with a stagecoach, a tepee, a jail, and a horse and buggy—all of which keep active buckaroos busy while their parents lounge under a tree and relax. Cushing is also the only park in Englewood with an area specifically for skateboarders.

## Genesee Park
### Interstate 70 West to the Genesee exit, Genesee
How many cities boast parks that house a herd of buffalo? The best reason to head here is to see the 30 or so bison roaming right off the highway. Once you see these gentle giants, you won't care that there aren't all the other fancy trappings of city parks.

## Washington Park
### Louisiana Avenue and Downing Street
This is one of Denver's most popular park destinations. Originally a prairie, it has two lakes that allow fishing (don't forget your license) and a lawn bowling/croquet green. Best of all, most of the streets are closed to vehicular traffic, so your family can in-line skate, bike, or walk without fear of being mowed down.

## The Denver Zoo
### City Park, East 23rd Avenue and Steele Street (near the Denver Museum of Nature and Science)
### (303) 376-4800
### www.denverzoo.org
You can't miss with a zoo, and the Denver Zoo may well be Greater Denver's most popular kid place of all. The zoo has some wonderful special events centered around the seasons. For more on the zoo, see our Tours and Attractions chapter and also our Annual Events and Festivals chapter.

Winter admission to the zoo is $9.00 for ages 12 to 64, $7.00 for seniors age 65 and older, and $5.00 for ages 3 to 11. Kids younger than age 3 get in free. Add $2.00 to each for summer admission prices. The zoo is open every day of the year 10:00 a.m. to 5:00 p.m. Summer hours begin an hour earlier and last an hour longer.

## Hudson Gardens Events Center
### 6115 South Santa Fe Drive, Littleton
### (303) 797-8565
### www.hudsongardens.org
Metro Denver's newest public gardens, this is a beautiful place to walk on a clear, warm day. Sixteen different "rooms" make up this floral wonderland, and kids can

sniff at the Fragrance Garden, wander through the Secret Garden, and look for butterflies in the Butterfly Bank Garden. The gardens are open daily 9:00 A.M. to 5:00 P.M. in May, September, and October. They stay open until 6:00 P.M. June through August, except on Wednesday nights, when they invite you to beat the heat and enjoy the sunset until 8:00 P.M. Adults pay $5.00, children $2.00.

**Rocky Mountain Arsenal National Wildlife Refuge**
**72nd and Quebec Streets**
**Commerce City**
**(303) 289-0232**
**www.fws.gov/rockymountainarsenal/**
Take a two-hour bus tour of one of the country's former toxic waste sites, now overrun with all kinds of wildlife. On this tour you hear the history of the area as well as its environmental cleanup. If you're lucky you'll also see eagles, hawks, mule deer, and prairie dogs. If the wildlife is out romping, this will be one of those "WOW!" experiences. Call for current schedule. Though the tour is traditionally free, reservations have always been a must.

## MUSEUMS

**Children's Museum of Denver**
**2121 Children's Museum Drive**
**(303) 433-7444**
**www.mychildsmuseum.org**
There's a wealth of things to do here, all of them aimed specifically at kids and all educationally oriented. There's a miniature grocery store, where kids can shop or be the checkout person, and a Denver Nuggets exhibit, where kids can compare their sizes to basketball players' sizes. There are laboratories where kids can work with earth sciences and natural phenomena and play educational games on computers. You'll find a light room and sound room, plant and animal exhibits, woodworking, and a traveling exhibit that changes every three months. Play Partners is a special toddler play area set up

like the Three Bears' house. It's a great museum, but a very busy one that's often crowded. The museum recommends coming between 2:00 and 5:00 P.M. on weekdays, when it's least crowded. Admission is free for members and kids younger than age 1, $5.00 for seniors, and $7.00 for all others. Hours are 9:00 A.M. to 4:00 P.M. Monday through Friday, 10:00 A.M. to 5:00 P.M. Saturday and Sunday.

Worthy of note is the museum's annual Halloween party, Trick-or-Treat Street, which runs for nearly a week, including Halloween. This is Denver's non-scary trick-or-treat alternative. Multitudes of kids show up in costumes to pass through the many exhibits and receive candy. The event includes pumpkin carving, performances, and other activities.

New to the museum is the Parent Resource Center and the Center for the Young Child, a developmentally age-appropriate area for newborns to 4-year-olds. The museum can be a little tricky to reach, so here are some directions: It's right off 23rd Avenue and Interstate 25. If you exit from Interstate 25, go east on 23rd and take the first right onto Seventh Street and then an immediate right onto Children's Museum Drive.

**Four Mile Historic Park**
**715 South Forest Street**
**(303) 399-1859**
**www.fourmilehistoricpark.org**
This museum is covered in our Tours and Attractions chapter but should be noted here as well. Kids enjoy walking through the living-history farmstead, where they can see old machinery, reconstructed barns, outhouses (not for use and odor-free), root cellars, chickens, ducks, calves, and horses. Older kids may also enjoy the tour of Denver's oldest house, led by costumed tour guides. During special events there are more kid attractions such as demonstrations of blacksmithing, butter churning, and other crafts of yesteryear as well as horse-drawn wagon or stagecoach rides. The number of events annually varies, but the museum has a few stan-

*Children's Museum of Denver dental hygiene exhibit.* THE DENVER POST/GLENN ASAKAWA

dard events: a July Fourth old-fashioned family picnic, the Pumpkin Harvest Festival in early October, and the holiday open house in December. Admission is $3.50 for adults, $2.00 for kids and seniors, and free for kids younger than age 6. The park also does special programming with special rates for groups of 10 or more.

Hours are noon to 4:00 P.M. Wednesday through Friday from April through September, 10:00 A.M. to 4:00 P.M. weekends. Winter hours are Saturday and Sunday noon to 4:00 P.M.

### Littleton Historical Museum
**6028 South Gallup Street, Littleton**
**(303) 795-3950**
**www.littletongov.org/museum**

This museum is covered in our Tours and Attractions chapter, but it's one of our favorites for kids. As a living-history museum, it's particularly fascinating to

kids interested in the past. But it's also a great way to let the kids see lots of animals and explore a fantasy world of the past. It's a working homestead and farm, with sheep, oxen, pigs, cows, chickens, horses, and other animals. Costumed staff and volunteers go about their antiquarian life chores, keeping to the roles and speaking in the manner of people from the late 19th century. As you walk around, you may encounter them working in a garden or barn or fields, cooking in the house, blacksmithing in the 1903 blacksmith shop, or teaching in the 1860s schoolhouse. If you're lucky in the winter, you may catch them harvesting ice from the lake for the 1900 icehouse, although the ice in recent years often has not been thick enough to harvest. Admission is free. Hours are 8:00 A.M. to 5:00 P.M. Tuesday through Friday, 10:00 A.M. to 5:00 P.M. Saturday, and 1:00 to 5:00 P.M. on Sunday.

# MAKING MONEY

**United States Mint**
**320 West Colfax Avenue**
**(303) 405-4764**
**www.usmint.gov**
Ever wondered what 40 million coins look like? Take the 30-minute tour of the U.S. Mint and you may get some idea. This free tour starts with an exhibit on the history of money and then proceeds to the observation room where you can look down on 60 high-speed presses that produce as many as a billion coins a month. In the next room you see machines count, sort, and bag coins. You learn that 70 percent of the coins stamped in Denver are pennies. Stop in at the Numismatic Sales Room where you can gaze on—even purchase—special coins, medallions, and commemorative coins. Tours start at 8:00 A.M. and go every 15 minutes until 2:45 P.M. Monday through Friday. Reservations are strongly encouraged, and the tours regularly fill up early. Go to the Web site above and click on "Make a Reservation."

**Young Americans Center for**
**Financial Education**
**311 Steele Street**
**(303) 321-2954**
**www.yacenter.org/**
This foundation was launched in the late 1980s by Bill Daniels, one of Denver's most famed citizens for being a pioneer of the cable TV industry, an industry in which Denver now plays a leading role. Now deceased, Daniels was chairman of Daniels Communications Inc., a broker/dealer of major cable systems around the country, and started the foundation to give kids an early grounding in the business culture. Most widely known is the Young Americans Bank, a real FDIC-insured bank of which the foundation is the nonprofit holding company. Designed for ages 21 and younger, it's the only bank in the world exclusively for kids. They can have their own savings and checking accounts, ATM and credit cards, and mutual funds. It emphasizes individual attention to children, with small teller booths designed with steps so kids can look the teller in the eye, and tellers who teach the kids one-on-one about deposit slips, interest, and so on.

Be Your Own Boss is a program for kids interested in starting and/or owning their own companies. This program is offered during the summer as a weeklong day camp for ages 10 to 12. Kids are taken step-by-step through the entrepreneurial process, from basic education on things like financing to the writing of their own business plans.

Young AmeriTowne is another nifty program, involving students role-playing in 16 different jobs and running their own town. It's accessed through schools, but parents can help by hustling their children's teachers to get their classes involved. During the school year, students learn first in their classrooms before coming in for a one-day program. Kids can also go to Young AmeriTowne on an individual basis during its summer programs: the Undergraduate Program (for kids who have completed 4th or 5th grades), the Girls Can Program (for girls who have completed 5th or 6th grades), the International Towne Program (for kids who have completed 5th or 6th grades), and the Junior Money Matters Program (for kids who have just completed 2nd or 3rd grades).

# AMUSEMENT PARKS (INDOORS AND OUT)

**Fat City**
**9670 West Coal Mine Avenue, Littleton**
**(303) 972-4344**
**www.fatcityinfo.com**
This is a 3½-acre indoor fun center for all ages. Activities include 40 lanes of bowling, roller-skating, an 18-hole miniature golf course, more than 150 video games, two restaurants, an ice-cream shop, a sports bar, and Laser Runner, a laser tag

game. There are also six major rides. There's no admission fee; you pay by activity, which ranges from $2.25 to $6.00. Hours begin at 11:00 A.M. daily in the summer and 4:00 P.M. the rest of the year. Closing varies from 10:00 P.M. to 2:00 A.M., depending on the day of the week.

### Funtastic Fun
**3085 South Broadway, Englewood**
**(303) 761-8701**
**www.funtasticfun.com**
This used to be called Funtastic Nathan's when it was located in the Cinderella City mall, but in 1994 it moved and changed its name. It's popular among kids of Greater Denver's south side. This fun center includes a Ferris wheel, a carousel, a train, swings, an air castle, and a lot of things kids can do on their own. A room of plastic balls with slides and games such as skee ball and air hockey will also keep the kids happy. Funtastic Fun has a room for younger kids, which includes a smaller air castle, so the squirts don't get rough-housed by the bigger kids. Individual admission is $9.95 for all day, except on Tuesday and Wednesday, when it's $6.95. Adults pay $2.95. Hours are 10:00 A.M. to 9:00 P.M. daily.

### Heritage Square
**I-70 West to exit 259;**
**go right for 1 mile, Golden**
**(303) 279-2789**
Out in the open all by itself, up against the foothills, Heritage Square is a great place to go for family entertainment. It's what appears to be a small Western town, with porticoed boardwalks along the front of retail stores, restaurants, and entertainment options lining its streets. The hill on the west side of town has an alpine slide that operates in summer, and it's just the greatest fun, except that all too often, if you don't go fast enough, some gung-ho geek comes racing up behind you with a bump. Heritage Square claims more than 40 attractions counting stores, restaurants, and amusement rides. It has

bumper boats, go-karts, and a family arcade. The Heritage Square Music Hall usually has a fun show to offer, and you can rent the town hall and wedding chapel for parties.

Admission to Heritage Square is free, as is the parking. It's fun just to stroll around. Summer hours are 10:00 A.M. to 8:00 P.M. Monday through Saturday, noon to 6:00 P.M. Sunday. Spring, fall, and winter hours are noon to 5:00 P.M. every day.

### Lakeside Amusement Park
**4601 Sheridan Avenue**
**Just south of I-70, Lakeside**
**(303) 477-1621**
**www.lakesideamusementpark.com**
Amid the grand hoopla of Elitch Garden's whopping new amusement park that opened in 1995, don't forget Lakeside. It remains an old-fashioned park, with art deco that marks it as having changed little since the 1940s, although, of course, it has more-recent rides. Among the sentimental favorites of Greater Denverites are the little trains that run around the lake, and everybody likes to scream when they go through the funky old tunnel. It has an extensive kiddieland with 15 rides sized for the tots. Lakeside still lets you bring in your own food for a picnic, and you don't have to pay big bucks to get in. Admission is $2.00. Inside, you pay 50 cents per coupon, and it takes two to four coupons per ride. Sometimes we just like to swing in for a ride on the Cyclone, the big roller coaster, and then call it a day. Unlimited ride passes are $12.75 during the week and $17.75 on Saturday, Sunday, and holi-

*For cold-weather fun, take the kids tubing down a ski slope at Keystone. For around $10 per hour for adults and about half that for kids, you get a gondola ride to the tubing spot and rope-tow rides back to the top. See our Ski Country chapter or call Adventure Point at (970) 496-4386.*

days. It opens weekends in May and full-time in June and closes after Labor Day weekend. The kiddie playland is open during the week from 1:00 to 10:00 P.M. and on Sunday and most Saturdays from noon to 10:00 P.M. The rest of the park rocks and rolls from 6:00 to 11:00 P.M. during the week and from noon to 11:00 P.M. on Sundays and most Saturdays. Parking is free.

**Six Flags Elitch Gardens**
**I-25 and Speer Boulevard (exit 212A)**
**(303) 595-4386**
**www.sixflags.com/parks/elitchgardens**
Elitch Gardens is Denver's oldest fun park, dating from 1890 when it began as a botanical and zoological garden and had no mechanical rides. Since then it has become Denver's flashiest amusement park. Now it's even bigger, expanding in 1995 from its old 28-acre site to a new 68-acre site along the South Platte River across from the Children's Museum. In 1997 it was purchased by Premier Parks, Inc., the fourth-largest theme-park company in the United States. The new Elitch Gardens has more than 45 rides, including a tropical waterpark. Among the rides is the Boomerang—a high-speed forward and backward looping coaster. Disaster Canyon is another beauty, a raft ride on white water and through a spray tunnel that will soak you. One of the great new features is the Observation Tower, which reminds one of Seattle's Space Needle. It's 250 feet high with a 360-degree viewing platform. In 1997 the park added the Mind Eraser, a looping steel suspended roller coaster, and the 200-foot free-falling Tower of Doom. Buying tickets online is the easiest and least expensive way to go because they're discounted and you can print them out at your computer. Adult admission at the gate is $44.99, online it's $34.99 (adult admission is required for anyone more than 48 inches tall). Restricted admission tickets for kids shorter than 48 inches are $32.49 at the front gate, $22.49 online. Season passes are available online for $79.99. Elitch's opens in May on weekends only. After

Memorial Day it is open daily 10:00 A.M. to 10:00 P.M. until Labor Day. Most days and some midweek days it closes at 8:00 P.M. Call for hours on specific days.

Getting to Elitch Gardens is no problem, since it now has its own exit from the Speer Boulevard viaduct, with its own traffic-light intersection on Speer. Coming across the viaduct toward downtown Denver, it will be a right turn. Coming from downtown, it will be a left turn. There is also an access from 15th Street.

## SOMETHING DIFFERENT

These entries defy categorization. They're still great fun, so check them out!

**Colorado Renaissance Festival**
**I-25 about 25 minutes south from Denver to Larkspur (exit 173), then follow the signs**
**(303) 688-6010**
See our Annual Events and Festivals chapter for more on the Renaissance Festival, but it's such a killer kid-pleaser that it cannot be omitted from this section. It's a dizzying fantasy world full of battling knights, cavorting jesters, and associated monsters and grotesques, where hundreds of food vendors, craftspersons, and performers dress, act, and speak appropriately to their setting in this re-created 16th-century village. It's an event rather than a place, however, so remember it's only around for eight weekends in June and July. Admission is $16.95 for adults, $8.00 for children ages 5 to 12. Kids younger than age 5 get in free. Discount tickets are available at King Soopers supermarkets.

**Denver Puppet Theatre**
**3156 West 38th Avenue**
**(303) 458-6446**
**www.denverpuppettheater.com**
The Denver Puppet Theatre is a delightful experience for kids age 3 and older. With six different plays performed each year—classics, world stories, new plays—kids can

come back every two months for a new show. Marionettes and shadow puppets make up the characters, and visitors can see all the puppets after each perfor- mance. (No autographs, however.) Perfor- mances are on Thursday and Friday at 10:00 A.M. and 1:00 P.M. and Saturday at 1:00 P.M. Tickets are $5.00 per person.

**Tiny Town**
**6249 South Turkey Creek Road**
**Morrison**
**(303) 697-6829**
**www.tinytownrailroad.com**
Hidden away in a mountain canyon south- east of Greater Denver, this is a curious and charming town of 110 miniature build- ings constructed at one-sixth scale on six acres. Kids can actually go inside some of the buildings, but it's a place where fami- lies enjoy just walking around. You can ride a miniature train pulled by a real—but tiny—steam engine over a mile-long course. They have a snack bar, a gift shop, and puppet shows on weekends. Part of the magic of this place is that it looks rather ancient, and it is. It's the oldest miniature town in the United States. George Turner was the owner of a Denver moving and storage business just after the turn of the 20th century, and this was his mountain property. His granddaughter was chronically ill, so he built a few minia- ture houses in the pasture for her to play in, then kept adding to the tiny town. Turkey Creek Road was dirt then, and people would stop their cars and delight their kids with the magic little town. By the 1920s and 1930s, it was one of Col- orado's major tourist attractions. After World War II it went through several decades of decline, including a flood and a number of failed attempts to make it a profitable tourist business. Now it's oper- ated by the Tiny Town Foundation, which donates 30 percent of the profits to chari- ties and uses a lot of volunteers. Admis- sion is low: $3.00 for adults and $2.00 for kids ages 3 to 12, and children age 2 and younger get in free. Pay an extra $1.00 if you want to ride the train. It's open 10:00 A.M. to 5:00 P.M. weekends only in May, September, and October and daily Memo- rial Day through Labor Day. Take C–470 to U.S. Highway 285, travel about 4 miles southwest on US 285, turn left onto Turkey Creek Road, and go about 0.25 mile. You'll see Tiny Town on the right.

# ANNUAL EVENTS AND FESTIVALS

Love a lively parade or jumpin' jazz fest? Denver and its surrounding communities offer enough parades, concerts, rodeos, art shows, and ethnic celebrations—pick a reason, we've got a festival—to keep your calendar full year-round. And we've included as many as possible, from those with instantaneous name recognition, like the Cherry Creek Arts Festival, which draws more than a quarter-million people every July Fourth weekend, to the lesser-known ones like the Olde Golden Christmas, held in December in downtown Golden.

The following list should be viewed as a practical guide to those festivals and events with a designated date and location, but a few words of warning: Dates can change from year to year, often well after this guide is published, so an event listed in September, for example, may actually turn out to be in October. Telephone numbers can also change after this guide has been published, although the old number can usually steer you toward the new number. And, of course, prices can change as well.

Two sources of last-minute information changes are the Denver Metro Convention & Visitors Bureau's outdoor special events hotline at (720) 913–8244 and the calendar of events at www.denvergov.org/event. Or if you find that one of our information numbers is outdated by the time you try to use it, just call the bureau and ask for the correct number. Folks there may have it.

While the bureau's events guide is not as descriptive as the subsequent listings, it has one significant advantage. Our listings include only annual events, those that happen every year. The bureau's guide includes many events that happen just once, such as a performance by a specific musical or dance group.

Many events in this chapter are not one-of-a-kind, and similar events can be found throughout the year. Between the city of Golden, the Buffalo Bill Museum, and the Buckhorn Exchange, for example, you can find enough Buffalo Bill events to keep you buffalo crazy all year. There are mountains of mountain-man rendezvous. Nearly every community has its own yearly celebration, from the Carnation Festival in Wheat Ridge to Western Welcome Week in Littleton. Mountain communities and ski areas, ditto. Remember that whenever you go to an event in some community or ski area, you're also placing yourself in a position to enjoy the other attractions there and nearby.

Some festivals and events, such as the Bolder Boulder 10K run, are one-shot deals. Others, such as the World's Largest Christmas Lighting Display at the Denver City and County Building, may stretch out over weeks.

For the most part these entries are confined to the Greater Denver area, but you'll notice that we've also covered events during the year at nearby ski areas and mountain communities. This list goes far afield: Cheyenne, Wyoming; Estes Park; and Colorado Springs—all easy day trips.

In some cases you can expect to experience exactly what we have described in the following entries. We can't guarantee that a festival or event will be exactly the same every year, but we can tell you what to expect based either on promises by the organizers or on the experiences of past years.

Once again, we certainly haven't covered *everything* there is to do. On the Fourth of July, for example, communities and organizations all over Greater Denver and the surrounding area have fireworks shows. Looking out across the plains from the mountains, the entire landscape seems to be erupting in fireworks. We recommend driving up in the evening to any foothills road with an east-facing view, parking, and enjoying the show.

And, of course, if you're looking for festivals and events, you may want to go beyond those annual events that a book like this clearly can provide. Many of the organizations and communities included here have events that are not offered every year, while many other organizations and communities have the same event on a regular basis. Take the **Colorado Rockies** baseball team (call 303-762-5437, or ROCKIES) as an example. They're playing constantly from spring to fall. Fashionable **Cherry Creek** has what it calls summer strolls from June through August and gallery walks in February, May, September, and December. The **Colorado Railroad Museum** at several points throughout the year has what it calls "steam ups," in which it fires up and moves Colorado's oldest locomotive, No. 346. The **Denver Botanic Gardens** offers a wonderful series of concerts during the summer, too many to list individually here. These are just a few of countless sources of entertainment.

Beyond this list, the best advice we can give is that you should check the Friday weekend sections of the *Denver Post, Rocky Mountain News,* and Boulder's *Daily Camera,* where the goings-on are listed in considerable detail. And don't miss the impressive events and activities section each week in *Westword,* Denver's leading weekly newspaper that's available free in dispensers all over Greater Denver beginning on Wednesday and continuing until the dispensers are empty.

# JANUARY

**Denver Boat Show**
**Colorado Convention Center**
**700 14th Street**
**www.boatcolorado.org**
This is boathead heaven in early January. The year's biggest boat show usually lasts four days, spanning a weekend and jammed with aquatic craft, rubber rafts, and gear and accessories fore and aft. It's great fun to goggle at the huge luxury boats. Tickets are $8.00 for adults; $5.00 for children.

**Chef's Cup Race and**
**Benefit Dinner Dance**
**West Portal Station, Winter Park Resort**
**Winter Park**
**(970) 726-1590**
**www.skiwinterpark.com**
During this early-January event, Fraser Valley chefs compete on the slopes and in the kitchen to benefit the Winter Park Competition Center. The day begins with a trip down the racecourse, after which the chefs head to the kitchen to prepare a specialty dish. The results are served at a benefit dinner, during which guests can sample the fare, bid on items in a silent auction, and dance to live music. Guests can watch the race for free from the resort's base. Tickets to the evening events can be purchased from the Competition Center at the number listed above.

**Ullr Fest**
**Locations throughout Breckenridge**
**(970) 453-5579**
Helmets with horns on them are the height of fashion at this free weeklong festival in honor of Ullr (pronounced "ooler"), the Norse god of winter. If you don't have a horned helmet, you will most certainly be able to find someone willing to sell you one. (They are also handed out free at the parade.) Ullr Fest starts on a Friday and runs for a week in early January. It includes a parade, kids' activities, and a variety of different events daily.

Other activities include a version of the Dating Game, an ice-skating party, and children's concert. And the Ullympics feature coed teams competing in crazy events, such as Broom Ball and volleyball with snowshoes.

### Chinese New Year
### Various locations throughout
### Greater Denver

Denver has a relatively small Chinese population, but come January they turn out in force to sponsor Chinese New Year celebrations. Events are publicized by the Denver Buddhist Cultural Society, 2530 West Alameda Avenue; Denver Chinese School at George Washington High School, 650 South Monaco Parkway, www.denver chineseschool.org; and at the Far East Shopping Center, on South Federal Boulevard between West Alameda and West Mississippi Avenues. Events usually include lion dances and religious celebrations.

### Colorado RV Adventure Travel Show
### Colorado Convention Center
### 700 14th Street
### (303) 892-6800
### www.bigasalloutdoors.com

This is Greater Denver's version of hog heaven for the recreational-vehicle enthusiast. Admire and wander through the shining state-of-the-art in anywhere from 100 to 200 new recreational vehicles, see the latest in RV accessories, and meet exhibitors from lodges and resorts that cater to the RV crowd. This event is held in early January, and the cost is $8.00 for adults, $7.00 for seniors; kids younger than age 12 get in free.

### National Western Stock Show & Rodeo
### National Western Complex
### 4655 Humboldt Street (Brighton
### Boulevard exit off Interstate 70)
### (303) 297-1166
### www.nationalwestern.com

Founded in 1906, the National Western is the largest annual event in Denver—and it's growing. You'll be in the company of more than 600,000 people, but the event is spaced over 16 days in mid-January, so there's plenty of room and time to tour the show competitions of everything from horses, sheep, and cattle to chickens and rabbits in more varieties than you dreamed existed.

Rodeo events go on every day, with the nation's top horse and bull riders, calf ropers, you name it, competing for nearly $500,000 in prizes. Between the big events, you can see all kinds of oddball fun: rodeo clowns, Western battle re-creations (cover the kids' ears if loud noises scare them), and a sheepdog herding sheep with a monkey in a cowboy suit riding on its back. Tickets start at about $10. Tickets to the Professional Bull Riders are the most expensive. The National Western begins with a colorful parade through downtown Denver.

Also check out what Denver calls the World's Largest Display of Christmas Lights at the City and County Building downtown. The lights are on from the first Thursday in December until January 1, but they're turned on at night during the stock show as well.

### Annual Colorado Cowboy Poetry
### Gathering
### Arvada Center for the Arts and
### Humanities, 6901 Wadsworth Boulevard
### Arvada
### (720) 898-7272
### www.arvadacenter.org

Tales grow tall under a wide-open sky, and nobody spends more time under a wider sky than cowboys and cowgirls. Once a year in mid-January, the poetic cream of the ranching and cowpunching community brings its Western oral tradition of tales and humor to Arvada from Colorado and beyond. Expect about 40 poets, balladeers, and yodelers from 14 states and Australia to perform during the four-day event. Guests can attend on-stage concerts as well as theme-poetry and western music sessions. Tickets are in the $12 to $25 range.

### International Snow Sculpture Championships
### Locations throughout Breckenridge
### (970) 453-5579

In late January the city of Breckenridge lends its front-end loaders to fill wooden forms with 20-ton blocks of snow. Four-person sculpting teams from around the world climb on top and tromp and stomp until the snow is packed tight. The forms are removed, and what happens to each big block of snow is up to the contestants, who use only hand tools. Sculptures run the gamut from geometric to free-form to recognizable shapes and scenes. The sculptures can last up to 10 days, depending on the weather. The event is free whether you participate or just watch.

### Sports Authority's International Sportsmen's Exposition
### Colorado Convention Center
### 700 14th Street
### (800) 545-6100
### www.sportsexpos.com

This pure hunting and fishing show sometime in late January features products and services related to archery, firearms, and fishing. This is a how-to show with a lot of demonstrations designed to improve your hunting and fishing skills. You can sit in a U-shaped theater-seating section, for example, to watch a presenter on stage explain how he ties flies or wraps fishing rods. Video monitors allow you to see the small work. Top-name seminar speakers from magazines such as *Field and Stream* and *Outdoor Life* will be here. Expect around 350 exhibitors and crowds in the low 30,000s. Price is $10 for adults; kids age 12 and younger are free.

## FEBRUARY

### Registration for Ride the Rockies
### www.ridetherockies.com

See the June entry, Ride the Rockies, for more on the largest and longest public group bicycling tour of the year, but right now is when you need to register if you're interested in taking part. It's a lottery, and you need to get on the stick if you want in. The *Denver Post,* sponsor of the ride, usually makes applications available in the first week of February, and they're due by the last week of February. Call (303) 820-1338 for information.

### Wells Fargo Cup
### Winter Park Resort, Lower Hughes Ski Trail, Winter Park
### (303) 316-1545
### www.nscd.org

The Wells Fargo Cup, the largest fund-raiser of the year for the National Sports Center for the Disabled (NSCD), brings together world-class disabled ski racers, Denver Broncos alumni, and amateur skiers of all abilities. Teams of amateur skiers take to the slopes in the pro-am race, and a timing run enables casual skiers to compete against more aggressive skiers with racing experience. The *Denver Post* Celebrity Challenge brings together local media personalities, political leaders, and the occasional former football star, who team up with two racers from the NSCD's Winter Park Disabled Ski Team. The highlight of the weekend, the World Disabled Invitational, is the only race in which disabled skiers compete head-to-head on parallel courses, a format used in professional racing events.

### CHSAA State Wrestling Championships
### The Pepsi Center, 1000 Chopper Place
### (303) 344-5050
### www.chsaa.org

Don't expect to see bellowing meso-morphs in outlandish costumes. Do expect to see real mainstream wrestling, as the top high-school contenders square off for the state titles. At any one time you will be able to see simultaneous contests on 10 different mats. The competition starts in mid- to late February and runs on a Thursday, Friday, and Saturday. Admission has ranged from $5.00 to $10.00 in the past.

**Columbia Crest Cup**
**Winter Park Resort, Winter Park**
**(970) 726-1548**
The length and steepness of the course combined with the quality of competition make this one of the most demanding races for disabled skiers in the country. It is usually held in late February or early March. See some of the best disabled skiers in the Rocky Mountain region in the super giant slalom, the giant slalom, and the slalom. Benefits the National Sports Center for the Disabled.

**Fat Tuesday Celebration**
**Bars and restaurants throughout**
**Breckenridge**
**(970) 453-6018**
Breckenridge hosts a modest version of Mardi Gras, which consists of ceremonies around the village. Beads, costumes, and seafood abound on Fat Tuesday, usually in late February. Food and drink prices vary; everything else is free.

**Buffalo Bill's Birthday**
**The Buckhorn Exchange**
**1000 Osage Street**
**(303) 534-9505**
This is the first of Greater Denver's many annual celebrations of Buffalo Bill, a celebrated local citizen. The Mountain Man Association descends in full costume on The Buckhorn Exchange, Denver's oldest restaurant (see our Restaurants chapter), to celebrate Bill's February 26 birthday. Everybody at the restaurant dresses in costume, too. You can come for lunch or dinner, savor the color, and enjoy gunfights on the hour throughout the afternoon. Reservations are suggested for dinner, if you want to get a table.

**Buffalo Bill's Birthday Celebration**
**The Buffalo Bill Grave and Museum**
**987 1/2 Lookout Mountain Road, Golden**
**(303) 526-0747**
**www.buffalobill.org**
This celebration takes place on the grounds of the Buffalo Bill Museum on Lookout Mountain, where the buffalo meister's grave is located. Past celebrations included bluegrass music, free ice cream and cake, and a birthday ceremony. Buffalo Bill look-alikes lend atmosphere. This party is held on a weekend close to Bill's February 26 birthday.

Take I-70 west to exit 256, where the sign says LOOKOUT MOUNTAIN and BUFFALO BILL'S GRAVE, and follow the well-placed signs to the top of Lookout Mountain. The celebration is free.

# MARCH

**Denver Auto Show**
**Colorado Convention Center**
**700 14th Street**
**(303) 831-1691**
**www.denverautoshow.com**
Shop among, or just enjoy looking at, all the new cars under one roof. (No driving from lot to lot and being stalked by salespeople.) The show includes imports and domestics, sometimes exotics, futuristics, and prototypes. Attendance at this five-day affair in early March has exceeded 170,000. Plan to pay $10.00 at the door to get in, $2.00 for children age 6 to 12. Children 5 and younger are free.

**Colorado RV, Sports,**
**Boat and Travel Show**
**National Western Complex**
**4655 Humboldt Street (take the**
**Brighton Boulevard exit off I-70)**
**(303) 892-6800**
**www.bigasalloutdoors.com**
This is a general outdoor product show (mainly related to fishing and boating) with the largest display of RVs in the region. It's in early March. Adults pay $8.00, and kids younger than age 12 are admitted free.

**CHSAA State Basketball Tournament**
**Locations to be determined**
**(303) 344-5050**
**www.chsaa.org**
See the final competitions of Colorado's high-school basketball season. A perma-

nent venue for this event is still being sought. Tickets range from $5.00 to $10.00 per person.

### St. Patrick's Day Parade
### Streets of downtown Denver
### (303) 368-9861
### www.saintpatricksdayparade.com

This is big, folks, the second-largest St. Patrick's Day parade in the country (New York City is first). The devil, you say. Yes, it's true. It never seems to end. Past parades have taken more than four hours for 250 floats, bands, and other colorful entrants to pass as clowns, leprechauns, and vendors ply the awesome crowds of spectators. There are ancillary events during the entire week, including the Running of the Green, a 5-kilometer race, and Irish entertainment at various pubs throughout town.

### Denver March Pow-Wow
### Denver Coliseum
### 4600 Humboldt Street (take the
### Brighton Boulevard exit off I-70)
### (303) 934-8045
### www.denvermarchpowwow.org

Don't miss this one in mid- to late March. More than 1,000 Native Americans of tribes from most of the United States as well as Canada dance simultaneously in full costume. At the edges of the dancing, groups of men surround huge drums and make the whole coliseum vibrate. The big en masse dancing, the Grand Entry, happens Friday and Saturday at noon and 7:00 P.M. and Sunday at noon, with other activities scattered throughout those days. And you'll get plenty of opportunities to see the costumes close up: The seats around you will be filled with Native American families related to the dancers. Costumed competitors will be sitting next to you and walking past you.

There's a modest Native American market downstairs. Expect between 40 and 50 drum groups to be at the pow-wow, along with representatives of 60 to 70 tribes and a total three-day crowd in the neighborhood of 80,000 (not including children younger than age 6 and adults older than age 60, who get in free). For

everyone else, admission is about $6.00. If you plan to bring a video camera, you must purchase a permit. Video permits cost $30 for Friday, $20 for Saturday, and $10 for Sunday.

### Annual Spring Home & Patio Show
### National Western Complex
### 4655 Humboldt Street (take the
### Brighton Boulevard exit off I-70)
### (303) 892-6800, (800) 457-2434
### www.bigasalloutdoors.com

There's nothing like a nice trade show in late March to get you ready for spring. So get in the mood for cleaning and summer grooming of house and yard by visiting the 300 exhibitors of home and garden products and services. Adults get in for $8.00, seniors for $6.00, and kids younger than age 12 for free.

## APRIL

### Easter Sunrise Service
### Red Rocks Amphitheatre (north of
### Morrison on Hogback Road; take I-70
### West to the Morrison exit, then go
### south), Morrison
### www.redrocksonline.com

One of the most inspirational places you'll ever find for an Easter sunrise service is this gargantuan natural amphitheater of red sandstone facing east over the plains. The event is nondenominational, free, and open to the public, attracting upwards of 12,000 people. Gates open at 4:30 A.M., and music begins at 6:00 A.M. The service has been cancelled only five times in six decades due to weather.

### Spring Splash/Closing Day
### Winter Park Resort, Lower Hughes Ski
### Trail, Winter Park
### (970) 726-1564
### www.skiwinterpark.com

This is one of those events that public relations people love because they get to use the word "zany." In most years the sun is out, everybody wears sunglasses, and ski-babes in bikinis and ski-bozos in goofy costumes come barreling down the hill trying to hydroplane across a puddle of ice water. Most belly flop at the bottom with a big splash. The event is always held on the closing Sunday of the season (typically mid-April). It has become one of the quintessential Colorado outdoor spectacles, with viewers jockeying for position on the balconies of the base lodge. Spectating is free; participating will cost you a lift ticket plus an entry fee.

# MAY

## Furry Scurry
**Washington Park, East Louisiana Avenue and Downing Street**
**(303) 696-4941, ext. 379**
**www.ddfl.org**
This annual 2-mile walk/run for humans and their canines benefits the Denver Dumb Friends League. Participants register for a fee of about $45 and collect pledges as well. Dogs on leashes are welcome if they are at least six months old, have been spayed or neutered, and have current ID and rabies tags. Treats are available for people and their pets along the route and at the finish line. The event is usually held the first weekend in May.

## Cinco De Mayo
**Civic Center Park, between Colfax Avenue and 14th Street**
**(303) 534-8342**
**www.newsed.org/cinco.htm**
This is Denver's celebration of its Hispanic heritage, the largest of its kind in the United States, attracting more than 400,000 participants over two days in early May. Many confuse this with Mexican Independence Day, which is on September 16. Cinco de Mayo is held in remembrance of la Batalla de Puebla, the Battle of Ciudad Puebla, which took place during the Mexican battle for independence from France. Mexicans, equipped with little more than farm implements, whipped one of the greatest armies on Earth, although the French came back five days later and made

up for it. Still, it's a spiritual moment for Mexico and has become a big holiday in Denver. It starts with the Celebrate Culture parade, intended to celebrate diversity, and a traditional Mariachi mass in the park's Greek Amphitheater. Past celebrations included about 250 exhibitors, a carnival, arts and foods, entertainment on six stages, ethnic-fashionwear showings, and Latin, jazz, rap, and contemporary music. Activities are also provided for children. The event is free.

## Denver Botanic Gardens Plant and Book Sale
**Denver Botanic Gardens**
**1005 York Street**
**(720) 865-3500**
**www.botanicgardens.org**
The Gardens' annual plant and book sale serves as the unofficial start of the gardening season for hundreds of Denver-area green thumbs. It's one of the facility's most popular fund-raisers, offering thousands of flowers, herbs, and vegetables that are especially suited to Colorado's climate. Among the most popular in recent drought years are the water-smart plants, although regulars plan their beds around the large stock of annuals, roses, water plants, and perennials. Crowds can be fierce, especially during the first few hours of the sale, and parking is limited. Shuttle buses run continuously between the Church in the City parking lot, at 1530 Josephine Street, and the Gardens. Members can preview the sale at 8:30 A.M. Friday, with the public welcome after 10:00 A.M. Admission is free.

## KBCO/Miller Lite Kinetic Sculpture Challenge
**Boulder Reservoir**
**5100 North 51st Street, Boulder**
**(303) 444-5600**
**www.kbco.com**
This has become one of the biggest and most colorful spring events in the Denver area, and it's certainly the looniest event of its size. The hijinks at the Boulder Reservoir can attract as many as 20,000 specta-

tors. The kinetic conveyances, sometimes called kinetic sculptures, are crafts powered by human muscle. They must be capable of going on land and water; and at the Challenge, they are required to go through a mud pit as well. The competition is judged not just on speed, but also on creativity, team costumes, and team spirit. There's also a beach volleyball tournament, live music, and a food court. A warning: Expect a big crowd, small access roads that are often muddy, and limited parking. Carpooling is a good idea.

Many locals park in surrounding neighborhoods and bicycle in. Gates open at 6:30 A.M., and it's best to arrive early for best seating. A 5-kilometer race begins about 9:00 A.M., and the kinetic conveyance teams begin their race about 11:00 A.M. Live music and dancing last until about 2:30 P.M. Be sure to prepare for all kinds of weather, with rainproof gear as well as sunscreen, lots of water, and binoculars for viewing teams as they travel across the far side of the reservoir. No pets, cans, glass containers, tents, or boats are permitted. If you'd like to catch a shuttle to the reservoir, they are available from downtown Boulder. Call for details. Admission is $12 per person, plus another $10 to park your car or $40 to park an RV. The event is held the first Saturday of May, weather permitting.

## Boulder Creek Festival
**Central Park and the Library–Municipal Building Complex, Canyon Boulevard (along the Boulder Creek Path), Boulder (303) 652-4942**
**www.bouldercreekevents.com**
In 1984 a group of volunteers agreed to meet along the banks of Boulder Creek over Memorial Day weekend to pick up trash along the 5.5-mile corridor from Eben G. Fine Park to the intersection of Pearl and 55th Streets. Their reward was an after-party that became so popular it turned into the Boulder Creek Festival. Now the trash cleanup is held the Saturday before Memorial Day weekend and is followed by a three-day festival that attracts more than 400 exhibitors and

150,000 participants. Booths display arts and crafts, outdoor equipment and services, health alternatives, and technology. Performers dance and play music, and food and beverage vendors sell a wide range of edible treats. Admission and entertainment are free.

## Bolder Boulder
**First National Bank of Boulder**
**30th and Iris Streets, Boulder**
**(303) 444-RACE**
**www.bolderboulder.com**
Since 1979 the Bolder Boulder has been a Memorial Day tradition in this athletic college town. The 10K race that began with 2,700 participants has become one of the world's 10 largest road races. It now attracts more than 50,000 runners, walkers, and wheelchair racers, including professional racers who compete for the world's largest non-marathon prize purse. The largest group of entrants are the "citizens," who leave the starting line in 68 waves that take several hours to stage. Faster runners are assigned to the early waves and must qualify for them by proving they can run the course in 60 minutes or less. Slower participants, including walkers and walk/joggers, are assigned to the latter waves and feel free to cover the 6.8 miles at their own pace. The course winds its way through neighborhoods, around the downtown area, and into the University of Colorado's football stadium. Along the way, participants are cheered by more than 100,000 spectators who show their support by wearing costumes, belly dancing, spraying sweaty runners with a hose, and playing music of all types. (Don't be surprised to pass a formally

*Find specifics on festivals and events each week by looking at the Friday sections of the* Denver Post, Rocky Mountain News, *and Boulder's* Daily Camera. *Also check the events listings in Denver's weekly newspaper,* Westword.

dressed string quartet on one corner and a troupe of high-stepping grannies on the next.) The race starts at the north end of 30th Street near the First National Bank of Boulder and finishes in Folsom Field. Registration fees start at about $26 for adults who preregister and climb from there depending on how late you register and what kinds of race T-shirts or paraphernalia you'd like to include. Two things you should know: Baby strollers and Walkman-type music systems are not allowed, and local traffic slows to a standstill most of race day. On Memorial Day, study the race route and carefully plan any outings in Boulder that require you to drive.

## JUNE

**Hot Sounds at the Pavilions**
**Denver Pavilions**
**16th Street Mall between Tremont and**
**Welton Streets**
**(303) 260-6001**
**www.denverpavilions.com**
Catch an outdoor concert each Thursday evening from June through mid-July at the Denver Pavilions. Featuring top names on the local music scene, the concerts are free, with proceeds from the sale of food and drinks going to local charities such as the Children's Hospital. Music starts at 5:00 P.M.

**Capitol Hill People's Fair**
**Civic Center Park**
**Between Colfax Avenue and 14th Street**
**(303) 830-1651**
**www.peoplesfair.com**
Capitol Hill is one of Denver's most colorful and historic neighborhoods. The annual festival that raises money for its neighborhood organization has, for more than 30 years, been held on the first weekend in June. Organizers claim this event is Colorado's largest arts and crafts festival, with about 500 exhibitors as well as food, dance, and entertainment on six stages, and kids' activities such as putt-putt golf, face painting, and more. In past years it has attracted crowds of 275,000; admission is free.

**Compass Bank Elephant Rock**
**Cycling Festival**
**Douglas County Fair Grounds**
**Castle Rock**
**(303) 282-9020**
**www.elephantrockride.com**
With bike tours of various lengths—from the 8-mile family loop to the 25-mile fat-tire course to road bike routes of 32, 50, 65, and 100 miles—the Elephant Rock festival is a bicyclist's paradise. Held the first Sunday in June, the event begins and ends in the Douglas County Fair Grounds and sends participants down country roads and through rolling hills, across ranch lands, and through the Black Forest. The free Kids' Race is held on a special loop around the area. Entry fees are $50 for adults for the 100-, 65-, and 50-mile courses, $35 for the 32-, 25-, and 8-mile courses. Children younger than age 14 are charged $25 for any course. To reach the Fair Grounds, take Interstate 25 south from Denver to exit 181 east.

**Western Heritage Day and Burial**
**Commemoration**
**Buffalo Bill Grave and Museum on**
**Lookout Mountain**
**987 1/2 Lookout Mountain Road, Golden**
**(303) 526-0747**
**www.buffalobill.org**
This is a commemoration of Buffalo Bill's burial, one of the biggest events in Colorado history. Bill Cody died in January 1917. He lay in state in the Colorado State Capitol Building one weekend while 50,000 mourners and gawkers filed by. During the six months before he was buried, his body had to be embalmed six times. For his interment on June 3, next to what is now the Buffalo Bill Grave and Museum, 25,000 people walked or rode horses up the narrow Lookout Mountain Road. Bill had once said he wanted to be buried in Cody, Wyoming, a town he founded, and its residents thought that was a good idea. They threatened to steal the body, so Denver stationed a military tank at the grave. It was a colorful event, and today people make it a colorful cele-

*Sandwiched between City Hall and the State Capitol is Civic Center Park, the site of the annual Capitol Hill People's Fair.* DENVER METRO CONVENTION AND VISITORS BUREAU

bration. This free event, which includes entertainment and educational activities, is held on the weekend closest to June 3.

**Estes Park Wool Market**
**Stanley Park Fair Grounds, Community**
**Drive off U.S. Highway 36, Estes Park**
**(970) 586-6104**
**www.estesnet.com/Events/wool**
**market.htm**
Sheep ranching is a big part of Colorado's history and economy. This event, held the third weekend in June, is dedicated to those who raise and shear them. You'll find spinning and weaving classes; dyeing classes; showings of sheep, llamas, and alpacas; spinning and weaving demonstrations and contests; spinning wheels for sale; and commercial exhibits related to the wool industry. All events are free, but it costs $3.00 to park.

**Colorado Renaissance Festival**
**Off Interstate 25 South, Larkspur**
**(303) 688-6010**
**www.coloradorenaissance.com**
Renaissance festivals are ripping good fun, and this is truly one of the best. Spread out across a huge site beneath the trees, the festival re-creates a 16th-century marketplace filled with costumed characters and ruled by King Henry and Queen Anne. More than 200 costumed crafters sell handmade goods. One of the main attractions is the battling, strutting, and jousting by knights on foot and horseback. You'll also enjoy strolling minstrels, jesters, jugglers, medieval food, rides, and games galore for eight weekends in June and July. Admission is $16.95 for adults, $8.00 for children ages 5 to 10. From Greater Denver, take I-25 South to the Larkspur exit, then follow the signs to the festival.

**Opera Pops "An Evening with the Stars"**
**Ellie Caulkins Opera House**
**14th and Curtis Streets**
**(303) 292-6500**
A benefit for the Central City Opera, this event features the Festival Orchestra and International Cast of Artists in their only

Denver performance of the year. Tickets are available for just the performance of opera's "greatest hits" for $45, or there is a VIP dinner and ticket package for $135 per person or $250 per couple. The VIP package includes cocktails at 5:00 P.M. and dinner at 6:00 P.M., usually presented by one of Denver's great chefs, such as Kevin Taylor (2006), followed by the concert at 7:30 P.M.

**Breckenridge Music Festival**
**Riverwalk Performing Arts Center**
**Park Avenue and Four O'Clock Road**
**Breckenridge**
**(970) 547-3100**
**www.breckenridgemusicfestival.com**
Nearly every day from mid-June to mid-August, visitors can enjoy performances by the National Repertory Orchestra, the Breckenridge Music Festival Orchestra, and nationally know performers, such as the Glenn Miller Orchestra. More than 45 concerts showcase classical, jazz, show tunes, and children's music. Tickets for the regular performances run from $20 to $30 and are available in discounted packages.

**Juneteenth**
**Five Points Business District, Welton**
**Street (between 24th and 28th Streets)**
**(303) 832-3770**
**www.juneteenth.com**
A major festivity of Denver's African-American community, Juneteenth celebrates June 19, the day that slavery ended in the United States. For three days over Father's Day weekend, participants can choose from booths with food, arts and crafts, games, exhibits at The Black American West Museum (see our Tours and Attractions chapter), a senior luncheon, a large parade, a Sunday gospel fest, and more. The event is free.

**Summer Concert Series**
**Arvada Center for the Arts and Humanities**
**6901 Wadsworth Boulevard, Arvada**
**(720) 898-7200 (box office)**
**www.arvadacenter.org**
For a mixture of country, Big Band, jazz, and Cajun music, come to the Arvada

Center's outdoor amphitheater. You can picnic on the grounds before the shows and browse the art gallery. If you'd like, you may bring your picnic inside for the concert. The center also stages a musical every summer. Ticket prices range from $15 to $45 depending on the performer and your seating choice.

### Ride the Rockies
### Statewide, a different route every year
### (303) 820-1338
### www.ridetherockies.com

If you have thighs like a *Tyrannosaurus rex,* Ride the Rockies is for you. At the very least, participants should be experienced bike riders who are comfortable covering at least 50 miles a day. To enjoy the event, they also should be accustomed to riding at high altitudes and climbing mountain passes that leave small cars choking for air. This event lasts six to seven days, during which time a stream of about 2,000 bicyclists push their pedals for more than 400 miles. Past trips have taken them through such resort towns as Steamboat Springs, Telluride, Copper Mountain, and Vail and more "everyday" towns such as Walsenberg, Durango, Cortez, and Granby. At night they camp on high-school sports fields or in their gyms. Communities provide nightly low-cost meals and various forms of entertainment. Not everyone can take part. The event's title sponsor, the *Denver Post,* holds a lottery in February. If you win, you're in. The registration fee has been about $290 and includes camping space, restrooms and showers, transportation of one suitcase, a jersey, aid stations, and medical support.

### Summer Concerts
### Denver Botanic Gardens
### 1005 York Street
### (720) 865-3500 (information)
### (866) 468-7624 (tickets)
### www.botanicgardens.org

Sitting on the grass in the midst of the Denver Botanic Gardens on a summer evening is a great way to listen to world-class artists. Past performers have included Shawn Colvin, Arlo Guthrie, k.d. lang, Los Lobos, and Keb Mo. This series of outdoor concerts is aimed at families in an informal setting. Bring an elegant picnic and a blanket and you're set for a fun evening. Tickets range from $45 to $50.

### Scandinavian Midsummer Festival
### Bond Park
### Virginia Street and Elkhorn Avenue,
### downtown Estes Park
### www.estesmidsummer.com

June 24 is midsummer in the Scandinavian countries, which prompts their biggest celebration next to Christmas. Estes Park's version of the big, traditional Scandinavian festival features arts and crafts, ethnic foods, educational mini-seminars and demonstrations, and the raising of the maypole with appropriate Scandinavian folk dancers every hour. At least one dance group usually comes from Scandinavia. There's also a bonfire, which is how Norwegians celebrate midsummer. Not surprisingly, this free festival is held the Friday and Saturday closest to June 24. There's no phone number; so use the Web site listed for more information.

### Greek Festival
### Assumption Greek Orthodox Cathedral,
### 4610 East Alameda Avenue
### (303) 388-9314
### www.assumptioncathedral.org

Assumption Greek Orthodox Cathedral, with its gold dome, is a familiar landmark. Denver's Greeks and Grecophiles convene on the church grounds each year in mid-June for "wonderful food prepared by the ladies of our church," live music, and Greek dance shows done by groups ranging in age from children to adults. Calamari, Aegean beer, wine, and beverages are served, and there is usually a gift shop and a small carnival area for kids. All proceeds benefit the church. Admission is $1.00; the price for food and drink varies.

**Yellow Rose Ball: Opening Night**
**Central City Opera House**
**124 Eureka Street, Central City**
**(303) 292-6500**
**www.centralcityopera.org**
In late June or early July, the Central City
Opera's season begins, usually with the
annual presentation of the Central City
Flower Girls, followed by a dinner at the
Teller House and a performance. Tickets
for both are $275; for the performance
only, $50 to $90.

**Genuine Jazz Breckenridge Festival**
**Maggie Pond at the base of Peak 9 and**
**Main Street Station, Breckenridge**
**(866) 464-2626 (ticket sales)**
**www.genuinejazz.com**
Breckenridge's three-day, late-June jazz
festival features Colorado artists. Evening
sessions take place at local bars. Free daytime performances occur at Main Street
Station and at Maggie Pond, where a stage
is built over the water and spectators sit
on the shore. A weekend pass costs $69,
while single event tickets are $39.

**American Red Cross Fat Tire Classic**
**Locations throughout Winter Park and**
**Fraser Valley**
**(303) 722-7474**
**www.denver-redcross.org**
This two-day mountain-bike pledge ride is
held the last weekend in June to benefit
the American Red Cross. It's not a race;
it's just a tour, with events for all levels of
riders. You should be in shape, though.
Even the beginner's ride is a 15-mile off-
road event. You'll find gourmet food, live
musical entertainment on Saturday night,
prizes for different categories of riders,
and a raffle. Riders can pay the entire
$160 registration themselves or raise
money from pledges. Prizes are awarded
for raising pledges of $300 or more.

**Cherry Blossom Festival**
**Sakura Square, Lawrence Street**
**(between 19th and 20th Streets)**
**(303) 295-1844**
**www.tsdbt.org/cherryblossom**

This celebration of Japanese culture is
held at Sakura Square, the heart of Denver's Japanese community. If you love
Japanese food, check out the food made
by volunteers in the adjacent Denver
Buddhist Temple. Also watch martial arts
displays, bonsai demonstrations, taiko
drumming, poetry singing, and traditional
folk dancing. The festival, held in late
June or early July, is free and open to the
public. Food and beverages may be purchased.

## JULY

See June entries for:
**Hot Sounds at the Pavilions**

**Colorado Renaissance Festival**

**Summer Concert Series, Arvada Center**
**for the Arts and Humanities**

**Summer Concerts, Denver Botanic**
**Gardens**

**Breckenridge Music Festival**

**Race to the Clouds**
**Pikes Peak, outside Colorado Springs**
**(719) 685-4400**
**www.ppihc.com**
You can enjoy this famous annual Pikes
Peak hill climb even if you're not one of the
top race-car drivers who come here to test
their skills on one of Colorado's 14,000-
foot peaks. But you do need tickets ($35)
ahead of time to drive up, park, and watch
the race from designated areas on the
mountain. In preceding weeks other
smaller races lead up to this big race, held
the last week of June or first week of July.

**OBON: Gathering of Joy**
**Sakura Square, Lawrence Street**
**(between 19th and 20th Streets)**
**(303) 295-1844**
**www.tsdbt.org**
A gathering in honor of those who have
passed away, the OBON service is held in

the heart of the Japanese cultural and business center. The event is usually held in late June or early July.

## Cherry Creek Arts Festival
**Cherry Creek North (on Second and Third Avenues between Clayton and Steele Streets)**
**(303) 355-2787**
**www.cherryarts.org**
Pulling some 300,000 visitors for this event, Denver's upscale retail shopping area hosts a sidewalk festival during Fourth of July weekend that features fine arts and crafts. About 200 artists from around the nation and Mexico come for the juried show. National and international performers provide entertainment. Local chefs cook up their best for a block-long culinary-arts extravaganza. Browsing is free, but prepare to pay top dollar for the artworks.

## Independence Day Celebration
**Four Mile Historic Park**
**715 South Forest Street**
**(303) 399-1859**
**www.fourmilepark.org**
Four Mile Historic Park, Denver's living-history park, throws a good old-fashioned, family-style Fourth of July party each year. This is a day of patriotic music, games, food, and costumed actors who do historical reenactments. Past events also included historic and craft demonstrations such as blacksmithing, quilting, weaving, lace making, and butter churning. Admission is $7.00 per adult, $4.00 per child, age 5 and younger free.

## Drums Along the Rockies
**INVESCO Field at Mile High Stadium**
**(303) 424-6396**
This booming good time in mid- to late July is the annual regional drum and bugle corps championships. About ten of the best drum and bugle corps from the western United States and Canada compete in the Drum Corps Regional Championships, usually including four or five of the top-ranked corps in the world. Tickets range from $15 to $80 each.

## NHRA/PowerAde
**Mopar Mile-High Nationals**
**Bandimere Speedway**
**3051 South Rooney Road, Morrison**
**(303) 697-6001**
**www.bandimere.com**
This is motorhead heaven. Between 600 and 700 cars and the nation's top racers gather for three days of competition in pro-stock dragsters, top fuel cars, and nitro funny cars in mid-July. Tickets range from $15 to $47, and all seats are reserved.

## Alpine Artaffair
**King's Crossing, downtown, Winter Park**
**(800) 903-7275**
**www.skiwinterpark.com**
At this two-day, outdoor, judged and juried art event, you can expect about 90 booths exhibiting photography, oil painting, pottery, jewelry, and more. Live entertainment and craft demonstrations keep things upbeat at this third-weekend-in-July event. Admission is free.

## Buffalo Bill Days
**Locations throughout Golden**
**(303) 384-0003**
**www.buffalobilldays.com**
The city of Golden hosts this Western celebration, which started in Buffalo Bill's honor, on the last weekend of July. In past years it has included a parade and other activities on Main Street and in Parfet Park, 10th Street and Washington Avenue, and Clear Creek Living History Park. There has been musical entertainment, a golf tournament, country and western dance contests, living-history reenactments, a talent contest, 6K and 10K races, a burro race, and the Golden Derby for Young Racers. Admission is free.

## Cheyenne Frontier Days
**Frontier Park, Cheyenne, WY**
**(800) 227-6336**
**www.cfdrodeo.com**
This is a nine-day Western theme event centered around rodeo events, but it also includes a carnival, evening shows by some of the biggest names in country-

western music (in past years Toby Keith, Willie Nelson, Alan Jackson, and Chris LeDoux), parades, free pancake breakfasts, a chili cook-off, a performance by the Air Force Thunderbirds team, and a free entertainment area with music and other acts. Cheyenne is only 100 miles from Denver, so it makes an easy day trip. About 300,000 people show up during Frontier Days, but parking is generally no problem in the gravel lots around the stadium. The event starts on a Friday and runs through the last weekend in July. Rodeo tickets range from $11.50 to $22.00, night shows range from $28 to $50.00. To get to Frontier Park, take I-25 North to Central Avenue (exit 12). Go east on Eighth Avenue and turn right. After 0.25 mile, turn right onto Carey Avenue. The park is on your left.

**Rooftop Rodeo**
**Estes Park Fairgrounds**
**Community Drive off US 36**
**Estes Park**
**(970) 586-6104**
**www.estesnet.com**
A rodeo plain and simple, this six-day event in mid-July offers a rodeo parade and six Professional Rodeo Cowboy Association rodeos. On Western Heritage Day, these are joined by a mountain-man rendezvous, an Indian village, gold panning, and Western entertainment. Other past attractions include cowboy cartoonists and poets, a dirt dance, and concerts. The rodeo parade is free; the rodeo's admission ranges from $5.00 to $15.00.

**Weld County Fair**
**Island Grove Regional Park**
**425 North 15th Avenue, Greeley**
**(970) 356-4000, ext. 2085**
**www.co.weld.co.us/weldcountyfair/**
Weld County, north of Adams County, brings in the nation's fourth-largest amount of agricultural revenue, contains the world's two largest feedlots, and accounts for about a quarter of Colorado's agriculture. Its county fair, therefore, is the

real thing. It doesn't have a carnival midway, but it does have a lot of animal showings and competitions, including about 1,400 4-H and FFA kids, with an animal-catching contest, food booths, a fun fair, a concert night, a dance, and a livestock auction. The fair is free to the public.

# AUGUST

See June entries for:
**Summer Concert Series, Arvada Center for the Arts and Humanities**

**Summer Concerts, Denver Botanic Gardens**

**Breckenridge Music Festival**

**Adams County Fair and Rodeo**
**Adams County Fairgrounds**
**9755 Henderson Road, Brighton**
**(303) 637-8000**
**www.adamscountyfair.com**
Adams County claims the largest county fair in Colorado, and it has included such attractions as rodeos, tractor pulls, more than 150 exhibits and livestock shows, 4-H events, a children's pavilion, petting zoo, multicultural village, artisans bazaar, free entertainment, and top-name concerts. Past entertainers include Alan Jackson and Mel Tillis. There's also a Mexican Cultural Day at the fair. Look for this event the first weekend in August. Admission to the fair is free; parking costs $5.00. To reach the fairgrounds, take Interstate 76 north from Denver to U.S. Highway 85 (exit 12) and follow it north to Henderson Road. Turn left there.

**Colorado Scottish Festival and Highland Games**
**Highlands Heritage Park, 9651 South Quebec Street, Highlands Ranch**
**(303) 238-6524**
**www.scottishgames.org**
Wake up and smell the heather on the first weekend in August. Enjoy the competitions: bagpiping and drumming, highland

athletic events, and highland dancing. You'll also find vendors selling merchandise from the British Isles, exhibitions of highland cattle and dogs, and Scottish food and beverages. Admission is $12.00 for adults, $8.00 for seniors and children age 7 and older. Take C–470 east to Quebec Street and go south to the intersection with Lincoln Avenue. The park is on the southwest.

## The International at Castle Pines Golf Tournament
**Castle Pines Golf Club**
**1000 Hummingbird Drive, Castle Rock**
**(303) 660–8000, (800) 755–1986**
**www.golfintl.com**
One of the world's great courses hosts one of the most unusual and challenging tournaments of the year for the Professional Golf Association's best golfers from around the world. You're welcome to walk the holes with them, thrill to their mighty drives, and stand behind ropes at each hole and clap or moan as they sink or muff their putts. You can attend golfing clinics, and if the pros are good Joes, you may even be able to talk with them. This event is held during July 4th week. Daily tickets range from $20 to $48. Weeklong patron passes start at $150.

## Rocky Mountain Wine, Beer and Food Festival
**Winter Park Resort, Winter Park**
**(303) 316–1545**
**www.nscd.org/events/winebeerfood.htm**
Gourmet foods, fine wines, and tasty beers are featured at this event benefiting the National Sports Center for the Disabled. Highlighting the festival is a combined wine, beer, and food extravaganza on Saturday. Visitors can sample specialties from local restaurants to complement select vintages, while beer enthusiasts can choose from more than a hundred varieties—the perfect counterparts to bratwurst and barbecue. Seminars are offered before the tasting begins. Tickets cost about $40 each. Seminar tickets are extra. Three nights of festival dinners also

take place at designated Winter Park restaurants. Call ahead for a list of participating restaurants. You'll need to make your own reservations.

## Sculpture in the Park Show and Sale
**Benson Sculpture Garden**
**29th and Taft Streets, Loveland**
**(970) 663–2940**
**www.sculptureinthepark.org**
Loveland bills this as one of the largest outdoor juried exhibitions of sculpture in the United States. The Benson Sculpture Garden ordinarily is home to about 40 pieces, but on this day during the second weekend in August, it attracts about 180 artists from around the United States and Canada who show and sell their work. The event features entertainment, demonstrations by artists, a silent auction, and speed-sculpting (artists who sculpt while you watch). Proceeds from this event buy new art for the Sculpture Garden. Tickets are $5.00; children age 14 and younger are free.

## Douglas County Fair
**Douglas County Fairgrounds**
**410 Fairgrounds Road, Castle Rock**
**(720) 733–6900**
**www.douglas.co.us/eventscenter**
This is an old-fashioned August shindig with a rodeo, carnival, and all the accoutrements. Simultaneously with the county fair, Castle Rock holds a community fair that includes a parade to celebrate the 4-H winners, with more than 100 parade entries and a barbecue in the Courthouse Square.

## Western Welcome Week
**Various locations in Littleton**
**(303) 794–4870**
**www.westernwelcomeweek.com**
This is Littleton's big yearly celebration, which runs for 10 days beginning the second Thursday in August. You'll find arts and crafts and continuous entertainment on Littleton's Main Street, with a circus, a parade, concerts, fireworks, a barbecue, pancake breakfasts, and used-book sales. Most events are free.

**Kaiser Permanente Moonlight Classic**
**State Capitol**
**Broadway and Colfax Street**
**(303) 282-9020**
**www.moonlight-classic.com**
Imagine cycling through the deserted streets of downtown Denver with the glow of the moon defining the course for you. Imagine doing so alongside thousands of other riders. The Moonlight Classic begins and ends at the State Capitol. The 15-mile course (an 8-mile shortcut is also available) passes through the business district, LoDo, and by landmarks such as Coors Field and the Cherry Creek shopping district. The event benefits Seniors, Inc., and is followed by the Lunar Breakfast, a breakfast with music and prizes. The first wave of cyclists leave at 12:15 A.M., and all must have helmets and front and back lights and reflectors. Registration is $35.

**Carnation Festival**
**Albert E. Anderson Park, 44th and Field**
**Streets, Wheat Ridge**
**www.wheatridgecarnationfestival.org**
Wheat Ridge was founded by farmers who supplied Denver with wheat, produce, and, in the 1940s, carnations. The Carnation Festival celebrates that heritage with a jolly small-town parade along 38th Street from Harlan to Upham Streets on the third weekend in August. Some floats are covered with carnations, but most just carry bigwigs and their families. The carnival in the park has rides for children, and the carnival midway has food and arts and crafts. There's also a fireworks display on Friday night. Admission is free.

**Rocky Mountain Folks Festival**
**US 36, Lyons (on the way to Estes Park)**
**(800) 624-2422**
**www.bluegrass.com**
This festival in mid-August features folk-music performers, in the past including Warren Haynes, Indigo Girls, Norah Jones, and Dan Sheridan. There is also

the Song School, with workshops and activities geared toward future musicians, and a song seminar that includes sessions on songwriting, copyrighting, and bookkeeping. Tickets are $40 to $45 per day, and campsites are available for an additional fee.

**Gilpin County Historical Society's**
**Annual Cemetery Crawl**
**Various historic cemeteries in**
**Central City**
**(303) 582-5283**
**www.gilpinhistory.org**
Lend an ear to the living dead at this entertaining and educational event portraying the life of Gilpin County 100 years ago. Members and friends of the Gilpin Historical Society transform into "spirits" of former residents, leaders, and movers and shakers of the period. The spirits share their stories as visitors walk through a different historic cemetery each year in mid-August. Admission is $12.00.

**King of the Rockies**
**Mountain Bike Festival**
**Base of the Winter Park Ski Area,**
**Winter Park**
**(970) 726-1590, (303) 316-1590**
**www.epicsingletrack.com**
This festival in mid- to late August features races and guided tours for all levels of mountain bikers as well as a mountain-bike and summer-sports expo.

**Lakewood on Parade**
**Heritage Center at Belmar Park**
**Wadsworth Boulevard and Ohio Street,**
**Lakewood**
**(303) 987-7000**
**www.lakewoodonparade.com**
The city of Lakewood's community festival, this free event is held the weekend before Labor Day weekend. It typically combines food, games, entertainment, a parade, golf tournament, car show, and art show.

**River Run's Annual Wine, Jazz &
Art Festival
Keystone Resort
U.S. Highway 6, Keystone
(800) 354-4386
www.keystone.snow.com/**
In late August Keystone's River Run base
area remakes itself for a weekend of
smooth jazz, art, and wine tasting. Patrons
can sample more than 300 wines from
around the globe, and when they're not
attending food and wine seminars, they
can enjoy the music and meet the artists
whose works are for sale.

**Winter Park Famous Flamethrower's
High-Altitude Chili Cookoff
The Village, Winter Park
(800) 453-2525
www.skiwinterpark.com**
Held the last weekend in August, this two-
day event is an opportunity to sample different types of chili and salsa produced
especially for the cookoff. Costumed chili
chefs vie for the Flamethrower title and
the opportunity to represent the Rocky
Mountain region in the World Chili
Cookoff in Reno, Nevada. Guests can buy
tickets to sample entries after they have
been judged, at noon, 1:00, and 2:00 P.M.
each day. The event benefits the National
Sports Center for the Disabled.

**Colorado State Fair
State Fairgrounds
1001 Beulah Avenue, Pueblo
(719) 561-8484, (800) 876-4567
www.coloradosfair.com**
The city of Pueblo is two hours south of
Denver on I-25, but this is the state fair.
It's one of the state's largest annual events
and is well worth the drive. In addition to
the full range of rodeo events, expect
parades, art exhibitions, a Latin Fiesta
Weekend, livestock sales, horse shows,
cooking competitions, midway carnival
rides, games, and lots of good food. Big-
name entertainers in past years have
included Pat Benatar, Tom Jones, Chicago,
and Julio Iglesias. The fair runs for two

weeks, late August to early September.
General admission is $5.00 to $7.00. Tickets for concerts and rodeos are extra.

**Taste of Keystone
Keystone Village at Keystone Resort,
Keystone
(970) 496-4FUN, (800) 354-4386
www.keystone.snow.com**
Held in late August or early September,
the Taste of Keystone offers visitors the
chance to sample food from Keystone's
best restaurants. Food tickets are available at the event for $1.00 each; food is
one to four tickets.

# SEPTEMBER

**AIDS Walk Colorado
Cheesman Park, between Eighth and
13th Avenues east of Lafayette Street
(303) 837-0166, (303) 861-WALK
www.coloradoaidsproject.org**
Every year thousands of people converge
on Cheesman Park in late August or early
September to raise money for the Colorado AIDS Project and other AIDS
organizations throughout the state. From
there they follow a 10-kilometer walking
route that brings them back to the park
for an afternoon party. In 2006 a registration fee-based 5-kilometer run was
added to boost fund-raising opportunities. Volunteers are usually needed, along
with walkers.

**The Festival of Mountain and Plain:
A Taste of Colorado
Civic Center Park, between Colfax
Avenue and 14th Street
(303) 295-6330
www.atasteofcolorado.com**
One of Denver's largest annual gatherings,
A Taste of Colorado runs four days over
the Labor Day weekend and attracts more
than 400,000 people. Organizers usually
even block off a street or two. You can
sample culinary delights from more than
50 Greater Denver restaurants, so it's a

good way to find new restaurants dear to your tastes. In addition to the food, the festival offers entertainment on seven stages, kids' activities, cooking demonstrations, arts and crafts booths, a carnival midway, stages with live entertainment, and a kaleidoscope of buskers and vendors. Entertainment is free; food can be purchased with tickets.

### Colorado Springs Balloon Classic
**Memorial Park, Pikes Peak Avenue and Union Boulevard, Colorado Springs**
**(719) 471-4833**
**www.balloonclassic.com**
The Balloon Classic is a grand spectacle. Typically about 125 hot-air balloons from around the nation are invited to ascend en masse at 7:00 A.M. on Saturday, Sunday, and Monday of Labor Day weekend. They are preceded by the "dawn patrol," about five balloons going up at 5:30 A.M. and dangling strobe lights, just to let folks know that the big event is coming. About 50 balloons light up Saturday and Sunday nights in the "Balloon Glo." (Albuquerque trademarked the name "Balloon Glow," so the folks in the Springs had to drop the "w.") The Kiwanis Country Breakfast is served in a big tent from 5:30 to 9:30 each morning. Other regular events include a hula-hoop contest, a photo contest, a scavenger hunt, and evening concerts on Saturday and Sunday. Admission is free.

### Longs Peak Scottish-Irish Highland Festival
**In the Stanley Park area; evening events at various locations in Estes Park**
**(970) 586-6308**
**www.scotfest.com**
Held the weekend after Labor Day, the Highland Festival celebrates the Celtic tradition for four straight days—Thursday night through Sunday night—with performances and competitions by bagpipe bands, highland dancers, Irish step dancers, highland dogs herding sheep, and Scottish athletes throwing the hammer and the caber. There are parades, medieval reenactments and folk concerts, perfor-

mances on the Celtic harp, and fiddle and tin-whistle contests. Each year organizers schedule a special seminar topic such as Scots and the military. Expect a $20.00-per-day gate fee; $5.00 for kids.

### Castle Rock ArtFest
**Old Courthouse Square**
**301 Wilcox Street, Castle Rock**
**(303) 688-4597**
**www.castlerockartfest.com**
This arts festival is held in mid-September, with family entertainment, continuous musical performances, and food. It features more than 130 artists displaying, selling, and working in a full range of media. Admission is $4.00 for adults, $3.00 for seniors; children age 12 and younger are free.

### Summerset Festival
**Clement Park, Bowles Avenue and Pierce Street, South Jefferson County**
**(303) 973-9155**
**www.summersetfest.com**
This end-of-summer (second weekend after Labor Day) outdoor celebration generally draws more than 50,000 people. Events include hot-air balloons, a muscle car show, three stages of entertainment, a fishing derby, a pancake breakfast, a softball tournament, midway games, arts and crafts booths, and a skate festival. Admission is free.

### Gateway to the Rockies Parade and Festival
**Colfax Avenue, between Dayton and Florence Streets, Aurora**
**(303) 361-6169**
**www.aurorabusiness.org**
Each year in mid-September the city of Aurora likes to celebrate the end of summer by organizing a festival and parade through the city's original downtown area. The free party attracts about 15,000 participants and includes a morning farmers' market, afternoon musical entertainment, an all-day arts festival, food vendors, and such kids' activities as face painting and a petting zoo. The event gets its name from East Colfax Avenue, which is the original

U.S. Highway 40 leading into the Rocky Mountain area. Aurora was the first town that westbound visitors hit on their way into Greater Denver.

### Miniatures, Dolls & Toys Fall Show and Sale
### Hotel Denver Tech Center
### 7801 East Orchard Road
### Greenwood Village
### (303) 322-1053

This is a benefit for the Denver Museum of Miniatures, Dolls & Toys, though the show and sale is never held at the tiny museum. It typically includes more than 100 national artists who specialize in making miniatures, dolls, teddy bears, and toys. They display and sell their wares during a two-day weekend in mid-September. The sale is preceded by three days of workshops that are open to the public but require preregistration. Admission is usually $5.00.

### Mexican Independence Day
### Civic Center Park, between Colfax Avenue and 14th Street
### (303) 534-8342

Held in conjunction with the Mexican Consulate, this free event celebrates Mexican Independence Day, which is September 16. There is Latino entertainment including continuous live music, dancers, artists, and food vendors. Performances on the Civic Center's Greek Amphitheater stage usually crank up around 6:00 P.M. Also look for international handcrafted items, an artists' gallery, an Aztec market, and children's games.

### Breckenridge Festival of Film
### Various locations in Breckenridge
### (970) 453-6200
### www.breckfilmfest.com

This four-day fest in mid-September includes premieres of documentaries, feature films, and children's features as well as parties in local clubs and bars. Past years have seen visits by James Earl Jones, Mary Steenburgen, Elliott Gould, and Angie Dickinson. The Peak Ten Pass costs $199 and includes admission to all the films and

events, plus a festival T-shirt. The Peak Nine Pass goes for $149 and gets you into all the films. Or you can opt for a four-punch pass for $34 or individual film tickets for $10.

### Oktoberfest
### Larimer Square, Larimer Street
### (between 14th and 15th Streets)
### (303) 534-2367
### www.oktoberfestdenver.com

Denver's main bow to the famous harvest festival of Munich (and the nation's second-largest Oktoberfest celebration, according to sponsors) is filled with polka bands and beer-drinking and sausage-eating fun. You'll see plenty of jolly Germanic costumes. One of the highlights of Larimer Square's festival year, this event is free unless you eat and drink. Oktoberfest includes Kinderplatz, a kids' area that has included Prince Ludwig's Castle, where kids can enjoy the Black Forest Maze and German storytellers, "the world's shortest parade," and more than 100 opportunities to do the Chicken Dance. The festival is usually held for four days in mid-September.

*Dancers entertain at the Oktoberfest celebration in Larimer Square.* DENVER METRO CONVENTION AND VISITORS BUREAU

# Nature's Annual Events

Nature puts on her own annual events: the changing of the aspen in the fall, which draws Denverites out of the city to high-country roads; the ritual of elk bugling from mid-September to mid-October at Rocky Mountain National Park; and the blooming of a sea of irises at Long's Iris Garden, 3240 Broadway, Boulder, in late May/early June, where you can gaze, photograph, or dig your own clumps for a reasonable price.

**Spanish Market and 1840s Rendezvous**
**The Fort Restaurant**
**19192 Colorado Highway 8, Morrison**
**(303) 697-4771**
**www.thefort.com**
The last week in September, Morrison's unique Fort Restaurant opens its gates to a quintessentially Western event. Fine Spanish artists from Colorado and New Mexico gather on the grounds to display and sell their creations. They're joined by reenactors dressed as 1840s traders and interpreters for a weekend of entertainment, storytelling, competition, and dancing. A patron preview party is held on Friday night, followed by the market on Saturday and Sunday. To get to the Fort from downtown Denver, take I-70 west to C-470 (exit 260). Follow C-470 south to U.S. Highway 285 south (Fairplay exit), then go 1.5 miles to the Highway 8 Morrison exit. The Fort is on the right.

**Great American Beer Festival**
**Colorado Convention Center**
**700 14th Street**
**(303) 447-0816**
**www.beertown.org**
This is America's biggest beer bash, usually held in late September or early October. Bring an ID that proves you are at least 21 and a designated driver because there are more than 1,600 beers to taste, the product of some 300-plus American breweries, microbreweries, and brewpubs. Tickets run about $35 per session.

## OCTOBER

**Rocky Mountain Snowmobile Expo**
**Denver Merchandise Mart, off I-25**
**at 58th Avenue exit**
**(303) 892-6800**
**www.bigasalloutdoors.com**
Snowmobiles are one way of enjoying snow, so you may want to check out the latest in snowmobiles and accessories and snowmobile services and travel destinations. Admission to the event, held in early October, is $8.00 for adults; kids younger than age 12 are free.

**Fall Crafts Bazaar**
**Eastridge Recreation Center**
**Highlands Ranch**
**(303) 791-8958**
This crafts show in early October features more than 100 artists. You'll find a crafts bazaar, entertainers and exhibitors, a pumpkin-carving contest, food, and kids' activities.

**Great Pumpkin Harvest Festival**
**Four Mile Historic Park**
**715 South Forest Street**
**(303) 399-1859**
**www.fourmilepark.org**
Usually held in early October, this event takes place in the park's 12-acre historic farm. Activities include old-time music, dancing, hayrides, and scarecrow making. The event is free, and pumpkins are available for sale.

**Cider Days Harvest Festival**
**Lakewood's Heritage Center, 797 South**
**Wadsworth Boulevard, Lakewood**
**(303) 987-7850**
In the early 20th century, apple trees were so common in Lakewood that the area was called Cider Hill. On the first weekend in October, the town celebrates its heritage with demonstrations of cider making, antique farm machinery, a vintage tractor-pull competition, food vendors, and live music.

**Pumpkin Festival at Chatfield**
**Nature Preserve**
**8500 Deer Creek Canyon Road**
**Littleton**
**(303) 973-3705**
**www.botanicgardens.org**
Bring a wheelbarrow and pick your own pumpkin(s) from the pumpkin patch. From tennis-ball size to behemoth, the sale of these orange globes raises money for the arboretum. There are also hay-rack rides and crafts and food booths. This event is usually the second Saturday in October and costs $5.00 per adult, $3.00 per child. (The pumpkin is extra.) Take C-470 to the Wadsworth exit, then follow Wadsworth south to Deer Creek Canyon Road. Turn right; the entrance is 0.25 mile down on the left.

**Annual Ski and Sport Extravaganza**
**Winter Park (exact location determined**
**a month before the event)**
**(970) 726-1590**
**www.skiwinterpark.com**
Winter is knocking at the door. Here's a chance to get new and used equipment, clothing, and accessories—anything related to skiing or snowboarding—and a chance to dump your old stuff. Ski shops from around the Rocky Mountain region put their goods on sale in mid-October and proclaim, "Outstanding bargains with prices reduced up to 60 percent." Guys and gals just like you will be selling their equipment, and you can, too. Just check in several days before the sale starts. If you're shopping rather than selling, the Friday evening preview fee is minimal; Saturday and Sunday are free.

**Victorian Horrors**
**Molly Brown House Museum**
**1340 Pennsylvania Street**
**(303) 832-4092**
**www.mollybrown.org**
This is a nice way to see the house once owned by Colorado's "Unsinkable Molly Brown." As visitors tour the house during mid-October, they encounter costumed characters reading selected bits from horror writers like Mary Shelley, Bram Stoker, and Edgar Allan Poe. There are refreshments in the carriage house. The cost is $16 for adults and $13 for seniors and kids.

**Boo at the Zoo**
**Denver Zoo in City Park**
**East 23rd Avenue and Steele Street**
**(303) 376-4800**
**www.denverzoo.org**
Celebrate Halloween at the zoo on the last weekend in October. Trick-or-treat doors are set up throughout the zoo, and kids get a food or toy item at each door. There is also a medieval village offering storytelling and face painting. The event is free with paid admission to the zoo, which is $9.00 for adults, $7.00 for seniors, $5.00 for kids ages 3 to 11, and free for kids younger than age 3.

# NOVEMBER

**Starz Denver International Film Festival**
**Various Denver locations**
**(303) 595-3456**
**www.denverfilm.org**
This 10-day festival showcases more than 175 top feature, documentary, and short films from around the world, screened at the Starz FilmCenter in the Tivoli Center, at the Buell Theatre at 14th and Curtis Streets, and at the King Center, on the Auraria Campus. They're all located downtown. Usually held the second week in November, it draws a host of actors, directors, and producers. Previous festivals have drawn

celebrities such as Robert Altman, Geena Davis, Sean Penn, and Shirley MacLaine. After some film showings, enjoy a question-and-answer session with the director, producer, actors, or others involved in the film's genesis. Call for ticket information.

### L'Esprit de Noel
**Locations in Denver vary each year**
**(303) 292-6500**
**www.centralcityopera.org**
Each year the Central City Opera Guild stages this fund-raiser to support the opera's education and community programs. Local florists donate their time to decorate upscale homes for the holiday season, then open the finished products for three days of tours. It's held the weekend before Thanksgiving, featuring homes in high-end developments. The event is kicked off with a patron preview party, then is opened to the public. Tickets are $18 at the door, $16 at King Soopers stores or from guild members.

### Starlighting
**Old Courthouse Square**
**301 Wilcox Street, Castle Rock**
**(303) 688-4597**
**www.castlerock.org**
The annual lighting of the Christmas star on top of Castle Rock, the monolith that towers above the city of Castle Rock has been going on since 1936. It goes along with a ceremony in Courthouse Square that includes carolers, Santa, and hot chocolate. It is followed by a fire-department-sponsored chili supper and dance (indoors), all on the Saturday before Thanksgiving. Everything is free except the chili, which will only set you back a couple of dollars.

### Winterfest
**Larimer Square, Larimer Street**
**(between 14th and 15th Streets)**
**(303) 534-2367**
**www.larimerarts.org/e_winterfest**
Starting just before Thanksgiving and running through the month of December, this festivity attracts the diehards who believe cold weather is another excuse to have

fun. Expect a square lighting ceremony, as well as a holiday concert and appearances by Dickens's Christmas characters. In a slightly wacky vein, 350 tuba players provide a little music. Every tuba is decorated for the holiday season.

### Come-Catch-the-Glow Christmas Parade
**Through downtown Estes Park**
**(970) 586-4431**
**www.estesnet.com/events**
The Christmas season starts the Friday after Thanksgiving in this mountain town. Start off this free event by visiting with Santa and various character animals, then watch the evening light parade.

### Wild Lights
**The Denver Zoo in City Park**
**East 23rd Avenue and Steele Street**
**(303) 376-4800**
**www.denverzoo.org**
This memorable family event begins the day after Thanksgiving and runs through December, from 5:00 to 9:00 P.M. Thousands of sparkling lights strung on trees create Christmas light sculptures of colored animals. There's nightly entertainment, storytelling, holiday refreshments, and an appearance by Santa Claus (until Christmas). Amid all the lights, it's fun to visit the animals and see what they do with their time on a winter night. Be aware that some of the animals are not out, but the seals and sea lions often make visitors laugh with their antics. Admission is $7.00 adults, $6.00 seniors, $4.00 children ages 3 to 11. Children age 2 and younger are free.

### Botanic Gardens Holiday Sale
**Denver Botanic Gardens**
**1005 York Street**
**(720) 865-3500**
**www.botanicgardens.org**
Plants are for sale as well as herbs, oils, and vinegars that volunteers have been producing all yearlong. Ornaments are crafted and purchased. You'll also find books on gardening, tools, and other botany-related subjects. Held toward the

end of November, the sale is free, as is admission to the gardens.

# DECEMBER

**Wild Lights**
See November entry.

**Holiday High Teas**
**Molly Brown House**
**1340 Pennsylvania Street**
**(303) 832-4092**
**www.mollybrown.org**
Held on select dates throughout December and early January, the teas are traditional in their offerings of sandwiches, pastries, scones, and hot tea. Cost is $23 per person and includes a tour of the home. Call the number given here for specific dates and reservations.

**LoDo Holiday Lighting of Union Station**
**17th and Wynkoop Streets**
**(303) 628-5428**
**www.lodo.org**
Join as many as 3,500 people as they gather to watch the lighting of Union Station on the Wednesday after Thanksgiving. The LoDo district is seeking to expand coverage and promotion, making this a bigger event each year. Already it is a favorite among local residents.

**World's Largest Christmas**
**Lighting Display**
**City and County Building, between**
**Colfax Avenue and 14th Street (across**
**from Civic Center Park)**
**(720) 913-4900**
**www.denvergov.org**
If light were music, the Denver City and County Building would be the world's largest pipe organ. About 30,000 flood-lights turn this huge government building into one big neon sign. It has become a Denver holiday tradition to walk around and ogle on a frosty winter evening. Bundle up the kids. The display is up from the first Thursday in December until mid-January, after the National Western Stock

Show has finished its run (see January entry).

**Olde Golden Christmas**
**Throughout downtown Golden**
**(303) 279-3113**
**www.goldencochamber.org**
Golden may be growing, but it's still one of the last Greater Denver communities with a real small-town feel about it. And here's an old-fashioned, small-town Christmas festival. Holiday festivities begin the first Friday in December with candlelight walks through downtown Golden. Everybody carries a candle and files down to Clear Creek to see the tree lights ignited. Santa Claus shows up. In the past the event has featured a clog-ging dance troupe and dancing kids. The first three Saturdays of the month are cel-ebrated with Christmas carolers, sleigh rides, carriage rides, reindeer, and cookie decorating as well as hot chocolate, cookies, and candy. At the Clear Creek Living History Ranch, in restored cabins from the turn of the 20th century, folks serve up cowboy beans, doughnut holes, coffee, and great entertainment. At the Pioneer Museum, 923 10th Street, there's live musical entertainment, hot cider, cookies, and a big bonfire.

**Parade of Lights**
**Streets of downtown Denver**
**www.denverparadeoflights.com**
This is truly one of the great public events of Denver's calendar: a night parade that lasts more than an hour and features floats, clowns, marching bands, and giant balloon figures, all lit up or fes-tooned with lights. The whole event is one big Roman candle of multicolored holiday illumination. The crowds are big enough that special shuttles run into downtown from select bus stations. Check with RTD for schedules. You might consider bringing extra wraps, blankets, and a thermos of something hot and comforting. And as with all parades, if you want to position a folding chair for a front-row seat, get there an hour before

the show. The parade is held the first Friday and Saturday night in December.

## Handel's *Messiah*
**Boettcher Concert Hall**
**14th and Curtis Streets**
**(303) 893-4100**
**www.coloradosymphony.org**
Holiday music lovers adore this one: classic Christmas music with the Colorado Symphony Orchestra and the Colorado Symphony Chorus performing Handel's *Messiah*. This is typically held the first or second weekend in December. Call for ticket prices.

## Christmas with Cody
**Buffalo Bill Grave and Museum**
**987 1/2 Lookout Mountain Road, Golden**
**(303) 526-0747**
**www.buffalobill.org**
This is the museum's free early-December Christmas event. Santa Cody rides in on his white horse to present gifts to all the good little cowpokes. Holiday music and crafts add to the festivities.

## A Colorado Christmas
**Four Mile Historic Park**
**715 South Forest Street**
**(303) 399-1859**
**www.fourmilepark.org**
Find an old-fashioned Christmas atmosphere at Four Mile Historic Park during this two-Saturday affair in mid-December. St. Nick, or Father Christmas, will be there; Christmas music will be performed; and bobsled rides (if snow conditions permit) will be offered along with crafts, activities, food, and drink. The cost is $7.00 per adult, $4.00 per child age 6 to 15 and seniors, free for children age 5 and younger.

## Blossoms of Lights
**Denver Botanic Gardens**
**1005 York Street**
**(720) 865-3500**
**www.botanicgardens.com**
During the month of December, the Denver Botanic Gardens does for plants what the Denver Zoo does for animals (see November listing). There are giant flowers of Christmas lights and lights draped all over plants and other objects. There's nothing more invigorating than a stroll through a wonderland of lights on a frosty evening, and this event provides a different way of seeing Denver's beloved Botanic Gardens. Nightly entertainment is included, along with holiday refreshments.

## A Colorado Christmas
**Boettcher Concert Hall**
**14th and Curtis Streets**
**(303) 893-4100**
**www.coloradosymphony.org**
This is a benchmark in our year, a favorite way to celebrate the Christmas season. The concert, usually held in late December, features the Colorado Symphony Orchestra, the Colorado Symphony Chorus, and the Colorado Children's Chorale. Tickets run from $5.00 to $55.00.

## Christmas Eve Torchlight Parade
**Winter Park Resort, Winter Park**
**(970) 726-1564**
**www.skiwinterpark.com**
On Christmas Eve guests begin by caroling around a bonfire at the base of the mountain. Santa Claus then leads a procession of torchbearers on skis as they make their way down Lower Hughes Trail. Their progress is punctuated with a fireworks display, followed by a nondenominational church service. Also on Christmas Eve, the mountaintop Lodge at Sunspot stays open for an elegant holiday dinner. Seating begins at 6:00 P.M., and reservations are required; call (970) 726-1446.

# THE ARTS

We admit it. We love Denver's cultural scene. In fact there aren't enough hours in a weekend to do all we'd like. We are richly rewarded both in and out of official venues.

In addition to theaters and theater companies, we've compiled a large section of art galleries in this chapter as well as a section on art museums (for other museums, see our Tours and Attractions chapter). And given that one person's definition of culture may overlap with another person's idea of popular entertainment, check our Nightlife chapter, too. Movie houses and bars and restaurants with music or other kinds of entertainment are in our Nightlife chapter.

In this chapter we begin by describing the Denver Performing Arts Complex. Next we describe performing groups, theaters, theater companies, dinner theaters, and popular music venues. We move on to visual arts found in Greater Denver's art museums, community art centers, and art galleries. Finally, we detail the literary arts by describing the many writers' organizations in town.

## PERFORMING ARTS

**Denver Performing Arts Complex**
**Speer Boulevard and Arapahoe Street**
**(303) 893–4100, (800) 641–1222**
**www.denvercenter.org**
The Denver Performing Arts Complex, a 4-block, 12-acre site, boasts more than 11,260 seats in nine performance venues and is the largest complex in the nation in terms of the number and variety of performance spaces, the number and size of support facilities, and the variety of activities taking place. It is second only to New York's Lincoln Center in terms of seating capacity.

Performances are offered by many tenants, the largest of which is the **Denver Center for the Performing Arts** (DCPA). In addition to Broadway touring shows and the region's largest resident professional theater company, the complex houses a state-of-the-art television, video, and recording production facility; offers the nation's only congressionally chartered graduate acting school; and conducts research with the world's only voice research laboratory associated with a performing arts center. Other tenants of the complex include the Colorado Symphony, Colorado Ballet, Colorado Children's Chorale, and Opera Colorado, all of which are described here. Tickets to all of the tenants' performances may be purchased by calling the numbers above.

The largest theater in the complex is the **Temple Hoyne Buell Theatre,** which opened in 1991 and has 2,830 seats. **Boettcher Concert Hall,** a unique 2,634-seat concert-hall-in-the-round, dates from 1978. The **Ellie Caulkins Opera House** is a grand old (1908) European-style theater with 2,268 seats. It was completely renovated in 2005.

The **Helen Bonfils Theatre Complex,** built in 1979, houses four smaller theaters. **The Stage** (770 seats) is a thrust stage; **The Space** is theater-in-the-round (well, it's actually more of a pentagon) with 427 seats; the **Ricketson Theatre** is a 250-seat informal proscenium; and the Jones Theatre, with 200 seats, is an intimate experimental thrust stage. The **Donald R. Seawell Grand Ballroom,** named for DCPA's chairman of the board, opened in 1998. The 10,000-square-foot glass-and-steel ballroom has a maximum capacity of 1,029 people, and it can accommodate a variety of functions with smaller configurations. Also in the complex is the **Garner Galleria Theatre,** which presents cabaret shows.

At intermission patrons spill out into the high, arched, glass-ceilinged galleria to stretch their legs and get some fresh air (or, conversely, to smoke a cigarette). The unique ceiling connects the diverse theaters.

**Denver Center Attractions, a division of the Denver Center for the Performing Arts**
**Speer Boulevard and Arapahoe Street**
**(303) 893-4100 or (800) 641-1222 (tickets), (303) 893-4000 (information)**
Broadway musical hits such as *Big River* and the national touring premiere of *The Lion King* make Denver Center Attractions a preferred stop on the touring circuit. The division is also known for its own productions of cabaret musicals including *Forever Plaid* and Denver's longest-running production, *Always . . . Patsy Cline*.

**Denver Center Theatre Company, a division of the Denver Center for the Performing Arts**
**Speer Boulevard and Arapahoe Street**
**(303) 893-4100 or (800) 641-1222 (tickets), (303) 893-4000 (information)**
The Denver Center Theatre Company, recipient of the 1998 Tony Award for Outstanding Regional Theatre, is the region's largest resident professional theater company and features an 11-play season, including traditional and contemporary drama and world premieres.

*Don't let the names confuse you. The Denver Performing Arts Complex is the city-owned facility that is rented by various performance companies. The complex comprises nine performance theaters offering more than 10,000 seats. The Denver Center for the Performing Arts is an organization that presents and produces Broadway touring shows and live theater through its two companies: Denver Center Attractions and the Denver Center Theatre Company.*

# Music

### Colorado Children's Chorale
**2420 West 26th Avenue, Suite 350-D**
**(303) 892-5600**
**www.childrenschorale.org**
The Colorado Children's Chorale, a 400-member chorus that tours nationally and internationally, celebrated its 32nd anniversary in 2006. Each year it joins the Colorado Symphony Orchestra for a very special, very popular holiday concert. It started with 50 members and now involves 20,000 children each year through its outreach program.

### Colorado Symphony Orchestra
**821 17th Street, Suite 700**
**(303) 893-4100**
**www.coloradosymphony.org**
The Colorado Symphony Orchestra, with 80 members, plays classical music and popular classics in Boettcher Concert Hall during its season, which lasts from September to May. Each season there are also several low-priced Sunday-afternoon concerts.

### Denver Brass/Aries Brass Quintet
**2253 Downing Street**
**(303) 832-4676**
**www.denverbrass.org**
Formed in 1981, the 12-member Denver Brass is one of very few symphonic brass ensembles in the country. Concerts feature something for everyone, from splendid brass fanfares to Big Band music. Performances, including an annual Christmas concert, are held at the Auditorium Theatre, Boettcher Concert Hall (both part of the performing arts complex), and Bethany Lutheran Church, 4500 East Hampden Avenue.

Also under the same management is the Aries Brass Quintet. Founded in 1976, Aries has toured the United States, Europe, and South America; performed its fresh and vibrant renditions of chamber music live on National Public Radio; and recorded several albums. Aries is a resident company at St. John's Episcopal Cathedral in

Denver, 1313 Clarkson Street, and at the Lamont School of Music at the University of Denver.

### Denver Young Artists Orchestra
**2828 North Speer Boulevard, Suite 230**
**(303) 433-2420**
**www.dyao.org**
The Denver Young Artists Orchestra was formed in 1977 as a means for Colorado's talented young musicians (ages 12 to 23) to rehearse and perform under professional standards. The orchestra plays three concerts each year in Boettcher Concert Hall, including a joint concert with the Colorado Symphony.

### Opera Colorado
**695 South Colorado Boulevard, Suite 20**
**(303) 357-2787 (tickets)**
**(303) 778-1500 (office)**
**www.operacolorado.org**
Opera Colorado presents three grand operas each winter and spring, all performed at the new Ellie Caulkins Opera House. "The Ellie" used to be the Denver Auditorium Theatre, which was renovated into a state-of-the-art performance venue featuring world-class acoustics and four levels of seating. Performances are sung in the original language, but patrons are treated to seat-back titling at every seat in the house, in one of only three opera houses nationwide, nine worldwide, that provides such an amenity. Opera Colorado also performs at special holiday concerts and summer festivals throughout the state. The Opera Colorado for Children program includes children's opera workshops, matinee performances for students, and an in-school puppet opera.

## Dance

### Cleo Parker Robinson Dance
**119 Park Avenue West**
**(303) 893-4100 (tickets)**
**(303) 295-1759 (office)**
**www.cleoparkerdance.org**
Cleo Parker Robinson Dance is a multi-cultural performing arts institution with a professional modern dance company and a dance school based in a historic African Methodist Episcopal Church. The ensemble performs regularly in Denver and extensively around the country and is one of the city's best-known exports in the arts field.

### Colorado Ballet
**1278 Lincoln Street**
**(303) 893-4100 (tickets)**
**(303) 837-8888 (office)**
**www.coloradoballet.org**
The Colorado Ballet was established as the Colorado Concert Ballet in 1961. The resident company of 31 dancers is under the artistic direction of Gil Boggs and is the only dance company in the state to perform with a live orchestra. Its repertoire includes full-length classical and one-act ballets. Performances are held in either the Buell Theatre or Ellie Caulkins Opera House from fall through spring. In 1993 the company made its exciting New York debut and was praised by *New York Times* dance critic Anna Kisselgoff for its "surprising maturity, presence and solid technique of its performers."

### David Taylor Dance Theatre
**1760 Glen Moor Drive**
**Lakewood**
**(303) 789-2030**
**www.dtdt.org**
David Taylor Dance Theatre, which marked its 25th season in 2004, is Denver's foremost professional contemporary ballet company. In addition, it's one of the region's major presenters of *The Nutcracker,* which is performed annually at the Lakewood Cultural Center and on tour throughout the state and the country. The main focus of the company, however, is original contemporary works. The *Rainforest Ballet* is one of its most popular productions. Although the company is headquartered in Lakewood, where it offers ballet classes for children and adults, it performs in different venues throughout Greater Denver from September through May.

**Kim Robards Dance**
**1379 South Inca Street**
**(303) 825-4847**
**www.kimrobardsdance.org**
Kim Robards Dance was established in 1987 as the Colorado Repertory Dance Company and is an important center for modern dance in Colorado. The dynamic collection of works in the company's repertoire includes pieces by artistic director Kim Robards along with works by selected international guest choreographers. The professional touring company, which consists of 8 to 10 dancers, has performed in New York and California, among other places. Locally the company presents a winter and spring season at different venues in metro Denver, along with a statewide educational outreach program. Its school, established in 1990, offers classes for beginners (ages 4 to adult) and professionals.

# Theaters and Theater Companies

### Aurora Fox Arts Center
**9900 East Colfax Avenue, Aurora**
**(303) 739-1970**
From fall to spring the Aurora Fox Arts Center is home to the Aurora Fox Theatre Company and the Aurora Fox Children's Theatre Company. The adult theater company mounts five major productions each season, including musicals such as *You're A Good Man Charlie Brown* and dramatic classics such as *Death of a Salesman.*

### Denver Civic Theatre
**721 Santa Fe Drive**
**(303) 309-3773**
**www.denvercivic.com**
The Denver Civic Theatre has been in its present location on Santa Fe Drive since 1991. The Arts Theatre stages well-known plays, including Broadway musicals and original works, year-round. The building was built in 1923 as a movie theater and over the years has been used for many

different purposes—it was a meatpacking plant in the 1950s and 1960s and later a photographer's studio. Now it houses two theaters: a main stage proscenium with 285 seats and an intimate black-box theater that seats 104. The Denver Civic Theatre was renovated in 2003.

Continuing programs at the Arts Theatre of the West include a theater series for children and a school touring program.

### Denver Victorian Playhouse
**4201 Hooker Street**
**(303) 433-4343**
**www.denvervictorianplayhouse.com**
The Denver Victorian Playhouse in northwest Denver is a restored and refurbished 1911 house with a 75-seat theater. Children's shows and a full range of adult comedies, dramas, and musicals are performed here year-round.

### El Centro Su Teatro
**4725 High Street**
**(303) 296-0219**
**www.suteatro.org**
El Centro Su Teatro was formed in 1971 by students at the University of Colorado at Denver as a forum for those interested in the Chicano civil rights movement. It has grown into a multidisciplinary cultural-arts center that sponsors concerts, drama, performance art, dance, festivals, workshops, and art exhibitions. Theater performances emphasize original works by Chicano and Latino playwrights, including Su Teatro's director Tony Garcia. El Centro Su Teatro is housed in a former elementary school.

### The Center for American Theatre at Historic Elitch Gardens
**Tennyson Street and West 38th Avenue**
**(no phone or Web site yet)**
Until about 1990 the historic Elitch Theatre was a Denver landmark. After Elitch Gardens amusement park moved to Denver's Central Platte Valley in 1994, the venerable theater sat vacant for more than a decade. In 2006 a $14.2 million renovation was begun, and by 2008 the building will begin its second lifetime as a playhouse

and community resource center. In the meantime it is being used year-round for music, dance, and film programming. The Elitch Theatre was built in 1891, modeled after Shakespeare's original Globe Theater, and welcomed big name stars such as Douglas Fairbanks, Sarah Bernhardt, Vincent Price, Edward G. Robinson, and Grace Kelly over the years. It stopped operating as a summer-stock company in 1963 and switched to single performances. In 1991 it closed completely.

### Festival Playhouse
**5665 Old Wadsworth Boulevard, Arvada**
**(303) 422-4090**
**www.festivalplayhouse.com**
There's plenty of history behind the Festival Playhouse. The Denver Players Guild, formed in 1936, stages eight plays a year—primarily Broadway comedies—in this converted Grange building in Olde Town Arvada. The Players Guild believes it is the oldest community theater group in the country under the same family management, and the playhouse is even older. Built in 1874, it's the second-oldest standing Grange hall in Colorado and the oldest building in the city of Arvada.

### Germinal Stage Denver
**2450 West 44th Avenue**
**(303) 455-7108**
**www.germinalstage.com**
Germinal Stage Denver was founded by four Denver actors in 1973, making it one of the longest-living small theaters in the region. Performances are held in an air-conditioned, 100-seat converted storefront, 5 blocks east of Federal Boulevard. The repertoire includes traditional to more arcane and experimental plays. The Germinal has an excellent reputation for producing quality theater.

### The Physically Handicapped Amateur Musical Actors League
**P.O. Box 44216, Denver 80201**
**(303) 575-0005**
**www.phamaly-colorado.org**
The Physically Handicapped Amateur

Musical Actors League (PHAMALy) gives physically handicapped actors a chance to perform. This group does only one musical a year, which in recent years has been staged during the summer at the Denver Performing Arts Complex. Performances are always wheelchair-accessible, and arrangements are made to provide assistance to hearing-impaired and visually impaired audience members.

### The Theatre on Broadway
**13 South Broadway**
**(303) 777-3292**
The Theatre on Broadway presents Denver premieres of new Broadway and off-Broadway shows in a small black-box theater. The theater is one of two venues for the Theatre Group, which began in 1972 as the Lakewood Players. Artistic Director Steven Tangedahl joined it in 1979. The group also performs at the Phoenix Theatre at 1124 Santa Fe Drive, which opened in April 1997 with *The Compleat Works of Wllm Shkspr (Abridged)*.

## Dinner Theaters

### Country Dinner Playhouse
**6875 South Clinton Street, Englewood**
**(303) 799-1410**
**www.countrydinnerplayhouse.com**
Country Dinner Playhouse is an Equity theater that presents Broadway hits and family entertainment year-round, with a buffet dinner preceding the show. The playhouse offers performances in the round for up to 470 audience members Wednesday through Sunday.

## CLOSE-UP

# Germinal Stage Denver

Ed Baierlein played to perfection the buffoon role of Major Petkoff in George Bernard Shaw's comedy *Arms and the Man,* scowling and bellowing, gaping and grinning and lolling his tongue, his face a writhing parade of expressions so foolish that the audience sometimes laughed loudest when he was saying nothing at all.

*Ed Baierlein and his wife, Sallie Diamond, in A. R. Gurney's* The Golden Fleece.
STRACKER EDWARDS

"That's some play you're running," a fan told him over the telephone one night an hour before the curtain went up. "You're quite a comedian."

"Well, thanks," Baierlein said. "We're doing pretty well. You wanted how many reservations now? Would that be Visa or MasterCard?"

More than a comedian, Baierlein is also one of the Denver area's most respected serious actors, but that doesn't mean he is above taking reservations, cleaning the theater, maintaining the mailing lists, and doing the books at the Germinal Stage Denver theater in northwest Denver.

"The thing that makes Ed unusual is that he's in a category that's almost gone," said Jackie Campbell, former theater critic at the *Rocky Mountain News.* "He's manager, producer, director, and actor. Because he is all of those things, his theater has his stamp very clearly."

So does Greater Denver. Since its founding in 1973, Germinal Stage has built a faithful audience with more than 130 plays including everything from experimental, first-run productions to Ibsen, Shaw, and Shakespeare. Those

**Heritage Square Music Hall**
**18301 West Colfax Avenue**
**(U.S. Highway 40), Golden**
**(303) 279-7800**
**www.heritagesquare.info**
Heritage Square Music Hall is a Victorian-style theater staging original comedies with melodramatic overtones and musical revues. A buffet dinner precedes the show, but it's possible to buy a ticket for the performance only. Performances are Wednesday through Saturday evenings, with Sunday matinees.

plays have earned the theater a reputation and influence all out of proportion to its 100-seat facility in an old 5,000-square-foot building.

While the large theaters of the Denver Performing Arts Complex are a point of pride and a focus of entertainment on Denver's cultural landscape, Germinal Stage and the more than a dozen other smaller local theaters perhaps provide a truer measure of that landscape's cultural depth.

"In the smaller theaters the artists tend to be in primary control," Baierlein says. "They tend to be more eclectic, with a more specialized audience and repertoire. The problems today are fairly similar to what they were when we started out—on the one hand, maintaining the integrity of our repertoire, and on the other hand, being popular enough so that people will pay to see your next failure."

Baierlein and Sallie Diamond, his wife and partner in the nonprofit Germinal Stage and one of the area's most versatile and respected actresses, are among the many who came to Denver by chance and stayed by choice.

"I was in the Air Force and was shipped here in 1968 and spent most of my time in the service at Lowry Air Force Base," Baierlein said. "My wife and I

decided this was the nicest place we had ever lived. My philosophy is, find a place where you like to live and then make the work happen there."

It was the city that attracted them, Baierlein said. The city is where they and their son, Thaddeus, who was born here in 1980, spend most of their time. From their home just a block away from the theater, they take periodic trips to Glenwood Springs, a three-hour drive to the west, to enjoy the world's largest outdoor hot pool.

"That's our favorite vacation, just to let the city seep out of us in the pools," Baierlein said. "We're not great outdoors people. We don't ski, and we don't camp."

Even so, Baierlein said they try to get to the mountains as much as possible, just to enjoy the beauty and solitude that is never far away from the lives and thoughts of even the most urbane of Greater Denverites.

"When you're away from here for any period of time, you really miss just the presence of the mountains," he said. "There's no other place I know where you can have the amenities of a big city and still, in a half hour, be absolutely isolated in a place where you feel nobody has ever been before."

## Variety Theaters

### The Bluebird Theater
**3317 East Colfax Avenue**
**(303) 322-2308**
The Bluebird Theater is Denver's newest old movie theater to offer a variety of

musical and other programming. Built in 1914 and originally used to show silent films, the Bluebird fell upon hard times and closed in the late 1980s. The restored theater reopened in fall 1994. On Sunday night the Bluebird shows cult movie classics and music movies. On

Wednesday through Saturday night, there's a wide variety of live music including rock, reggae, Latin, jazz, folk, and blues.

### The Ogden Theatre
### 935 East Colfax Street
### (303) 830-2525

A vaudeville-era theater that later became a movie house, the Ogden Theatre's newest incarnation is as a concert hall presenting a wide variety of local and national acts. It's located in the heart of Capitol Hill, along with the Bluebird Theater and the Fillmore.

### Paramount Theatre
### 1621 Glenarm Place
### (303) 830-8497 (tickets)

The historic Paramount Theatre has more than once been on the verge of falling to the wrecker's ball. Built in 1930 by Temple Hoyne Buell, a prominent Denver architect, the theater is the epitome of art deco style and has one of only two Mighty Wurlitzer organs in the country (the other is at Radio City Music Hall in New York City). During the summer of 1994—under new management yet again—the Paramount underwent extensive remodeling. The Paramount seats 1,950 and presents a mixed bag of theater, comedy, pop music, children's programming, and ballet.

## Popular Music Venues

Outdoor rock and other popular music concerts are held at INVESCO Field at Mile High, Coors Amphitheatre, and Red Rocks Amphitheatre. Indoor venues include the Pepsi Center and the Ogden Theatre and Paramount Theatre (the latter two are described in the Variety Theaters section as they're not limited to popular music events). Tickets for all concerts at virtually all venues are most conveniently purchased at TicketMaster outlets (cash only) or by calling TicketMaster at (303) 830-TIXS, but a trip to the box office can generally (though not always) save you from paying a service charge. You can also purchase tickets for most concerts at Rocky Mountain Teleseat by stopping in any King Soopers.

Red Rocks and Coors Amphitheatre are the venues for the Summer of Stars series, which brings major recording artists in for concerts during the summer.

### Coors Amphitheatre
### 6350 Greenwood Plaza Boulevard
### Englewood
### (303) 220-7000
### www.hob.com/venues/concerts/coors_denver/

Coors Amphitheatre is a huge 18,000-seat amphitheater just west of Interstate 25 between Arapahoe and Orchard Roads. You can opt to sit on the lawn, which costs a little less than reserved seats. It's also a little less comfortable. For info on concerts and tickets, call (303) 220-7000.

### Fillmore Auditorium
### 1510 Clarkson Street
### (303) 837-0360
### www.thefillmore.com/fillmoredenver.asp

Formerly the Mammoth Events Center, this Capitol Hill landmark fell into disrepair until it was purchased and remodeled to resemble San Francisco's Fillmore Ballroom. It opened in May 1999, holds 3,600 people (it seats a whole lot less than that), and has become one of Denver's

*The Pepsi Center.* DENVER METRO CONVENTION AND VISITORS BUREAU

premier venues for acts as diverse as country star Robert Earl Keen and the Indigo Girls.

### INVESCO Field at Mile High
**1701 Bryant Street**
**(720) 258-3000**

By far the biggest, offering 80,000 seats, Denver's newest venue hosts popular concerts featuring nationally known artists. The stadium opened in August 2001 with a performance by the Eagles, the group's only North American stadium appearance in 2001. Can't see from the nosebleed seats? No problem. Giant video screens show everything that's happening on the stage so far away.

### The Pepsi Center
**1000 Chopper Place**
**(303) 405-1111 (box office)**
**www.pepsicenter.com**

Home to the Denver Nuggets and the Colorado Avalanche, the Pepsi Center also hosts big-name shows. The arena seats up to 16,000, and the custom full-range speakers blaring music are crowd-pleasers.

### Red Rocks Amphitheatre
**Interstate 70 West to the Morrison exit**
**Morrison**
**(303) 295-4444 (information)**
**www.redrocksonline.com**

Red Rocks Amphitheatre is one of the most spectacular settings anywhere for a concert. About half the size of Coors Amphitheatre, Red Rocks is a natural red sandstone amphitheater set deep into the foothills on Hogback Road near Morrison (take I-70 west to the Morrison exit and follow the signs). It was renovated in 2003 to include a $16 million visitor center.

### Swallow Hill Music Association
**71 East Yale Avenue**
**(303) 777-1003**
**www.swallowhill.com**

The venerable Swallow Hill Music Association is Denver's center for folk and traditional acoustic music. Concerts are held at their two theaters, the largest of which seats 300. Swallow Hill also presents concerts elsewhere in the city, including summer concerts at Four Mile Historical Park.

# VISUAL ARTS
## Art Museums

**The Denver Art Museum**
**100 West 14th Avenue Parkway**
**(720) 865-5000**
**www.denverartmuseum.org**
The Denver Art Museum is the largest art museum between Kansas City and the West Coast and is especially noted for its superb collections of Native American, pre-Columbian, and Spanish colonial art. Its seven floors also house impressive displays of American, Asian, African, and contemporary art and galleries devoted to design, graphics, and architecture.

The museum building itself, completed in 1971, is artistically noteworthy. Designed by Milan architect Gio Ponti in association with Denver architect James Sudler, the fortresslike seven-level building has a 28-sided tiled exterior with uniquely shaped windows. Most of the collections have been reinstalled in recent years as part of a seven-year renovation. In 1997 the museum added a new entrance onto Acoma Plaza and an underground connection with the new Central Library. Also opened was the entirely new American and Western art exhibit on the seventh floor. After winning a referendum in 1999 for its expansion, the Art Museum continues to grow, adding another 146,000 square feet, almost doubling its size. The expansion was designed by architect Daniel Libeskind and was completed in 2006. It houses traveling exhibits and permanent modern, contemporary, African, Oceanic, and western American collections.

Choice Tours are free with admission and are scheduled at 1:30 P.M. daily with an additional tour at 11:00 A.M. on Saturday. Tours can be scheduled at other times, so call ahead. Family programs are held every Saturday. The museum has a shop and full-service restaurant.

The museum is open 10:00 A.M. to 5:00 P.M. Tuesday through Saturday (extended hours until 9:00 P.M. on Wednesday) and noon to 5:00 P.M. on Sunday; it's closed Monday and major holidays. Admission is $6.00 for adults, $4.50 for seniors and students with ID, and free for children age 12 and younger. Saturday is free for Colorado residents, thanks to funding provided by the Scientific and Cultural Facilities District. Membership is available for $70 for families; $45 for seniors, students, and teachers; $50 for individuals.

**Kirkland Museum of Fine and Decorative Art**
**1311 Pearl Street**
**(303) 832-8576**
**www.vancekirkland.org**
Vance Kirkland may be Colorado's best-known painter. His work spans realism, surrealism, abstraction, abstract expressionism, and Dot Paintings, and his career stretched from 1926 to 1981. The museum showcases more than 600 of his paintings as well as housing a 2,000-object decorative arts collection and more than 300 works from Colorado artists. The building itself is worthy of note. Built in 1910–1911, it's the second-oldest commercial art building in Colorado, designed in the Arts and Crafts style, and it served as Kirkland's studio. The museum is open 1:00 to 5:00 P.M. Tuesday through Sunday, with tours at 1:30 P.M. Children younger than age 13 are not admitted; children age 13 to 17 must be accompanied by an adult. Admission is $6.00 for adults and $5.00 for seniors, students with ID, and teachers.

**Museo de las Americas**
**861 Santa Fe Drive**
**(303) 571-4401**
**www.museo.org**
Denver's newest museum is the only one in the Rocky Mountain region dedicated to Latin American art, history, and culture. Officially opened in July 1994, the Museo de las Americas showcases art from all

the Americas, including the Caribbean, in changing exhibitions. The museum supplements its temporary exhibitions with lectures, workshops, and other educational programs and has built a small permanent collection. It has twice shown an exhibition jointly with The Denver Art Museum, with some of the material at the art museum and some at the museo. The museum is open 10:00 A.M. to 5:00 P.M. Tuesday through Friday, noon to 5:00 P.M. Saturday and Sunday. Admission is $4.00 for adults, $3.00 for students and seniors, and free for kids younger than age 13.

**Museum of Outdoor Arts**
**1000 Englewood Parkway, Suite 2–230**
**Englewood**
**(303) 806–0444**
**www.moaonline.org**
More than 50 outdoor sculptures comprise this "museum without walls" in the 400-acre Greenwood Plaza Business Park area. You can do a self-guided tour or call to schedule a guided group tour. We recommend the children's art classes that are offered year-round. Visitors can view the art on their own during daylight hours for free. Guided tours can be arranged for groups; call in advance.

# Community Art Centers

**Arvada Center for the Arts and Humanities**
**6901 Wadsworth Boulevard, Arvada**
**(720) 898–7200 (box office)**
**www.arvadacenter.org**
The major contender in this category is the Arvada Center for the Arts and Humanities. The center has two galleries, which display changing exhibits of contemporary art, folk art, design, and crafts. There's also a small historical museum. In addition, the center has both an indoor 500-seat auditorium and an outdoor amphitheater with 1,200 seats (600 covered, 600 on the lawn).

The Arvada Center keeps up an impressive schedule of performing arts programming that includes children's and adult professional theater, dance, and music concerts. One resident company, the Arvada Center Chorale, calls the center home, but many groups perform here. It's the site each winter of a cowboy-poetry gathering. A highly regarded deaf-access program makes many programs accessible to the hearing-impaired.

After 24 years the Arvada Center became a full-equity professional theater in 2000. Hours are 9:00 A.M. to 6:00 P.M. weekdays, 9:00 A.M. to 5:00 P.M. Saturday, and 1:00 to 5:00 P.M. Sunday. Admission to the gallery and museum is free.

**The Foothills Art Center**
**809 15th Street, Golden**
**(303) 279–3922**
**www.foothillsartcenter.org**
The Foothills Art Center is much smaller than the Arvada Center and does not offer a performing arts program. However, the center is home to two prestigious national exhibitions—the biannual North American Sculpture Exhibition and Colorado Art Open and the annual Rocky Mountain National Watermedia Exhibition. It also hosts the statewide annual Colorado Clay exhibition. The remainder of the center's schedule is composed of changing exhibits of national and regional arts and fine crafts. Admission is $3.00 for adults, $2.00 for seniors.

# Art Galleries

## DOWNTOWN

Greater Denver's contemporary art galleries tend to be clustered in the Lower Downtown (LoDo) and Ballpark neighborhoods although galleries are sprinkled throughout Denver. Working on the assumption that there's strength in numbers, the LoDo galleries have banded together to form a Lower Downtown Arts District and to coordinate openings and other special events. The most significant program to come out of this cooperative effort is First Fridays, in which more than two dozen LoDo galleries stay open until 9:00 P.M. the first Friday of each month. Especially in the summer, there's kind of a street festival atmosphere as patrons go from one gallery to the next, stopping to compare notes with friends on the sidewalk. For more information call the LoDo District at (303) 628–5424.

Gallery openings are usually held on Friday and are, with rare exceptions, free and open to the public. Check *Westword* or the Friday edition of the *Denver Post* and the *Rocky Mountain News* for a list of openings and current exhibit information. Most galleries close on Monday, but this varies so call ahead to be sure.

Think of art galleries as a wonderful free smorgasbord of exciting things to see. Of course, the bottom line is that galleries must sell art to stay in business, but unlike art dealers in some cities, Denver dealers are notably low-key and happy to educate browsers without pressuring them to buy. Dealers know that the best way to develop customers is to make people feel comfortable, and high-pressure sales tactics aren't going to do that. On the other hand, if you are a serious buyer, you should be aware that virtually every gallery in town adds the phrase "and by appointment" to its set hours. This may be especially important to visitors whose time in the city is limited.

The heart of Denver's avant-garde arts district is the 1700 block of Wazee Street. You'll find several galleries in the surrounding district. LoDo's high rents forced several galleries to relocate in 1998. Many have chosen the areas north and east of downtown for their affordability and Bohemian appeal.

## Camera Obscura Gallery
**1309 Bannock Street**
**(303) 623-4059**
**www.cameraobscuragallery.com**
Near The Denver Art Museum is Camera Obscura Gallery, devoted exclusively to photography. Owner Hal Gould is supremely knowledgeable; spend a little

time talking with him, and he'll show you the vintage treasures he keeps upstairs.

## David Cook Gallery
**1637 Wazee Street**
**(303) 623-8181**
**www.davidcookfineart.com**
David Cook Gallery offers a wide range of artists and styles, but its specialty is historic American Indian art, from Navajo rugs to Pueblo pottery, from beadwork to baskets. You can also find antique jewelry as well as paintings of the Rockies by early Colorado artists.

## EDGE Gallery
**3658 Navajo Street**
**(303) 477-7173**
**www.edgegallery.org**
Open Friday 7:00 to 10:00 P.M., Saturday and Sunday 1:00 to 5:00 P.M., EDGE is an independent exhibition space that is run cooperatively by the artists who are shown there. It has nonprofit status, which means that it doesn't have to depend on sales for its survival. As a result, the contemporary art shown there can be edgier and more contemporary than that seen in more traditional galleries. EDGE moved to its present site in Denver's historic Little Italy in 1992.

## Knox Gallery
**1512 Larimer Street, Suite R-5**
**(303) 820-2324**
**www.knoxgalleries.com**
Knox Gallery specializes in realistic bronze sculpture. The gallery represents local and regional painters and sculptors.

## The Metropolitan State College of Denver Center for the Visual Arts
**1734 Wazee Street**
**(303) 294-5207**
**www.mscd.edu/news/cva/**
Technically a college gallery, Metro seldom shows student work, but rather puts on some of the best and most provocative exhibitions in town. Traveling exhibits are booked years in advance for the purpose of art education. Past

exhibitions have included contemporary Chinese painting, African-American quilts, and baseball paraphernalia from local collections.

### Old Map Gallery
### 1746 Blake Street
### (303) 296-7725
### www.oldmapgallery.com
If you're in the market for antique maps, this is the place. You'll find historic maps such as ones from the 16th century or maps of Louisiana before it was purchased. Maps range from $35 to several thousand dollars.

### +gallery
### 2350 Lawrence Street
### (303) 296-0927
### www.plusgallery.com
Since 2001 Ivar Zeile has been showcasing the works of emerging as well as nationally known talents in his Ballpark neighborhood gallery. Shows rotate every six weeks and include sculpture, photography, painting, video, paper, and installation art. The gallery is open noon to 6:00 P.M. Wednesday through Sunday and by appointment at other times.

### Redshift Framing and Gallery
### 2266 Broadway
### (303) 293-2991
### www.redshiftframing.com
Redshift Framing and Gallery opened in 1990 and features the work of local and national emerging artists. The art here—which includes paintings and sculpture—is affordable and original.

### Robischon Gallery
### 1740 Wazee Street
### (303) 298-7788
### www.robischongallery.com
Robischon Gallery is Denver's premier gallery for abstract, representational, and symbolistic painting and sculpture. It represents such well-known artists as Robert Motherwell, Christo, and Manuel Neri as well as emerging young artists.

### The Sloane Gallery of Art
### 1612 17th Street
### (303) 595-4230
### www.artnet.com/net/galleries/gallery_home.aspx
The Sloane Gallery of Art, located next to the Oxford Hotel in LoDo, is devoted exclusively to contemporary Russian art. It exhibits oils, acrylics, drawings, pastels, and sculpture.

### Spark Gallery
### 900 Santa Fe Drive
### (720) 889-2200
### www.sparkgallery.com
Spark Gallery is an artists' cooperative (Denver's oldest) that's open Thursday through Saturday from noon to 5:00 P.M. It features original paintings, sculpture, and photographs sold directly by the artists.

### William Matthews Gallery
### 1617 Wazee Street
### (303) 534-1300
### www.williammatthewsgallery.com
The William Matthews Gallery exhibits the Western watercolors of William Matthews. It also features limited-edition prints, posters, and note cards.

## CHERRY CREEK AND OTHER CENTRAL DENVER GALLERIES

Most of the galleries in Cherry Creek are more commercial and more geared toward Santa Fe–style art than those downtown. For this reason, we've listed many of them in our Shopping chapter rather than here.

## WEST OF CHERRY CREEK
### Artyard
### 1251 South Pearl Street
### (303) 777-3219
Artyard is a wonderful out-of-the-way place that feels like a discovery even when you've been there a dozen times. The indoor space doubles as a studio for acclaimed kinetic artist Robert Mangold as well as gallery space for a variety of artists; outdoors is a large sculpture gar-

den that features changing exhibitions of sculpture by well-known artists.

## The Chicano Humanities and Arts Council
**772 Santa Fe Drive**
**(303) 571-0440**
**www.chacweb.org**
CHAC, the Chicano Humanities and Arts Council, has a gallery that is open Wednesday and Thursday 10:00 A.M. to 4:00 P.M., Friday noon to 10:00 P.M., and Saturday and Sunday noon to 4:00 P.M. In addition to these eclectic hours, CHAC sponsors a number of special events and programs throughout the city, including a Day of the Dead exhibition, the annual Chile Harvest Festival held at Four Mile Historic Park in August, and Las Posadas at the gallery during December. CHAC is a consortium of artists, individuals, and organizations dedicated to the preservation and promotion of Chicano/Latino cultures.

## Core New Art Space
**900 Santa Fe Drive**
**(303) 287-8428**
**www.corenewartspace.com**
Core New Art Space is a cutting-edge cooperative gallery that primarily features local artists who work in oil, photography, ceramics, and papermaking.

## Platte River Art Services
**350 North Santa Fe Drive**
**(303) 571-1060**
**www.platteriverartservices.com**
This premier frame shop is more of a conservation studio than an art gallery, but it is still the place to go when you want something unusual. The shop offers exquisite frames, including hand-carved, hand-gilded ones and restored antique frames.

## Rule Gallery
**227 Broadway**
**(303) 777-9473**
**www.rulegallery.com**
The peripatetic Rule Gallery, which used to be on Wazee Street, then on Wynkoop, is now housed on Broadway across from the Mayan Theater. This gallery specializes in modern and contemporary painting, sculpture, and photography by regional artists.

## Sandy Carson Gallery
**760 Santa Fe Drive**
**(303) 573-8585**
**www.sandycarsongallery.com**
The Sandy Carson Gallery shows contemporary painting, sculpture, and photography as well as ceramics and glass. In business since 1980, this gallery acquires arts from all over the country and also has quite a reputation as art consultant.

## William Havu Gallery
**1040 Cherokee Street**
**(303) 893-2360**
**www.williamhavugallery.com**
Named Top Art Gallery by readers of *5280* magazine, the gallery specializes in regional contemporary fine art.

## WESTSIDE GALLERIES

As LoDo has changed and rents have gone up, many artists have moved their studios from the Platte River area to the area just west of I-25. In this transitional neighborhood you'll find the following galleries.

## The Bug Theatre: Performance and Media Arts Center
**3654 Navajo Street**
**(303) 477-9984**
**www.bugtheatre.org**

*A funky collection of galleries in fast-changing northwest Denver is a fun and different way to spend a Friday or Saturday evening. Galleries such as Bug Theatre and Pirate are located in the 3600 block of Navajo Street. Have dinner at Patsy's Inn Italian Restaurant (3651 Navajo Street) and stroll through the galleries afterward.*

The buzz is good on the Bug Theatre, a renovated movie house that's now an avant-garde showcase for emerging artists and their artwork, including poetry, music, film, and new media. Call the Bugline at (303) 477-5977 to find out what's coming.

### Pirate, A Contemporary Art Oasis
**3655 Navajo Street**
**(303) 458-6058**
**www.pirateart.org**
Pirate, A Contemporary Art Oasis has what are generally regarded as the hippest openings in town. It is one of the most experimental galleries in Denver, showcasing stunning paintings and sculpture. Pirate is only open on weekends, and shows change frequently.

### RIVER NORTH ARTS DISTRICT
**Northeast of downtown Denver**
**www.rivernorthart.com**
This emerging arts district was once home to Denver's early-day foundries, smelters, ironworks, and the blue-collar families who made them run. For the past decade it has drawn artists and real estate investors priced out of nearby LoDo and the Coors Field area. They banded together to form the informal River North Arts District, called RiNo for short, and now sponsor district-wide studio tours and individual events. The group's name comes from its location along the northern edge of the South Platte River, roughly bounded by I-25, and I-70, Park Avenue West, and Lawrence Street. News is posted on the group's Web site, as are details about each of its 41 members.

## LITERARY ARTS

If you love the written word—or the company of those who write—Denver has several writers' organizations that appeal to both beginning and advanced scribes as well as writers in a variety of genres.

### Colorado Authors' League
**P.O. Box 24905, Denver 80224**
**(720) 981-9357**
**www.coloradoauthors.org**
Founded in 1931, the Colorado Authors' League is one of the oldest professional writers' organizations in the state. Counting such notables as Clive Cussler, Clarissa Pinkola Estes, and Joanne Greenberg among its ranks, this organization has monthly meetings with speakers on topics from spotting trends to writing with a collaborator. Dues are $40 a year.

### Columbine Poets, Inc.
**P.O. Box 6245, Westminster 80021**
**(303) 431-6774**
Part of the National Federation of State Poetry Societies, the purpose of this organization is to promote poetry throughout the state by offering contests, workshops, and monthly critique groups. Their fee structure is complicated. You can belong to the National Poetry Society for $12 or you can join the local FlatIrons Chapter for $35, which includes the $12 entry fee for the national society but also allows you to attend the chapter's weekly workshops. They offer a third supporting member category, $25, which allows you to do everything with the local chapter except attend the weekly workshops.

### Denver Woman's Press Club
**1325 Logan Street, Denver 80203**
**(303) 839-1519**
**www.denverwomanspressclub.org**
This club was formed in 1898 by 19 members whose mission included "functioning as a stimulating gathering place for people in literary journalism and media endeavors." Today the club meets regularly for lunch and dinner programs, offers Saturday seminars for the community at large, and has afternoon teas featuring authors in town on book tours. Housed in a charming historic landmark, this organization of women writers is the oldest in the state. Dues run $75 a year.

**Mystery Writers of America**
**(Rocky Mountain Chapter)**
**Bonnie Ramthun, Chapter President**
**(303) 665-3992**
**www.rockymountainmysterywriters.com**
Monthly meetings and bimonthly programs keep the published and unpublished members of the regional chapter
of Mystery Writers of America busy.
Members get to attend all bimonthly programs for free. One of the highlights of
each year is the annual meeting, where
the featured speaker might be an FBI
agent or a judge from a criminal court.
National dues are $95, which allows
membership locally.

**Rocky Mountain Fiction Writers**
**P.O. Box 260244, Denver 80226**
**(303) 331-2608**
**www.rmfw.org**
This popular fiction-writing organization is
geared to writers of commercial novels. Its
400 members are both published and
unpublished and enjoy monthly meetings
where speakers talk about anything related
to writing and researching. Monthly
newsletters offer market news, and critique
groups are held all over Greater Denver.
The annual conference in September is a
much-awaited event; big-name writers, six
or seven editors, and several New York
agents attend. Dues are $45 a year.

**Women Writing the West**
**8547 East Arapahoe Road, Suite J-541**
**Greenwood Village, CO 80112**
**(303) 773-8349**
**www.womenwritingthewest.org**
This organization has 250 members from
all over the United States, Canada, and
Australia. The motto here is "We don't do
meetings, and we don't do T-shirts." What
they do do is work on marketing themselves—all of whom are interested in writing about "a new view of the women's
west." Members get a quarterly newsletter, displays at booksellers associations,
and a major opportunity to network—all
for $50.

# PARKS AND RECREATION

Greater Denver is a recreational heaven. Where else can you enjoy some of the best skiing in the world on Saturday, then play 18 holes of golf on Sunday—all on a sunny March weekend?

It doesn't stop there. We've got biking trails, hiking trails, climbing spots, and picnicking galore. You can boat, swim, fish, snow ski, water-ski, or windsurf. You can hunt wildlife or simply admire it from afar. You name it, we've got it. And it's all in the city or just minutes outside its limits.

We have organizations, facilities, rental companies, and tour guides for everything—bicycling, climbing, fishing, hunting, running, in-line skating, sailing, waterskiing, and horseback riding, to name a few. We even have ranges for skeet, trap, pistols, and rifles. Skiing, of course, is Colorado's most popular and famous form of recreation as well as one of the state's biggest money-earners. In addition to some brief tips in this chapter, we've given skiing a chapter of its own called Ski Country.

Major facets of Greater Denver's recreation are its beautifully groomed urban parks. The ones listed below will add a delightful serenity to your day. In general, Denver's parks are open from 5:00 A.M. until 11:00 P.M. and do not allow camping.

## PARKS

## Urban Parks

City and county parks and recreation departments are much more than fabricated facilities and structured activities. The parks themselves offer pleasant havens throughout Greater Denver's urban fabric. Pockets of greenery, playing fields, play-grounds, and surfaces for running, biking, and skating are just some of the amenities.

The city parks offer a lot more than we sometimes suspect. Denver Parks and Recreation, for example, is the agency responsible for such widely varied facilities as the Denver Zoo, the city's golf courses, and 100 miles of foliated center strips on major streets.

Denver has about 250 parks, ranging from small triangles to enormous open spaces, as well as a trail system guesstimated at about 130 miles. And, of course, there are the 14,000 acres of Denver Mountain Parks, including a variety of named and unnamed parcels of natural area.

### Chatfield Nature Preserve
### 8500 Deer Creek Canyon Road
### Littleton
### (303) 973-3705
### www.botanicgardens.org

This little gem is operated by the Denver Botanic Gardens and offers historic sites, trails, and naturalist guides. It's a great place for a picnic, and the traditional playground next to the historic schoolhouse is fun for kids. Down the path along Deer Creek, you can see the foundation where the schoolhouse was before they moved it. Look for the piece of chain on one of the cottonwood branches above the path, the remnant of the swing where kids played more than 100 years ago. Chatfield Nature Preserve is just off Wadsworth Boulevard south of C-470 and is open 9:00 A.M. to 5:00 P.M. seven days a week. Admission is charged.

### Cheesman Park
### Between 8th and 13th Avenues
### east of Lafayette Street

Cheesman Park is a Denver jewel just east of downtown. This vast urban oasis fea-

*Visitors to Denver's City Park enjoy rides on these whimsical paddle boats.* THE DENVER POST/BRIAN BRAINERD

tures a great 1.5-mile walking/jogging path, enormous trees throughout, manicured flower gardens, and an impressive pavilion at the eastern edge. And the mountain view from the pavilion is stunning. The compressed dirt jogging path is easy on the body and popular with nearby residents. The park was established in 1892 on the city's former first cemetery lot. It is adjacent to the Denver Botanic Gardens, which charges a small entry fee and is open daily. To get there, take 14th Avenue east out of downtown to Lafayette, then head south 1 block to the park.

### City Park
### 17th Avenue Parkway and
### Colorado Boulevard

The lake at City Park is ringed by acres of grass and mature trees that offer wonderful picnicking and relaxing. There also is an extensive path that is great for biking, walking, and in-line skating. The historic City Park Pavilion was restored and fea-

tures musicians in the bandstand on the lake's west shore. In the summer you can rent paddleboats seven days a week for only $5.00 an hour. The east end of the park is home to the Denver Zoo and the Museum of Nature and Science. To get there take 17th Avenue east out of downtown to York Street. The park lies between York Street and Colorado Boulevard.

### Commons Park
### Between 15th and 19th Streets
### on Little Raven Drive

Commons Park was Denver's most unusual urban park when it opened in 2001. Reclaimed from decades worth of neglect, the land that held Denver's earliest settlers was envisioned as the crown jewel in a string of riverfront parks that bisect the city. Forward-thinking city fathers (and mothers) spent more than two decades amassing the land, scraping away the rail yards and hobo shanties, and planning for redevelopment. First came the city park, a grassy knoll in Denver's urban core that offers visitors a place to stare at the skyline to the east and the mountains to the west. Visitors can dabble their feet in the waters of the South Platte River or listen to a concert staged in the outdoor arena. Then came the pricey high-rises that attracted families and retirees, empty nesters, and urban professionals. Connecting them all are: to the south, an amusement park (Six Flags Elitch Gardens) and a sports arena (the Pepsi Center, home to Denver's professional basketball and hockey teams); to the north, a free city-owned 50,000-square-foot skateboard park that attracts 200 to 300 skaters a day. Reach this rich cultural stew by riding the 16th Street shuttle west to its end point, then walking across the Millennium Bridge. By car, follow Interstate 25 to Speer Boulevard, then exit south. Turn right at Elitch Circle, and keep turning right until you're on Little Raven Street. The park runs alongside Little Raven Street between 15th and 20th Streets.

### Dinosaur Ridge
**Outside Red Rocks Amphitheatre**
**Morrison**
**(303) 697–DINO (3466)**
**www.dinoridge.org**

This unexpected park is a treasure of exposed dinosaur bones and tracks, along with plant and other fossils. The best way to get there is to take Interstate 70 west to the Morrison exit and head south on Highway 26. A couple of miles downhill, you'll see the right turn that takes you to Red Rocks. Don't take that! We're offering it only as a landmark to help you identify the turnoff across the road (which will be a turnoff to the left) on West Alameda Parkway. At that left turnoff, there is a sign that says NATURAL NATIONAL LANDMARK, which is Dinosaur Ridge. The road swings uphill, and on the north side of the road, you'll see a stone building and barn. That's the Dinosaur Ridge Visitor Center, where you can get information about Dinosaur Ridge

*The must-see view of Greater Denver and the Rocky Mountains is from the entrance to the Denver Museum of Nature and Science, in City Park at Colorado Boulevard and Montview Street. The sweeping vista of treetops, skyscrapers, and snowcapped peaks is the best in town.*

hours, tours, and directions as well as buy T-shirts, books, casts of dinosaur footprints, and other dinosaur-relevant things.

Dinosaur Ridge is essentially an outdoor experience, however. Continuing east on West Alameda Parkway, you'll find on the uphill slope exposed dinosaur bones in the hillside. This is where the first dinosaur bones in the western United States were found in 1877. It's wheelchair accessible. Over the hill and starting down, you come to another display, this one of exposed dinosaur footprints. The Friends of Dinosaur Ridge holds Open Ridge Day one Saturday each month from May through October, when the road is closed to cars and volunteers station themselves at the various stops along the road to tell you what you're looking at. You can also join one of the Dinosaur Ridge guided tours. Call the visitor center, (303) 697–DINO, for information. Admission is free, but donations are accepted.

As long as you're out there, you may want to combine your Dinosaur Ridge visit with a visit to the Morrison Natural History Museum, where they have some of the original bones that were taken out of the first dinosaur dig site as well as other exhibits. To get to the museum, get back on Highway 26 and go south into the town of Morrison, turn right in the center of town at the intersection by the Morrison Inn (a great place to stop for American-Mexican food, by the way; see our Restaurants chapter), go about 0.5 mile to the last stoplight, turn left onto Highway 8, and go about 0.5 mile to the museum. You'll see the log-cabin structure on your right.

### Sloan Lake Park
### 17th Avenue and Sheridan Boulevard

Sloan Lake is one of the more popular lakes/parks in the north end of town. Like other Denver parks, it is dotted with trees and offers a great place to have a picnic, play Frisbee, or just hang out. A running trail circles the park and soccer fields. A large playground is great for kids. To get there, take Colfax Avenue west to Sheridan Boulevard, then right to 17th Avenue.

### Washington Park
### Louisiana Avenue and Downing Street

This is perhaps the most popular park for a variety of sporting events. For starters, there's a great path around the park for bicycling, walking/jogging, and in-line skating. In the middle are two lakes for fishing (especially good for kids). There are soccer games and impromptu volleyball games nearly every warm, sunny weekend of the year. The flower gardens on the western edge, along Downing Street, are perfection and the backdrop for great tourist photographs. But most of all, "Wash Park," as it's known, is a wonderful spot to relax and enjoy Denver's blue skies and manicured landscapes.

## State Parks and Recreation Areas

Moving farther out from the urban area, you encounter county park and open-space systems. Jefferson County has the largest, but Adams, Douglas, and Arapahoe also have their county park systems. As you get into the mountains, you also encounter the Denver Mountain Parks system, 14,000 acres of mountain parks scattered through four counties. Red Rocks Park is one of these, as is the Winter Park ski area (see our Ski Country chapter for details). When people want to enjoy the great outdoors without driving way into the mountains, the first places they often think about are the four state parks and two state recreation areas right in Greater Denver. But they're all exceptionally fine, and you can get more information by calling each park or by contacting the Colorado Division of Parks and Outdoor Recreation's Metro Region office, (303) 791-1957, or visiting the Web site at www.parks.state.co.us. All state parks charge a $3.00 to $6.00 per vehicle admission fee.

### Barr Lake State Park
### Northeast of Denver about 20 miles near Brighton
### (303) 659-6005
### www.coloradoparks.org

Barr Lake is a 2,700-acre state park surrounding a 1,900-acre prairie reservoir. Decades ago the reservoir used to be something of a sewage dump, and people would roll up their car windows when they drove past it on Interstate 76. But please, that was long ago. Today it's a charming and tranquil place with more than 300 species of birds. It's the area's best place to watch eagles that hunt around the lake and nest in the trees at the lake's southern half, which is designated as a wildlife refuge (no pets allowed in this area). It's also the biggest lake in the Denver area, where you can canoe, kayak, or otherwise go boating without being buzzed by Jet Skis, power-boats, and water-skiers. The only boats allowed on the lake are sailboats, hand-propelled craft, and boats with electric trolling motors or gas engines of 10 horsepower or less. Hiking here is pleasant because the lakeshore is lined with cottonwoods. There are plenty of aquatic plants and marshes, where it's always interesting to watch the big carp rooting and sucking. On both the north and south ends of the lake, you can walk out on wooden boardwalks extending into the water and watch wildlife from the gazebo at the end. Bring binoculars. Camping is not allowed at Barr Lake, but the park is open 5:00 A.M. to 10:00 P.M. year-round. To get there, take I-76 northeast out of Denver about 20 miles to exit 22, Bromley Lane, east to Picadilly Road, and south to the park entrance. There's also a nature center with displays and information and a bookstore.

## Castlewood Canyon State Park
## South of Denver near Castle Rock
## (303) 688-5242
## www.coloradoparks.org

Castlewood is one of those delightful discoveries that people often make only after years or decades of living in the area. To those used to thinking of Colorado as a mountainous place, this may seem more like some hidden natural gorge refuge on the far plains of Kansas. Part of Colorado's Black Forest, it's a popular place for short- and medium-range hiking as well as bird-watching. There are viewing points and hiking trails aplenty. You can follow Cherry Creek along its scenic cut in the landscape and visit the stone ruins of Castlewood Canyon Dam, which look like something left over from the Egyptians. There's also a nifty trail that leads up to a cave: a small cave, but very delightful for kids. Dogs are allowed on a 6-foot leash. No camping is allowed. Take I-25 south to Castle Rock, go west on Highway 86, turn south just before Franktown on Douglas County Road 51, and you'll see the park entrance after about 3 miles.

## Chatfield State Recreation Area
## 1 mile south of C-470 and Wadsworth Boulevard
## (303) 791-7275
## www.parks.state.co.us/

Here you'll find Greater Denver's widest range of outdoor experiences, from powerboating to appreciating nature in remote surroundings. The northern end is the reservoir, a place popular with boaters, water-skiers, swimmers, and anglers (check our Boating and Windsurfing section in this chapter for details). It's probably the area's greatest general recreational resource in terms of variety and scenery. As you get toward the south end, where the South Platte River flows into the reservoir, and head on south from there, you're in the nature part of the park. The South

Platte Valley along here is heavily wooded beneath a striking canopy of old-growth riverbottom cottonwoods. People bike, hike, and horseback-ride on the paths following the river, and the river here is also a charming place to cast a line. On the west side, between the river and U.S. Highway 75, the Chatfield Wetlands is a newly created area with ponds and flora engineered to be a natural Colorado wetland. There are lots of waterfowl and animals. You can walk the wetlands from either side. There's a viewing platform just off US 75 on the west side. And if you keep on US 75 farther south, you get to the Waterton Canyon Recreation Area, about 4 miles south of C-470. You can take a trail up the canyon, where there are lots of nature observation opportunities (including the canyon's own bighorn sheep herd), picnic spots, fishing, historic spots, and ultimately a connection into the Colorado Trail, which goes all the way to Durango.

The north end of Chatfield, however, is where you'll find the more civilized activities concentrated. The swimming beach is large and first-rate; it is open Memorial Day through Labor Day. The campgrounds have more than 150 sites with all the amenities, but we suggest reservations, (303) 470-1144. The Chatfield Marina, (303) 791-5555, has extensive facilities and extensive capacity for renting boats, as outlined in our Boating and Windsurfing section. You can also rent paddleboats, water toys, and pontoon boats there, and you can ride on a hot-air balloon that takes off near the swimming beach. The U.S. Army Corps of Engineers has also been offering summer tours of the Chatfield Dam.

Chatfield Stables, (303) 933-3636, offers horseback riding. Note that dogs are not allowed in the Waterton Canyon Recreation Area. Dogs are allowed in Chatfield on a leash not longer than 6 feet and in a dog exercise area where they're allowed off-leash on the north side of the dam, in the Chatfield State Recreation Area. To get to Chatfield, take I-25 or I-70 to C-470, then C-470 to the Wadsworth Boulevard exit. Or just take Wadsworth Boulevard south, if you're near it on the west side. Just south of C-470 on Wadsworth, you'll see the park entrance on the left.

### Cherry Creek State Park
**Interstate 225 and South Parker Road**
**(303) 690-1166, (303) 699-3860**
**www.coloradoparks.org**
Like Chatfield, Cherry Creek is based on the existence of a large reservoir, in this case Cherry Creek Lake. It's less nature-oriented and more activity-oriented than Chatfield. However, there are wetlands, including beaver ponds. The recreation area gets a lot of school groups for its trails and guided nature walks. The south end is the most nature-oriented, where Cherry Creek and Cottonwood Creek flow into the reservoir. There is a mountain-bike trail and a lot of cottonwood trees and aspens. Along the trail systems you may see mule deer and white-tailed deer, owls, coyotes, foxes, and the like.

One of the big advantages of this recreation area is that it's so centrally located. It's right off I-225, surrounded by Aurora, Denver, the Denver Tech Center, and Centennial Airport. A lot of people who come here to visit friends or family opt to stay at the recreation area, where they can camp or park their RVs. Cherry Creek Lake is not much smaller than Chatfield Reservoir, and the folks at Cherry Creek Park think their campground is nicer. Call (303) 470-1144 for camping reservations, and plan to make them at least three or four days ahead of time. It has 102 campsites on five loops, and most of them are shaded by trees. It has a marina, (303) 779-6144, which we describe in our Boating and Windsurfing section in this chapter. Cherry Creek has a riding stable, (303) 690-8235. The recreation area is 1 mile south of I-225 on Parker Road.

### Golden Gate Canyon State Park
**Outside of Golden off Golden Gate**
**Canyon Road**
**(303) 582-3707**
**www.parks.state.co.us**

This is the mountainous park among Greater Denver's six nearby state parks and recreation areas. It's where you go for vistas, and it's heavy on the aspens, which means you're not likely to find a nearby place with better viewing of the autumn gold—from Panorama Point especially, at the top of the park on its northern edge. A lot of people like to drive up to Panorama Point on those autumn days of blue skies and green and gold mountains. A little path from the parking lot and picnic area leads to a multilevel megagazebo on the brim of a westward-sloping mountainside, where you can look across deep valleys and up to more than 100 miles of snowcapped peaks along the Continental Divide.

The park's 14,000 acres range from 7,600 to 10,400 feet in altitude, and it has 35 miles of trails for foot and hoof, 275 picnic sites, and more than 130 campsites as well as more than 20 backcountry shelters and tent sites. Two yurts and fire cabins are a recent addition to camping choices. Reservations are recommended and can be made by calling (303) 470-1144 or online at reserveamerica.com. Once there, your first stop is always at the visitor center on the park's lower east end (open 9:00 A.M. to 4:00 P.M. daily), where there's a pond full of big, tame trout to watch and a museum to browse through. Right outside the visitor center is a nature trail designed for accessibility to the physically impaired. You can reach the park by turning west off of Highway 93 onto Golden Gate Canyon Road and driving about 15 winding miles to the park.

### Red Rocks Park
**Off Morrison Road, Morrison**
**(303) 295-4444**
**www.redrocksonline.com**
Entrance to Red Rocks is free and open year-round (when there's not a concert going on) and definitely worth the visit. The natural rock formations are splendid to see. Much of the area is wheelchair accessible, too. You can even bring a guitar and play on the natural amphitheater's stage. To get there, just take I-70 west

to Morrison Road, go south, and follow the signs.

## Roxborough State Park
**South on Santa Fe Drive past Littleton**
**(303) 973-3959**
**www.coloradoparks.org**

Roxborough is the most natural of Greater Denver's local state parks. It was Colorado's first state park to be designated both a Colorado Natural Area and a National Natural Landmark. There is only one building, the visitor center. Camping, rock climbing, and pets aren't allowed, and there are no picnic sites. What you do have is the opportunity to take a number of lovely hikes through some dramatic and unique natural terrain. The hikes are gentle; a brochure is available at the visitor center at the entrance. The geology is spectacular. The Dakota Hogback runs north-south along the west side of the metro area. The park hides behind it to the west, with the spectacular red-rock moonscape of the Fountain Formation.

There are numerous guided nature hikes and nature programs. The park also has an "extended golf cart" ride, known as the Rocks Ride, that is available to people who can't hike because of health reasons or disabilities. It has a limited schedule, and reservations are required. Reach Roxborough by following U.S. Highway 85 (Santa Fe Drive) south from Denver to Titan Road. Take a right onto Titan Road and go 3.5 miles. Follow Titan Road left onto Rampart Range Road. Go 3 miles and turn left onto Roxborough Park Road, then take an immediate right onto the park access road. The entry fee is $5.00 per car and well worth it.

# RECREATION

# Bicycling

## PAVEMENT BICYCLING

Cities in the Greater Denver area have put significant effort and money into building superb trails that allow bicyclists to take rides that can last all day long. These paths were designed both for bicycling and in-line skating so rather than repeat our listings, we've described several paths in our In-line Skating section in this chapter.

For bicycling in Denver, your first resource should be the Colorado Lottery, which provides money for the State Trails Program and offers free trail maps. Visit the Web site at www.coloradolottery.com. In addition, consider the following for relaxing or challenging rides (you set the pace).

## Cherry Creek Bike Path

Running east-west through Denver's urban core, the Cherry Creek Bike Path is one of a kind. It begins at Confluence Park, the birthplace of Denver, at the intersection of the South Platte River and Cherry Creek, and wanders through some of the ritziest areas of Cherry Creek before dumping riders out in Aurora. For much of the way, it follows the creek and is worlds away from the roadways above. Riders share the paved path with in-line skaters, joggers, and walkers, but in exchange they see everything from the Cherry Creek Country Club to beaver ponds.

## East Seventh Avenue Bike Route

This ride takes you through city streets, so watching for traffic is a must. But if you're more interested in sampling Denver's scenery and architecture than getting a real workout, this is a nice ride. Start just south of downtown at Broadway and East Seventh Avenue, then head east on Seventh and follow the bike route signs. You can take it for 4 miles before it dead-ends at Colorado Boulevard, through Denver's oldest neighborhoods, replete with mansions and stunning old trees.

## The Highline Canal

This Denver-area highlight was built in the 1880s and is now lined by huge cotton-woods in what amounts to a river of ancient trees through the city. This favorite trail runs from Waterton Canyon in the west to Aurora's Environmental Park in the east. Depending on the time of year, the canal will either be swollen with spring runoff or bone dry. Watch for horses, as the dirt areas are popular with equestrians.

### Platte River Greenway Trail

This is a major bike trail in Greater Denver that runs from Chatfield Reservoir in the southwest to the city of Thornton in the upper north metro region. The trail passes through more than a dozen parks. Access points are legion; consult the Colorado Lottery Map for details. Two popular access points are Confluence Park at 15th and Platte Streets near Lower Downtown and Ruby Hill Park near Evans Street and Broadway.

## Resources

The State of Colorado has urban trail maps for four different areas of the state. One of those is for the metropolitan Denver area: *Urban Trails in Colorado, Denver Metro Area*. The state also has a very useful *Colorado Trails Resource Guide*. These references are available free if you stop by or write Trails Guides, 1313 Sherman Avenue, Room 618, Denver, CO 80203. Provide a self-addressed, stamped return envelope with six first-class stamps; the envelope should measure at least 6 by 9 inches. Some bike shops will have urban trail maps available as well.

A nonprofit group called Bicycle Colorado, (303) 417-1544, is perhaps the biggest single source of bicycling information. It has a general guide to public-lands trails and other tips, and it also has a Web site at www.bicyclecolo.org.

Among the other bicycling resources that may be helpful are the Denver Bicycle Touring Club, (303) 756-7240; Team Evergreen, (303) 674-6048, one of the friendlier local bicycle clubs with about 700 members, weekly road-bike and mountain-bike rides, its own newsletter, and other attractions; and the American Cycling Association of Colorado, (303) 458-5538.

## Rentals

There are numerous bike rental shops in the Denver area; your best bet is to consult the yellow pages. Expect to pay from $15 to $25 a day depending on the quality and expense of the bike. We'll give you an idea of a few good shops that have been around for a long time.

### Adventure Cycling
### 4361 South Parker Road
### (303) 699-2514

Adventure Cycling rents bikes and is convenient to those in the southeast part of town.

### The Bicycle Doctor
### 860 Broadway
### (303) 831-7228
### www.bicycledr.com

Located near downtown Denver, the Bicycle Doctor is a full-service shop that works on bicycles when it's not servicing skis. It also rents both, with bikes running between $15 and $40 a day, depending upon the model you choose. The store is open weekdays from 10:00 A.M. to 7:00 P.M. and Saturday from 10:00 A.M. to 5:00 P.M., although those hours can change with the season. It's closed on Sunday.

### Sports Rent
### 8761 Wadsworth Boulevard
### (303) 467-0200

This shop rents three types of bikes, depending on the terrain you plan to tackle.

### Treads Bicycle Outfitters
### 3546 South Logan
### (303) 781-1162
### www.treads.com

This shop rents everything from trail bikes for pavement to high-performance mountain bikes and has maps and brochures for sale.

## MOUNTAIN BIKING

If any outdoor sport could be said to define Colorado, mountain biking would probably run a close second to skiing. Hikers are still the primary users of Colorado backcountry, but increasingly they are having to share the path with mountain bikers. Mountain bikes have fat nubby tires, super-light frames, and gearing low enough to ride up the steepest hills.

Mountain bikers can pretty much go on any hiking trail or off-trail. Polite bikers slow when passing hikers, or get off the trail for people on horses. In fact, consideration for others is among the International Mountain Biking Association's official Rules of the Trail: (1) Ride on open trails only, (2) Leave no trace, (3) Control your bicycle, (4) Always yield the trail, (5) Never spook animals, and (6) Plan ahead.

Where trails are closed specifically to mountain biking, in places like Boulder Mountain Parks, it's most likely because mountain bikes in excessive numbers are viewed as destructors of trails. You can't mountain bike in Roxborough State Park, in city of Boulder open space, or on about half the trails in Golden Gate State Park. Trails in virtually all national forests along the Front Range and nearby areas over the Continental Divide are open to mountain bikes. Generally, if you don't see a sign prohibiting mountain biking, you can take to the trails.

A lot of great mountain-biking rides are available in Jefferson County on Denver's immediate west side. These are wonderful places for their terrain, scenery, and/or technical aspects. All of them are accessible to anyone with reasonably fit lungs and legs.

### Deer Creek Park Trail

This area is about 4 miles up Deer Creek Canyon from Wadsworth Boulevard, in Jefferson County Open Space. Steeper areas like Deer Creek aren't for beginners or those who haven't been working out. Deer Creek Park has one hiker-only trail.

### Hayden–Green Mountain Park Trails

These intermediate trails also challenge riders. They wind through the park before climbing 1,200 feet to the Green Mountain

*The Sand Creek Regional Greenway Trail is a well-kept secret and will be until the 13-mile east-west walking and biking trail is completed. The mostly unpaved trail connects the Platte River Greenway in Commerce City with the High Line Canal in Aurora and completes a 50-mile loop through wetlands, along creek beds, and beneath an old airport runway.*

summit. To get there, take Sixth Avenue west to the Union Street exit, go south to Alameda Avenue, then right. The park is on the right side.

### Mount Falcon

Take U.S. Highway 285 west past C–470 to the Morrison exit, then right. Follow the clearly marked signs. From the Morrison trailhead, you can head up the Castle Trail to the pavilion at Walker's Dream Shelter. You can ride several loops above this point, with moderate technical skills. Avoid the area's hiker-only trail.

### Waterton Canyon

Take Wadsworth Boulevard south from its junction with C–470, 4 miles to the Waterton Canyon Recreation Area sign, and turn left to park. You are now at the South Platte River just upstream from the Chatfield Recreation Area. There are lovely, gentle trails around the recreation area, but up the canyon it gets a little more dramatic. No dogs are allowed because the canyon is home to a herd of bighorn sheep. A 6-mile dirt road heads up past Cottonwood Gulch, Mill Gulch, and Stevens Gulch to the Colorado Trail.

### References

One of the best overall references for these and other rides is *The Best of Colorado Biking Trails* (revised edition), published by Outdoor Books & Maps Inc. of Denver and available in many local bookstores, bike shops, and outing stores. Other good mountain-biker references include *Mountain Biking Colorado,* by

Stephen Hlawaty, *Bike With a View: Easy, Moderate, Mountain Bike Rides to Scenic Destinations,* by Mark Dowling; and *Colorado Gonzo Rides,* by Michael Merrifield.

# Boating and Windsurfing

Boaters and windsurfers have a lot of lakes and reservoirs to choose from around Greater Denver, but if you're into powerboating, only a few select places are either large enough or allow enough horsepower to do more than putt from one fishing spot to the next.

The most popular lakes for powerboating are the big boys: Cherry Creek Lake and Chatfield Reservoir. Both of them are big reservoirs and, as part of state recreation areas, are nice environments in which to split the water. You can find more general descriptions of these areas in our State Parks and Recreation Areas section in this chapter, but boaters will be interested to know that both of them have extensive marinas offering a lot of rentals.

### Aurora Reservoir Marina
### 5800 South Powhaton Road, Aurora
### (303) 690-1286

This newer facility is 7 miles east of Quincy Reservoir in Arapahoe County. Powerboaters pay it little attention, since gas motors aren't allowed on the water. But the water is clean, and it's popular with sailors and windsurfers. There's a little marina with a general store, where you can rent electric motorboats, rowboats, sailboats, sailboards, paddleboats, and canoes. It also features a paved bike path that stretches about 8 miles around the lake. You'll find the reservoir by driving about 2 miles east of Gun Club Road on East Quincy Avenue and turning right at Powhaton Road. Hours vary depending on sunrise and sunset, but generally run from dawn to dusk, and visitors will be

charged a $5.00 daily vehicle pass fee. Electric boats cost $12.00 an hour and canoes and pedal boats cost $8.00 an hour.

### Bear Creek Lake Park
### Off Morrison Road near C-470 Lakewood
### (303) 697-6159 (park rangers)

There are three water areas here: Bear Creek Lake, Little Soda Lake, and Big Soda Lake. Bear Creek is mainly for fishing as it allows no motors greater than 10 horsepower. There also is some sailing. Hours are 6:00 A.M. to 10:00 P.M. from Memorial through Labor Days, and an admission fee is charged. There are no rentals at Bear Creek Lake. The access point is easy to see off Morrison Road, once you exit C-470.

Big Soda Lake is open to the public for nonmotorized boats and has its own Soda Lake Marina, (303) 697-1522, where you can rent paddleboats, kayaks, sailboards, and canoe. The marina is open noon to 7:00 P.M. weekdays and 10:00 A.M. to 7:00 P.M. weekends. Big Soda has also added a swim area. Admission to the lake is $4.00 per car.

Little Soda Lake isn't open for public boating. However, it is open for the Soda Lake Ski School, (303) 697-0121. Hours and costs vary.

### Chatfield Marina
### 11500 North Roxborough Park Road
### Littleton
### (303) 791-5555

This marina for the Chatfield Reservoir includes a store with boating and fishing supplies, groceries, and take-out food. It's Denver's only on-the-water grill and deli restaurant with a patio and an observation deck. The season runs from April through October. Hours are 9:00 A.M. to 7:00 P.M. Monday through Thursday, 9:00 A.M. to 8:00 P.M. Friday, 8:00 A.M. to 8:00 P.M. Saturday, and 9:00 A.M. to 7:00 P.M. Sunday. The marina rents fishing boats, pontoon boats, and paddleboats by the hour or by the day. Rates vary depending

# Public Recreation Centers and Programs

Public parks and recreation departments are your greatest resource for year-round recreation, so use them often. Public recreation centers, ubiquitous throughout Greater Denver, are your best bets for finding indoor and outdoor swimming pools. No matter where you are, there is more than one nearby. If you're a member of the community, the cost is minimal. If you come from another community, the cost is only slightly higher. Parks and recreation departments are also your best bet for youth team sports ranging from basketball to soccer, and if they don't run their own programs in some sport—T-ball for the kiddies or tennis for adults—they will certainly be able to refer you to the nearest local organizations that do.

The offerings at the following public centers are too vast to catalog here, so we've just listed the numbers for you to call. However, we have listed specific programs under other headings, tennis or climbing, for example, to steer you in the right direction.

## Denver

Denver Parks and Recreation Department, (720) 913-0696

## Adams County

Adams County Parks and Community Resources Department, (303) 637-8000

Aurora Parks and Recreation Department, (303) 739-7160

Brighton Recreation Center, (303) 655-2200

Commerce City Parks and Recreation Department, (303) 289-3789

Hyland Hills Park and Recreation District, Federal Heights, (303) 428-7488

Northglenn Parks and Recreation Department, (303) 450-8800

Thornton Recreation Center, (303) 255-7800

## Arapahoe County

Arapahoe Park and Recreation District, (303) 730-6109

Aurora Parks and Recreation Department, (303) 739-7160

Englewood Parks Department, (303) 762-2680

South Suburban Park and Recreation District (also covers a small area of Douglas County), (303) 798-5131

## Douglas County

Castle Rock Recreation Center, (303) 660-1036

Parker Recreation Center, (303) 841-4500

## Jefferson County

Arvada Parks and Recreation Department, recreation handled by North Jeffco Park and Recreation District (below), (303) 424-2739

Broomfield Recreation Center, (303) 464-5500

Edgewater Recreation Center, (303) 237-4817

Foothills Park and Recreation District, (303) 409-2100

Golden Recreation and Parks Department, (303) 384-8100

Lakewood Recreation Department, (303) 987-7800

North Jeffco Park and Recreation District, (303) 424-2739

Westminster Parks and Recreation Department, (303) 430-2400

Wheat Ridge Recreation Center, (303) 231-1300

on the boat, between $100 to $160 an hour, and require a refundable damage deposit. Call ahead for reservations.

**The Cherry Creek Marina**
**Aurora**
**(303) 779-6144**
**(303) 699-2501 (yacht club)**
**www.cherrycreekmarina.com**
The marina is on the west side of the reservoir; just follow the signs after entering. It has slips, water access, and rentals of canoes, motorboats, sailboats, rowboats, pontoon boats, and bicycles. This marina also has a little restaurant. It's open weekdays from 10:00 A.M. to 6:00 P.M. every day April through October. Weekend hours are extended from 8:00 A.M. to 8:00 P.M. June through August. All hours are weather permitting. Rental prices vary greatly. Sailboats, for example, rent for $17 an hour, fishing boats for $25 an hour, and eight-person pontoons for $90 an hour. Discounts often apply to multiple-hour rentals.

**Standley Lake**
**9805 West 88th Avenue, Westminster**
**(303) 425-1097**
**www.ci.westminster.co.us/res/recfac/SL**
Standley Lake, the big north Jefferson County lake bordered on the north and east by Westminster and on the south by Arvada, is a popular location for windsurfing. Motorboats are allowed there between May 1 and September 30, but you need a permit for boats with more than 20 horsepower, and the number of permits is limited. Boats with less than 20 horsepower can use the lake for $10 per day. Call the city of Westminster's office at the lake at the number above. There are no rental facilities at Standley.

# Climbing

Climbing isn't exactly the kind of sport you just decide to try on a Saturday morning. It can be dangerous—and deadly—even for those who've been doing it for years. But it also can be an unparalleled challenge for people into getting the most from their workout.

There are many climbing opportunities in Colorado. Most require getting out of the Denver area, but you can start by taking lessons and learning the ropes in town. A number of businesses and recreation centers have their own in-house climbing walls. From there you can graduate to climbing areas just outside of Boulder, where the terrain is internationally known. There also are climbing groups that put together excursions.

**City Park Recreation Center**
**10455 Sheridan Boulevard, Westminster**
**(303) 460-9690**
City Park has its own climbing wall in its gymnasium, where people can practice or take climbing lessons while the basketballs bounce behind them. Classes are offered for beginner, intermediate, and advanced climbers. Or you can take a short orientation, then pay a low drop-in fee of $3.25 for residents or $4.75 for nonresidents.

**Colorado Mountain Club**
**710 10th Street, No. 200, Golden**
**(303) 279-3080**
**www.cmc.org**
Technical climbing instruction is available from the grandfather of Colorado mountaineering organizations, the Colorado Mountain Club, but classes are offered only once a year. Basic rock climbing is offered in May and June, and the intermediate class is usually in August or September. Membership is required and runs about $100 for year-round, in-state membership and about $35 for a Friends of Colorado Mountain Club membership for out-of-staters. From there you will receive a schedule of events, including climbing excursions, twice a year.

**Eldorado Canyon State Park**
**9 Kneale Road, Box B, Eldorado 80025**
**(303) 494-3943**
**www.parks.state.co.us**

No discussion of mountain climbing in the Denver metro area can occur without mentioning Eldorado Canyon State Park. It's where athletes from around the world gather to practice their skills, swap stories, and train for the really big mountains. The park is day-use only and boasts 500 routes that rise as much as 1,500 feet above the canyon floor. The easiest are used for climbing lessons; the most challenging are reserved for the experts. Because the area is a state park, expect to pay a use fee and then relax at picnic tables or by biking or fishing in the stream.

### Paradise Rock Gym
**6260 North Washington Street, No. 5**
**(303) 286-8168**
**www.paradiserock.com**
This is an indoor rock-climbing gym built around technical climbing, with 7,500 square feet of climbing wall and structure as well as lessons, a small amount of climbing accessory retail, and cross-training facilities such as weight machines, stationary bicycles, and stair machines. Beginners are welcome here for lessons. The Monday-night lesson for beginners costs only $20, including equipment. More advanced lessons are offered in a complete instruction program; call for information.

### REI (Recreational Equipment Inc.)
**1416 Platte Street**
**(303) 756-3100**
**www.rei.com**
This gigantic store tempts visitors with its climbing wall at the entrance. REI offers a variety of classes for all levels. Cost is $15 to $35 per class. Kids climb free on Saturday, and free clinics are offered monthly. Call for details and times. REI's wall is designed for an introduction to climbing so it isn't equal to the rock gyms mentioned above. Beyond the wall, the store offers a full range of retail equipment for climbing and mountaineering. Walls and lessons also are available at REI stores at 1789 28th Street, Boulder, (303) 583-9970; 9637 East County Line Road, Englewood, (303) 858-1726; and 5375

South Wadsworth Boulevard, Lakewood, (303) 932-0600.

### Thrillseekers
**1912 South Broadway**
**(303) 733-8810**
**www.thrillseekers.cc/proshop.html**
This climbing gym offers more than 12,000 square feet of climbing space, including a 35-foot roof climb, 40 top ropes, 5 lead walls where climbers can get horizontal, and a separate "bouldering" area where you can free-climb. A complete lesson program is available for all levels, and a full retail section will fill your every climbing need. Lesson prices vary depending on level and number of people, so call ahead. Thrillseekers also offers a team-building seminar.

# Fishing

One-third of the state's land area is open to public hunting and fishing. Colorado is a national destination for these activities, the kind of place where people come from the Midwest and both coasts to cast a fly in rushing mountain streams.

Fishing in Colorado, of course, isn't just a matter of mountain trout streams. The state has flatland rivers, large lakes, and reservoirs aplenty. Colorado's 6,000-plus miles of streams and 2,000-plus lakes and reservoirs open to public fishing include high-country fishing for cutthroat, brook, brown, lake, and rainbow trout. There's also a lot of warm-water quarry such as walleye, largemouth and smallmouth bass, catfish, crappie, yellow perch, wiper, bluegill, and muskie. A lot of warm-water fishing is available right in Greater Denver. The state's record tiger muskie (40 pounds, 2 ounces) was caught in Quincy Reservoir, a half-mile east of Buckley Road on Quincy Avenue in Aurora.

The Denver daily papers publish a weekly fishing and stocking report provided by the Colorado Division of Wildlife. In the *Denver Post,* it's called "Colorado's

Best Bets," and in the *Rocky Mountain News,* it's called "Colorado's Hot Spots." Both offer anglers up-to-the-minute scoops on hot fishing spots.

Recorded information about fishing (license fees, locations, etc.) is available from the Division of Wildlife, (303) 291–7533; information on specific fishing conditions throughout the state is available from mid-April through Labor Day weekend at (303) 291–7534. You can also visit the Colorado Division of Wildlife's Web site at wildlife.state.co.us and click on "Fishing" in the index.

## LICENSES

Fishing licenses are required; you can get yours at most major sports and outdoors stores or online at www.wildlifelicense .com/co/. Cost is $26 per year for Colorado residents, $56 for nonresidents. A day license costs $9.00 for residents and nonresidents, and a five-day license is $21.00, nonresidents only. There are discounts for senior citizens and people with disabilities; children younger than age 16 do not need a license. Anglers receive a complete rules and regulations brochure when they purchase a license. Brochures are usually available where you buy your license. There are various size and quantity limits as well as rules on allowable bait, depending on the waters and type of fish. Consult the brochure you receive during licensing, call the DOW at (303) 291–7533, or check its Web site for details at www.wildlife.state.co.us.

## FISHING SPOTS

Although Colorado has been suffering through drought conditions that have affected reservoir levels and stream flows, the state remains world-famous for its Gold Medal trout waters. These lakes and streams have a high-quality aquatic habitat, a high percentage of trout 14 inches or longer, and a high potential for trophy fish. The Colorado Division of Wildlife has a booklet on the state's 11 Gold Medal waters; call (303) 297–1192 or go to www.wildlife

.state.co.us/fishing/wheretogo.

The South Platte River is one of the best rainbow and brown trout fisheries in the nation and is world-famous among fly fishers. This Gold Medal river is for the serious fishing enthusiast and has it all: proximity to Denver, lots of big fish, consistent insect hatches, and incredible scenery. The Cheesman Canyon section of the South Platte holds approximately 5,200 trout per mile that average 15 inches in length (although some locals will tell you it also seems to have at least that many fishermen).

The two best ways to reach Cheesman Canyon both involve traveling south to the Deckers area and then working your way back north along the river. Take US 285 west from Denver, then turn south onto County Road 126 at Pine Junction. Follow CR 126 for 20 miles toward Deckers; the Gill Trail parking lot is just off CR 126. The Gill trailhead is a 20-minute hike from the Gill Trail parking lot. If the hike to Gill Trail doesn't sound appealing, just continue on CR 126 into Deckers; parking and open fishing is plentiful right along the road north of town.

For those looking for an enjoyable but less rigorous fishing expedition, Denver-area reservoirs offer a wide range of opportunities.

Aurora Reservoir is home to some hefty rainbow and brown trout, with fish up to 17 inches not uncommon, and also contains many warm-water species such as largemouth bass, crappie, yellow perch, and walleye. The reservoir is open year-round from dawn until dusk. Take I–25 or I–225 to Sixth Avenue and follow it until it turns south to become Gun Club Road. Quincy Avenue is about 2 miles past the BFI landfill. The reservoir is about a half-mile east at 5800 South Powhaton Road. The daily access fee is $4.00 per car.

Chatfield Reservoir is one of the Denver metro area's most popular recreation spots. The 1,100-acre reservoir is an impoundment of the South Platte River described earlier in this section and offers fishing access to the river both above and below the reservoir itself. A Colorado State

Parks permit is required, which can be purchased for $5.00 a day after Labor Day through April 30 or $6.00 a day from May 1 through Labor Day. From Denver, take Wadsworth Boulevard (Highway 121) south past C-470, and turn left into the park at the Deer Creek entrance. As an alternate route, take Santa Fe Boulevard south to Titan Road and turn west. Go to Roxborough Park Road, and turn north to the Plum Creek entrance.

# Golf

The Denver area is a great place to plan a golf vacation. There are more than 70 golf courses in the Greater Denver area, 90 percent of them are public, and getting a tee time is much easier than in years past. Not only that, but if you want to make a day of it, there are another 20 or so spectacular mountain-area courses, all within a one- to two-hour drive from downtown Denver.

As with many major metropolitan areas, Denver city courses are typically smaller, older tracts, but they often have more character than the treeless suburban courses that tend to show up in housing developments. While these inner-city layouts might not attract tournament golf, they almost always present more of a challenge than you would expect, the price is usually easier on the wallet, and you can get to most of them by cab, avoiding the freeways around Denver.

On the other hand, there is nothing like teeing off in the Rocky Mountains at one of the nearby mountain courses. It's not unusual for a first-time player to return from a day of golf in Breckenridge or Winter Park only to find he can't remember how he played—he spent too much time looking around at the scenery!

Most courses require advance tee times but limit how far in advance you can call, usually not more than seven days. This is only a problem if you need a weekend tee time, when courses are most crowded, or if you have no flexibility in your schedule. Otherwise, local experience reports that many courses can fit you in with a same-day call, and sometimes you can even "walk-on" without a tee-time reservation. Resorts typically allow you to make tee times when booking your vacation.

There are several excellent publications and Web sites that you can use to get course information in the Denver area, plus we're going to highlight some of the more exceptional courses in this chapter.

*Colorado AvidGolfer Magazine* is available online at www.coloradoavidgolfer .com, by subscription at (720) 493-1729, or at local newsstands monthly.

*Colorado Golf Magazine* is available online at www.coloradogolf.com, or via quarterly subscription at (303) 688-5853.

*Colorado Golfer Newspaper,* (303) 699-GOLF, sells an annual issue that has listings and fees of all the courses in Colorado.

*GOLFViews Magazine* is available online at www.golfviews.com, or phone (303) 797-8700.

**Arrowhead**
**10850 West Sundown Trail, Littleton**
**(303) 973-9614**
**www.arrowheadcolorado.com**
Designed by Robert Trent Jones Jr. in 1971, Arrowhead is a par 72, 18-hole course that winds 6,682 yards through a landscape of scrub oak and magnificent red sandstone rock formations. Arrowhead is regarded as one of the most beautiful and challenging courses in the state, and it regularly makes *Golf Digest*'s top 20 list of places to play in Colorado. Tee times can be made up to seven days in advance, with greens fees ranging from $129 weekdays up to $135 on weekends including the mandatory cart. No denim is allowed, and collared shirts are required. Take I-25 south to C-470 west, exit onto Santa Fe Drive, and go south 4 miles to Titan Parkway. Turn right onto Titan Parkway, follow it until it becomes Rampart Range Road, then follow the signs to Arrowhead.

## Breckenridge Golf Club
200 Clubhouse Drive, Breckenridge
(970) 453-9104
www.breckenridgegolfclub.com

Breckenridge Golf Club has the distinction of being the only municipally owned
Jack Nicklaus–designed course in the
world, and it is a masterpiece. Rated one
of "America's Top 75 Upscale Golf
Courses" by *Golf Digest,* Breckenridge
features 27 holes that include some of
the most beautiful valley vistas on any
course anywhere. Like most mountain
courses, the layout incorporates many of
the surrounding area's natural settings,
with tree-lined fairways, rock outcrop-
pings, and hazard areas filled with mountain bushes and flowers. Greens fees are
typical for mountain courses, at $99 plus
$16 for a cart; tee-time reservations can
be made four days in advance. Breckenridge is about 90 miles west of Denver.
Take I-70 west to exit 203 and turn south
onto Highway 9. Go 7 miles to Tiger
Road. Turn left onto Tiger Road and proceed to your first right turn.

## Fox Hollow
13410 West Morrison Road, Lakewood
(303) 986-7888
www.lakewood.org

Fox Hollow is a 27-hole course you play
by booking two of the three 9-hole venues, each of which offers a unique layout
ranging from wide-open links to tree-
lined river bottom to rugged canyon-
lands. *Colorado Golf Magazine*'s player
poll ranked Fox Hollow the third-best
public course in the state in 2001. Call
for tee times up to six days in advance,
wear appropriate golf attire to the
course, and think about adding a third 9
holes to your round for an extra $24.
The 18-hole greens fee is $48 Monday
through Thursday, $52 Friday through
Sunday, plus $14 per person for the
optional cart. Take C-470 south to the
Morrison Road exit, then go east on
Morrison Road for 3.5 miles. The course,
which is well signed, will be on your
right.

## Legacy Ridge
10801 Legacy Ridge Parkway
Westminster
(303) 438-8997
www.ci.westminster.co.us/res/recfac/golf

Although parts of Legacy Ridge's 18-hole,
par 72 course are laid out among housing
developments, the majority of the holes
either wind through protected wetlands or
traverse a ridge that offers spectacular
views of the Front Range of the Rockies.
Renowned Ohio architect Arthur Hills
designed this course in 1994, and it regularly makes the top 10 in player polls.
Greens fees are $39 during the week and
$45 on weekends, plus $14 per person for
the optional cart. If you play late in the
day, be sure to enjoy a classic Colorado
sunset from the outdoor deck of the clubhouse bar and grill. From Denver take I-25
north to U.S. Highway 36 west, toward
Boulder. Exit US 36 at the 104th Avenue
exit, and head east on 104th Avenue to
Legacy Ridge Parkway. Turn left and
watch for the clubhouse on your left.

## Pole Creek
P.O. Box 3348, U.S. Highway 40
Mile marker 220, Winter Park 80482
(970) 887-9195, (800) 511-5076
www.polecreekgolf.com

When Pole Creek opened in 1985, it was
named "Best New Public Course in the
United States" by *Golf Digest*. Surrounded
by 13,000-foot snowcapped peaks, at an
elevation of 8,600 feet, Pole Creek is quintessential Colorado mountain golf. The original 18-hole layout, designed by Gary Player
and Ron Kirby, has been expanded by Denis
Griffiths to 27 holes that play up into the
lodgepole pines, back down into the riverbottom meadows, and through some of the
most beautiful scenery in the state. At this
elevation golfers can expect an extra 15 percent distance on their shots, just one of the
many benefits of making the drive up from
Denver to play here. Tee times can be made
five days in advance, and greens fees are
very reasonable for the short-season mountain courses, at $85 including a cart. Pole
Creek is located 78 miles from Denver. Take

I-70 west to exit 232 onto US 40, then follow US 40 to Winter Park. Pole Creek is 11 miles beyond the town of Winter Park. Turn left at the 220-mile marker and follow the signs to the course.

### Red Hawk Ridge
**2156 Red Hawk Ridge Drive, Castle Rock**
**(720) 733-3500**
**www.ci.castlerock.co.us/**
Red Hawk Ridge, south of Denver in Castle Rock, is a virtual cousin to nearby private Castle Pines, the country club famous for the International pro-golf tournament. Designed by Jim Engh and opened in 1999, the par 72, 6,942-yard Red Hawk Ridge received immediate rave reviews in national golf publications for its dramatic setting and design, including the 15th hole, a 528-yard, par 4 that shoots blind to a plateau, then downhill into a valley where the green lies at the bottom. Fees are a little higher, at $47 to $72 weekdays and $50 to $77 weekends (depending on the season), including a cart. Tee times can be made up to seven days in advance. From I-25 take the Wolfensberger exit and turn west after approximately 0.5 mile. Turn right onto Red Hawk Drive and go about another 0.25 mile; the golf course is on the left.

### Riverdale Dunes
**13300 Riverdale Road, Brighton**
**(303) 659-6700**
**www.riverdalegolf.com**
Riverdale Dunes is a true hidden gem. Designed by Pete and Perry Dye in 1985, this course garners national praise every year from leading golf magazines. Rated as one of the "Top 75 Public Courses" in the country by *Golf Digest,* and the "#1 Public Course in Colorado" by *Colorado Golfer Newspaper,* the Dunes is an 18-hole, par 72 course that plays 6,398 yards in a Scottish-style links layout. Though hard to find, this reasonably priced, immaculately maintained course is worth the effort. From Denver go north on I-25 to the 120th Avenue exit, then east to Colorado Boulevard and turn left. Follow Colorado Boulevard to 128th Avenue and turn right. 128th Avenue ends at Riverdale Road, and you will feel as though you're in the middle of nowhere, but turn left onto Riverdale Road and follow it about 1.5 miles to the enormous new clubhouse, which you will see on your right.

## Hiking

Hiking is the most common way of enjoying Colorado's backcountry. For information on hiking safety and our favorite places to hike, see our The Great Outdoors chapter.

## Horseback Riding

What's more quintessentially Western than an outing on the back of a horse, especially when you're riding on the prairies or foothills of the Rockies? Riding in the Denver suburbs may not compare with the more remote horse experiences in the high country and points west, but it beats a canter through Midwestern cornfields.

A lot of people on the outskirts of Denver have their own horses, but if you don't, there are some fine stables to choose from for a daily rental ride. The two state recreation areas on Greater Denver's south side are nice places to ride, simply because they have large and carefully cultivated natural areas and their own stables on-site, where you can pay to ride the nature trails.

### Chatfield Stables
**11500 North Roxborough Park Road**
**Littleton**
**(303) 933-3636**
**www.painthorsestables.net**
These stables at the Chatfield State Recreation Area provide a serene riding setting with great foothill views. Rides are available beginning in March or April, depending on how wet the spring is, and usually end around October or November,

again depending on weather. Reservations are required and there is a two-horse rental minimum and a 210-pound weight limit. A one-hour rental costs $24, an hour-and-a-half rental costs $35, and a two-hour rental costs $45 per person. Chatfield Stables is open every day from 9:00 A.M. to 5:00 P.M. but might close on Monday, so call ahead. Hay rides are available year-round, weather permitting. To get there from C–470, take the Wadsworth exit south and turn left at the third stoplight, into the park. From there, follow the signs.

**Paint Horse Stables**
**4201 South Parker Road, Aurora**
**(303) 690–8235**
**www.painthorsestables.net**
At the Cherry Creek Reservoir State Recreation Area, this is a great spot for a ride. The area is wooded and has lots of open meadows with natural grasslands. You need reservations to ride here; a day or two in advance is fine. Paint Horse Stables also runs the Chatfield Stables, and rental rates are the same (see the listing for Chatfield Stables). It's open from 9:00 A.M. to 6:00 P.M. in the summer; winter hours vary.

**Stockton's Plum Creek Stables Ltd.**
**7479 West Titan Road, Littleton**
**(303) 791–1966**
**www.stocktonsplumcreek.com**
Stockton's has access to the 7,000 acres of Chatfield State Recreation Area via its own private entrance. The area is beautiful, with plenty of bird-watching opportunities on native prairie grasses. Find the stables by going about 4 miles south of C–470 on Santa Fe Drive and turning right on Titan Road. Call for information on hayrides and special events.

---

*If you want to hunt on private land, you have to ask the owner; it's legal in Colorado to hunt on private land with the owner's permission.*

**A Worthy Ranch & Stables**
**West Parker Road, Parker**
**(303) 841–9405**
On the other side of Greater Denver's south side are a couple of stables in the town of Parker, which you can reach by taking I–25 a little more than a mile south of its intersection with C–470, then traveling east about 2.5 miles on Lincoln Avenue (exit 193) before turning right on a little dirt road called West Parker Road. A Worthy Ranch & Stables is about 2 miles down West Parker Road on the left. It offers lessons as well as riding, with miles of trails. Guided rides are given by reservation only and cost $25 per hour with a two-hour minimum.

# Hunting

Hunting, together with fishing, is a $3 billion a year industry in Colorado. That's second only to the ski industry in terms of economic impact. As vast as the numbers are, so are the locations and types of hunting available in Colorado. Hunting is legal on certain public lands as well as on private land with permission. In fact, you might see bumper stickers that say "Ask first . . . before hunting or fishing on private land."

## LICENSES AND SEASONS

All hunting, including on public land, requires licenses that can be purchased at any major sports and outdoors stores (such as Kmart or Sports Authority [formerly Gart Sports] stores). The cost varies depending on the game hunted.

For example, a resident deer license costs around $31; nonresidents pay $295. Rare game such as moose will cost much more to hunt—$251 for residents and more than $1,600 for nonresidents. There are limits on the number of licenses issued, with more reserved for residents. A lottery is held for some big-game hunting where numbers are kept to a minimum. Call the Division of Wildlife (DOW), (303) 297-1192, for a complete list of prices and limitations. Brochures for the various types of hunting are available from the DOW beginning in February and March, depending on the game. The yearly updates spell out the rules and regulations.

Most hunting is confined to specific seasons, whose dates vary from year to year. To find out the parameters of specific game, contact the Division of Wildlife at (303) 297–1192 or use the following recorded information lines: big-game hunting, (303) 291–7529; small game, (303) 291–7546; game birds, (303) 291–7547; and waterfowl, (303) 291–7548.

The state is most famous for big game, including elk, mountain lion, black bear, mule deer, bighorn sheep, mountain goat, white-tailed deer, and pronghorn antelope. But 105 of the state's 113 species of sport game are small game, including ducks and geese, wild turkey, ring-necked pheasant, mourning dove, band-tailed pigeon, quail, grouse, rabbit, and coyote.

There's a lot of winter trapping as well for beaver, muskrat, bobcat, weasel, marten, mink, badger, and fox.

# In-Line Skating

Commonly called "Rollerblading" for the trademark brand name, this sport is more properly called "in-line skating" for the same reason you say "copying" instead of "Xeroxing." If you're a beginner you might want to try the safe route of renting in-lines at a local indoor roller rink. Xpress Sports, 8412 North Huron Street, Thornton, (303) 429–4999, in north Greater Denver rents both in-line and traditional rollers in a safe, indoor atmosphere of neon lights and music.

Outdoors is a different story; it's where you go when you want to get a little more serious about in-line skating. Outdoors, there's the temptation to go faster, which in-lines can do, and the tendency to fall harder with rougher landings. Experts always recommend wearing helmets, knee pads, and wrist guards.

There are plenty of places around Greater Denver where in-lining can be slow and easy, where people of all experience levels can enjoy the sport. Check Denver's city bicycle maps (see the Pavement Bicycling section in this chapter) for the city bike paths where in-line skating is good. If it's a good pavement biking path, then it's a good blading path.

### Chatfield State Recreation Area
### South on Wadsworth Boulevard
### off C–470
Follow the signs to this state park for smooth in-line skating. As with other paths, you'll share it with bikers and joggers, but there's plenty of room. The mountain views are better here than at Cherry Creek, but both are perfect spots for people of all levels of expertise. There aren't too many shady spots on the Chatfield path, so brings lots of water. One word of caution: Watch for park traffic on cross streets.

### Cherry Creek Greenbelt Path
### Various access points from Confluence
### Park to Cherry Creek Reservoir
This cement path begins (or ends, depending on your perspective) at Confluence Park, which is the confluence of the South Platte River and Cherry Creek, off 15th Street just west of Lower Downtown. It follows the creek past the Denver Country Club, through the Cherry Creek neighborhood to the east side of town, and out to Cherry Creek Reservoir. The entire length is approximately 15 miles of smooth surface and quiet spaces. It's one of the most esteemed blading zones due to its pleasant and fashionable location and the many connecting bike paths along its length. The streets of Cherry Creek also have a great reputation: It's a fun place to be, and the roads tend to be new and smooth.

### Cherry Creek State Park
### South on the Parker Road exit off I–225
Just follow the signs off Parker Road to enter the paths that wind through this state park area. The terrain is smooth and

flat and surrounded by prairie grasses and groves of trees where you can rest and cool off. The path is open year-round, and it's great on sunny winter days, too. As with Chatfield State Recreation Area, watch for park traffic on cross streets, especially on weekends.

### Colorado Highway 470 Path
### Various access points along C–470 from Highlands Ranch to I–70

One place that's "totally happening," according to one in-liner jock, is the bike path that follows C–470 along its eastern side in Jefferson County. It has good uphills and downhills, sharp corners, and a smooth surface built for speed. The path parallels C–470 on the east side all the way to I–70.

### Crown Hill Park
### On the east side of Kipling Street between 32nd and 26th Avenues
### Wheat Ridge

This is popular for the seamless concrete path surrounding Crown Hill Lake. The park atmosphere is friendly and inspiring for all the amateur athletes who take to the path year-round. You'll share the path with bikers and joggers, but mostly joggers, and like all Denver-area paths, it can get crowded at times. Just watch out for speed demons.

### Platte River Greenway
### Access points from downtown Denver through Littleton

This path also starts (or ends) at Confluence Park and extends in both directions along the Platte to Chatfield State Park. It's just as good as the Cherry Creek path: wide open and lots of smooth skating. This one might be slightly slimmer than Cherry Creek, however.

### Washington Park
### Between South Franklin and South Downing Streets just north of I–25

Washington Park is always filled with skaters, bikers, walkers, and joggers. An asphalt street rings the park and has lanes for all of them. Inside the park the scenery is interesting, with soccer and volleyball games going on and colorful flower beds and two lakes along the way, but the asphalt surface can be rough.

### Rentals

In-line skating rentals can be found in every area of town. Reservations aren't necessary, as most places rent by the hour on a first-come, first-served basis. The cost will vary, so you need to check with the individual shops. You can expect to pay at least $4.00 an hour and up to $8.00 (24-hour rentals priced as low as $15.00). Sports Plus, 1055 South Gaylord, (303) 777-6613, rents to a lot of Washington Park skaters.

# Running

Runners are everywhere in Greater Denver: in the streets of downtown and the suburbs, in the city parks and greenbelts, and along the mountain paths. You can run anywhere. Most people run in their own neighborhoods. But there are some popular running venues for those who want to run where others are running, in pleasant settings and on motorist-free trails.

Washington Park, between South Franklin and South Downing Streets just north of I–25, probably has Denver's highest runner density. That may be because it's one of Denver's biggest and most pleasant parks, or it may be because it's in an area with a lot of upscale empty-nesters who believe in exercise and don't have to get it by pushing their kids on the park's swings. Closer in, City Park, between Colorado Boulevard and York Street, 2 blocks north of East Colfax Avenue, is another popular running area where folks can get away from cars and run through some semblance of foliated quietude. Greenbelts, including the popular Highline Canal in Littleton, the Cherry Creek Bike Path, and the South Platte River trails at Chatfield Reservoir, are particularly nice places to run for that same aesthetic. If you like running on natural terrain, which is healthier because it avoids the repetitive, one-dimensional joint-pounding of flat terrain, you may want to try the many fine trails along the Front Range. See some of the suggested mountain-biking trails outlined in our Mountain Biking section.

A lot of runners are solitary souls. You see them at dawn while you're driving to work, and you see them in the evening when you're coming home, running alone and happy about it. But for those who enjoy the group experience, there are plenty of events and clubs. Greater Denver's largest annual running events include the 5-mile Cherry Creek Sneak in April, the Governor's Cup 5K in September, the Run for the Zoo 5K and 10K in October, the Race for the Cure 5K in October, and the 4-mile Turkey Trot on Thanksgiving morning.

Among the larger running clubs are the Colorado Masters, for the older-than-30 crowd, www.comastersrun.org, and the Rocky Mountain Road Runners, (303) 871-8366. Don't forget that walkers have found increasing acceptance in the area's big running events. The Front Range Walkers, (303) 377-0576, is perhaps the area's biggest walking club.

Some running stores also serve as information clearinghouses on running clubs, events, and race series and are places where you can sign up for races. This includes Runners Roost Ltd., 1685 South Colorado Boulevard, (303) 759-8455.

# Skiing

You'd expect skiing to be the top entry in any guide to Greater Denver recreation, but we're placing it down here because it's well covered in our Ski Country chapter. That chapter gives you an abundance of information on all the major ski areas near Denver, along with plenty of tips on tickets, lessons, and the ski season.

Skiing is certainly recreation, however, and if you're a beginner or a want-to-be beginner, you may want to know about

*One of the best bargains in fitness is the Denver Parks and Recreation membership. Depending on the recreation center and the offerings chosen, Denver residents can lift weights, play basketball, and swim for $150 a year. Nonresident fees are $200. Check with your nearest rec center for details or visit www.denvergov.org and search "recreation."*

some of the information sources that can help you get into the sport.

Colorado Ski Country USA, (303) 837-0793, a trade association for all the ski resorts in the state, publishes the *Colorado Ski Country Consumer Guide*. Within about 130 pages, it contains a lot of the information you may want to know about skiing in Colorado. Colorado Ski Country USA will mail it to you free if you give them a call.

You may also want to know about Sniagrab (bargains spelled backward), the big annual ski equipment and apparel sale held every year by Sports Authority (formerly Gart Sports) outlets around Greater Denver. It starts on the Saturday before Labor Day and runs through much of September. You can find some fine deals on new and used equipment.

One of the best ways to get into skiing is to link up with a ski club. It's not only a social event, but also a way of letting the more experienced take you under their wing via group outings to local ski areas where all you have to do is show up, get on the bus, and have a good time. A lot of health clubs and recreation districts have ski clubs, and it's not unlikely that you'll find a ski club at your place of employment.

# Tennis

Greater Denver has plenty of tennis facilities, both private and public. Of course, you don't have to contact any organizations or join any leagues to play tennis. You can find courts in just about any major city park.

In Denver, try Washington Park, between South Franklin and South Downing Streets just north of I-25, and City Park, between Colorado Boulevard and York Street, 2 blocks north of East Colfax Avenue. Park play is free and usually runs on a first-come, first-served basis as long as there are no tournaments or lessons going on.

Beyond public courts, there are many organized centers and city recreation departments that offer players a chance to join group play, take lessons, and play in tournaments.

Greater Denver's central tennis resource is the Colorado Tennis Association, (303) 695-4116. If you're looking for courts or are interested in finding out how to get into organized tennis leagues or sanctioned tournaments, the CTA can help steer you to the right place. It also has copies of tournament schedules for adults and juniors as well as general information brochures. It's the local branch of the U.S. Tennis Association as well, so you can get USTA memberships and publications through the CTA.

### Arvada Tennis Center
### Corner of 65th and Miller Streets
### Arvada
### (303) 420-1210

This is a fine public facility with eight courts and sanctioned USTA play. If you want to take to the courts, we suggest making reservations in advance. It is open from about 5:00 until 9:00 P.M. nightly and on Saturday and Sunday from 7:30 A.M. until noon. Cost is $5.00 per hour per court, $7.00 after dark.

### Aurora Parks and Recreation
### Aurora-area parks
### (303) 326-8700

Aurora has a good reputation for its public tennis program. Pros offer beginning, intermediate, and advanced lessons for one-week or two-week sessions as well as evening and Saturday lessons. Tourna-

ment play is available, too; check the summer brochure. Aurora maintains 72 courts on a first-come, first-served basis. Very few courts are lighted; one exception is Del Mar Park at Sixth Avenue and Peoria Street.

### Denver Parks and Recreation
### Denver-area parks
### (720) 913-0696

The city recreation district maintains a few dozen courts across the city for daytime play. There are junior programs and adult lesson programs throughout the Denver area. The USTA youth tournament program runs seven weeks of instruction in the summer and one week of tournaments beginning in early June. Adults age 18 and older can join the Congress Park (Eighth Avenue and York Street east of downtown) program or the Berkley Park (46th Avenue and Sheridan Boulevard northwest of town) program in June and July. Call for information on other programs.

### Gates Tennis Center
### 100 South Adams Street
### (303) 355-4461
### www.gatestenniscenter.com

This popular facility is just south of the Cherry Creek mall and consistently rated as one of the top public tennis facilities in the country. You don't need a membership, court times are reasonable, and lessons are competitively priced. It has one of the nation's largest tennis ladders, a challenge arrangement in which you sign up at a certain level and begin to play and move up and down the ladder. Gates has more than 1,000 people on its computerized ladder, enough to offer specialized ladders for singles, doubles, etc. There's even a coed ladder reputed to be a good place for singles to meet. It's a 20-court facility complete with clubhouse, locker room, and pro shop. Pros will teach you, and ball machines will test you.

### Holly Tennis Center
### 6651 South Krameria Way, Englewood
### (303) 771-3654

Holly offers the most USTA-sanctioned tournaments in Colorado. It offers programs on a total of 40 courts, including use of courts in the South Suburban Recreation District. Six of Holly's courts are lighted. League play varies from $40 to $46 and includes practice and matches. Junior and adult private and group lessons cost between $40 and $50.

### Ken Caryl Ranch Community Center
### 1 Club Drive, Littleton
### (303) 979-2233

Ken Caryl has four indoor courts and six outdoor courts. You won't find prettier surroundings; the Ken Caryl Ranch community is in the red-rock moonscape of the valley hidden behind the Hogback Formation that runs north-south along C–470. The facility is actually owned by Jefferson County Open Space. Offered here are leagues, tournaments, and lessons for resident and nonresident youths and adults. You also can purchase a membership to the center. Cost varies depending on the program. Tennis clinics, for instance, vary from $20 to $50 per person.

# Wildlife Watching

While hunting wildlife is more traditional, recent years have seen a tremendous growth in the stalking of wildlife either to photograph, or just for the joy of seeing it as close as is possible or safe. There are few things as magical as watching a herd of elk feeding in a mountain field or catching a glimpse of a red fox as it darts amid trees. Colorado offers more than 100 places to view wildlife year-round. The best time to view is early morning and late evening (dawn and sunset).

As you travel Colorado's roads and highways, watch for signs that depict a pair of binoculars and say WILDLIFE VIEWING AREA, and follow the signs. One such area is just outside Denver International Airport. Another is in the mountains, along I-70 just east of Georgetown (about an hour and a half from Denver). But there are dozens more. Contact the Division of Wildlife at (303) 297-1192 for a list, or pick up a wildlife viewing book at any major bookstore. The *Colorado Wildlife Viewing Guide* is available through the Colorado Wildlife Heritage Foundation for $12.95. Call (303) 291-7212 or visit online at www.wildlife.state.co.us/CWHF/shop/.

By the way, wildlife viewing has its own etiquette that keeps wildlife—and people—safe and healthy. For instance, keep binoculars handy because wildlife should be viewed from a distance. Of course, never chase or spook animals; not only is it frowned upon, but it's also illegal. And don't approach wildlife too quickly, as you can scare them away and ruin everyone's enjoyment.

In recent years bird-watching has become an increasingly popular pastime. Reported as the nation's fastest-growing form of outdoor recreation, bird-watching attracts a well-educated and serious crowd in Colorado. Denver even boasts another kind of distinction—it's home to a best-selling mystery writer whose lead character is a bird-watcher. Among the sinister plots Christine Goff has written about are meadowlarks that are ousted from their habitat by vintners (*Murdered by Merlot*). Anyone interested in joining Denver-area bird-watchers should call the Audubon Society, (303) 973-9530.

# THE GREAT OUTDOORS

As a diverse three-dimensional universe, the mountains offer unparalleled opportunity for adventure. You can venture deep into the Colorado Rockies for long trips or drive less than a half-hour and be surrounded by great exploring territory.

Camping, hiking, and biking abound in Colorado's great outdoors, and we've offered a few tips to enjoy them.

More than one-third of Colorado's land area is owned by and is available to the public, including 8.3 million acres of Bureau of Land Management tracts and 14.3 million acres of national forest. There are 11 national forests in Colorado, covering major parts of the state. The national forests are basically undeveloped areas where you can hike, fish, hunt, ride, and camp just about anywhere. They are also where the vast majority of wilderness can be found, and if you want to hike to some remote and beautiful backcountry refuge anywhere in the United States, the likelihood is that you'll do it in a national forest.

## NATIONAL FORESTS

While national forests are generally open to timber sales, mining, and other activities that purists might find at odds with the idea of a natural setting, wilderness areas are those set aside specifically under the 1964 Wilderness Act, allowing no permanent roads, structures, timber sales, or mining other than those that already exist. These areas are wild country, accessible only by trail and closed to anything but on-foot transport. No bikes are allowed, but horses are OK.

Three of Colorado's national forests are located immediately to the west, northwest, and southwest of Greater Denver: Pike National Forest, Arapaho National Forest, and Roosevelt National Forest. You can seek information on these from the USDA Forest Service's Rocky Mountain Regional Office, (303) 275-5350, or call each national forest office itself.

## Arapaho and Roosevelt National Forests

Arapaho and Roosevelt National Forests, (970) 295-6600, are combined into a jurisdiction that spans the Continental Divide from the Wyoming border to just south of Interstate 70, west of Denver. Roughly speaking, the Roosevelt National Forest comprises that section east of the Continental Divide. The Arapaho National Forest lies west of the Continental Divide, although it comes east to cover the area south of I-70 to mid-Jefferson County.

Together they make up some 1.3 million acres in the Rocky Mountains and foothills, wrapping around Rocky Mountain National Park and including 47 national forest campgrounds and a number of wilderness areas such as the Rawah Wilderness on the Wyoming border, the Indian Peaks Wilderness west of Boulder, and the Cache La Poudre Wilderness around the Cache La Poudre River that flows through Roosevelt National Forest and down to Fort Collins.

## Pike and San Isabel National Forests

Another combined jurisdiction, the Pike and San Isabel National Forests, (719) 553-1400, consist of 2.3 million acres. The San Isabel is, at its closest, about 100 miles of winding, two-lane U.S. Highway 285 away from Denver; at its farthest, it winds south almost to New Mexico.

The Pike National Forest, at 1.1 million acres, is Greater Denver's national forest neighbor south of I-70 and west of Interstate 25, reaching southwest of Colorado Springs (Pikes Peak is part of this national forest). It contains several converging sources of Greater Denver's South Platte River as well as that river's most scenic stretches before it reaches the Flatlands. It has a half-dozen of the state's peaks higher than 14,000 feet, sharing Mount Evans with Arapaho National Forest. Its vegetation is drier than Arapaho and Roosevelt National Forests, with more juniper, oak brush, and bristlecone pine. Its major wilderness area is the Lost Creek Wilderness, 106,000 acres on which Pikes Peak granite has been eroded into domes, spires, turrets, and crests, with a lot of big-boulder slopes. Lost Creek is less popular than Indian Peaks and the other big wilderness areas to the north, and it's a good place to backpack and find a bit of solitude. One unique feature of the Pike is 118 miles of motorcycling trails in a designated area around Sedalia.

## HIKING

Hiking—with backpack, daypack, or no pack—is the most common way to enjoy the backcountry. You can hike just about anywhere on national forest land as long as it isn't posted as off-limits. Before we get into the details of where to hike in the Denver area, however, it's important to emphasize safety and preparedness. Even a short hike up a seemingly innocent, well-groomed trail just outside the city can turn into a nightmare if you underestimate the power of nature in these rugged mountains. Having said that, there are a number of common sense, and sometimes not so obvious, rules and guidelines, and if you are careful to follow them, you will come away with memories of a wonderful, exhilarating experience.

Before we get into these rules and guidelines, however, a brief discussion of altitude sickness is in order. Altitude sickness can affect anyone coming from a lower altitude to a higher one. Most people in good health will experience nothing more than a slight headache, light-headedness, and shortness of breath. Usually these symptoms are not severe and can be treated with aspirin and rest. More serious symptoms can include dizziness, nausea, and impaired mental abilities. Severe altitude sickness, called high altitude pulmonary edema, can lead to seizures, hallucinations, coma, brain damage, and death.

To avoid altitude sickness, refrain from strenuous activities for your first few days at a new altitude while your body acclimates. While it actually takes a few weeks for your body to fully acclimate, each passing day spent at a higher elevation helps your body create the extra red blood cells it needs to capture the limited oxygen at higher altitudes. Take the time to get used to the altitude here before you charge off in pursuit of the high country. Getting off the plane from sea level one day and going on a 6-mile hike to 10,000 feet the next is asking for big trouble.

The most important rule for hiking in the mountains is to be prepared; even in the summer months, Rocky Mountain weather can be unpredictable and merciless. Wherever you hike, the scenery becomes more beautiful—and the necessity of preparedness more important—the higher you go. You will probably start out in the lower forests of aspen and ponderosa pines or in dark, moody groves of spruce and fir, but eventually, as you rise, the forest will break open into the "krummholz," or crooked wood zone, where trees stunted by altitude and twisted by relentless winds make a border before you reach the alpine meadows above. When you're above tree line, you're in the fragile alpine meadows, home to a stunningly beautiful landscape covered with wildflowers. You're also in the heights prone to drastic weather changes and a climate not unlike the arctic zones of the world.

Mountain-savvy folks will tell you the most important way to dress is in layers. When you start hiking down low during the warm months, you'll most likely want to wear a T-shirt and shorts. But there are few things more miserable than reaching the beauty of the high alpine meadows in those clothes as bad weather moves in, dropping temperatures into the 40s or lower with high winds, sometimes a cold rain or snow, and usually a good afternoon lightning storm. If you plan to hike up high, bring along a sizeable backpack into which you've packed a long-sleeved wool or flannel shirt. Bring a sweater or sweatshirt to put over that and a windbreaker/raincoat to put over that. A hood is always nice, but you should at least have a knit cap and warm gloves. Bring trousers, or at least sweatpants, to put on over or instead of the shorts.

During colder months, including the spring and fall, make certain that *none* of these clothes are made of cotton, especially your socks. Instead, choose wool or garments made from the many synthetic fibers specifically designed to wick moisture away from the body and to dry quickly, keeping you both warm and dry. Cotton clothing retains moisture and will not dry quickly when wet, presenting the very real possibility of hypothermia.

Carry plenty of fresh water with you, and never drink stream or lake water without boiling it for at least 10 minutes, using disinfectant pills, or first passing it through a portable disinfectant pump. Drinking untreated water can lead to a nasty case of giardia, and your vacation will come to an abrupt end. You will need to pack a sizeable water bottle, at least 32 ounces per person, and use the water disinfectant tablets or filtering pump as your backup for providing additional drinking water. Make sure you understand how to use the tablets or the disinfectant pump before leaving for the day.

As obvious as it might seem, don't forget your boots. Remember, you'll be on your feet most of the day, and good boots are a must. We don't recommend hiking in anything but hiking boots; sneakers, running shoes, and sandals might be attractive and look better with your shorts, but you'll be glad you left them behind if you encounter cold, wet weather, and your feet will thank you at the end of the day.

A good map is not only an essential emergency item, it adds to the enjoyment of planning your hike. Get yourself one of those "quadrangle" maps on a 1:24,000 scale, where 1 inch equals about 0.4 mile. You may need more than one to cover the area of your interest. Another great resource is the *Delorme Colorado Atlas & Gazetteer,* a road-atlas-size book that contains topographical maps of the entire state. Here the scale is more like 1 inch equals 2.5 miles, but you still get good detail, contour lines, and trail routes. You can find quadrangle maps and the *Delorme Colorado Atlas & Gazetteer* in well-stocked outdoor stores, bookstores, and even some gas stations. You can also get maps from the Bureau of Land Management in Lakewood, (303) 239–3600, or from the U.S. Geological Survey at the Denver Federal Center in Lakewood, Map and Book Sales, (303) 202–4700.

You don't have to be a technical climber with ropes, carabineers, ice axes, and all the other gear to mount most of Colorado's highest peaks. If you want to do such technical climbing, many instructors are available in the metro area to teach you how, and lots of gyms and recreation centers now have their own climbing walls with simulated rock faces on which you can practice. (See our Parks and Recreation chapter for more details.)

Most people just want to climb the mountains, not scale them. Hundreds of trails make that possible, ranging in difficulty from easy to extremely hard. Unless you are an experienced hiker and are acclimated to our high elevations, avoid the 500 or so Colorado peaks that rise higher than 12,000 feet. An elite group of climbers like to "bag the 14ers," or climb to the summits of all 56 peaks that are 14,000 feet or higher. Doing so can be dangerous if attempted by novices, so we recommend that you hook up with experienced climbers if that's what you're after. They can be found through staff in most outdoor recreation stores.

For our purposes, we've listed a range of moderate day hikes that are within easy driving range of Denver. Find more trails in books such as *Hiking Colorado,* second edition, by Maryann Gaug (Falcon) and *Hiking Trails of Central Colorado* by Bob Martin (Pruett Publishing). Three books by Tracy Salcedo focus more closely on the Denver area: *Best Easy Day Hikes Denver, 12 Short Hikes Denver Foothills Central,* and *12 Short Hikes Denver Foothills South* (all Falcon). A good book for families is *Best Hikes With Children in Colorado* by Maureen Keilty (Mountaineers Books). And don't think just in terms of summertime hiking; the trails of summer become the snowshoe and cross-country ski trails of winter. Check out *Winter Trails Colorado: The Best Cross-Country Ski and Snowshoe Trails,* second edition, by Andy and Tari Lightbody (Globe Pequot Press) or *Snowshoeing Colorado* by Claire Walter (Fulcrum Publishing).

## Green Mountain Trail
**About 4 miles north of Morrison**
**Jefferson County Open Space**
**Department**
**(303) 271-5925**
**Map: Jefferson County Open Space map for Hayden's Green Mountain Park**
This easy trail in Denver's foothills wanders 3.5 miles one way (7.25 miles round-trip) and climbs 600 feet, from 6,200 to 6,800 feet. To reach it, drive west from Denver on Sixth Avenue past I-70 and turn left onto U.S. Highway 40. After a short distance, turn left onto Rooney Road and drive south to the parking area to the east. Walk across C-470 on the pedestrian bridge to join the Green Mountain and Lonesome Trails. Take the Green Mountain Trail for the best nature experience. From the top of the mountain, you'll have panoramic views, and along the way you may see mule deer, foxes, coyotes, rabbits, and up to 150 species of birds. If you'd like to do a round-trip loop, take the Lonesome Trail back, but be aware that it follows Alameda Parkway much of the way back to the parking area.

## Highline Canal
**Near Chatfield Reservoir, between**
**Waterton and the Rocky**
**Mountain Arsenal**
**Denver Water Department, Office of**
**Community Relations, (303) 628-6340**
**Map: USGS Front Range Corridor map, sheet 2**
Another easy trail south of Denver, this one runs a total of 71 miles along the irrigation ditch completed in 1883 by Scotsman James Duff. Only 58 of those miles are hikeable, but they can be traveled in segments long or short enough to suit any appetite. Most of the trail is wheelchair and stroller accessible, and it's open year-round to walkers, hikers, joggers, horseback riders, bikers, and in-line skaters. It can be reached in Englewood on South Santa Fe Drive, County Line Road, or Hampden Avenue and in Aurora on Havana Street or Colfax Avenue.

## Mesa Trail
**West of Boulder**
**Boulder County Parks and Open Space**
**(303) 441-3950**
**Maps: Boulder and Eldorado Springs USGS quad maps**
This easy trail runs 6 miles and climbs 900 feet, from an elevation of 5,600 to 6,500 feet. It's good year-round and provides wonderful views of Boulder, the plains, and the Flatirons. The trail begins in Boulder's Chautauqua Mountain Park and winds south to South Boulder Creek near the town of Eldorado Springs. To reach the trailhead, drive west on Baseline Road to Grant Street, turn left into Chautauqua, and hike south about 0.5 mile on the paved road near the ranger station. If you decide to hike the entire span of the trail, you'll need to leave a car at the Eldorado Springs trailhead for your return. Reach it by driving south from Boulder on Highway 93 to Highway 170 and the sign for Eldorado Springs. Travel west on that road for about 1.5 miles to the trailhead parking area on the right.

White Ranch Park
Northwest of Golden and
southwest of Boulder
Jefferson County Open Space
(303) 271–5925
Maps: USGS Ralston Buttes quad or
White Ranch Park map (available at
the park)

Ute and Arapahoe tribes camped and
hunted on this land before Welsh immigrants James and Mary Bond settled on it.
Originally on their way to California, they
decided to stop here after a young son
fell beneath the wagon's wheels and was
killed. The land is now open space owned
by Jefferson County. It is crisscrossed by
trails of varying difficulty that range from
0.3 to 4.5 miles. Several are good for children, and the relatively easy 1.6-mile
Sawmill Trail leads to a campground (an
advance permit is required to stay there,
available from the Jefferson County Open
Space office). To get to White Ranch Park,
drive north from Golden on Highway 93 to
Jefferson County Road 70 (Golden Gate
Canyon Road). After 4.1 miles, turn right
onto Jefferson County Road 57 (Crawford
Gulch Road) and drive another 4.1 miles.
Turn right to enter the park.

# CAMPING

Finding a location to camp on national
forest land is simple once you've determined whether you want to "car camp," as
it's called, or backpack in for a more
remote location. The main distinction is
simple: Car camping usually means you'll
be near your car, won't have to hike in,
and will likely be at a designated campground with amenities such as outhouses
and running water. If you car camp, you'll
likely be near others—anywhere from 50
feet to a few hundred feet depending on
the campground—and have a designated
fire pit. You'll also pay a small daily fee of
around $6.00 to $12.00 per site. If you
backcountry camp, you can go virtually
anywhere on national forest land and

camp for free, but you won't have any
amenities.

The rules for backcountry camping are
fairly simple, but important: You must pick
a spot at least 100 feet from a roadway,
trail, or stream and at least a half-mile from
standing water. Unless fire danger is high,
as it has been for several years, fires are
allowed for cooking and warming but must
be in a contained pit. You must restore the
fire area when you leave. Your car can be
as much as 300 feet off the road but not
parked in a bog; if you have a catalytic
converter, do not park over grass as it can
start a fire.

Making a reservation for car camping
in designated campgrounds is highly recommended and nearly imperative on holiday weekends (see our list of phone
numbers). Backcountry camping does not
require a reservation and can be done anywhere as long as the rules are followed.

If you car camp, you can get to a
campground early and take your chances
at cruising around looking for an empty
space or finding people who look like they
are about to leave. Usually you need to
show up by 7:00 P.M. or your reserved
spot could be taken. The rules are somewhat loose and depend on individual
campgrounds. The national forests have a
toll-free number, and in any part of Colorado, a certain percentage of the forest
service campgrounds are part of that
reservation system. You can call (877)
444–6777 or go to www.reserveusa.com.
Make sure to have ready not only the
name of the campground you want, but
also a selection of other campgrounds in
the vicinity. Many times they'll tell you the
one you want is not open to reservations
but operates on a first-come, first-camp
basis. The person you're talking to on that
toll-free number is actually sitting in Cum-
berland, Maryland, where Biospherics, the
company that has the contract with the
federal government, is located. If you ask
the reservationists at Biospherics to suggest another reservations-accessible
campground nearby, they will know as

much about Colorado campgrounds as they do about campgrounds in Australia.

Following is a helpful list of national forest campgrounds in Colorado that are under the Biospherics reservation system. Note that a road atlas or Colorado state map is likely to have a little tree symbol representing each campground but no name. The *Delorme Colorado Atlas & Gazetteer* often has the name of a lake or creek that coincides with the nearby tent symbol indicating a campground. One resource that names each campground on the map is the national forest visitor map, one for each national forest, produced by the USDA Forest Service itself and available for $6.00 to $7.00. You can get such maps from the USDA Forest Service's Denver Regional Office. You can either call them at (303) 275-5350 and ask that they fax or send you an order form, or you can drop in to the Regional Office at 740 Simms Street, Lakewood, and pick up the map(s) of your choice. You can also buy these maps at some sporting goods stores.

# Campgrounds

Following are just a few of the national forest campgrounds; there are many more. The daily fees average $14. For a full list you can call the USDA Forest Service's Denver Regional Office at (303) 275-5350. They'll mail you the free brochure, "Rocky Mountain Region Campgrounds." Not only does it list all the campgrounds in Colorado, but it lists campgrounds in national forest and national grasslands in Wyoming, Kansas, Nebraska, and South Dakota.

### Arapaho/Roosevelt National Forest
**(970) 295-6600**

**Boulder Ranger District, Boulder**
**(303) 444-6600**
Campgrounds:
Kelly Dahl
Olive Ridge
Pawnee

**Canyon Lakes Ranger District**
**Fort Collins**
**(970) 498-2733**
Campgrounds:
Chambers Lake
Dowdy Lake
Mountain Park
West Lake

**Clear Creek Ranger District**
**Idaho Springs**
**(303) 567-3000**
Campgrounds:
Cold Springs
Echo Lake
Guanella Pass
Pickle Gulch (group campground)
West Chicago Creek

**Pike National Forest**
**(719) 553-1400**
**Pikes Peak Ranger District**
**Colorado Springs**
**(719) 636-1602**
Campgrounds:
Meadow Ridge
Pike Community (group campground)
Red Rocks (group campground)
Thunder Ridge

**South Park Ranger District, Fairplay**
**(719) 836-2031**
Campgrounds:
Aspen
Jefferson Creek
Lodgepole

**South Platte Ranger District, Morrison**
**(303) 275-5610**
Campgrounds:
Buffalo
Kelsey
Lone Rock
Meadows (group campground)

**Sulphur Ranger District, Granby**
**(970) 887-4100**
Campgrounds:
Arapahoe Bay
Green Ridge
Stillwater

You can find a lot of books about camping, but a good basic reference is *Camping Colorado* by Melinda Crow (Falcon). For more information about recreation in other areas of Colorado, pick up copies of the *Insiders' Guide to Boulder and Rocky Mountain National Park* by Roz Brown and Ann Alexander Leggett and the *Insiders' Guide to Colorado's Mountains* by Linda and Jim Castrone (Globe Pequot).

## Resources

There are umpteen books on how to enjoy Colorado's recreational, scenic, and natural opportunities. A pass through a major bookstore will load you down with more than you need. Following are a few other informational resources.

**Bureau of Land Management**
www.co.blm.gov

**Colorado Department of Regulatory Agencies, Division of Registration (outfitters registration office for hunting and fishing)**
(303) 894-7778
www.dora.state.co.us/registrations

**The Colorado Directory**
(303) 499-9343

**Colorado Division of Wildlife Headquarters, Denver**
(303) 297-1192
www.wildlife.state.co.us

**Colorado Mountain Club**
(303) 279-3080
www.cmc.org

**Colorado State Parks (camping, boating, and recreation)**
(303) 866-3437
www.coloradoparks.org

**Denver Audubon Society**
(303) 973-9530
www.denveraudubon.org

**Dude Ranchers Association (serving all western states including Colorado)**
(307) 587-2339
www.duderanch.org

**National Park Service camping reservations**
(800) 365-2267 (CAMP)
http://reservations.nps.gov

**USDA Forest Service camping reservations**
(877) 444-6777
www.reserveusa.com

# SKI COUNTRY

Admit it. You've envisioned spending your days gliding down pristine, sunlit mountains and your nights snuggled cozily, brandy in hand, by a roaring fire. In Colorado Ski Country USA, the dream is just moments away from downtown Denver.

Although Denver is on the plains, it's only a little more than an hour or so from some of the best skiing on the continent. In good snow years (and with the help of snowmaking), the ski season can stretch from mid-October through June. Remember, snow can be falling like crazy in the mountains while it's 60 degrees and sunny in Denver. Most ski resorts are open from Thanksgiving to mid-April.

Colorado is home to 25 ski areas, ranging from rope-tows to world-famous resorts such as Aspen and Steamboat Springs. Seven major areas are day trips from Denver, including Vail, one of the country's premier destination ski resorts. Overnight trips offer even more variety.

If, despite all the descriptions of champagne powder and unbelievable scenery, downhill skiing just isn't your thing, don't despair. The resorts have realized that not everybody skis, and they've come up with winter activities for nonskiers. Sans skis, you can ride the chairlift up to the Lodge at Sunspot at Winter Park simply to enjoy the view and have lunch, then ride back down again. Other widely available winter activities include ice skating, snowmobiling, snowshoeing, horse-drawn sleigh rides, and dogsledding.

Cross-country skiing is very popular and getting more so. Groomed cross-country tracks are available at most downhill areas and many backcountry trailheads—including some that connect with the 10th Mountain Division Hut Association hut system, named for the elite World War II U.S. ski troops who trained in the area, which are within a few hours' drive from Denver.

All the big ski areas offer adult and child lessons, child care, and specialized lessons; call the general information number given for each resort for prices and special packages. We've given prices for the current season whenever possible, but at press time some resorts hadn't determined their lift ticket prices. Discounted lift tickets are sold at Front Range King Soopers, Albertsons, and Safeway supermarkets and REI sporting goods stores. Availability varies, so call ahead.

The fun doesn't stop when the snow melts. There are as many things to do and sights to see in summer as in winter. Mountain biking? How about an easy lift up with your bike on the gondola and a wild ride down. Music festivals? Ski slopes make great outdoor amphitheaters in the summer. Boating? There's nothing like a mountain lake or reservoir ringed in jagged peaks.

During the past 10 years or so, most of Colorado's ski areas have concentrated on becoming year-round resorts. In fact, Colorado resorts consider cruise vacations to be their stiffest competition, so they're doing all they can to make sure the slopes remain the vacation of choice. As a result, ski resorts account for more than $3 billion a year in tourism dollars.

To appeal to a wide audience, resorts have developed golf courses and established annual festivals and events such as A Taste of Vail. Drifting over the Vail Valley in a hot-air balloon is a great way to spend the afternoon. And the more than 50 miles of paved bike paths that extend from Breckenridge to Vail are unsurpassed.

It's crucial to take altitude into consideration when traveling to the mountains. Even folks accustomed to Denver's 5,280 feet above sea level can get dizzy after a high-speed chairlift ride to 12,000 feet. Drink plenty of water, give yourself time to adjust, and slow down if you get a headache or feel nauseated. Alcohol makes matters worse, so take it easy.

Also, no one should set out on backcountry trails, either on foot or on skis, without sound knowledge of avalanche awareness, direction-finding skills, and adequate clothing, food, and water. Even people going on day trips should be prepared to spend a night outside, as weather conditions in the mountains change in seconds. Local bookstores are filled with trail guides—buy one that has basic safety information as well as backcountry routes. And always let someone know where you're going and when you expect to be back. If you want to enjoy the great outdoors when the snow is gone, see our The Great Outdoors chapter for hiking and climbing information.

Eldora Mountain Resort, near Boulder, is covered in the *Insiders' Guide to Boulder and Rocky Mountain National Park*. For more information on ski areas, see the *Insiders' Guide to Colorado's Mountains*.

We've listed and described below some ski areas that make feasible day trips from Denver. (Aspen, Colorado's most famous area, is too far away to qualify as a day trip.) We've included information about winter and summer activities, dining, shopping, and accommodations, should you decide to extend your day trip into a weekend or longer.

If you're a beginner or a want-to-be beginner, you may want to know about some of the information sources that can help you get into the sport:

Colorado Ski Country USA, (303) 837–0793, www.coloradoski.com, a trade association for all the ski resorts in the state, publishes the *Colorado Ski Country Winter Journal.* Within about 160 pages, it contains a lot of the information you want to know about skiing in Colorado. Colorado Ski Country USA will mail it to you free if you give them a call or go online and ask for it.

You may also want to know about Sniagrab (bargains spelled backward), the big annual ski equipment and apparel sale held every year by Sports Authority outlets around Greater Denver. It starts on the Saturday before Labor Day, and you can find some fine deals on new and used equipment.

One of the best ways to get into skiing is to link up with a ski club. To get a list of local ski clubs, send your request and a self-addressed, stamped envelope to National Ski Club News, P.O. Box 4704, Englewood, CO 80155; call (303) 689–9921; or visit www.skiclubnews.com.

We've given resource phone numbers in each section and at the end of the chapter as well. Most phone numbers are in the (970) area code, although a few resorts retain Denver direct-dial numbers, and some have toll-free numbers. In general, for activities on the ski mountain itself, call the resort; for lodging, dining, and other activities, call the chamber of commerce

## LOVELAND

The closest major ski area to Denver, just 53 miles west, Loveland is at the Eisenhower Tunnel, an easy hour's drive west on Interstate 70. Take exit 216, just before the tunnel entrance. Loveland, the ski area (as opposed to the town, which is miles away on the plains), is strictly for skiing—there's no lodging, and there's very little in the way of restaurants. However, a traditional cafeteria-style lunch is available on the mountain with deli fare, soups, baked goods, and specialty pizzas.

There's also a 5,000-square-foot shopping space that sells everything ski and snowboard related. Here you'll find clothes, gloves, skis, boards, and the like.

Loveland also grew in 1998 with the addition of the world's highest quad lift: more than 12,600 feet above sea level. It serves 450 acres of expert terrain, bringing the total to more than 1,300 acres served by lifts.

With an average annual snowfall of 385 inches and lower prices than other close-in areas, there's plenty to pull you off the highway before the tunnel. Snowboarders enjoy a snowboard-only park. Ladies get special treatment in women's programs offered at special rates. Call for information about this year's program. Loveland opened an expanded and renovated rental shop in 1997, featuring the addition of telemark rentals. Loveland also offers an end-of-day bonus—no tunnel traffic. One-day adult lift tickets are $50. One drawback to skiing Loveland is that it can get windy, especially on trails above tree line. The direct-dial phone number from Denver is (303) 571-5580. The Web site is www.skiloveland.com.

## WINTER PARK

Although it's 70 miles away from Denver (less than two hours from DIA), Winter Park is a city of Denver park—hence the name. The resort (Colorado's fifth-largest in skier visits and a favorite with Front Range skiers) was developed in the 1940s and doubled its capacity in the 1970s. Winter Park is among the more friendly and laid-back of Colorado resorts and doesn't suffer from some of the snobbery of other destinations such as Vail and Aspen.

In all, there are three interconnected mountains, a high alpine bowl, and Vasquez Cirque, all accessible with one lift ticket. Winter Park and Vasquez Ridge offer a mix of beginner, intermediate, and advanced cruising runs. Mary Jane is where mogul enthusiasts test their knees (No Pain, No Jane, as the advertisement goes). The high-alpine Parsenn Bowl, at 12,060 feet, is known for its gladed tree skiing and above-timberline vistas.

## Useful Phone Numbers

**Winter Park Resort, (970) 726-5514; direct dial from Greater Denver, (303) 892-0961; www.skiwinterpark.com; Snow Conditions, (303) 572-SNOW.**

**Winter Park/Fraser Valley Chamber of Commerce, (970) 726-4118; (800) 903-7275.**

> ℹ️ *To avoid driving in weekend ski traffic to Winter Park, try the Ski Train, which departs from Union Station on Friday, Saturday, and Sunday from late December through March. Call (303) 296-4754 for reservations.*

## Getting There

To get to Winter Park from Denver, drive west on I-70, exit onto U.S. Highway 40 West at the Empire town exit (watch out for those speed traps) and continue over majestic Berthoud Pass to Winter Park, which sits at the base of the north side of the pass. There are two entrances to the ski area. Expert skiers turn off at Mary Jane, while beginners and intermediates continue to the main Winter Park base. The town of Winter Park is a few miles farther down the road from the ski area, and Fraser is 5 miles farther. Both towns have grown up alongside the resort, and all remain casual. A free shuttle connects the ski resort with the towns of Winter Park and Fraser. Both have restaurants, shops, and places to stay, although Fraser is known as the place where locals also shop for necessities—it has a Safeway store, for example.

If you balk at driving over a pass, you can make the trip by train. On weekends the Denver Rio Grande Ski Train departs Denver's Union Station at 7:15 A.M., dropping skiers within walking distance of the lifts, and leaves Winter Park at 4:15 P.M. just after the lifts close. The train runs weekends-only during ski season and Friday as well during February and March. The trip takes two hours each way and passes through the Moffat Tunnel. Originally trains traveled over the Continental Divide via the Rollins Pass Road over Corona Pass. The 6.2-mile Moffat Tunnel was completed in 1927, drastically reducing the time it takes trains to travel between Denver and the mountains. Cost is $40 to $45 same-day round-trip for adults, depending on the month, and $70 in first-class. Discounted lift tickets are available on the train. For information and reservations call (303) 296–4754; the Web site is www.skitrain.com.

## Skiing

Eight high-speed quad lifts carry skiers and snowboarders to 2,886 acres of terrain. Snowboarders have three terrain stations ranging from beginner to advanced, plus two half-pipes. Nonskiers can ride the Zephyr Express lift to the top of the Winter Park ski area and meet the rest of the group for lunch at the beautiful Lodge at Sunspot. One-day lift tickets are $72 for adults.

Winter Park is renowned for its ski program for the disabled and is home to the National Sports Center for the Disabled, (970) 726–1540. Its 39 full-time staff members and more than 1,000 volunteers can handle the needs of more than 40 different disabilities.

## Cross-country Skiing

Down-valley from the downhill area is a top-notch cross-country center called **Devil's Thumb Ranch,** (970) 726–8231 or (800) 933–4339. Skate-skiers love the 125 kilometers of groomed trails at Devil's Thumb, which fan out into the forest from an expansive meadow. To get there, drive west from Winter Park to the town of Fraser and turn right onto County Road 83. Tickets are $15.00 for adults, $6.00 for children younger than age 12 and seniors older than age 60. Lessons and equipment rental are available. Devil's Thumb Ranch is open year-round, with gourmet dining in the Ranch House Restaurant & Saloon and private or bunkhouse-style accommodations available. Ask about moonlight sleigh rides in the winter and horseback riding, trout fishing, rafting, and kayaking in the summer.

Backcountry skiers like the trails on top of Berthoud Pass and the Jim Creek Trail that begins directly across from the Winter Park ski area. No one should set out on these trails without knowledge of avalanche awareness, adequate clothing, food, water, and a trail guide or maps.

## Dogsled Rides and Other Winter Activities

Dogsled rides are a newly popular winter activity in Winter Park. The price is high, but Insiders say it's worth it. Call Dog Sled Rides of Winter Park, (970) 726–8326. Prices vary, and rides last for two hours. If you'd rather be pulled by horses than dogs, go for a sleigh ride. Call **Grand Adventures,** (970) 726–9247, or **Devil's Thumb Outfitters,** (970) 726–1099.

Winter Park also has a free public ice-skating rink (rentals can be arranged at the Cooper Creek Square rink). Ice skaters can try the **Fraser Ice Rink,** 601 Zerex Avenue (US 40 just before the Safeway Plaza), (970) 726–4708. The rink is also free, but bring your own skates. It is outdoors and features bonfires at night.

You can also ride a snocat to the top of the mountain for $38 for adults and for kids older than age 3. Lap-sitters age 3 and younger are free. There are three tours that offer lunch stops; call (970) 726–1616 or (303) 316–1616.

Snowshoe tours, including shoes and poles, start off with a ride up a lift and conclude with a gentle descent through wooded terrain. Cost is $30 per person, $25 if you bring your own snowshoes. (Not recommended for kids younger than age 7.) Call (970) 726–1616 or (303) 316–1616.

## Summer Fun

Every summer the green slopes of Winter Park are the site of acclaimed musical events. The Winter Park Jazz Festival attracts a stellar lineup of great jazz musicians, including Harry Connick Jr. It is usually held in July. If you go, bring a lawn chair and rain gear.

Other summer activities available for less than $10—check summer prices at (970) 726-5514—include the alpine slide at the base of the mountain (Colorado's longest); Mountainside Mini-Golf, located at the base of the Zephyr lift, offering a Winter Park Valley history theme with railroad and mining holes; and the Human Maze, also located at the base of Zephyr, known for trapping adults while kids get through in record time.

## Mountain Biking

Winter Park has worked hard to attract mountain bikers and is known as Mountain Bike Capital USA. More than 600 miles of marked, mapped, and maintained trails wind through the Fraser Valley. At the ski area itself, riders can take the easy way up via the Zephyr Express chairlift to connect with another 45 miles of steep, exciting trails. Pick up a trail map at local bike stores or the Chamber of Commerce Visitor Center on the east side of US 40 downtown. Bike rentals are available at any number of local stores. Try **Grand Sports,** in town at 78786 US 40, (970) 726-1092, with a good selection and knowledgeable staff, or **Ski Depot Sports,** (970) 726-8055, 257 Winter Park Drive, and **Slopeside Gear & Sport,** located in the Village Plaza shops, (970) 726-1664. Tips on where to go are free from staff.

The Fraser River Trail is paved and the easiest, most mellow ride for families; it's good for in-line skaters, too. Valley trails go up from there, to rides even locals find frightening. Helmets, of course, are highly recommended. An all-day park pass for all activities, including the Zephyr lift for mountain biking, is $49, $39 if you book in advance at (970) 726-5514. Half-day passes are $44. Otherwise, a Zephyr ticket for mountain biking is available.

## Golf and Other Recreation

Golfers will enjoy the beautiful 27-hole **Pole Creek Golf Club,** (970) 887-9195, about 10 miles northwest of Winter Park in the town of Tabernash. Pole Creek consistently rates one of the top public courses in Colorado. There also is the **Grand Lake Golf Course,** (970) 627-8008 or (800) 551-8580, about 40 miles farther west. It's not quite Pole Creek, but it's easier to get on.

Nongolfers can choose among fishing, hiking, horseback riding, jeeping, and rafting. Much of the Fraser Valley that isn't privately owned falls within the boundaries of the Arapaho National Forest. The Winter Park/Fraser Valley Chamber of Commerce can provide more information, or contact the **USDA Forest Service** in Denver at (303) 275-5350.

## Dining

Winter Park has traditionally been a day-use area for Denver families and doesn't have the range of restaurants and stores that the Summit County areas or Vail can offer. But things are picking up.

**Gasthaus Eichler,** in downtown Winter Park on US 40, (970) 726-5133, is noted for its Austrian and German specialties. Reservations are suggested.

**Deno's Mountain Bistro,** (970) 726-5332, is also located in downtown Winter Park on US 40. Locals have been coming here since 1973 for steaks, pasta, pizza, and some of the best burgers in town. Its après-ski atmosphere is one of the most mellow in town. It's open for breakfast, lunch, and dinner.

**Carvers Bakery & Cafe,** (970) 726-8202, is a popular breakfast location, but it can be hard to find. It's tucked behind Cooper Creek Square, but locals agree it's worth the search. Housed in a quaint log building, it's known for home-baked breads and pastries. Its lunches are just as good, featuring homemade soups, stews, and vegetarian dishes.

**Lodge at Sunspot,** (970) 726-1444, at the top of Winter Park mountain, serves a buffet for $29.95 or a five-course dinner for $39.95. It's open Thursday through Saturday nights and more during holiday seasons. Reservations are suggested. It's a great experience if you're looking for something a little more memorable.

For more casual dining and nightlife—actually it can get wild at times—there's the **Crooked Creek Saloon & Eatery** at 401 Zerex Avenue off US 40 in Fraser, (970) 726-9250, which serves Mexican and American food and no small amount of beer.

# Accommodations

Accommodations in Winter Park range from condominiums on the mountainside to bed-and-breakfasts in town. **Winter Park Central Reservations,** (800) 979-0332, can arrange lodging in more than 50 condominiums, motels, hotels, lodges, inns, and bed-and-breakfasts.

If full-service hotels are what you're after, check into the **Vintage Hotel,** (800) 472-7017. Its restaurant, **Tipper's Tavern,** is a reasonably priced family place, featuring American home-style food, sandwiches, and pizzas. There's a pool on-site. **Arapahoe Ski Lodge,** (970) 726-8222 or (800) 754-0094, offers moderately priced lodging packages with breakfast and dinner or breakfast only. The closest thing in Winter Park to ski-in/ski-out is the **Iron Horse Resort and Retreat,** Central Reservations, (800) 979-0332. **The Pines Inn of Winter Park,** (970) 726-5416, is a bed-and-breakfast inn

---

ℹ️ *Buy reduced-price lift tickets at Greater Denver locations including King Soopers, Albertsons, and Safeway supermarkets; Total gasoline stations; and Sports Authority, Christy's, and REI sporting goods stores.*

---

conveniently located just 600 yards from the ski area. It provides free shuttles to and from the lifts, boasts an outdoor Jacuzzi, and sponsors Murder Mystery Weekends (call for dates).

The bulk of available lodgings are condominiums in larger complexes. **Beaver Village Resort,** (800) 666-0281, is one well-run and centrally located, although not lavish, choice. **The Viking Lodge,** (800) 421-4013, is great for small budgets, and it's clean and well maintained.

## SUMMIT COUNTY

The Summit County ski areas include Breckenridge, Keystone, Arapahoe Basin, and Copper Mountain. Collectively these four areas attract more skiers than any other ski destination in North America. And why not? There's tremendous variety, good shopping and restaurants, dependably fine snow, and easy access from Greater Denver.

Breckenridge and Keystone tickets are also valid at A-Basin, Vail, and Beaver Creek. To ski Copper, you must buy a Copper Mountain lift pass. All areas offer discount prices for multiday or advance tickets. Check with each for details.

Summit County is about one and a half hours west of Denver on I-70. The Eisenhower Tunnel, opened in 1973, saves motorists 10 miles of driving over Loveland Pass on U.S. Highway 6, a steep, twisting road. Still, US 6 is hard to beat for sheer scenic grandeur, as it crosses the Continental Divide and drops down past Arapahoe Basin before flattening out as it heads toward Keystone and the towns of Dillon and Silverthorne. When time permits and road conditions are favorable, this is a recommended alternate route and the most direct approach to Arapahoe Basin.

The crowds have been coming to Summit County in the summer in record numbers. Among other things, they come for the more than 50 miles of well-marked, paved bike path that winds through Summit County from Breckenridge to Frisco to

Copper Mountain and beyond. It is an unmatched public amenity in Summit County, luring even day-trippers from Denver with its motor vehicle–free lanes and grand mountain scenery.

If you're planning a trip to Summit County, you might find it worth your while to read through the entire Summit County section that follows. We've treated each Summit County area separately, listing first ski information, then other winter and summer activities, and finally restaurants, shopping, and lodging. But things are close enough so that a person might ski at Breckenridge, eat in Dillon, and stay overnight in Frisco. An excellent free public transportation system, the **Summit Stage,** makes getting around without a car easy. Pick up a schedule at the visitor center in Frisco, 011 South Summit Boulevard (at the intersection of Summit Boulevard and Main Street), or in Dillon, on US 6 about 1 mile south of I-70 at the Dillon Dam Road. The visitor centers are open daily year-round.

## BRECKENRIDGE
# Useful Phone Numbers

**Snow Conditions, (970) 453-6118**

**Breckenridge Ski Resort general information, (970) 453-5000, (800) 789-SNOW**

**Breckenridge Outdoor Education Center (disabled skiing), (970) 453-6422, (800) 383-BOEC**

**Breckenridge Resort Chamber and Central Reservations, (970) 453-2913, (800) 221-1091**

**Breckenridge Resort Chamber Guest Services & Activities, (970) 453-5579, (877) 864-0868**

**Town of Breckenridge trolley information, (970) 547-3140**

# Getting There

To get to Breckenridge, take the Frisco exit from I-70 and drive south on Highway 9 for 9 miles.

# Skiing

Breckenridge, the oldest and largest of the Summit County communities, is a former mining town that got its start when gold was discovered nearby in 1859. A National Historic District, Breckenridge boasts a Main Street lined with handsome Victorian buildings that now house great shops, art galleries, and restaurants. Breckenridge has 27 lifts and more than 2,208 skiable acres spread across four distinct peaks. In the last few years, it has been either the most popular or second most popular ski area in North America. Snowboarding is not only permitted but promoted, as Breckenridge considers itself the "Rocky Mountain Capital of Snowboarding." There's close-in pay parking near Beaver Run and the Peak 8 base, but most skiers park in one of the town's public lots and take the free shuttle to the slopes. Adult full-day lift tickets are $59.

# Cross-country Skiing and Other Winter Activities

There is a **Nordic skiing center** adjacent to the ski area; call (970) 453-6855 for more information. Other winter activities in Breckenridge include the usual—sleigh rides, snowmobiling, ice skating—and the unusual—the annual Budweiser International Snow Sculpture Championships every January.

Ice-skating is available at **Maggie Pond** at the Village at Breckenridge, (800) 847-5445, and **Breckenridge Ice Rink,** built in 1997, (970) 547-9974.

ℹ️ *Escape the ski resort crowds—at the Frisco Nordic Center, alongside Dillon Reservoir about 5 miles north of Breckenridge. Snowshoers and cross-country skiers find serenity among snow-covered evergreens and sloping trails. Stop at the horse barn and have lunch on the seat of a sleigh. Rentals and maps are available at the center's outpost. Call (970) 668-0866.*

Snowmobilers can book rides with **Good Times** at (970) 453-7604 and **Tiger Run** at (970) 453-2231. Snowcat tours run by **Chicago Ridge Snowcat Tours,** (719) 486-2277, are out of **Ski Cooper,** a ski area near Leadville.

For disabled skiers, adaptive skiing with special seats and equipment is offered by the **Breckenridge Outdoor Education Center,** (970) 453-6422.

## Summer Fun

In summer there's hiking in the Arapaho National Forest and outstanding golf at the Jack Nicklaus–designed municipal course, the **Breckenridge Golf Club.** It's our favorite mountain course, and in 1991 *Golf Digest* named the Breckenridge Golf Club the top public course in Colorado. Call (970) 453-9104.

The Pioneer Trail is an easy and popular trail for mountain bikers. Start at the top of the Colorado SuperChair and wind down the front side of Peak 8, through thick forests and wide-open ski runs. Breckenridge offers lift rides up for mountain bikers.

The **Breckenridge Recreation Center** at 880 Airport Road, (970) 453-1734, is open every day except Christmas and has indoor and outdoor tennis courts, a pool, racquetball courts, a steam room, a hot tub, and separate locker room facilities for men and women. Visitors can purchase a daily admission.

If you'd like to see the Ten Mile Range of the Rockies from the back of a horse rather than on foot, **Breckenridge Stables,** (970) 453-4438, prides itself on its gentle horses. Two 90-minute rides are available at $45 each, one of which is a breakfast ride.

The Blue River, which runs through Breckenridge, is a favorite fly-fishing locale. Fishing licenses are required and can be purchased at various locations in town, i.e., sporting goods stores where fishing equipment and bait are sold. A water activity in Breckenridge that's fun for the whole family is paddleboating on Maggie Pond in the Village at Breckenridge.

Several once-booming town sites near Breckenridge still hold allure for visitors. Also within the town itself are a number of buildings reputed to be haunted. Call the resort's main number for information, (970) 453-5000.

The **Breckenridge Outdoor Education Center,** (970) 453-6422, also offers disabled visitors summer recreation events such as kayaking and rope courses.

## Dining

Breckenridge has superb dining and shopping. Among the fine restaurants in town are the **St. Bernard Inn,** 103 South Main Street, (970) 453-2572, for northern Italian food (dinner only) and **Cafe Alpine,** 106 East Adams Avenue, (970) 453-8218, noted for its tapas bar, which features appetizers and 40 wines by the glass. Reservations are strongly suggested at both places. One of the state's first brewpubs, **Breckenridge Brewery,** is at 600 South Main Street, (970) 453-1550—try the Avalanche Ale or their pub-brewed root beer. Locals favor the **Blue Moose Restaurant,** 540 South Main Street, (970) 453-4859, for its affordable natural food and friendly atmosphere, and **Mi Casa Mexican Restaurant & Cantina,** 600 South Park Street, (970) 453-2071, for its Mexican lunch and dinners (no reservations) with daily specials.

# Shopping

Breckenridge's shopping also rates superlatives. A few hours spent walking up and down Main Street will acquaint you with the very best the town has to offer. Of course, there's the usual array of T-shirt and souvenir shops, but there also are numerous spots that offer something special. Two galleries to check out are **Hibberd McGrath,** 101 North Main Street, for fine crafts, and **Breckenridge Fine Art Gallery,** 124 South Main Street. You can get a complete list of local galleries at the Visitor Information Center, 309 North Main Street, (970) 453-6018.

You won't want to miss **The Twisted Pine,** 505 South Main Street, for Western apparel, especially men's clothing and hats. For women's gear check out the sister shop at 100 South Main Street. For a free catalog call (970) 453-6615. **Goods,** 105 South Main Street, is the most popular basic clothing shop in town.

# Accommodations

Accommodations in Breckenridge range from luxury condominiums to Victorian-style bed-and-breakfasts in historic homes. **Barn on the River,** 303 North Main Street, (970) 453-2975, is an especially well-appointed 19th-century trio of buildings with period furniture and antiques, but guests also enjoy the modern pleasures of whirlpool tubs for two, private balconies, and sumptuous breakfasts. Rates range from $149 to $289, depending on the season. The Breckenridge Resort Chamber can provide information about the other bed-and-breakfasts in town or book a condominium or hotel room. **The Village at Breckenridge,** (877) 593-5260, is a huge complex with athletic facilities. **Pine Ridge Condominiums,** (800) 333-8833, have full kitchens and washer/dryers in the units. The complex has two common hot tubs and a pool. **The Lodge & Spa** at Breckenridge has the distinction of

being the world's highest athletic club and spa. The fitness center features individualized training for all levels, (970) 453-9300. The **River Mountain Lodge,** (800) 627-3766, offers the convenience of being in town and is of high quality. **Allaire Timbers Inn,** (970) 453-7530, is a high-end bed-and-breakfast with each room decorated individually. **Beaver Run Resort,** (800) 525-2253, is a ski-in/ski-out resort that's popular with visitors.

# KEYSTONE
## Useful Phone Numbers

**Keystone Resort general information and reservations, (970) 496-2316, (800) 239-1639; keystone.snow.com**

**Summit County Chamber of Commerce, (970) 668-2051, (800) 530-3099**

# Getting There

Exit onto US 6 at the Dillon-Silverthorne exit 205, turning left at the traffic light. Keystone is 6 miles down the road.

# Skiing

When Keystone opened for business in 1969-1970, it was widely considered a good spot for beginners and intermediates but not challenging enough for experts. The addition of steep and bumpy North Peak in 1984 and the expansion into the powder-filled glades of the Outback and the Outback Bowls in the 1990s have greatly changed the character of the area and made it more attractive to advanced skiers. Keystone is noted for its snowmaking capability, which often allows it to open earlier than its neighbors. It is also the only ski area in Summit County to offer night skiing, until 8:00 P.M. Snowboarding debuted in 1996, as did specially designated terrain, which is also lit. Keystone runs daily NASTAR races, including a self-timing system that allows skiers to improve with practice runs.

In summer 1998 Keystone owner Vail Resorts spent $18 million on the mountain. The biggest project was Keystone's fifth high-speed quad, which replaced the Santiago triple chair. It is in the midst of a multiyear $1 billion renaissance of the base area, including River Run, Ski Tip neighborhood, Mountain House, and Keystone Village. They have already added hundreds of condos, town homes, restaurants, and shops to River Run.

## Cross-country Skiing and Other Winter Activities

In the 2000–2001 season, **Keystone's Cross-Country Center** relocated to the New River Course Golf Clubhouse on the west side of the resort. The center has 16 kilometers of groomed trails and 57 kilometers of packed trails in the White River National Forest. They offer lessons in cross-country skiing, snowshoeing, ski-skating, and telemarking. Call (970) 496–4386 or (800) 354–4FUN for more information. There is a **Nordic Center** in Frisco, too, designed by Olympic silver-medalist Bill Koch with close to 40 kilometers of trails near Dillon Reservoir. Call (970) 668–0866 for prices and rental information.

If you'd rather strike out on your own, some of the best cross-country skiing in Summit County is found by continuing along the road to Montezuma past the Ski Tip Lodge. Peru Creek (for beginners) and St. Johns and Wild Irishman Mine (for intermediates) are favorite tours for Front Range skiers. Remember to take precautions: Let someone know where you're going and when you expect to return.

As for other winter activities, Keystone is home to Keystone Lake, the largest

maintained outdoor skating lake in the country. It's right in the center of the village, and skate rentals are available. Sleigh rides and snowmobiling can be arranged by calling the Keystone Activities Center, (800) 345–4FUN. For a chilly thrill ride that all ages will love, try tubing in Keystone's designated area. For about $15 (adult price), you get to slide down the mountain on an inner tube and catch pulley rides back to the top.

## Summer Fun

In summer Dillon Reservoir—locally known as Lake Dillon—provides landlocked Coloradans with one of the state's greatest recreational assets, a 3,000-acre reservoir (the country's highest) ringed by mountains. The lake can accommodate sailboats, kayaks, and fishing boats; charters are available. Weather and water-level permitting, the marina is open from the end of May through the last weekend in October. Swimming is allowed but only recommended for the hearty, as this mountain reservoir is ice-cold even in August. For information call the Dillon Marina at (970) 468–5100.

There's golf at the **Keystone Ranch Golf Course,** (970) 496–4250, designed by Robert Trent Jones Jr.; the **River Course at Keystone,** (970) 496–4444; and the **Raven Golf Club at Three Peaks,** (970) 262–3636.

The main fishing artery in Summit County is the Blue River, where anglers aim for trout. Contact a local fishing shop or the Colorado Division of Wildlife for more information, (303) 291–7533.

Mountain bikers can sign up for a **Dirt Camp** weekend, in which elite-level coaching and training techniques are taught by world-class professionals. Call (800) 711–DIRT.

Try the **Llama Lunch Trek,** where you have the fun and the llama carries your lunch. The trek stops for hiking along the way. Call (800) 354–4FUN.

# Dining

**The Alpenglow Stube,** atop Keystone's North Peak, serves Bavarian-accented contemporary cuisine for lunch and dinner and is reached via enclosed gondola chairlift. The Stube has earned the AAA four-diamond rating and is closed during the spring and autumn shoulder seasons, when the gondola doesn't operate. The rustic **Keystone Ranch,** also awarded the AAA four-diamond rating and voted Colorado's best restaurant by the Zagat Survey, is a restored ranch with six-course dinners. It's open year-round. To make a reservation at either restaurant (required), call Keystone's Dining & Activities Center, (970) 496–4386 or (800) 354–4386.

**The Old Dillon Inn,** (970) 468–2791, on Highway 9 in Silverthorne, is always packed on weekends with skiers who come for the Mexican food and margaritas, the impressive 19th-century bar, and the rollicking music. For a quieter evening, cook your own steaks on the grill at **The Mint** in Silverthorne, 347 Blue River Parkway, (970) 468–5247. In one of the oldest buildings in Summit County, The Mint is a fun-for-the-whole-family dining spot. For a hearty pre-ski or pre-sail breakfast, take your appetite to the **Arapahoe Cafe & Pub,** 626 Lake Dillon Drive, Dillon, (970) 468–0873. **The Snake River Saloon,** 23074 US 6 in Keystone, (970) 468–2788, is locally famous for its spirited après-ski and late-night entertainment. **The Ski Tip Lodge,** (970) 496–4950, offers American regional cuisine, including several wild-game dishes, in a rustic atmosphere. This historic spot was Colorado's first skiers' lodge. Seating is limited so reservations are essential.

**Der Fondue Chessel,** (800) 354–4FUN, entertains diners with Bavarian music while serving them a Swiss-style four-course fondue dinner. Dinner sleigh and wagon rides (winter and summer), (800) 354–4FUN, pull riders up to the **Soda Creek Homestead** and serve a Western-style meal while a cowboy performer leads the crowd in a sing-along. **Garden Room Steak House,** (970) 496–4386 or (800) 354–4FUN, is in the village at Keystone and is open in the winter.

# Shopping

The factory outlet stores in Silverthorne are reason enough to drive up from Denver. Clustered in three malls just off I-70 at exit 205 are bargain outlets for 80 well-known manufacturers, including **Bass Shoes, Eddie Bauer, Nike, OshKosh B'Gosh, Great Outdoor Clothing,** and **Wilson's Leather.** The stores are open seven days a week and claim a 40 percent average savings over retail. For information call (970) 468–5780.

# Accommodations

Accommodations in Keystone are plentiful, with 1,600 lodging units available at the resort in seven neighborhoods. They include the luxurious **Keystone Lodge** and the truly deluxe **Chateaux d'Mont.** There are also condominiums of all sizes and private homes available for rent. Contact Keystone Reservations, (970) 496–4242 or (800) 222–0188. **Western Skies Bed and Breakfast,** (970) 468–9445, features a secluded 10,500-foot elevation and reasonable rates. **The Ski Tip Lodge,** (970) 496–4950, offers good access to cross-country trails in a funky, authentic Colorado setting.

Simpler but charming and comfortable lodging can be found in Frisco, Dillon, and Silverthorne. **The Galena Street Mountain Inn,** (970) 668–3224 or (800) 248–9138, is a pretty, modern bed-and-breakfast in Frisco tucked a half-block back from Main Street and near the bike path. Rooms cost around $99 to $199, depending on the season and the accomodations. Summit County Central Reservations, (800) 525–3682, can provide more possibilities.

The **Best Western Ptarmigan Lodge,** (970) 468–2341 or (800) 842–5939, is on

Lake Dillon at 652 Lake Dillon Drive (take exit 205 off I-70). The lodge has deluxe motel accommodations, kitchenettes, and condominiums with fireplaces and serves continental breakfast year-round. Rates vary, depending on the season and type of accommodation selected, but are generally midrange for this area. Kids younger than age 12 stay free. Newly remodeled to be more wheelchair accessible, the lodge now has a hot tub, sauna, and more cable TV channels.

There is a second Best Western lodge in Summit County, the **Best Western Lake Dillon Lodge** at 1202 North Summit Boulevard in Frisco, (970) 668-5094 or (800) 727-0607. More of a full-service hotel than the Ptarmigan Lodge, it has large rooms, an indoor pool, a hot tub, a restaurant, a ski shop, and a lounge on-site. It also has family rooms available with three double beds. Again, rates vary tremendously, but are moderate for the area and comparable with the Holiday Inn described below.

The 217-room **Holiday Inn** at 1129 North Summit Boulevard in Frisco (across the street from the Best Western Lake Dillon Lodge) provides comfortable overnight accommodations in a location just off I-70 that's more convenient than scenic. There's an indoor pool, sauna, hot tubs, restaurant, lounge, gift shop, and ski shop on the premises, and you are also within walking distance of Frisco shops and restaurants. Rooms can cost anywhere from $70 to $190, depending on the season. For reservations call (800) 782-7669. The local phone number is (970) 668-5000.

Both the Best Western Lake Dillon

**i** *With ski traffic mounting every year, think about renting a condo for the weekend to avoid day-skiing hassles. On Saturday take a shuttle to the slopes. To avoid the heavy weekend traffic through Idaho Springs on Sunday, be the first on the slopes and the first to leave, or stay another night and drive down in the morning.*

Lodge and the Holiday Inn are close to the bike path and a Summit Stage bus stop. To reach them take exit 203 off I-70.

# ARAPAHOE BASIN
## Useful Phone Numbers

**Main number and central reservations,** (970) 468-0718; www.arapahoebasin.com

**Nursery–day care (18 months and older),** (970) 468-0718

## Getting There

To get to Arapahoe Basin, take I-70 to exit 205, Dillon/Silverthorne. Follow US 6 for 12 miles; Arapahoe Basin is 5 miles past Keystone.

Situated 5 miles away from Keystone at a (gasp!) base altitude of 10,800 feet above sea level, Arapahoe Basin is where Insiders head for unbeatable spring skiing. (It stayed open until August 10 in 1995 due to late snows.) It offers the highest lift-served terrain on the North American continent; the summit is at 13,050 feet above sea level. It's not unusual late in the season to see skiers in shorts and T-shirts. A-Basin is characterized by tough terrain and tough weather conditions—but a good day here is a great day. Don't forget the sunscreen.

Arapahoe Basin is a full-service resort, if not glamorous. The most important thing you'll find here is great skiing (490 acres; 40 percent expert). There is also a cafeteria, bar, ski school, rental shop, and retail store. For information call the main number.

# COPPER MOUNTAIN
## Useful Phone Numbers

Snow Report, (970) 968-2100, (800) 789-7609

Copper Mountain Resort general information, (970) 968-2882, (800) 458-8386, www.coppercolorado.com

Central reservations, (888) 219-2441

Copper Mountain Chamber of Commerce, (970) 968-6477

Summit County Chamber of Commerce, (970) 668-2051, (800) 530-3099

# Getting There

Copper Mountain is about 75 miles west of Denver. To get there, take I-70 west and get off at exit 195.

# Skiing

Copper Mountain was constructed as a self-contained resort in the early 1970s. It is the home of Club Med's first North American ski center, and it's a very enticing place for intermediate and expert skiers, as more than three-quarters of the trails are intermediate to expert.

In January 1996 Copper opened a new double lift that serves the 700-acre Copper Bowl. A second lift was opened in 1997, bringing the total to 22 lifts. The expansion makes Copper the biggest ski area in Summit County, with more than 2,400 acres.

More than $500 million has been spent refurbishing Copper Mountain's base area since 1998. Among the components of the mountain's new look are expanded base restaurants near the Super Bee lift, Commons, and Union Creek; additional snowmaking capacity; and a new Super Pipe Dragon for carving out a larger half-pipe.

Copper has also put a great deal of effort into its ski school program, so beginners will feel comfortable here as well. In the past Copper has even offered free skiing on its easiest lifts, K and L. In all, the K and L lifts access 53 acres of terrain and have an easy grade just right for the first-

time skier or boarder. To find out about the K and L lifts, call (800) 458-8386, ext. 4INFO.

The mountain is naturally divided between harder and easier skiing. Still, Copper has a reputation as a prime destination for serious skiers who are looking to maximize time on the slopes and are turned off by the glamorous atmosphere of Vail. Snowboarding is permitted; the resort's first snowboard park opened in 1996–1997 and its second opened in 1999. A one-day adult lift ticket to Copper Mountain costs $72.

# Cross-country Skiing and Other Winter Activities

The cross-country skiing tracks at Copper Mountain begin near the Union Creek base area and branch off into the rolling, wooded valleys of the Arapaho National Forest.

Dinner sleigh rides are offered nightly in winter and in summer (on wheels) and include a gourmet meal midmountain. Call the Copper Mountain Stables at (970) 968-2232.

# Summer Fun

The **Copper Creek Golf Club** is the highest-altitude championship golf course in America. (Elevation is 9,650 feet, meaning your ball will fly 15 percent farther than at sea level.) Summer activities include a 35-foot freestanding outdoor climbing wall, a quad-powered bungee jump on a trampoline, and, new in 2006, Copper Go-Karts. Hikers, backpackers, and horseback riders enjoy challenging themselves on the Wheeler-Dillon Pack Trail, which begins across the highway from Copper Mountain and climbs rapidly into the rugged Gore Range in the Arapaho National Forest. The Colorado Trail, a 469-mile trail that extends from Denver to Durango, passes near Copper Mountain, too. You can also arrange a breakfast or dinner horseback ride out of Copper Mountain Stables.

In the summer you can ride the American Eagle lift free daily from mid-June to about Labor Day. For information about any summer activity at Copper Mountain, call Copper Mountain Resort, (800) 458-8386.

Frisbee golfers will love the 18-hole course through the base of the village. It's a disc-thrower's delight—and free!

For $14 a day mountain bikers can ride up the lift and ride down on either the mountain road or a twisty single-track. Bike rentals are easily found. Try Gravitee, (970) 968-0171. Intermediate riders might want to try the Ten Mile Canyon ride, which follows the old railroad grade along Ten Mile Creek.

## Dining

**Endo's Adrenaline Cafe,** (970) 968-3070, is the place to chow down on huge sandwiches and specialty drinks. It's located in the Mountain Plaza Building. At **Double Diamond,** (970) 968-2880, in the **Foxpine Inn,** you'll find a selection of steaks, sandwiches, pizza, and burgers. **Creekside Pizza,** (970) 968-2033, features pizzas made with homemade dough and fresh ingredients. They also offer pasta, salads, and sandwiches and are located in Snowbridge Square.

## Shopping

Since Copper's village expansion, shopping has improved considerably. There are now more shops near the Super B lift and in the village. Its offerings are still eclipsed by the surrounding towns, but you can find almost anything you need for a ski vacation. Try **Christy Sports** in the center of the village, (970) 968-2086.

## Accommodations

Virtually all the overnight lodging at Copper Mountain is in condominiums. Call **Copper Mountain Resort,** (888) 219-2441, for rental information.

## VAIL AND BEAVER CREEK
## Useful Phone Numbers

Ski Area information, (970) 476-5601

Snow Report, (970) 476-4888

Vail/Beaver Creek Reservations, (970) 845-5745, (800) 525-2257

Vail Valley Tourism & Convention Bureau, (970) 476-1000, (800) 525-3875

## Getting There

Vail is along I-70 about 100 miles west of Denver; Beaver Creek is 11 miles farther west.

## Skiing

For as long as Vail has been a playground of plenty, Front Range residents have had a love-hate relationship with it. They love the skiing—acres and acres of varied, magnificently designed slopes—but hate the crowds, glitz, and high prices. Driving to Vail from Denver also means navigating Vail Pass, which can be treacherous in bad weather and an incentive to exit at Copper Mountain or sooner. Still, every self-respecting skier should try Vail. It's the largest single ski-mountain complex in North America: three base areas, more high-speed quad chairlifts than any other ski area, and vast powder-filled back bowls that spread out across 5,200 acres of spectacular alpine terrain. China Bowl alone is as large as many ski areas. Intermediates especially can ski all day and never go down the same run twice. A heated and lighted gondola, the Eagle Bahn, was added in 1996. During the summer of 1998, Vail spent $10 million to improve its on-mountain restaurants and its Adventure Ridge mountaintop activity center featuring an outdoor skating rink, snowmobile tours, and other winter fun. Also look for Chaos Canyon for kids only, which features an obstacle course and other kid-friendly attractions.

A ticket at Vail is interchangeable with one at Beaver Creek, Vail's little (but even richer and more exclusive) sister 11 miles farther west on I-70. First opened in 1980-1981, elegant Beaver Creek attracts an international elite clientele as well as local skiers who praise the area for its spectacular natural beauty, lack of crowds, free parking, and intimate feel. About 65 percent of the runs at Beaver Creek are intermediate or advanced. Snowboarding is permitted at Vail and Beaver Creek.

One-day adult lift tickets, good at Vail, Beaver Creek, Breckenridge, and Keystone, are $81. Kids do not ski free here: A child ticket for ages 12 and younger is a hefty $49. There are, however, a total of 12 kids-only areas (in addition to the large Chaos Canyon) featuring historical Indian tepee villages, a mountain lion's den, ski-through mock gold mines, and a fort. Parking can add another $15 to your Vail tab, so carpool if you can.

With more than 4,600 acres of trails and only 100 miles from Denver, Vail remains a top destination for serious skiers. Its international clientele means that you never know who might be in the gondola with you—a neighbor from Denver or a visitor from Europe or Mexico.

Modeled after a Tyrolean village, Vail is a charming town that caters to pedestrians. Free buses link all the base areas and run from morning to late night. Vail is home to the **Colorado Ski Museum,** at the Vail Transportation Center, (970) 476-1876, and is the frequent site of World Cup ski races.

# Cross-country Skiing and Other Winter Activities

Vail and Beaver Creek each have a cross-country ski center: the **Vail Cross Country Ski School,** (970) 479-3210, located at the Vail Golf Course, with backcountry access to Vail Mountain and the White River National Forest; and **Beaver Creek Nordic Center,** (970) 845-5313, at the bottom of Strawberry Park lift (chair 12). At Beaver Creek skiers ride the lift up to McCoy Park, which is home to a system of groomed trails. Equipment rentals, tours (including snowshoe tours), and lessons are available at both areas.

There are abundant opportunities for backcountry touring throughout the Vail Valley; the summit of Vail Pass itself is often the first ski tour of the year for many Denver backcountry enthusiasts, as it receives plentiful early snow. The town of Vail and Vail Pass are the starting or ending points for several overnight tours to 10th Mountain Trail Association huts, including the luxurious (well, for a hut) Shrine Mountain Inn. Reservations are essential; call the **10th Mountain Division Hut Association,** (970) 925-5775.

The bobsled run at Vail is a thrilling ride. Snowmobile and sleigh rides can be booked through local companies, and Vail's world-class **John A. Dobson Ice Arena** is open for public skating. Admission is $5.00 for adults and $4.00 for children ages 5 to 12, skate rentals are $3.00 per person. Children ages 4 and younger skate for $2.00. Call (970) 479-2271.

**Adventure Ridge,** (970) 476-9090, is a mountaintop activity center featuring an outdoor skating rink, tubing hill, snowmobile tours, thrill sledding, ski biking, laser tag, snowshoeing, orienteering, and a free nature center. It's open in winter only until 10:00 P.M. and has three restaurants to choose from.

# Summer Fun

Summer is glorious in the Vail Valley. In fact, many Denverites who avoid Vail's winter glitz look forward to its more laid-back summer style. Hikers and backpackers can explore a large network of trails, either on foot or on horseback. Most of these trails are fairly steep, but the many lakes and waterfalls provide lots of resting and picnic spots. Much of the land around Vail is part of the White River National Forest; call or visit the **Holy Cross Ranger District Office** (off the West Vail exit ramp) for suggested routes and maps, (970) 827-5715.

Four chairlifts on Vail and Beaver Creek mountains make it easy to reach new mountain-biking heights and nearly 100 miles of world-class trails. Rentals are easy to find at any number of shops in town or at the Wildwood Shelter on top of the Wilderness Express lift at Vail.

There are several public and private golf courses in the Vail Valley, the most touted of which is the **Beaver Creek Golf Course,** (970) 845-5775, a Robert Trent Jones Jr. course. The par 72 **Cordillera Golf Club** opened in July 1997 with both mountain and valley courses, (970) 926-5100. A fun and affordable option is the **Eagle-Vail Golf Course** located between Vail and Avon, (970) 949-5267. Former site of the Jerry Ford Invitational Golf Tournament is **Vail Golf Club,** a par 71 public course with spectacular views of the Gore Range, (970) 479-2260.

Vail offers several summer getaway packages. For reservations and information call the tourism bureau at (800) 525-3875.

---

ℹ *If you'd like to hike or ride a mountain bike near the Holy Cross Wilderness Area near Vail, Aspen, or Copper Mountain but aren't keen on sleeping in tents, the 10th Mountain Division Hut Association huts are open in the summer from July 1 through September 30. Call (970) 925-5775 for more information or to make reservations.*

If you're looking for Vail glamour, try the **Spa at the Sonnenalp Resort,** offering the ultimate relaxation with a Scandinavian touch, (800) 654-8312. For the musically inclined, the **Bravo! Vail Valley Music Festival** will be in its 20th year in July and August 2007, featuring an array of classical music and jazz, (970) 827-5700 or (877) 812-5700.

# Dining

Two of the finest restaurants in the state are in Vail: **Sweet Basil,** 193 East Gore Creek Drive, (970) 476-0125, and **The Wildflower,** 174 East Gore Creek Drive in the Lodge at Vail, (970) 476-5011. Both are expensive but well worth it for special occasions; reservations are recommended. Sweet Basil serves inventive American cuisine in a pretty spot by Gore Creek. The Wildflower Inn offers up superbly creative American cuisine in an elegant setting. Less expensive is **Los Amigos,** (970) 476-5847, at the top of Bridge Street, which serves standard Mexican fare in a bustling atmosphere. Also more for the budget-minded, **Blu's,** 193 East Gore Creek Drive, (970) 476-3113, is a longtime favorite serving breakfast, lunch, and dinner. The food is eclectic American cuisine, including soups, salads, pizzas, great desserts, and coffee.

Dining in Beaver Creek is even more heavily tilted toward the expensive than Vail, and reservations are de rigueur. **Mirabelle,** located in a former home at 55 Village Road, (970) 949-7728, receives high praise for its romantic ambience, excellent service, and French cuisine with a twist. It's closed briefly during the spring and fall, between ski season and summer. Up on the slopes of Beaver Creek, **Beano's Cabin** offers more than just a meal. Reached by sleigh ride, this elegant log-and-glass lodge offers six-course gourmet meals as well as entertainment for adults and children. In the summer you can get there via horseback or horse-drawn wagon (about a one-hour trip) or by shuttle van (a 10-minute trip). Naturally, an experience like this does not come cheap: Adults pay $96 (tax, tip, and alcoholic beverages extra); children age 11 and younger, $50. For reservations call (877) 354-0061.

For a more casual meal, visit **Pazzo's Pizzeria,** 122 East Meadow Drive, (970) 476-9026, at the end of the Vail Village pedestrian mall.

## Shopping

Vail and Beaver Creek are known for their fine selection of shops and galleries. But this is not bargain shopping. Sticker-shock is common, as are full-length furs, custom-designed jewelry, and designer labels. For colorful, contemporary regional art, visit **Vail Village Arts,** 100 East Meadow Drive.

Vail and Beaver Creek offer resort-town shopping at its finest. **The Golden Bear,** 286 Bridge Street, has ladies' clothing and men's and ladies' jewelry, including earrings, pendants, bracelets, and other accessories featuring its trademark golden bear (available in sterling silver, too). **Pepi Sports,** 231 Bridge Street, is another long-time source for outerwear and sportswear as well as ski, bike, and in-line skate rentals. There's also **True North,** 100 East Meadow Drive, which stocks an array of Canadian-designed outerwear, sweaters, pants, and boots. **Slifer Designs** specializes in interior design and is located in nearby Edwards.

## Accommodations

A reasonably priced room can be hard to come by in the Vail Valley. When money is no object, grand lodges and luxury hotels are happy to oblige. Try **The Lodge at Vail,** (970) 476-5011; **Beaver Creek Lodge,** (800) 525-7280; and the truly special **Lodge at Cordillera,** (970) 926-2200 or (866) 732-ROCK. But the price will be steep, ranging from around $150 a night in the off-season to $950 in high season. A bed-and-breakfast some-

what off the beaten path is the **Minturn Inn,** 422 Main Street in Minturn, (970) 827-9647, a completely refurbished 1915 hewn-log home with prices ranging from $99 to $319 for a riverfront room. U.S. Highway 24 runs right through Minturn. **The Roost,** (970) 476-5451, touts itself as the least expensive lodging in Vail and offers continental breakfast. Check the Denver newspapers for special packages, or call **Vail/Beaver Creek Reservations,** (800) 525-2257.

## Ski Country Resources

### Arapaho National Forest
Dillon District Office, 680 Blue River Parkway, Silverthorne, (970) 468-5400; www.fs.fed.us/r2/arnf

### Colorado Cross-Country Ski Association
Information on cross-country centers, www.colorado-xc.org

### Colorado Division of Wildlife
Fishing information, (303) 291-7533; www.wildlife.state.co.us/fishing

### Colorado Ski Country
Daily ski conditions/reports (statewide), (303) 825-7669; www.coloradoski.com

### National Weather Service
Denver and central mountains, (303) 494-4221; road conditions within two hours of Denver, (303) 639-1111

### 10th Mountain Division Hut Association
Aspen, (970) 925-5775; www.huts.org

### USDA Forest Service
Denver Regional Office, 740 Simms Street, Lakewood, (303) 275-5350; www.fs.fed.us/

### U.S. Geological Survey
Topographical maps, (303) 202-4700; www.usgs.gov/

**White River National Forest**
900 Grand Avenue, Glenwood Springs,
(970) 945–2521; www.fs.fed.us/r2/white
river

# Recommended Guidebooks

*Hiking Colorado* (second edition) by
Maryann Gaug (Falcon)

*100 Classic Hikes in Colorado* (revised edition) by Scott S. Warren (Mountaineers
Books)

*Rocky Mountain Skiing* (second edition)
by Claire Walter (Fulcrum Publishing)

*12 Short Hikes® Denver Foothills Central* by
Tracy Salcedo (Falcon)

*Winter Trails Colorado* (second edition) by
Andy and Tari Lightbody (Globe Pequot
Press)

# SPECTATOR SPORTS

Spend a few days in Denver, and you're likely to think the term "sports town" was coined for the Mile-High City. This town is rabid about its sports.

In 1987, when the Denver Broncos lost their second Super Bowl, local media enlisted psychologists to help comfort downtrodden fans through newspapers and radio talk shows. People were encouraged to look at the loss not as a reflection of civic pride but for what it was—a game. (Of course, since the 1997 and 1998 Super Bowl championships, fans are still pounding their chests.)

When baseball's National League was looking for expansion cities, a majority of metro Denver fans anted up with a tax hike to fund a stadium. "Build it and they will come" became the local mantra. We have Coors Field to show for our efforts.

Today Denver is one of only a few cities that boast five big-league sports teams: football's Broncos, baseball's Colorado Rockies, hockey's Colorado Avalanche, basketball's Denver Nuggets, and soccer's Colorado Rapids.

Denver's two daily newspapers step all over each other to be the best source in sports news. When the Rockies expansion team formed, the *Rocky Mountain News,* which owns part of the team, declared itself the "Official Newspaper of the Rockies." The *Denver Post* quickly followed by dubbing itself the "Official Newspaper of the Fan."

No matter which paper visitors read, they quickly get a sense of Colorado's love of sports. The sour mood at the office on Monday morning is almost palpable if the Broncos lose on Sunday. Fans talk about players like they're family. Broncos former quarterback John Elway was once proclaimed "St. Elway" in a *Denver Post* headline.

Even when the favorite teams aren't winning championships, Denver fans remain loyal. Bronco fans are an especially devoted group. Season-ticket holders have reaped thousands of dollars in windfall profits by selling rights in the '80s and '90s that were free in the '60s. Rockies fans refuse to be outdone in their fervor. They broke nearly every attendance record on the books in the team's first season: the all-time Major League Baseball single-season attendance record, the largest opening-day crowd, largest attendance at a single game, and fastest team to reach one-, two-, three-, and four-million attendance levels. Over the years, crowds have thinned.

The newest and most spectacular addition to Denver's sports scene opened in the fall of 2001—INVESCO Field at Mile High. INVESCO Field hosted the first Monday-night game of the 2001 season when the Broncos met the New York Giants on September 10.

The Pepsi Center opened as home to the Denver Nuggets and Colorado Avalanche in 1999. It is also host to dozens of other events such as concerts, circuses, and ice shows. Groundbreaking on the $160 million, 675,000-square-foot arena began in 1997. The structure is located in the Central Platte Valley on the edge of downtown and next to the Six Flags Elitch Gardens amusement park. A pedestrian walkway connects it to Elitch Gardens, and it features 17 concession stands, a 236-seat club restaurant, 95 luxury suites, and fully upholstered cast-iron armchairs throughout the arena. It is within walking distance to Lower Downtown restaurants and shops.

For those who like playing to win, Greater Denver also has several racetracks. Lots of people would consider the National Western Stock Show & Rodeo the city's premier spectator sports event, but as it only happens once a year, we've covered it in our Annual Events and Festivals chapter.

# Colorado Rockies Bring Baseball, Big Bucks, and Beer to LoDo

The time is the 1970s, the place is a small section of Denver—dirty, a little rough, and definitely seedy.

Brown bags and empty booze bottles litter the streets like bad reminders of the night before. Graffiti covers plywood, which covers shattered warehouse windows. The only signs of life happen at night, and these aren't the signs of prosperity and possibility. If the place had a disclaimer, it would shout: "Danger: Go Away."

This is no place for America's favorite pastime.

Now fast-forward to the mid-1990s. Red brick surrounds gleaming windows in renovated warehouses. Litter is gone, replaced by bustling shops and streets and smiling pedestrians. Tourists lounge on the sunny patios of upscale joints and savor microbrewed beer. Above it all towers Coors Field, home of the Colorado Rockies.

This dramatic turnaround may sound like a scene from a developer's dream, but it's the reality of lower downtown Denver's revitalization. Much of the metamorphosis comes compliments of the Colorado Rockies and their new baseball stadium.

The Rockies have done wonders for Denver's economy and, specifically, the revival of the once-blighted area Insiders call "LoDo." An economic-impact study done in 1994 estimated the Rockies would prompt nearly $200 million a year in new spending. That's a lot of beer and hot dogs.

Of course, there's more to LoDo than beer and dogs. In fact, unless the beer

has a fancy name from one of 11 local brewpubs (Sagebrush Stout, anyone?) and the dogs are dressed up with freshly crushed green chile salsa and served in the center of a dazzling food display, it probably isn't in LoDo. Indeed, LoDo (sort of like SoHo, only not quite) is home of the hip, cool, and happening.

Development around the stadium in the past few years is remarkable. More than 40 new restaurants and brewpubs have sprung up in LoDo since Coors Field opened.

Residential living also has sprung up around Coors Field. Now that the abandoned warehouses around the stadium have been revived into posh lofts, many of which advertised "Coors Field access," developers have begun ground-up projects elsewhere in LoDo to sate public demand.

Also on the rise are hotel rates, not-so-good news for tourists but good for Denver's economy. Occupancy rates have climbed.

The city of Denver has done its part to build the area. Baseball-related infrastructure improvements include millions in road construction (at least $36 million for the city of Denver alone). Another $5 million has gone toward LoDo economic development projects and streetscaping.

In fairness to the LoDo area, much of the revival was launched pre-Rockies. But nearly everyone agrees the Rockies have stimulated business and interest in LoDo. The Rockies alone bring more than three million people to downtown during baseball season (of course, many of those are repeat customers). But the games lure people downtown who might not other-

*Coors Field is a home run for the Colorado Rockies.* DENVER METRO CONVENTION AND VISITORS BUREAU

wise have made the trek—like suburbanites who in the '80s stayed away from the city. Those same people, having sampled the excitement and vibrancy of LoDo, return to eat, shop, and party. In a downtown Denver survey, 37 percent of metro respondents said baseball was the main reason they went downtown.

"It's turned LoDo into a year-round destination," says Ben Wright, chief economist for the Denver Metro Chamber of Commerce.

To some extent, the phenomenon happened out of luck—and lack of parking. A dearth of spaces (only 15,000 spaces for 50,000 fans) was once a negative against Coors Field in its planning stages. But the paucity has forced fans to park in lots all over downtown and walk to the game—passing enticing restaurants and shops along the way.

A recent nationwide survey placed the Rockies and Coors Field 11th on the list of top tourist attractions. LoDo rose in popularity to seventh place. Publications around the nation and even in Canada have hailed the powerhouse effect of the Rockies on breathing economic life into LoDo. As proof, the Lower Downtown District Inc. maintains a drawer full of publications, including *Sunset Magazine, USA Today,* and the *New York Times,* which have written all about the revival.

How does a neighborhood achieve that kind of success while also balancing the quality-of-life issues that having a major-league team in your backyard brings?

If you're Coors Field and lower downtown Denver, you do it with a little luck and a lot of style.

## BASEBALL

**Colorado Rockies**
**Coors Field, 2001 Blake Street**
**(303) 762-5437 (ROCKIES)**
**www.rockies.mlb.com**
The Colorado Rockies was one of two expansion teams added to the National League in 1993. Despite a losing inaugural season, they won the hearts of Coloradans and received national media attention for the record-breaking attendance they attracted.

After two seasons playing in Mile High Stadium, the Rockies began their 1995 season in their new home, Coors Field, in Lower Downtown at Blake and 20th Streets. Designed by Hellmuth, Obata & Kassabaum, a Kansas City firm, the 50,249-seat all-baseball stadium is an updated version of a classic ballpark. Its exterior is built of two shades of red brick, and its seats provide views of the Rocky Mountains. The nation got a good look at Coors Field when Denver hosted the 1998 All-Star Game. The game was a weeklong celebration of baseball and Lower Downtown fun for thousands of local and visiting fans.

Such an intense focus on baseball in Colorado once made the best game seats hard to come by, but things have since eased up, and good seats are available for almost every game. Single seats go on sale for all games beginning in February and range from $4.00 to $49.00. During the season, purchase tickets at the stadium at Gate C between 20th and 21st Streets and Blake Street or at Rockies Dugout Stores and King Soopers supermarkets. Wheelchair-accessible seating is available. Day-of-game "Rockpile" seats go on sale at the stadium two hours prior to game time and cost $4.00 for adults, $1.00 for kids age 12 and younger and seniors age 55 and older.

---

*Coors Field has two "family sections" where alcohol is not served. Ask for sections 141 and 342.*

---

RTD (Regional Transportation District) provides special buses to and from Rockies games from 16 suburban park-and-rides. The fare is $6.00 round-trip for express routes. Regular service to and from Market Street Station also brings you within walking distance of the stadium but may not be as conveniently timed for evening games. For schedules and fare information, call (303) 299-6000, TDD (303) 299-6089.

## BASKETBALL

**Denver Nuggets**
**The Pepsi Center, 1000 Chopper Place**
**(303) 405-1100**
**www.nba.com/nuggets**
Under the guidance of head coach George Karl, the Nuggets continue to pursue their playoff goals with a lineup mixture of seasoned veterans and top draft choices, winning the 2005–2006 Northwest Division title.

Tickets range from $10 to $124, and there are a number of special deals, such as family and youth nights and group discounts. Handicapped seating is available on request. Nuggets tickets are available by calling the number above or through Ticketmaster at (303) 830-TIXS.

The Nuggets share the Pepsi Center, located in the Platte Valley next to Six Flags Elitch Gardens, with the Colorado Avalanche.

## FOOTBALL

**Denver Broncos**
**13655 Broncos Parkway, Englewood**
**(303) 649-9000**
**www.denverbroncos.com**
After losing three Super Bowls (1986, 1987, and 1989), the Broncos finally granted fans their ultimate wish—the 1997 championship. And then they followed with the 1998 championship. Broncos fans were joined by legions of John Elway supporters across the country who wanted to see the

*INVESCO Field at Mile High was built in 2001 as the new home of the Denver Broncos.* THE *DENVER POST*/ANDY CROSS

longtime quarterback win a Super Bowl title.

Although Elway has since retired, it's no surprise that virtually every home game is a sellout. If you want to attend, you'll have to call well in advance for tickets and information or show up at the game and take your chances that someone in the parking lot has a ticket to sell. The Broncos played their first regular-season game in their new stadium, INVESCO field at Mile High, in the fall of 2001. The new stadium comes compliments of metro-area voters, who in November 1998 approved partial public funding for Mile High to be demolished and replaced with a state-of-the-art facility. Tickets, if you can get them, range from $39 to $90 and are available by calling (720) 258-3333, through Ticketmaster at (303) 830-TIXS, or online at www.denverbroncos.com.

RTD's BroncoRide services all home games from a number of locations in Greater Denver, with special shuttles available for fans catching the BroncoRide along Federal Boulevard and at the Auraria campus. Call RTD at (303) 299-6000 for schedules and current fare information.

## HOCKEY

**Colorado Avalanche**
**The Pepsi Center, 1000 Chopper Place**
**(303) 405-1100**
**www.coloradoavalanche.com**

---

*The hottest spot to meet for pre-Broncos game beers, burgers, and boasting is Zang Brewing Company, 2301 Seventh Street, visible from INVESCO Field at Mile High. If you don't have tickets but want to experience Bronco fever, stop by any number of sports bars, including Jackson's Hole at Sixth and Kipling Streets, to cheer on the team via television.*

---

*The Broncos have developed a well-deserved reputation for finding little-known college running backs who become phenoms in the team's offensive system. Starting with Terrell Davis, Denver has introduced the NFL to Mike Anderson, Olandis Gary, and Clinton Portis.*

By mid-1995 Denver could boast of having four major-league teams when it was announced that the company that owns the Nuggets purchased the Quebec Nordiques. By 1996 Denver could really boast—and boast it did—when its new Colorado Avalanche won the Stanley Cup. They repeated that win in 2001 against the New Jersey Devils in Game 7 of the series. (A parade followed the next Monday with as many as 250,000 fans lining the downtown parade route.) Since then the NHL has seen its way through labor difficulties, a season-long shut down in 2004–2005, and a player's salary cap that has stripped many teams, including the Avalanche, of some of its top players. Nevertheless, the Avs remain an annual playoff contender, and they boast a legion of devoted followers.

Single-game tickets go on sale in early fall, with prices ranging around $90 to $120 in the lower level and $21 to $90 for balcony-level seats. Ask about group discounts. Season tickets are available. To purchase tickets call the number above or Ticketmaster, (303) 830-TIXS.

## SOCCER

**Colorado Rapids**
**The Pepsi Center, 1000 Chopper Place**
**(303) 405-1100**
**www.coloradorapids.com**
The Colorado Rapids kicked off their first home game in April 1996 and have been gaining momentum ever since. In 1997 the team captured the western conference championship. In 1998 four of its star play-

ers made the All-Star lineup: Marcelo Balboa, Chris Henderson, Paul Bravo, and Adrian Paz. Along with the 1997 title, the team also has the distinction of raising its win/loss record from "worst" in 1996 to "first" in 1997. The team is gaining popularity; attendance averages 15,000 per game. The Rapids moved to INVESCO Field at Mile High in 2002, although they are building their own stadium in Commerce City. Tickets are between $10 and $25. Call the Rapids at the number above or call Ticketmaster at (303) 830-TIXS.

## RACETRACKS

**Arapahoe Park Racetrack**
**26000 East Quincy Avenue, Aurora**
**(303) 690-2400**
Pari-mutuel thoroughbred, quarter horse, and other races take place Thursday through Sunday and holiday Mondays from June through early August at the Arapahoe Park Racetrack, just east of Gun Club Road. General admission is $3.00, clubhouse admission, $10.00 per table of four persons.

**Bandimere Speedway**
**3051 South Rooney Road, Morrison**
**(303) 697-6001**
**(303) 697-4870 (recording)**
**www.bandimere.com**
Championship drag racing events are held from April to October at Bandimere Speedway in Morrison (off C-470 between Alameda Avenue and Morrison Road). Events aren't limited to drag racing only; they include motorcycle and snowmobile events as well as such unusual shows as "most unique vehicle" and "stereo wars." Admission varies with events.

**Colorado National Speedway**
**4281 Weld County Road 10, Erie**
**(303) 665-4173**
**www.coloradospeedway.com**
This speedway has NASCAR and a variety of other races on a paved $3/8$-mile oval track, located off Interstate 25 at exit 232.

# INVESCO Field at Mile High

Nearly three years and $400 million after the unveiling of the proposed stadium design, INVESCO Field at Mile High, new home to the Denver Broncos, opened on August 11, 2001, with a concert featuring the Eagles in their only stadium appearance in North America in 2001. A pyrotechnics extravaganza followed, rivaling the millennium festivities in downtown Denver.

Throughout the development process, efforts were made to retain ties to the history of Mile High Stadium while creating a first-class, state-of-the-art facility. To that end, the new stadium logo incorporates the recognizable standing horse silhouette. And "Bucky" the bronco has been reconditioned and moved to a perch atop the new south scoreboard. The "Mile High" moniker was negotiated into the naming rights agreement.

The differences, however, are more striking than the similarities, particularly in terms of amenities. While the seating capacity has remained nearly identical, the total square footage of the stadium has doubled from 850,000 square feet to 1.7 million square feet. Approximately 8,500 club seats have been included, as well as 762 pairs of ADA-compliant seating. All seats have expanded in both width and length. Each seat now has a cup holder as well, a change welcomed by most but decried by a few for taking up precious leg room. Televisions, escalators, and a greater number of elevators have been added. The number of rest-rooms has doubled, and the number of concession stands has more than quadrupled. Finally, video boards have been added to each end of the field and increased in size over the one video board present in Mile High Stadium.

The naming of the stadium proved to be an emotionally charged issue for fans who had filled every seat in Mile High Stadium for every regular season game since 1970. Torn between reducing the public's debt load and retaining the historic "Mile High" name, the Metropolitan Football Stadium District was able to negotiate a naming rights agreement that incorporated "Mile High." INVESCO, a company that has had ties in the community for more than 70 years, will no doubt be on the lookout to prevent shortening of the name to "Mile High," but in agreeing to retain those words in the stadium name, they satisfied at least part of the public's desire.

The September 10, 2001, game between the Broncos and the New York Giants kicked off the 2001 Monday-night football season, while simultaneously being the first regular-season game in the new stadium. In addition to the Broncos, INVESCO Field at Mile High serves the Colorado Rapids soccer team (at least for a few seasons—the Rapids are building their own facility in Commerce City). INVESCO Field also hosts community events and festivities.

For more information on INVESCO Field at Mile High, log on to www.denver broncos.com.

Races are held Saturday night April through September. Colorado National Speedway is in Erie, 20 minutes north of Denver.

**Mile High Greyhound Park**
**6200 Dahlia Street, Commerce City**
**(303) 288–1591**

Live pari-mutuel races take place at Mile High Greyhound Park in Commerce City June through August and again in December and January. Matinee and evening races are scheduled throughout the week. General admission is $1.00; clubhouse admission is also $1.00.

# DAY TRIPS

Just to keep things reasonable, our day trips are destinations within about 100 miles of Denver. Even so, that still forces you to choose from more than 3,000 square miles of opportunities. Our recommendations tend to concentrate in the mountains and up and down the Front Range along Interstate 25. That's not a prejudice against the plains but simply a result of the fact that the Front Range and the mountains to the west have historically focused a lot more energy on tourism, and that's where the tourists tend to go. For most people who come to Denver, a ride to see the scenery seems automatically to mean heading into the mountains.

Anyone who loves the Great Plains knows that few landscapes are more tranquilizing than the endless rolling prairie, and few things are more magnificent than 180 degrees of sky. Towns and cities on the plains, furthermore, retain much more of their original historic feel because they haven't been so relentlessly populated by newcomers or so dolled-up to attract the tourist trade.

That being said, however, our recommendations are heavily weighted westward, wherein lie attractions on a larger scale connected by drives through flamboyantly awesome scenery. The landscape itself is a day trip. Almost anywhere you go in the mountains, you can get out of your car and take a walk. Parking at the top of Berthoud Pass on U.S. Highway 40 between Empire and Winter Park, for example, you may just want to hike eastward up the windswept slope to the top of Colorado Mines Peak for some great views and landscape. Loveland Pass, like almost any mountain pass in the state, offers a similar opportunity for wonderful views from a high-altitude parking spot.

We've mentioned a few scenic driving trips near Denver. But they are virtually infinite, given the combination of roads and off-road experiences. If you're looking for new ideas, you might check the "Hike of the Week" or "Ski Tour of the Week" features that run Sunday in the *Denver Post*.

Do bear in mind, however, that snowstorms can render high mountain roads treacherous, if not impassable, from September through May. You might consider calling (303) 639-1111 for the Colorado State Highway Patrol's report on road conditions before taking off on a mountain jaunt during these months. Most mountain lovers who've lived in Greater Denver for any period of time can tell you a horror story about sliding sideways on a snowy mountain pass, or worse. Particularly treacherous in heavy weather are high-altitude roads such as Berthoud Pass, Loveland Pass over the Continental Divide, the Eisenhower Tunnel under the Divide (on the way to Breckenridge, Arapahoe Basin, Keystone, and Copper Mountain ski areas), and Vail Pass (on the way to Vail and Beaver Creek).

If conditions are bad, it's advisable to make sure your vehicle has good snow tires or carry chains. If the chain law is in effect at a particular pass, those without chains will be turned back, no matter how good their tires are. And sometimes the road will just be closed, period. It's really a pain to pull out of Vail heading east up Interstate 70 and discover that they've swung the gates closed across the interstate.

Another worthwhile tip: I-70 and U.S. Highway 285 are Greater Denver's two

---

*When opening carbonated beverages in the car during high-altitude drives, remember that they have been bottled at a lower altitude and pressure. When opened, they can squirt in your face and all over the interior of your vehicle.*

main conduits into and out of the mountains. If there's any way to avoid it, do not return to Denver during the Sunday and Monday holiday rush hour, which runs from late afternoon to early evening. These highways become absolutely jammed with traffic, and spending hours in the jam can take the glow off your mountain experience. This problem is worse in winter, when the ski areas shut down their lifts between 3:30 to 4:00 P.M. This unleashes a concentrated wave of traffic in often-slick conditions when it's already dark. Return in early afternoon, if you can, or avoid the traffic by stopping for dinner in the mountains. Let the rush pass you by, then have a pleasant drive home.

With the exception of Winter Park, we haven't mentioned the mountain resort areas in this chapter because we've covered those in our Ski Country chapter. But they are certainly wonderful day-trip destinations year-round. We've chosen a few of our favorite day trips with outstanding special features sure to make you feel that a day's outing has been worth the drive.

One thing that's fun about day trips in Colorado is that the roads you travel are usually quite spectacular for their geography. There's always some amazing formation of land and rocks that makes you wonder how it got there. A good book for planning road trips is *Scenic Driving Colorado,* second edition, by Stewart M. Green (Falcon). You'll discover the wonders of Colorado's ecological and topographical diversity, multiethnic history, and magnificent beauty. Or, if you've got a couple days off, check out the suggestions in *Quick Escapes® Denver: 25 Weekend Getaways in and around the Mile High City* by Sherry Spitsnaugle (Globe Pequot Press).

## BOULDER

A day trip to Boulder could really turn into a weekend trip, there's so much to do in this college town. Should you decide to stay longer and want more extensive information, check out the *Insiders' Guide to Boulder.* That said, let's go.

When you're driving up U.S. Highway 36 from Denver to Boulder, watch for the exit to the cities of Louisville and Superior. Just beyond is a stunning vista of Boulder and its mountainside setting. In fact, if you haven't been to Boulder before, you should watch for a sign that says SCENIC OVERLOOK and take the exit to the right. During the warmer months the Boulder Convention and Visitors Bureau operates a visitor information kiosk at the overlook. More importantly, you need to absorb the view to get a full sense of what Boulder is all about, and Davidson Mesa, as this hill is known, is a primo vantage point.

Boulder nestles like a jewel in the scenic bowl of Boulder Valley. The most identifiable features of the mountainsides rising from its western edges are the Flatirons, enormous sandstone monoliths that lean against the slopes like a row of fossilized aircraft carriers. Losing that vantage point as you drive down the hill and into town, you encounter a city of tremendous charm and diversity.

Detractors used to call it "the people's republic of Boulder" during the Vietnam era when students at the University of Colorado at Boulder, CU's main campus, added antiwar protests to the already offbeat lifestyle of this university town. Profiles of Boulder in national magazines continue to emphasize the offbeat, and there's plenty of that. Boulder is a national mecca for alternative medicine, natural foods, spirituality, and outdoor sports such as bicycle racing, mountain biking, and technical climbing.

**Naropa University,** a national center for Buddhist studies, is here. It's the only fully accredited, Buddhist-inspired institution of higher education in North America, including bachelor's and master's degrees. And it's unconventional, colorful, and photogenic. It's open all day for those who want to drop in at 2130 Arapahoe Avenue, but it also has tours on weekdays at 2:00 P.M. Call (303) 444-0202 for more information. **Celestial Seasonings,** 4600 Sleepy-time Drive, now an international power in the herbal tea business, was founded here and remains headquartered here. Want to take a tour of the company? Call (303) 581-1202.

Celestial Seasonings is only one example of how Boulder's penchant for individualism and innovation also expresses itself in business entrepreneurism. This is a start-up town, where new companies pop up like spring flowers. Many are high-tech companies, and many have moved outward to other parts of Boulder County as they have grown. Storage Technology Corp., located in Louisville on the edge of Boulder Valley, for example, sprang from the Boulder high-tech community, and although it has been acquired by Sun Microsystems, its employees have gone on to found numerous other high-tech companies. High-tech spin-offs are a fundamental part of the local culture, and technology here is high indeed, including major federal government laboratories such as the National Center for Atmospheric Research and the National Institute of Standards and Technologies. The University of Colorado received more than $250 million in sponsored research awards for the 2003 fiscal year and is nationally prominent in fields ranging from molecular biology to telecommunications. It's one of the main reasons why high-tech companies locate or start up here, and it works closely with that community. Qwest Advanced Technologies, the research and development arm of Qwest Communications, is in the CU Research Park specifically to be close to its university research partners.

Despite the flaky image, often unfairly and shallowly reported by the outside press, Boulder has a wealth of cultural attractions and probably a greater concentration of good restaurants than you'll find in Denver, with the possible exceptions of Denver's downtown and Cherry Creek area. Boulder has everything from the fine cuisine of the **14th Street Grill** at 1400 Pearl Street, (303) 444-5854, to the hearty fare of family restaurants such as the **Red Robin Burger & Spirits Emporium** at 2580 Arapahoe Avenue, (303) 442-0320.

Boulder also belies its offbeat image by the impressive strength of its business community. Boulder County has, if not the highest, the state's second-highest percentage of employment in manufacturing, and it's way ahead in per-capita high-tech manufacturing. But don't expect to see Boulderites walking around in boardroom-elegant suits with grim, nose-to-the-grindstone expressions. Boulderites generally maintain an easygoing attitude. They're avid on the subjects of environmental responsibility and health consciousness.

All this is a rather long dissertation on one day trip, but Boulder is by far the biggest nearby trip in breadth of offerings. The **Pearl Street Mall** is the center of the city. Formerly the main street of old Boulder, it's now a pedestrian mall lined with unique shops, restaurants, art galleries, flower gardens, and street performers—a delightful stroll in any but the worst weather, except for the occasional panhandler or bourgeoisie-disdaining misanthrope. South on Broadway from Pearl Street and up the hill is **University Hill,** where you can enjoy a walk around the graceful campus of the University of Colorado at Boulder.

Go farther south on Broadway past the campus to Baseline Road, turn right onto Baseline, and go up a long hill. Just past Ninth Street you'll find on the left the entrance to **Chautauqua Park & Auditorium.** The auditorium is a lovely setting for a summer evening concert. For information call the Chautauqua ticket service at (303) 440-7666. One of Boulder's biggest treats is a summer breakfast, lunch, or dinner on the veranda of the **Chautauqua Dining Hall,** built in 1898, where you can gaze out at the mountains as you munch; call (303) 440-3776.

Chautauqua Park is also the city's prime entrance to **Boulder Mountain Parks,** some 8,000 acres of trails and rough climbing, including Bear Peak, Green Mountain, Flagstaff Mountain, and, of course, the Flatirons.

Another entrance to the park, and an attraction in its own right, is the **National**

ℹ️ *It's always cool in the mountains at night, even in the summer. Take a sweater, or shiver.*

**Center for Atmospheric Research,** commonly referred to around Boulder simply as NCAR (say it EN-car). An architectural masterwork by the renowned architect I. M. Pei, it perches like an Italian hill fortress on the redundantly named Table Mesa to the south of Chautauqua, with views of the mountains and plains that make it a great spot just for weather gazing. You find it by going still farther south on Broadway from Baseline to Table Mesa Drive. Turn right, and keep going until you stop at NCAR. You may see deer on the way. You can pick up a map in the lobby and take the self-guided tour from 8:00 A.M. to 5:00 P.M. Monday through Friday and 9:00 A.M. to 4:00 P.M. on Saturday, Sunday, and holidays. There's also a drop-in tour, which takes place daily at noon. The Science Store, opened in summer 2000, stocks a great selection of books and activities for children. And best of all, admission is free. The cafeteria is open to the public for breakfast and lunch from 7:30 to 9:30 A.M. and 11:30 A.M. to 1:30 P.M. To find out about NCAR's guided tours and other information, call (303) 497-1174. Outside NCAR, you can hike on 400 acres of the mesa top, including a wheelchair-accessible nature trail leading west behind the lab. And just west of the mesa, you get into the system of Boulder Mountain Park trails.

You can usually see climbers scaling the Flatirons, but the best place for close-up watching of technical climbers is **Eldorado Canyon.** Keep going south on Broadway from Table Mesa Drive until Broadway becomes Highway 93 as you pass into open country. Watch for the Eldorado Springs Drive turnoff on the right, just more than 5 miles out of Boulder. This is Highway 170, and about 8 miles of it takes you to **Eldorado Springs.** Back around the turn of the century this resort town used to be called "the Coney Island

of Colorado" because of all the people who flocked here for the resort hotels and 76-degree springs. Pass on through it and into **Eldorado Canyon State Park,** where you'll find a magnificent cut between high cliffs. You'll see little smudges of white all over the rocks; it's chalk from climbers' hands. In good weather you'll see people dangling all over the canyon walls.

## COLORADO SPRINGS

"The Springs," as locals call it, is an hour's drive south, 67 miles from Denver, and the largest single cluster of tourist attractions in our day-trip–defining radius of 100 miles. It doesn't have as many natural wonders as Rocky Mountain National Park, but it has some great ones. And it has plenty of other attractions of human contrivance.

**Pikes Peak** is the biggest show in town, of course. You can drive to the top by taking U.S. Highway 24 west to Cascade and hanging a left on the same road that brings top auto racers from around the world every year for the Pikes Peak Hill Climb. Or you can do the dizzying trip on the **Pikes Peak Cog Railway,** officially known as the Manitou and Pikes Peak Cog Railway. Reach its terminal by driving west from Colorado Springs on US 24 to the Manitou exit, west on Manitou Avenue, and left onto Ruxton Avenue.

This is the highest cog railway in the world. Established in 1889, it's a historical as well as a sensory experience. During the three-and-a-half-hour round-trip, you get more panoramas than you can stuff into your brain, including great views down on Manitou Springs and the Garden of the Gods. You get a great view of Denver on a clear day, just as Denverites can see Pikes Peak on a clear day. You can see a seemingly infinite expanse of mountains to the west, and you can even look into New Mexico.

Do take care not to exert yourself too much at the 14,110-foot summit: Oxygen is scarce up there, and altitude sickness is

*The Royal Gorge Bridge is the world's highest suspension bridge.* DENVER METRO CONVENTION AND VISITORS BUREAU

not a pleasant experience. Besides walking around and taking in the views, you can also unwind in the information center, the gewgaw shop, and the concession area.

The railway is only open from April to October and runs every day during that period. Reservations are required, since this is one of Colorado's big attractions. There's a $29 charge for adults and a $16 charge for children ages 3 through 11. Rates go up $2.00 for adults and 50 cents for kids in July and August. Call (719) 685-5401 for information.

**Garden of the Gods Park,** 1805 North 30th Street, (719) 634-6666, is another of Colorado Springs' most famous sights. A drive through the park reveals one of the most spectacular displays of dramatic red sandstone formations in Colorado. It's just northwest of downtown. **Cave of the Winds,** Highway 24 West in Manitou Springs, is the biggest commercial cave in Colorado, and well worth taking the tour through the underground passages and caverns. Call for tour information at (719) 685-5444. Cost is $16.00 to $20.00 for

adults and $8.00 to $12.00 for children ages 6 through 15 depending on the tour you select. There's also an outside laser light show each night at 9:00 P.M., costing $10.00 for adults and $5.00 for children, with kids ages 5 and younger getting in free.

If you want to go a bit beyond the 100-mile limit of our day-trip definition, you will certainly enjoy the Cripple Creek Narrow Gauge Railroad, (719) 689-2640. **Cripple Creek** itself is worth visiting, certainly, as one of Colorado's most famous old mining towns and a National Historic District in its own right, although the town has changed somewhat since limited-stakes gambling was legalized here in 1991. A little farther out Highway 115 is **Royal Gorge,** about an hour's drive from Colorado Springs, where you can drive across the world's highest suspension bridge 1,178 feet above the Arkansas River. Call Royal Gorge Bridge information at (719) 275-7507. By paying $19 for adults and $15 for children ages 4 through 11, you can drive or walk across the bridge as well as ride an aerial tram, a minitrain, and a carousel. They also have an incline railway, a cagelike ride that takes you all the way down to the bottom of the canyon to the river's edge.

There is so much more to see and do in the Colorado Springs area, including the Victorian town of **Manitou Springs** and its natural hot springs; the **Cliff Dwellings Museum,** (719) 685-5242, 5 miles west of Colorado Springs on US 24; the historic **Broadmoor Hotel,** (719) 634-7711, with its two great 18-hole golf courses; **Santa's Workshop at the North Pole,** (719) 684-9432, a little magic village/funland that kids can enjoy from mid-May through Christmas Eve; the **ProRodeo Hall of Fame** and the **Museum of the American Cowboy,** both at (719) 528-4764.

Of all Colorado Springs attractions, however, the very busiest is the **U.S. Air Force Academy.** Although access is limited during times of increased security, in normal times you can tour its 18,000 acres. The academy doesn't have any one attraction that will blow your socks off, but it's intrinsically interesting simply because of its importance in the military world of aviation. You can take a self-guided driving tour around the grounds daily between 9:00 A.M. and 5:00 P.M., or walk the nature trail that winds along the ridge behind the school, with plenty of wind-through-the-pines atmosphere and academy overlooks with benches. There's a very nice museum on the grounds. The most famous sight is the chapel, which is architecturally striking. Perhaps the best way to experience the academy is by attending its spring graduation ceremony, where you can see the now-ceremonial tossing of hats in the air by cadets and enjoy a performance by the Thunderbirds, the Air Force's famed jet-acrobatics team. You do need tickets in advance for this event, however. The tickets are free, and they generally become available about two weeks before the ceremony, which is always held on the first Wednesday after Memorial Day. Call the academy's visitor center at (719) 333-2025 for tickets and other information.

Directly across I-25 from the north gate of the Air Force Academy is a particular favorite of ours, the **Western Museum of Mining and Industry.** It's a nice place for a picnic, with 27 acres of rolling hills, trees, meadows, streams, beaver ponds, and picnic tables. Most important, of course, is the museum itself: more than 15,000 square feet of exhibits in four buildings, along with outdoor displays. It's a big treat to watch them fire up the 1895 Corliss steam engine and watch the 17-ton flywheel go. You can see mining and milling demonstrations and even pan for gold. Admission is $7.00 for adults, $5.00 for seniors and students, and $3.00 for kids ages 3 to 12. Kids younger than age 3 get in free with a paying adult. The museum is open 9:00 A.M. to 4:00 P.M. Monday through Saturday year-round; it's open till 5:00 P.M. June through August. For information call (719) 488-0880. To reach the museum get off I-25 at exit 156A, Gleneagle Drive.

## FORT COLLINS

We go to Fort Collins when we need a small-town (or smaller-town these days) fix. Just one hour north of Denver on I-25, this college town (home of Colorado State University) has seen tremendous growth in the last few years.

As you head north on I-25, take the Harmony Road exit and go right for a quarter of a mile until you see a farm with all kinds of shiny sculptures. This is the **Swetsville Zoo,** a menagerie of dinosaurs and mythical creatures made by owner Bill Swets. This self-styled artist makes his creatures out of old car parts and farm equipment. With more than 150 sculptures, this "zoo" makes a delightful diversion. Open every day year-round, the zoo is free, though donations are appreciated.

Once you're ready to head into town, get back on I-25 and go north to the Mulberry Street exit. This will take you through downtown and past it to Roosevelt Street, where you'll find City Park. Here you'll find the **Fort Collins Municipal Railway,** a fancy term for a restored trolley car that travels down its original route on Mountain

Avenue to downtown. Powered by 600 volts of electricity, the trolley runs on tracks that line the grassy median of one of the city's major thoroughfares. Don't be surprised when you reach downtown if the conductor gets out and smokes a pipe before returning to City Park. Remember, this is small-town living, not a New York subway. The 25-minute ride costs $1.00 for adults, 75 cents for seniors, and 50 cents for kids age 13 and younger. Open weekend afternoons and holidays from May through September.

Like most college towns Fort Collins offers shopping that transcends the typical mall experience. **Historic Old Town Square** at College and Mountain Avenues is a trove of art galleries, shops, and outdoor cafes all housed in historic buildings. Like the Pearl Street Mall in Boulder (though much smaller), this is a pedestrian-only area with places to sit and watch people when you're tired of shopping.

For beer drinkers a visit to Fort Collins wouldn't be complete without a free tour of the **Anheuser Busch Brewery,** off of I-25 at exit 271. Opened in 1988, the world's largest brewery offers free tours from 10:00 A.M. to 4:00 P.M. Thursday through Monday from October to May, 9:30 A.M. to 4:30 P.M. daily from June to August, and 10:00 A.M. to 4:00 P.M. daily in September. The 75-minute tour shows high-tech brewing processes as well as a chance to see the famous Clydesdale horses. Best of all, at the end, you can visit the Hospitality Center to taste a few brews.

We think a trip to Fort Collins must include a visit to the **Colorado State University** (CSU) campus. You might want to stop at the visitor center just south of College Avenue and Laurel Street if you want a map of the campus. Our favorite destination is Johnson Hall, where, in the summer, the CSU Theater Department puts on three plays in repertory. Usually light comedies such as *The Heidi Chronicles, Tuna Christmas,* and *Love Letters,* the plays are performed at the outdoor theater where the audience sits at cabaret tables. The student actors are an enthusiastic

bunch, and at $20 a ticket, this is a theatrical bargain—and a wonderful way to end a day in Fort Collins.

## GEORGETOWN

Georgetown is a historic mining town that has been lovingly maintained and restored with a turn-of-the-20th-century style that makes it look like one of those toy towns on an elaborate model railroad setup. John Denver used it as the site of one of his Christmas specials in the 1980s. It's a National Historic District that nestles deep in the head of a valley overshadowed by the steep slopes of several 12,000-foot mountains.

The biggest single attraction here is the **Georgetown Loop,** an old Western railroad train that hauls loads of tourists and train and history buffs from Georgetown uphill to **Silver Plume,** and back, which is about a 3-mile round trip. The train ride includes passage over a 100-foot trestle known as Devils Gate Bridge. We can't recommend this trip highly enough, and it's not just the scenery or the fun of riding. It's the historic element and the bits of cinder that fly from the stack of the horrendously puffing old engine and settle on the passengers behind. It's one of the few great antique train rides in Colorado and by far the closest one to Denver. For a special treat, do it in the fall when the aspens are at high color. The railroad costs $17.50 for adults and $12.00 for children ages 3 through 15, with no charge for kids age 2 and younger as long as they sit on a parent's lap. The train operates from May to October, and reservations are suggested. For reservations and information call (888) 456–6777.

Georgetown itself went from a mining camp in 1859 to style itself as the "Silver Queen of the Rockies" by the 1870s. Now it's just a fun place to stroll around; it has shops, restaurants, museums, galleries, and National Historic Register sites. The museums include the **Hotel de Paris,** the **Hamill House,** and the **Energy Museum,** which

> *Layering is the key for dressing in Colorado, especially in the mountains. Temperature changes often take visitors off-guard, but if you're prepared, it's not a problem. An inexpensive rain poncho for mountain showers can be a trip-saver.*

was recently renovated with help from the State Historic Fund. The Hamill House was built in the 1870s in the Gothic Revival style and has been restored to that period. The Hotel de Paris, owned by Louis Dupuy, included a fine dining room and is open for tours, as are all the museums. Reach Georgetown by taking I-70 exit 228, about 50 miles west of Denver.

You can also drive out of Georgetown south on the **Guanella Pass Scenic Byway,** which goes all the way to the city of Grant on US 285. The byway peaks out at Guanella Pass, elevation 11,669 feet, where you have wonderful views that include looking up at Mount Bierstadt. This pass is also a good place to get out of the car and look around, but don't stand up too fast in this altitude; the air is thin, and people have been known to faint from small exertions. Find a big rock and have a picnic.

Georgetown has another neat little element. The State of Colorado chose a spot near the lake just east of Georgetown as the state's first **Watchable Wildlife Viewing Station,** although there are others now. Stop and see if you can spot the herd of bighorn sheep on the mountainsides. You can even spot them from I-70 as you're whizzing by, although they've become hard to find because the herds were decimated by disease in 1994.

Georgetown visitor information has a toll-free number, (800) 472-8230.

## GRAND LAKE-GRANBY LOOP

We call this the Grand Lake–Granby Loop drive because those are the two towns

that anchor it on the western side of the Continental Divide. *National Geographic Traveler* mentioned this drive in its March–April 1994 edition, in an article titled "50 Great Scenic Drives." Nobody around here was surprised.

You can experience Grand Lake–Granby Loop by driving from Denver to Estes Park and over Trail Ridge Road (closed in winter) through Rocky Mountain National Park and down to Granby. Take US 40 from Granby south through Winter Park, over Berthoud Pass, connecting at Empire with I-70 back to Denver. It's almost 200 miles, a full day, especially if you stop along the way, which you should. Or, you may want to take the circle in the other direction. In fact, you may want to head the other direction only as far as Grand Lake, rather than making a full loop, and leave the Boulder, Estes Park, and Rocky Mountain National Park stops for a trip of their own some other day.

Grand Lake is both the name of the city and of the big lake on the edge of which the city perches. Just south of Grand Lake is Lake Granby. You'll travel along their western edges, and looking east at the mountains rising from the lakes' other sides into Rocky Mountain National Park and Arapaho National Forest, you can almost believe you're in Switzerland. The lakes are huge, deep blue, and clear, usually decorated with sailboats and always lined with small resorts. Grand Lake is the state's largest lake created by glaciers. Grand Lake is a quaint historic village with boardwalks along the main street. Walk around and maybe catch a bite to eat. Or, you might buy something and head out for a picnic at Lake Granby's Arapahoe Bay.

**Arapahoe Bay** is at the far southeastern end of Lake Granby. Its depths are a favorite fishing spot in June for the lake's big Mackinaw, or lake trout. You reach it by taking the first left turn off of U.S. Highway 34 at the southwestern tip of Lake Granby. A long gravel road passes over Granby Dam and skirts the southern edge of the lake. At the end of the bay, you'll find campgrounds and some nice short hiking trails. You can follow the trail east past Monarch Lake and go as far as you want up toward or into the Indian Peaks Wilderness. It's a pretty area that makes a pleasant stopping point on your loop.

Head south to meet US 40 just west of Granby. You may want to take an added excursion west, or right, on US 40 along the scenic highway toward Steamboat Springs, or at least as far as Hot Sulfur Springs. (See this chapter's section on Hot Sulfur Springs.) If not, take a left onto US 40 to get back to Denver by way of Granby, Tabernash, Fraser, Winter Park, Berthoud Pass, and down through Empire onto I-70.

Most people just hustle through **Empire,** but there are some nice places to stop for refreshments there. It's perhaps most famous as the location of **The Peck House,** Colorado's oldest operating hotel. Driving through Empire from Berthoud Pass, the Peck House, (303) 569-9870, is about three-fourths of the way through town, a half-block off US 40. You'll see it from the highway on your left, a big white building with red trim. It's a moderately priced hotel, ranging from $50 to $100 a night. Check it out and maybe dine in its restaurant.

## HOT SULPHUR SPRINGS

What was once our oddball recommendation is no longer such an oddball. This quaint town of about 375 residents has come alive again with the major renovation of Hot Sulphur Springs Resort, which reopened full-time in 1997. To reach this town located 90 miles northwest of Denver, take I-70 to US 40 and head west. US 40 has been widened and resurfaced, so slow down when you come to Hot Sulphur Springs.

You'll see the Riverside Hotel and Casa Milagro Bed and Breakfast on the close side of the Colorado River. Cross the river to get to the **Hot Sulphur Springs Resort,** which is nestled against 70 acres of sagebrush.

The Ute Indians once "took the waters" here to heal and relax. Today people come for the same reasons. You can soak in any of the 22 pools where 200,000 gallons of hot mineral waters flow at temperatures of 95 to 112 degrees year-round. Too darn hot? Go to the kid's pool that runs around 85 degrees.

This casual resort has private pools, pools with views, and cavelike pools. And if you're feeling particularly luxurious, you can go for a massage and a facial, too. If you're feeling invigorated, you may want to hike and picnic in the beautiful surroundings. The pools are open year-round from 8:00 A.M. to 10:00 P.M. A private pool is $12 per person per hour. The outdoor pool is $16.50 for adults in the summer, $14.50 in the winter. There is also a combo pass for $22.50 that allows you to use both the indoor and outdoor pools, and a no-expiration eight-visit pass for $110.00. Either way you'll return home totally relaxed. For information call (800) 510-6235.

**The Riverside Hotel,** across the bridge from the resort, is a blocky wooden structure that was built in 1903. Bought when it was rundown after being closed for a year and a half, the new innkeeper spent 10 months sprucing it up and opened for business in 1983. The 19 rooms are old-fashioned in appearance, like the hotel rooms you might see in a cowboy movie or find a bit more fancied up in a modern bed-and-breakfast. The hotel may be closed Monday through Wednesday in the winter months, when business slows down. Dinner is served seven days a week year-round. The dining room has a potbellied stove and looks out on the Colorado River. Call ahead for reservations, (970) 725-3589.

## IDAHO SPRINGS

Idaho Springs, 32 miles west of Denver on I-70, is the first resort town and erstwhile mining town you hit on the way west.

It's also the mining town that is most visible as a mining town, thanks to the yellow tailings spilling from holes that dot the mountainsides along I-70 here. If you want a closer look at this phenomenon, take the "Oh My God Road" from Idaho Springs to Central City, a narrow and scary road with even more holes and tailings dotting the hillsides.

Prospector George Jackson launched Idaho Springs in early 1859 when he pulled out nearly $2,000 worth of gold in one week. Miners flocked in, and the town was off. Two of your best choices for a look into the town's mining past are the **Argo Gold Mill** and the **Phoenix Mine.** You can't miss the Argo Gold Mill. It's the biggest structure on the north side of the valley, and the name is printed in large letters on its front. Where much of the local ore was processed is now a museum and National Historic Site that you can tour from May to October, (303) 567-2421. The Phoenix Mine, sunk in 1872, is once again a working mine that you can tour guided by an experienced miner. Learn about the history, geology, and art of gold mining; dig your own ore; and pan your own gold. Call (303) 567-0422.

Idaho Springs and the surrounding area have a lot of other attractions, too, and one of them is simply the **Clear Creek Ranger District Office, Arapaho National Forest,** (303) 567-3000, where you can stop in to find out about other opportunities nearby. It's at 101 Chicago Creek Road. Coming from Denver on I-70, take the Mount Evans exit, then turn left up Highway 103; it's the first brown building on the right-hand side.

And, of course, Idaho Springs has natural hot mineral springs. The **Indian Springs Resort,** a National Historic Site, offers hot baths and a covered mineral-water swimming pool. It's at 302 Soda Creek Road, just east of downtown. Call (303) 989-6666 for information.

For more information on these and other attractions, call the Idaho Springs Visitors Center at (303) 567-4382, (800) 685-7785.

## MOUNT EVANS

If you love mountains, this is the best day trip of them all. Not because there's a

resort or town or some paying attraction at the end of it—just because this is the fastest route to the greatest vistas in the region. For out-of-town visitors with only a morning or afternoon to see the mountains, this is the best recommendation we can make. For anybody else, it's a must.

It's simple. Highway 5 to the top of Mount Evans is the highest paved road in the world and your chance to go to the top of one of Colorado's "14ers" without having to huff and puff up thousands of feet of forest and alpine meadow. You park at about 14,260 feet, wander around, and look down and out 100 miles in every direction. The view is absolutely magnificent. It's more impressive than the view from Trail Ridge Road at the Continental Divide in Rocky Mountain National Park, and it's just up the hill from Idaho Springs.

Take I-70 west out of Denver to Idaho Springs, about a 30-minute drive. Get off at exit 240, which features a sign saying MOUNT EVANS, and get on Highway 103. It winds uphill, to the intersection with Highway 5 at Echo Lake. This is where rangers will collect the $6.00 per vehicle fee. The lake, by the way, is a nice place for a picnic and some fishing. Also, either on the way up or on the way down, stop at the **Echo Lake Lodge,** (303) 567-2138, located at the intersection. Pause for refreshments in their little restaurant and browse among their gifts and souvenirs. Make sure to look out the window at the hummingbird feeder. In summer you can expect to see the striking spectacle of broad-tailed hummingbirds swirling and hovering like bees just on the other side of the windowpane.

Head uphill on Highway 5 for another 14-mile trip to the top. Acrophobics should be warned that this stretch may produce whiter knuckles than any paved road in Colorado. The road is very narrow, especially on the ride down. Looking out from the passenger seat, you can easily imagine the car slipping off the side and cartwheeling into the abyss.

Once at the parking lot, you can climb a short trail to the highest point

*Echo Lake on the way to Mount Evans.* DENVER METRO CONVENTION AND VISITORS BUREAU

and look down to the west on the Continental Divide, east over Denver and the Great Plains, north over the Roosevelt National Forest, and south over the Pike National Forest. Bring along a state map; it's fun to try to identify some of the major peaks. If you like boulder fields, there are plenty to scramble around on. If you're a flatlander who hasn't been in Denver for at least three days, however, do bear in mind that there's only about half as much oxygen up here as there is at sea level. Don't exert yourself too hard or too long. Altitude sickness can hit you right away, or it can hammer you after you've been back in Denver for hours. Take it easy, drink lots of water, and you should do fine. The road to Mount Evans is open only in the warmer months, and even then, weather can turn bad. To check on road conditions or ask other questions, call the Clear Creek Ranger District of Arapaho National Forest at (303) 567-3000.

## THE PEAK-TO-PEAK

The Peak-to-Peak Highway is so called because it follows the eastern slopes of more peaks than you can shake a stick at. It's basically the road that runs below the Continental Divide from the tourist mecca of Estes Park on the north to the historic towns and gambling meccas of Black Hawk and Central City on the south. Along the way there are plenty of turnoffs westward that will get you closer to Longs Peak, Mount Meeker, Chiefs Head Peak, Isolation Peak, Ouzel Peak, Mount Alice, Mount Orton, Mahana Peak, and Copeland Mountain—and those are just some of the peaks along the first 10 miles. The highway is about 60 miles long and actually consists, north to south, of Highway 7, Highway 72, and Highway 119.

Take the Peak-to-Peak in either direction. The entire route is a winding road of beautiful vistas and lovely mountainsides. It's a worthwhile tour anytime but an especially great place to take in the views of autumn's golden aspens, generally in September. Ten miles south of Estes Park, you find the well-traveled turnoff for the Longs Peak trailhead. This may be the most popular ascent of a Colorado "14er." It's a heck of a long slog.

Another 4 miles or so along, you'll find on the right the turnoff for the **Ouzel Falls Trail** at Wild Basin. If you want to get out of your car for a pleasant walk to a gem-like waterfall in the cool forest, this is the opportunity. The falls are only about 3 miles up the trail.

All along the Peak-to-Peak there are not only turnoffs to the west to reach scenic areas and other attractions, but also turnoffs to the east that will take you back down to the flatlands in case you decide to bail out of the loop. You can come up these routes and travel only part of the loop. At one of these points, the historic mining town of Ward, you can head east downhill via **Lefthand Canyon** or you can head west up to **Brainard Lake.** This crystalline, high-mountain lake is a beautiful place where you can absorb spectacular views without walking more than a few steps from your car. Actually, you can just look out through the windshield, but the effect is better if you get out and inhale the mountain breezes.

Pass on south through Nederland (lots of nice drives west from here, too) and continue to Rollinsville. A drive west from here on a gravel road will bring you to the Moffat Tunnel, which connects Denver by railroad with points west. A trail up to the east of the tunnel makes a nice hike and is popular with cross-country skiers in winter.

From Rollinsville on down, the big tourist attractions are **Black Hawk** and **Central City,** which have become the places for Denverites to gamble since limited-stakes gambling was allowed by Colorado voters in 1991. For complete listings of lodging, casinos, and restaurants in Black Hawk, go to www.blackhawk colorado.com; for Central City visit www .centralcitycolorado.com. Also see our Nightlife chapter for more information.

Black Hawk is right next to Central City and was one of the first mining camps around Gregory Gulch, where gold was discovered in 1859. Central City, in the middle of Gregory Gulch, became the prominent population center because of its location, which claims the "richest square mile on Earth." It is a great old historic mining town, but a lot of people feel that its historic authenticity has been obliterated by all the new casinos. Central City has become a favorite evening and weekend excursion for a lot of people looking for a little Las Vegas in their own backyard, but it's still a nice historic district as well. The **Central City Opera House** is still one of Colorado's reigning opera performance centers during its summer season. In 1878 it was built on the site of the Montana Theatre, which had burned to the ground in 1874. Closed when the silver boom ended, it has been operating again since 1932. Call the Denver business office at (303) 292-6700 for opera information.

The **Teller House,** next to the opera, is Central City's historic hotel, perhaps most well-known for the "Face on the Barroom Floor." The mystique of that woman's face is probably due more to the faded paint job and her mysterious expression than to its origin, because it doesn't hail from the boom days. It was painted in 1932. The **Gilpin County Historical Museum** is a better bet for a bit of history on this gold and silver town of yore, and it's located right in town. Call (303) 582-5283 for more information about the museum.

Whether gambling has hurt or helped Central City and Black Hawk is a matter of opinion. Historic tourism wasn't paying the bills, supporters say, and gambling bolsters the economy so the historical aspects get their just due. Gambling drove real estate sky high, drove out a lot of authentic residents and their businesses, and required the gutting of historic buildings for new casinos, say detractors. At any rate, your Peak-to-Peak Highway tour is likely to run into heavy gambler traffic along here, bumper-to-bumper on busy gambling nights. This area is well patrolled by police.

# Special Summer Events

Denverites don't mind the 45-minute trip to Central City or Boulder for the following summer performing arts events.

The **Central City Opera,** (303) 292-6700, is a favorite summer tradition. Begun in 1932, the opera holds its performances in the historic Opera House in the old mining town of Central City, about 34 miles west of Denver. The incongruously grand opera house was built in 1878 and ceased operations from 1927 to 1932, at which time the Central City Opera Association took over the building and began restoration and performances. Such notables as Edwin Booth, Mae West, Helen Hayes, and Beverly Sills have performed here. The coming of gambling to Central City in 1992 has drastically changed the formerly sleepy nature of the town, but the opera remains as charming as ever. Three operas are performed each summer. Ask in advance about specially priced youth performances, round-trip bus transportation from Lakewood and Glendale, and reserved parking—the last is highly recommended if you plan to drive yourself.

The summer concerts at Boulder's **Chautauqua Auditorium** are another reason to head west. Boulder's Chautauqua dates from 1898, when a national movement brought the arts to numerous Chautauqua summer camps throughout the country. Before the evening concerts in the wonderful wooden auditorium, concertgoers can enjoy a picnic dinner under the big shady trees at the base of the foothills or a sit-down dinner at the Chautauqua Dining Hall, (303) 440-3776. Chautauqua concerts include both a popular music series, (303) 440-7666 (box office), and the Colorado Music Festival, (303) 449-1397 (year-round), (303) 449-2413 (summer ticketing), which emphasizes classical music.

The **Colorado Shakespeare Festival** (www.coloradoshakes.org or 303-492-0554) is another summer-only event in Boulder that draws audiences from Denver and beyond. Held at the outdoor Mary Rippon Theatre and indoor University Theatre on the University of Colorado–Boulder campus, the annual event features both traditional and modern renditions of Shakespeare's plays and non-Shakespearean classics. Three shows rotated during the 2006 season: *The Tempest, As You Like It,* and *The Merchant of Venice.* Film actor Val Kilmer took part in a production one year, and other top performers and directors have likewise been attracted to this highly regarded event. Falstaff's Fare, a box dinner, can be ordered and eaten on the lawn before the show begins. There are evening and matinee performances.

A short ride down the road will take you to I-70, if you're in a rush to get back home. But if you're here for the scenic route, you're well-advised to take a left on U.S. Highway 6 down scenic Clear Creek Canyon to Golden.

## ROCKY MOUNTAIN NATIONAL PARK

With the possible exception of Yellowstone in Wyoming, Rocky Mountain National Park (970-586-1206) is the nation's most famous. And you can't say too much about it, since it's Colorado's hugest single natural site that can be experienced by auto and/or short walks. It's a chance to see the full spectrum of Rocky Mountain nature in one gulp. You can roam from the darkest subalpine forests below to the sun-sprinkled meadows and granite grandeur of the continent's roof—265,000 acres of it well connected by roads and trails.

The best way to do the park by auto, of course, is Trail Ridge Road, 48 miles of US 34 that vaults over the park from Estes Park on the east to Grand Lake on the west. The drive over the top is one of the nation's great scenic routes, although its two lanes are jammed in the summer season. The opening of Trail Ridge Road by snowplow some time around Memorial Day is an annual Colorado event photographed for the Denver and Boulder papers. The road stays open until October. But you can access the park year-round. The east side has plenty of lovely drives and hiking opportunities. To reach the west side in winter, take I-70 west from Denver to US 40 at Empire, then US 40 north to Granby, where you go right on US 34 to the park. Autumn and spring visits are particularly enjoyable. Do check it out on late-summer or early-autumn evenings when the elk are bugling, particularly in the Kawuneeche Valley on the western side.

## WINTER PARK

Just because you don't ski doesn't mean a day trip to a ski resort should be crossed off your list—especially in the summer. Come Memorial Day weekend Winter Park Ski Resort gears up for the onslaught of visitors who want to get the heck out of Dodge—or Denver, as the case might be.

To reach Winter Park, located 67 miles northwest of Denver, take I-70 west to exit 232 (US 40) and follow US 40 over Berthoud Pass to Winter Park. However, if you're really feeling adventurous, consider going down to Union Station and catching the **California Zephyr** to Fraser (the town right next to Winter Park). The train leaves Denver daily at 8:05 A.M., arriving in Fraser at 10:07 A.M. This is a much more relaxing way to get there, and better yet, once you arrive in Fraser, a free shuttle bus will pick you up and take you to any number of fun destinations. The train costs around $60 round-trip, depending on availability, and leaves Fraser each afternoon at 4:10 P.M., arriving back at Union Station at 7:00 P.M.

Once you're there, consider a ride down the **Alpine Slide,** located at the base of Winter Park Mountain. It's the longest alpine slide in Colorado. Then head over to the **Zephyr Express Chairlift** to take a scenic ride to the 10,700-foot summit of the mountain. You can have lunch at the Lodge at Sunspot and then burn those calories off by hiking down to the base.

If you've brought a bike with you (or you can rent one at the resort), consider riding the 5-mile **Fraser River Trail,** built a few years ago and perfect for beginners and families. You can get on the road at the base of the mountain and follow it to the Trademark Condos where you'll pick up the Fraser River Trail. If your lungs and legs are in good shape, consider taking the bike to the top of the mountain on the Zephyr Express and choose any number of sky-high trail rides.

Should you happen to be visiting the Winter Park area on a Saturday in July or August, plan to catch some cowboy action at the **High Country Stampede Rodeo,** held at the John Work Arena in Fraser on County Road 73. This little rodeo pits cowboys against bucking broncos. You can even come a bit earlier and enjoy the barbecue dinner before the show.

And if you just want to spend the day shopping, summer is a great time to look for bargains. Look for sidewalk sales of closeout winter clothing and equipment. Also check out the specialty gift shops for items you won't find in a mall.

# RELOCATION ⌂

Colorado has always been a popular place to live, and population experts predict it will continue to be, regardless of the financial vagaries of its major industries. Starting with 19th-century gold mining, then continuing through the oil boom of the 1970s and the telecommunications explosion of the 1990s, Colorado has always attracted newcomers looking to make a fortune. These boom cycles are always followed by a bust, but they do little to stop the state's rampant growth. In 2000 the U.S. Census found Colorado to be the country's third-fastest growing state, adding new residents at a rate of 2.2 percent per year, while the U.S. average was just 1.2 percent. After the dot-com bust of 2001, however, growth cooled. By 2004 migration had flattened considerably, and the net population gain was nearly zero.

The same things attract newcomers today as attracted them in the 1880s— breathtaking mountains, blue skies, more than 300 sunny days a year, and the opportunity to live the kind of outdoor lifestyle so many Americans crave. Some Colorado transplants were hooked during college, coming to the University of Colorado or Colorado State University and falling in love with the state's beauty. Others were among the 26.2 million tourists who come here on vacation each year and leave with an appreciation of Colorado's charm. The state also appeals to entrepreneurs looking to locate in beautiful surroundings without compromising their business edge. Denver is the largest city between San Francisco and St. Louis, which makes it an excellent place to headquarter businesses serving the western half of the country. And Denver International Airport makes it easy for globally oriented businesses to connect with transportation hubs on the East Coast and in Europe.

Housing prices are among the nation's highest, however, which can be discouraging for transplants from cities other than urban hubs like Boston and San Francisco. Bargains can be found, but it takes some research and legwork to find them. The Neighborhoods and Real Estate Resources sections in this chapter have information about housing prices and the region's largest real estate firms, respectively.

Public schools in metro Denver are among the nation's best, and private-school options abound, from those with religious connections to those specializing in college preparatory programs. Colleges also abound. Colorado's state-financed junior college and university system offers a wide range of program and location options.

Greater Denver also has one of the nation's highest percentages of baby boomers (not to be confused with retirees), which may explain the broad support for public recreation centers, parks and open-space areas, arts and entertainment complexes, shopping centers, and fine restaurants. Younger families can also find the amenities they are looking for, from parks to child-friendly destinations (see our Kidstuff chapter for some places to get started) to good, dependable child care.

Like other cities, Denver has plenty of day-care homes and centers but lacks enough infant care. If you find yourself in the market for child care, we suggest several good places to get started. One good resource is *Colorado School Guides™* by Margerie Hicks (www.coloradoschool guides.com). Metro Denver Child Care Resource and Referral Partners, (303) 381–2990, can refer callers to child-care providers in their neighborhoods. The Colorado Office of Resource and Referral Agencies, (303) 290–9088, is an umbrella organization that can refer callers to other sources of child-care information in their area.

If you'd like to check the background of a day-care provider before hiring him or her, you can do so at the Colorado Division of Childcare, 1575 Sherman Street, Denver, (303) 866–5958. With the correct name and/or street address of the provider, this office can tell you if the person's license is current. If you want to know about complaints that may have been filed against your candidate, ask to speak to a counselor who can help you view the case file (72-hour advance notice is required).

Colorado does have its growing pains. The number of students in its public and private schools grew by 29 percent from 1990 to 2000, according to the state's Department of Education. And traffic problems have kept pace with the population. The *Denver Post* reported a 22 percent increase in traffic along one section of interstate during the same decade. Major thoroughfares are being widened and light-rail routes are being expanded as quickly as possible, but that means construction projects will inconvenience drivers in the meantime. See our Getting Here, Getting Around chapter for more information about the T-Rex expansion project on Interstate 25.

Newcomers to metro Denver needn't feel like they're alone, however. More than one in four residents has arrived within the past decade, and many remember what it feels like. Two groups are designed to help transplants settle in. The Newcomers Club, www.newcomersclub.com/co.html, arranges social events for people throughout the metro area. After the Boxes Are Unpacked faith-based workshops are offered in Highlands Ranch, Englewood, Castle Rock, and Colorado Springs; visit www.justmoved.org for details.

A line charting Denver home sales over the years looks like a wave—up, down, up, down, up, down, up, down. These days the wave is falling. Denver's housing market historically mirrors the state's "boom/bust" economy. In the late 1980s, for example, Denver was still recovering from a crash in the oil business, and real estate was seemingly impossible to give away. In the 1990s the economy rebounded, leaving buyers, sellers, and even Realtors scratching their heads over rising property values. The latest bust came in about 2001, when the economy softened nationwide. A shakeup in the telecommunications industry contributed to Denver's economic woes, and by 2003 real estate prices were beginning to fall. Today they are relatively flat. Even so, housing prices in the Denver metro area are among the nation's highest.

For a cursory look at Denver's real estate market, turn to the Internet, where you can find information on prices, neighborhoods, and agents and photos of properties. It's an easy way to scan listings.

If what you seek is the offbeat, then "cohousing" might be for you. Specially planned communities that house residents in individual homes but bring them together in jointly owned kitchens, greenhouses, nursery schools, gardens, and workshops can be found in at least eight Colorado locations. Closest to the city are two near Boulder and one in Golden. Some of Denver's neighborhoods are hotter and more expensive than others. Cherry Creek North, in the shadow of Denver's No. 1 tourist attraction, Cherry Creek Shopping Center, is booming. Tiny crackerbox houses once occupied by working-class families are being bought, demolished, and replaced with expensive townhomes and row houses fashioned in the old, East Coast style. Price tags rarely dip below $350,000 and easily climb as high as $1.2 million. (Walking distance to Saks Fifth Avenue has its price.)

Loft living is another hotter-than-hot trend. In the late 1980s developers began transforming rundown warehouses into empty, but very stylish, loft shells for as low as $90,000. You supplied the walls, kitchen, etc. Today's urban palaces can cost more than $1 million, but most cost around $350,000.

New-home sales have cooled a bit. The vast majority of the new-housing market is in the suburbs, where land is plentiful and opposition to development is minimal. New development in Denver tends to be small, exclusive infill projects on vacant lots. Two major redevelopment projects currently are being built. Stapleton Airport, which was replaced by Denver International Airport, and Lowry Air Force Base, which was closed by the federal government, are being redeveloped to include a "new urbanism" mix of residential homes, parks, open spaces, and retail.

The corner grocery store has made a strong comeback in Denver and is starting to show up in new developments. A housing project outside of Longmont features homes with Victorian-era styling and the amenities of days past. Other developers are watching sales closely to see if buyers will pay more for detailing and a city feel without the city problems. The 1999 redevelopment of the former Elitch Gardens site in northwest Denver incorporated new urbanism concepts.

A full picture of Denver's residential scene, from home prices to ambience, would require a book much larger than our entire guide. There are more than 70 officially designated neighborhoods in the city and county of Denver alone, and hundreds more in surrounding counties. Nonetheless, we've scanned several to give you an idea of Greater Denver's residential fabric.

The most important factor to remember is that prices within neighborhoods can vary greatly. In Capitol Hill, for instance, a lovely Victorian condo can be a mere 3 blocks from a mansion that commands ten times as much. Because no centralized data exists about housing prices, we've listed the most current figures available from each neighborhood, usually a range from low to high prices. Sometimes those figures came from property tax rolls, other times from real estate reports. As a direct result of climbing interest rates, Denver Metro housing prices are predicted to flatten and perhaps even fall in the predictable future.

# NEIGHBORHOODS

## Denver

As Greater Denver's urban center, the city and county of Denver covers the widest range of neighborhood types and home prices, from humble to haughty. The most general statement we can make, aside from highlighting some of Denver's more well-known neighborhoods, is that you can find any level of living you want in the city and county of Denver, from rural ranches to downtown high-rises.

**Downtown** includes the Union Station area on the north, the Auraria neighborhood to the west, and the Civic Center area on the southwest. It reaches east to Broadway, where it borders the North Capitol Hill and Capitol Hill neighborhoods. This is where you live if you like the downtown lifestyle, and here you almost certainly live in a condo.

**Lower Downtown,** the redbrick historic area between the central business district, Union Station, and the Central Platte Valley, is particularly popular of late. LoDo, as Denverites call it, is hot owing largely to the revitalization of the Central Platte Valley in general and the rise of Coors Field in particular.

Downtown Denver is très chic, but an anomaly as far as residential opportunities. Condo prices are high, and single-family homes are virtually nonexistent.

The **Uptown** neighborhood, just east of downtown and centered around 17th Avenue, is experiencing a revival that

*After an exodus of families from Denver to the suburbs in the 1980s, the inner city is experiencing a resurgence of popularity. The Denver Public Schools have done their part to improve test scores and the overall quality of education. In fact, in 1998 voters approved a bond to upgrade and build new schools in the core city to accommodate growth.*

The D & F Tower, built in 1909, anchors downtown's 16th Street Mall. *DENVER METRO CONVENTION AND VISITORS BUREAU*

includes several new infill projects. Most notable here are three-story, statuesque row houses, mixed with grand mansions that have been turned into law offices, graphic arts studios, and single-family homes. The feel is urban elegance. Prices haven't skyrocketed because of the neighborhood's proximity to East Colfax Avenue, known for sleaze and crime. Still, new row house developments command between $200,000 and $400,000.

Just east of downtown Denver, you'll find historic neighborhoods untouched by the revitalization boom shaking Lower Downtown. **North Capitol Hill** and **Capitol Hill,** bounded roughly by 20th and Sixth Avenues, Clarkson Street, and Broadway, were among the first of Denver's housing developments in the 1800s. While those in the working class were making their homes down by the river and in other outlying sections, the aristocrats were populating this area east and upslope from the business district. Here you find most of the historic mansions and a stretch of Grant Street once known as "Millionaires' Row." In recent years people have come to appreciate the historic charm of the area and its accessibility to downtown. Many of Capitol Hill's mansions have been converted to condominiums, offices, and bed-and-breakfast inns, and there are a lot of cultural and fine-dining opportunities close by. Home prices range from $203,000 to $316,000.

Because of Capitol Hill's reputation for crime, many prefer to live farther east in the Cheesman Park or City Park West neighborhoods. The **Cheesman Park** neighborhood, bounded by University Boulevard, Clarkson Street, and Colfax and Sixth Avenues, surrounds one of Denver's finer parks, Cheesman Park, and borders one of the city's finest amenities, the Denver Botanic Gardens. The Cheesman Park neighborhood contains two historic districts and has a feel of urban gentility with lots of pedestrians, coffee shops, and neighborhood gathering spots. Home prices range from $350,000 to $444,000.

Things start to get more expensive as you move south of Cheesman. Still relatively reasonable, however, is **City Park West,** an urban treasure trove of historic homes going back to Denver's silver boom of 1880–1893. Bounded by Clarkson Street, University Boulevard, and Colfax and 23rd Avenues, it's located between North Capitol Hill and City Park, Denver's largest central park, containing the Denver Zoo and the Denver Museum of Nature and Science. It's a moderate walk to the Botanic Gardens and a reasonable walk to downtown, and it has a hospital complex on its northern edge. The 17th Avenue strip of fine restaurants and entertainment runs right through it. Median house value is $289,000.

Washington Park is Denver's other big, well-known public green space, and the **Washington Park** neighborhood is one of Denver's most popular living areas. It has a lot of homes built in the early to mid-1900s. Home prices range from $246,000 to $858,000. It's convenient to transportation, bordering on I-25 to the south and Colorado Boulevard to the east. The Denver Country Club is just north of it, where home prices range from $440,000 to $1.1 million.

Just east of the Denver Country Club is fashionable **Cherry Creek.** Bounded by University Avenue, Colorado Boulevard, and Sixth and Alameda Avenues, it's an area of large- to moderate-size homes, expensive condos, and shopping nirvana. It's Greater Denver's premier retail and arts area. It has a gracious ambience and is a fun place to visit and shop. Its residences are highly sought after; prices range from $314,000 to $471,000.

Directly east of Cherry Creek is **Hilltop,** another prestigious living area of well-cared-for streets adjacent to the major north-south corridor of Colorado Boulevard. In Hilltop, prices range from $455,000 to $685,000. **Park Hill,** to the north, just west of City Park, is an area of handsome old homes and large mature trees. Home prices range from $164,000 to $543,000, with prices climbing the farther south you go.

**RELOCATION**

*East of Colorado Boulevard, two streets represent each letter of the alphabet. The second of these streets is usually related to a plant or group of plants: Ash, Birch, Cherry, Dahlia, Elm, Forest, and so on.*

One area that has become particularly interesting of late is the area known as **Far Northeast Denver.** These neighborhoods stand out not only geographically but also as a focus of growth expected as a result of the new airport.

**Montbello** and **Green Valley Ranch** are established, quiet neighborhoods, although there's been some complaining about noise since Denver International Airport opened. The oldest homes in Montbello were built in the 1970s, and homes range from $134,000 to $220,000. The oldest homes in Green Valley Ranch were built in the 1990s, and homes sold there range from $145,000 to $1.75 million. These are low-crime areas with panoramic views of the mountains, room for another 9,400 dwellings, and a lot of open space. They're still the extreme edge of Denver's urban fabric, places where residents can take a walk and see a deer or an eagle in flight and maybe even hear coyotes howling at night.

**Gateway,** between Montbello and Green Valley Ranch and directly bordering the airport on the north, is where Denver planners envision big-time development. Already launched are the beginning stages of a planned $1 billion Denver International Business Center just a few miles from the terminal. The local media has referred to Gateway as "our first 21st Century neighborhood" and represented it as a future community of 65,000 people with strong economic links to the airport. Although it was annexed by Denver to link the city with the airport, it's not yet officially a neighborhood. Denver planners envision it as a new employment area on the level of the Denver Tech Center, which is only one-sixth the size of Gateway.

**Southeast Denver** is a popular area with a variety of housing options. In general, houses tend to be more expensive and newer than their northwest counterparts. However, that doesn't necessarily mean homes are bigger. Southeast Denver offers anything from tiny frame two-bedroom homes on up. Neighborhoods such as Southmoor Park offer quiet residential living with plenty of trees and nearby parks. There also are plenty of upscale apartment, condo, and townhome choices. Homes in Southmoor Park sold from $61,000 for multifamily dwellings to $675,000 for single-family homes.

We've given a lot of mention here to the central and eastern parts of Denver, perhaps more than is fair. But this is where the oldest neighborhoods, the big-name neighborhoods, and the well-known neighborhoods are. A lot of people, however, prefer the west side of the city. It's the smaller part of the city, closer to the mountains, and it generally has a feeling of being near to its country roots.

**Northwestern Denver** is the city's smallest quadrant, bounded by West Colfax Avenue on the south, 52nd Avenue on the north, Sheridan Boulevard on the west, and the South Platte River on the east. The **Highland** and **Jefferson Park** neighborhoods, stretching west from the high ground above the South Platte, were where Denver put its first residential neighborhoods west of the South Platte. Around the turn of the 20th century, there was a large Italian neighborhood here. Descendants of truck farmers in what are now the western suburbs still tell of taking their produce downtown for delivery to Italian produce salesmen who would sell their wares in the streets. These neighborhoods now have a rich ethnic mix and some fine restaurants, including Latin American and Vietnamese establishments. Here, as elsewhere, prices are on the rise. Highland prices range from $120,000 to $550,000 (single family). Jefferson Park single-family homes range from $87,500 to $775,000.

**Sloan Lake, West Highland, Berkeley,** and **Regis** are some of the neighborhoods to the west that are pleasantly equipped with quiet streets and the greenery of lawns and parks around small lakes. These northwestern neighborhoods are as old as a lot of east Denver neighborhoods between downtown and Colorado Boulevard, but they're across the river, up the hill, and over the ridge from the central city. The feeling here is apart from the urban bustle. Sloan Lake prices range from $90,000 to $775,000, West Highland from $96,500 to $498,000, Berkeley from $80,000 to $525,000, and Regis from $88,000 to $320,000.

**Southwest Denver** is larger, more extensive, and more dynamic than the west side of the city. Certainly it has its older neighborhoods close in, such as **Val Verde** and **Sun Valley.** Val Verde, Spanish for "green valley," was a separate town established in 1873 and annexed into Denver in 1902. Bordered by Sixth and Alameda Avenues, the South Platte River, and Federal Boulevard, it is today an ethnically diverse neighborhood with a large industrial and warehousing base. As you move southwest toward southern Lakewood, however, you get a sensation of increasingly newer urban landscape. Not that there haven't been homes in this area since the 1800s, of course, but the neighborhood wasn't developed as early and extensively as the northwest. Val Verde prices range from $90,000 to $257,000 and Sun Valley range from $94,900 to $417,000.

One of Denver's few areas where major new development is taking place is the **Marston** neighborhood that juts down into unincorporated Jefferson County on Denver's farthest southwestern point. Near Marston Reservoir you'll find particularly high-quality residential living. Generally, however, southwest Denver vies with northwest Denver for the city's lowest overall housing prices, and a much larger percentage of its population consists of married couples and families. Homes now on the market average about $175,000 for condominiums to $350,000 for single-family homes.

## Adams County

Adams County is often viewed as the area's most blue-collar, working-class county, and that has a lot to do with the heavy industry and warehousing around **Commerce City,** northeastern Denver, and the Interstate 76 corridor leading northeast. Commerce City, Adams County's industrial–warehousing heartland, where twice as many people work as live, certainly has some of the county's lowest housing prices, $133,000 to $182,000.

One of the first things you may notice in driving north on I–25 to Thornton, Westminster, and Northglenn is a sensation of climbing to higher ground. **Federal Heights,** a community between Westminster and Thornton, is well named. From here you're actually looking down at the tops of downtown Denver's highest buildings. Much of this northern area seems to be on high ground, and since there is little in the way of high-rise buildings, Denver's northern suburbs have some of the grandest views of the Rockies. Homes sell for $139,000 to $235,000.

**Westminster** is Greater Denver's closest northside city to the mountains. Westminster spreads all over the place, so it isn't easily categorized. It's roughly centered around the Westminster Mall off U.S. Highway 36 at 88th Avenue, but the newest parts of the city stretch north to 120th Avenue. To the west, 88th Avenue contains extensive shopping complexes. To the north there are attractive housing developments clustered and scattered through a lot of open country with big-sky views. Another arm of Westminster protrudes west to wrap around two sides of Standley Lake, one of Greater Denver's best water recreation resources, on the edge of unincorporated Jefferson County. Westminster has lots of upscale townhomes and middle-class neighborhoods as well as established areas with mature trees and big lots. Home prices range from $175,000 to $539,000.

Westminster's eastern half, near **Northglenn** and **Thornton,** is where you'll find

# Movies Filmed in Denver

Even if you've never been to Denver, you may have seen it in the movies. The hit movie *Die Harder,* starring Bruce Willis, had major scenes filmed at the old Stapleton Airport. Portions of Woody Allen's 1973 film *Sleeper* were shot in Denver and vicinity, including the exterior of the National Center for Atmospheric Research in Boulder and a modernist home visible from Interstate 70 near Genesee that's known locally as the Sleeper House.

Between July 1996 and June 1997, 188 film productions took place in Denver, including 8 feature films, according to the Mayor's Office of Art, Culture and Film, which keeps tabs on such things. All this production activity tucked $32.8 million into Denver's coffers. John Sayles's *Silver City* is the most recent, filmed in downtown Denver in 2003.

Among the movies shot in Denver in past years were Warner Brothers' *Under Siege II: In Dark Territory,* with Steven Seagal, and Boat Drink Productions' *Things to Do in Denver When You're Dead,* starring Andy Garcia. *Under Siege II* has scenes in Lower Downtown (LoDo), including around Union Station and Coors Field. *Things to Do* was shot largely in the Five Points neighborhood at 26th and Welton Streets, including the historic Rossonian Hotel. For some key scenes the Rossonian's bar was transformed into a malt shop. *Elephant Man* (also known as *Nickel and Dime*), with Bill Murray, was also filmed in Denver and elsewhere in Colorado.

The made-for-TV film *Asteroids* was filmed in downtown Denver and prominently displayed the campus of East High School, one of Denver's beautiful, old schools. The remake of *The Shining* (also made for TV) was shot in Denver and Estes Park. And not surprisingly, *The Ellen Hart Peña Story* (she's the ex-wife of former mayor Federico Peña) was filmed in Denver.

the most building, with the newest developments ringing the well-respected Legacy Ridge Golf Course.

The **North Suburban Central** area, bordered by I-25 on the west, the South Platte River on the east, Denver on the south, and 144th Avenue on the north, contains the bulk of the city of Thornton, which has a moderate- to lower-income population and a suburban feel. Some newer developments, such as **Hunter's Glen** and **Thorncreek,** surround a golf course and are more upscale, but the mid-1970s two-story homes still dominate Thornton. Because of its outlying location, prices here haven't climbed as much as elsewhere.

**Brighton,** the Adams County seat to the northeast, is seeing a lot of growth but still has the benefit of a small-town, rural atmosphere within an easy 15-mile commuting distance to Denver. Here you'll find homes with acreage and space for horses. Some new developments have a minimum 35-acre requirement. Home prices are moderate, with sales prices between $135,000 and $425,000.

Southeast of Commerce City, the city of **Aurora** has its industrial centers in its northern Adams County side, along the I-70 corridor near Denver International Airport.

# Arapahoe County

Most of Aurora lies in Arapahoe County. This is where the bulk of the city's office and research/development centers are found. It's also where the homes are higher priced, ranging from $100,000 to $650,000. A typical, moderately priced Aurora development is **Tollgate,** where the homes are new, the neighborhood is clean, and the lawns are well manicured. The area is close to the Denver Tech Center business area on the south and is well-connected north-south by Interstate 225 to both I-70 and I-25.

Aurora's population is young, with a median age of 31. The city has always suffered from a lack of identity, due primarily to its proximity to Denver. It's known for its flat landscape and lack of mature trees, prompting the nickname "Saudi Aurora." But with a good supply of affordable housing, Aurora is popular with young families looking for starter homes or wanting more room for less money.

The region known among Realtors as the **Suburban Southeast,** roughly defined by the Arapahoe County line, County Line Road on the south, and Aurora on the north, contains most of the region's most expensive properties. The northwestern segment contains about half of Greenwood Village and most of Cherry Hills Village.

The bulk of this area lies in unincorporated Arapahoe County east, west, and north of Centennial Airport. It includes the Denver Tech Center. Home prices here tend to be skewed rather dramatically upward by prestige pockets such as Cherry Hills Village, one of Greater Denver's most upscale communities, with residences averaging $1.5 million and ranging from $400,000 to $3.5 million. **Cherry Hills Village,** for example, has virtually no commercial base, and the only nonresidential features are two private schools and the Cherry Hills and Glenmoor country clubs. **Greenwood Village,** just south of Cherry Hills, wrapping under the Denver Tech Center and up its eastern side, is another highly desired living area with distinctive custom homes. Many are on large lots and are tucked away from the street. Greenwood Village has condominiums priced from the low $100,000s to the low $200,000s. Single-family homes in some neighborhoods range from approximately $250,000 to $700,000, while many Greenwood Village homes start at $800,000 and can exceed $4 million.

Move a little to the west, and you'll find the area directly below the city of Denver known as the **South Suburban Central** region, which includes the cities of Littleton, Englewood, about half of Greenwood Village, and a substantial patch of unincorporated Jefferson County between Greenwood Village and County Line Road, Littleton, and I-25.

The unincorporated part of South Suburban Central is generally an area of clean, new neighborhoods with the kind of convoluted street patterns that make life confusing for pizza deliverers but peaceful for residents. It has a country feel, being the last neighborhood south of Denver before you arrive at Douglas County. There are some good shopping complexes along County Line Road, including Park Meadows; the Denver Tech Center is just up I-25; and C-470 provides fast access west and up to I-70 near Golden.

The city of **Littleton** grew from an old downtown established in 1890 on what is now its northwestern edge along the South Platte River. It still has that old, traditional community atmosphere, with ranch homes on big lots, but the city also has its newer areas reaching south to Douglas County and C-470. The South Platte River runs north-south through nearly the entire length of the city, and the extra green spaces make Littleton a particularly pleasant place to live. Littleton single-family homes for sale range from $219,000 to $3.6 million, according to Realtor listings.

**Englewood,** like Littleton, is one of the southern suburbs with an old downtown established in the 1800s along Broadway. Also like Littleton, it has a small-town appeal. But it's closer to Denver, and its business corridor along South Santa Fe

Drive on the city's west side is home to hundreds of manufacturing, industrial, and service companies. Homes are smaller frame structures. On the east side, the city borders Cherry Hills Village. Englewood single-family homes for sale range from $139,900 to $6.5 million, according to Realtor listings.

## Broomfield County

Just north of Westminster, mostly in Boulder County but with a good quarter of its population in the newly recognized Broomfield County, is the city of **Broomfield.** Originally a residential community, it's fast becoming a business-development area thanks to its strategic position between Boulder and Greater Denver and the rampant development of business and industrial parks along US 36. Broomfield is popular because it still retains its own identity, separate from Greater Denver, with enduring, solid 1950s brick ranches. This is attractive to people who work in Denver and Boulder and want more affordable living. Broomfield's home prices are climbing along with closer-in locales; they range from $155,000 to $520,000.

## Douglas County

Anyone who has lived in Greater Denver for 10 years or more is likely to be struck by the number of new residences in Douglas County, set well apart like estates, speckling the landscape from I–25 south. It's an area of rolling hills and open spaces, with views of the mountains and the feel of the Great Plains—at least for now. Douglas County in January 1999 lost its designation as the fastest-growing county in the nation, but it still ranks among the top five.

Douglas County certainly is the metro area's fastest-growing county, although figures can sometimes be misleading. Because the area had so few residents, the influx of several thousand new residents meant three-figure growth rates. It is a huge area with just a few old and well-established towns like **Larkspur, Franktown,** and the county seat of **Castle Rock.** Otherwise you'll find very little in the way of residential buildings that aren't either ranches, farm structures, or the large expensive homes that are popping up like crazy in exclusive planned communities with names like **Castle Pines Village, Deer Creek Farm,** and **The Meadows.** These are among the 20 to 30 planned communities along the Denver/Colorado Springs corridor that are expected to bring Douglas County's population as high as a half-million by the year 2030.

**Highlands Ranch** is the Douglas County community best known by Denverites, partly because it now represents a continuum of the Greater Denver urban fabric. It lies on the northern edge of Douglas County directly south from the city and county of Denver. With nearly 81,000 residents and growing like crazy, it's supposed to top out at a population of 90,000 by the year 2010. No one will be too surprised if at some point it is incorporated as a city. It's already starting to look like one, with well-established schools and community centers; a huge central green space, Northwest Community Park, that branches through the main, western cluster of the community; and the large Highland Heritage Regional Park on the growing eastern cluster. The average single-family home sells for about $300,000.

## Jefferson County

Here is where home buyers can choose from the widest variety of landscapes, simply because Jefferson County has both the bulk of Greater Denver's mountain communities and a large percentage of the area's flatland communities. The mountain communities are a big attraction. After a hot summer day at work in Denver, residents retreat to cool mountain evenings among the pines. Of course, the drive can be less appealing in the winter, when commuters are faced with severe mountain snowstorms. Sport-utility vehicles tend to be popular among mountain-community commuters.

Jefferson County's flatland communities, however, still offer the attraction of being near the mountains, and the county in general has a good reputation for quality-of-life factors such as good schools, relatively low crime, and nice neighborhoods. Actually, flatland is a bit of a misnomer here, because Jefferson County's eastern half is close to the mountains and tends to include lots of ridges and valleys. On average, Jefferson County's population is moderately well-to-do and well educated.

**Jefferson County South** is the county's most expensive housing region, bordering directly on Denver. The vast majority of residences here are in the area bounded roughly by U.S. Highway 285 on the north, Sheridan Avenue on the east, and C-470 on the south and west. Bulging into that area on the northeast corner is the city and county of Denver's Marston neighborhood, which surrounds Marston Lake. It's an unincorporated area, but one that envisions itself as a unique community on the edge of the mountains. It has rejected efforts at incorporation as a city, but it holds its own community festivals and has its own organization of homeowners associations known as the Council of Homeowners Organizations for Planned Environment.

South Jeffco also has some nice housing south and west of C-470; for example, in Ken Caryl Valley on the other side of the Dakota Hogback, where there's a mix of everything from townhomes to million-dollar mansions. **Ken Caryl Ranch** is a stable area with lots of horse property, surrounded by the foothills and tucked away from the big city. Houses range from $230,000 to $800,000, with most around $400,000.

North from Ken Caryl is **Green Mountain,** with stunning city views and prices from $170,000 to $370,000.

The city of **Lakewood** is the giant of Denver's southwest side and the third-most populous city in Greater Denver after Denver and Aurora. Unlike many suburbs, Lakewood is a major employment center, with the Denver Federal Center, strong retail communities, and substantial light industry. At the same time, it also has a lot of semirural areas inside the city limits. Lakewood's older neighborhoods lie to the east, where the city shares about half the western border of Denver. On the west it reaches into the foothills, where its 6,000 acres of parks include Green Mountain and the surrounding William Frederick Hayden Park. Lakewood touches the city of **Morrison,** a small town hidden in one of the red rock–rimmed valleys in the Rocky Mountains' first folds. Lakewood-area homes average $120,000 to $270,000 but can range higher than $600,000.

North of Lakewood is the city of **Wheat Ridge,** also bordering Denver. It has developed largely since World War II. Before then it was a farming area known for fruits, vegetables, and carnations. Wheat Ridge also has that uniquely rural flavor characteristic of many suburbs here, with older homes on larger lots. Foxes come into the neighborhoods at night from the Clear Creek greenbelt. Deer sometimes blunder into busy Wadsworth Boulevard at morning rush hour. Walkers in serene suburban neighborhoods sometimes see people passing on horses. Home sales range from $150,000 to $400,000.

Driving west on 32nd Avenue and passing out of Wheat Ridge as you go under I-70, you are on the way to the city of **Golden,** on the other side of South Table Mountain. Between I-70 and South Table Mountain, however, you notice nicely groomed new neighborhoods primarily on the left. You are on the north side of a loosely defined area known as **Applewood,** which includes bits of Lakewood, Golden, and Wheat Ridge but is mostly in

unincorporated Jefferson County. Applewood is a name often heard on the lips of westsiders considering a move to a new home, but it also includes older, established homes with mature trees. Applewood prices range from $180,000 to $450,000.

Keep going west on 32nd Avenue, around South Table Mountain, past a row of Adolph Coors Co. subsidiary companies, and finally past the brewery itself, and you'll enter Golden through the back door. Largely hidden from Denver by South Table Mountain and scrunched into the foothills on its western side, Golden has kept an identity apart from the rest of the metro area. It has an Old West downtown, and it is a charming small town. Once a Coors-company town, it's now mainly a high-technology and university town, largely influenced by the culture of the Colorado School of Mines just up the hill from Washington Avenue. New neighborhoods have been climbing up the side of South Table Mountain, growing south toward Heritage Square and Morrison and spreading east toward Lakewood. The level of education among Golden's population is one of the highest in the Greater Denver area. Homes range from $140,000 to $240,000, with many newer ones as high as $500,000.

Northeast of Golden and north of Wheat Ridge is one of the larger cities of Denver's west side, **Arvada.** Looking north from the top of the ridge that is the center of Wheat Ridge, you can see the historic center of Arvada, now known as **Olde Town Arvada.** But Arvada has spread considerably from that historic beginning, out to the "horse country" of the far west side. Arvada's central area consists largely of homes typically built in the 1950s and 1960s, but a rapidly growing high-end development called **West Woods Ranch** offers new homes centered around a golf course. Arvada is known for its family-oriented lifestyle and its easy access to Boulder and Denver. Home prices in Arvada range from $165,000 to $350,000. Custom-made homes in West Woods Ranch climb to $650,000.

Arvada and Westminster define the residential majority of the area known as **Jefferson County North.** The parts of the two cities in this area—north, east, and south of Standley Lake—are more like each other than they are like their respective city centers. A lot of new homes have gone in here in the last 5 or 10 years, primarily tract homes with some high-end custom homes and some of the patio homes preferred by empty-nesters. The area has a country feel because you're looking west across the last prairie before the mountains. It's a short shot north on Wadsworth Boulevard to Broomfield and on US 36 to Boulder.

West beyond Rocky Flats and Golden, off Highway 93, there are growing mountain developments up side roads such as **Coal Creek Canyon, Golden Gate Canyon,** and **Crawford Gulch.**

Greater Denver's big mountain communities, though, tend to be off I-70 and US 285. Communities such as **Genesee, Evergreen, Conifer, Aspen Park, Indian Hills, Kittredge,** and **Hidden Valley** offer a lot of new, high-end living across ridge tops with fantastic vistas and in hidden, pine-covered valleys and hillsides. The only drawback is the sometimes hazardous 30-minute commute from Evergreen to Denver, 45 minutes to an hour from areas farther out. The bulk of housing opportunities are in burgeoning, although tasteful, developments. Genesee homes are more in the foothills, with better access to Denver. Homes there range from $400,000 to more than $1 million. There are some older, less-expensive properties, though they're harder to find.

**Evergreen** is probably the largest, most-established community near I-70, about 8 miles south of it, actually, on Highway 74. There are more than 9,000 people in the city of Evergreen—45,000 including the nearby communities of **Kittredge** and **Bergen Park**—and there's even a downtown, just below the dam that holds back Evergreen Lake. Evergreen also has shops, restaurants, and the Little Bear bar, which pulls people up from Denver for its great musical evenings and singles scene. Housing here is among the most expensive in the region, ranging well into the millions.

Mountain communities down US 285, in the **Conifer** and **Aspen Park** area, have Denver commuting times closer to an hour, but here you'll find properties in all price ranges, with some horse properties and more available space. Here prices range from $250,000 to $350,000.

## REAL ESTATE RESOURCES

You can get more information on the local real estate market, Realtor licensing and ethics, and other information involving the sale or purchase of homes by contacting the following agencies.

**Colorado Association of Realtors Inc.**
**(303) 790-7099**
**www.coloradorealtors.com**

**Denver Board of Realtors**
**(303) 756-0553**
**www.dbrealtor.org**

**Douglas/Elbert Realtor Association**
**(303) 688-0941**
**www.derarealtors.com**

**Jefferson County Realtor Association**
**(303) 233-7831**
**www.jcar.com**

**North Metro Denver Realtor Association**
**(303) 451-5757**
**www.nmdra.com**

**South Metro Denver Realtor Association**
**(303) 797-3700**
**www.smdra.com**

## HOME BUILDERS

Colorado's home-building business thrived during the 1990s and early 2000s. Based on available space, most new home construction—master planned communities and tract-housing developments—occurred and continues to occur in the suburbs. Single units and smaller town home or condo developments make up the bulk of city infill projects. Perhaps the biggest trends are the growing number of upscale townhomes and row homes being built on vacant city lots and the pop-top phenomenon in older core neighborhoods, in which new owners remodel small homes into larger modern ones with all the amenities of the suburbs.

On a larger scale, redevelopment of both Lowry Air Force Base, a few miles east of downtown, and the old Stapleton Airport site are major projects that include residential, retail, and parks. Work on Lowry is nearing completion, while Stapleton construction will extend well into the future.

Another trend hitting Greater Denver is the revival of new urbanism, in which communities are built to look like the days of old, with "vintage" housing and neighborhood amenities just down the street. The Lowry and Stapleton sites include new urbanism, as does development in the Central Platte Valley, just west of downtown.

For more information on the hundreds of home builders, call the Home Builders Association of Metropolitan Denver at (303) 778-1400.

## REAL ESTATE FIRMS

The following are among Greater Denver's more well-known real estate brokerages.

**Century 21 Professionals Inc.**
**www.century21.com/meet/office_state**
**.aspx?st=co**
Century 21 is a worldwide company operating in 30 countries and territories. Each of the Denver/Front Range's 25 offices are

*In the central Denver real estate market, homes frequently sell for at or above the asking price. At best, bargaining is reserved for the overpriced or run-down homes. In general, your dollar buys a lot more square footage, and often lot size, in the suburbs.*

independently owned. Go to the Web site and click on the "Front Range" part of the Colorado map for the complete list of addresses and phone numbers.

**Co-Ka-Ne Consultants Inc.**
**405 Arapahoe Street, Kiowa**
**(303) 621-2555**
**www.co-ka-neconsultants.com**
This offices specializes in ranch and horse property, residential, acreage, and development in the southeast edge of suburban Denver and stretching east into rural territory. Four agents help people looking for a rural lifestyle, many with horses and small animals and some looking for multi-acre ranches.

**Coldwell Banker Residential Services**
**8490 East Crescent Parkway**
**Greenwood Village**
**(303) 409-1500**
After a merger in 1999, Coldwell Banker became the largest real estate services firm in Colorado, with more than 900 associates. Each office is staffed by experts who know their area or can help you anywhere across Colorado. This busy Greenwood Village office is in what's called South Suburban Central—an area known for its mountain views and mix of suburban living amid open space. Coldwell Banker is active all over the Denver area, north to Loveland and in Breckenridge, Frisco, and Winter Park. The company sells new construction as well as resales.

**Coldwell Banker Devonshire**
**105 Fillmore Street**
**(303) 758-7611**

Coldwell Banker Devonshire frequently produces several of the top 10 agents in the Denver area. The awards not only say a lot about the agency's expertise, but also about the high-end homes in which it specializes. "Cottages to Castles" is its slogan.

**The Kentwood Co.**
**5690 DTC Parkway, Greenwood Village**
**(303) 773-3399**

**44 Cook Street, Cherry Creek**
**(303) 331-1400**
Based in the Denver Tech Center, The Kentwood Co. specializes in upper-price homes and does most of its brokerage in the south metro area as well as some of the more-expensive properties in the inner city. It offers a complete range of real estate services, including corporate relocations, condo conversions, and new-home sales. The company's 53 sales associates average more than 15 years of experience. Average annual sales volume tops $300 million.

**Leonard Leonard**
**420 Downing Street**
**(303) 744-6200**
**www.leonardleonard.com**
When you see a Leonard Leonard "for sale" sign, you're almost sure to find a top-quality home inside. Founded in 1983, Leonard Leonard is known for specializing in the heart of Denver. Owner Sonja Leonard Leonard has built a staff of agents whose attention to detail shows in their high-quality properties. And their open-house tours, which often feature champagne and munchies at every stop, are a fun way to spend a few hours.

**Metro Brokers Inc.**
**4 Inverness Court East #200**
**Englewood**
**(303) 843-0100**
**www.metrobrokersonline.com**
Metro Brokers Inc. is a trade association of independent brokers that operate all over the state. With more than 60 offices and

1,800 agents, they have been working in Colorado for almost 30 years.

**RE/MAX**
**8390 East Crescent Parkway, Suite 500**
**Greenwood Village**
**(303) 770-5531**
**www.remax.com**
RE/MAX began in Denver in 1973 as a locally owned real estate office and has grown to become a global franchise network. RE/MAX offices are now open in more than 60 countries on six continents, with more than 114,000 sales agents working from 4,400 offices. Corporate headquarters are located in Greenwood Village, but to find an office near you, it's best to visit the Web site.

# EDUCATION

Choices, choices, and more choices. That best describes the educational scene in Greater Denver. Your child loves music and dancing? Denver Public Schools offer the Denver School of the Arts. You have a child who's goofing off and not living up to his or her potential? There are numerous private schools that offer a low pupil-teacher ratio and individualized instruction. You want your child to have rigorous college-prep courses? Several public schools offer the International Baccalaureate Program. No matter what you're looking for, chances are you'll find it here.

Better yet, Colorado's public schools were made more accessible in 1994 by legislation creating open enrollment statewide, meaning you can enroll your kids in any public school at no extra cost. Got your eye on a school with some real nice programs but live outside the traditional enrollment area? That problem has been eliminated by open enrollment. Of course, local children have priority, so it depends on whether space is available.

The state stands at the educational forefront in many ways. In 1993, for example, Colorado became the third state after Minnesota and California to enact charter schools, which are publicly funded but run by groups of parents, teachers, and other individuals who want to devise their own curriculum. Greater Denver now has charter schools in operation or pending in every one of its counties. Whether they opt for charter schools or not, Denver parents are involved in their children's education. Many schools are governed by cooperative decision-making teams, made up of parents, teachers, administrators, students, and local businesspeople. And, not surprisingly, in 1997 the end of 25 years of court-ordered busing in Denver Public Schools has already brought a tremendous amount of community support for what will now, once again, be neighborhood schools.

One of the best resources available to parents looking for information about both public and private schools is the searchable online database www.coloradoschool guides.com by Marjorie Hicks. It lays out just about everything you could want to know about Greater Denver's 15 public school systems, its school districts, and the individual schools and programs within each district, as well as giving complete reference for private elementary and secondary schools in the area. To purchase a 30-day membership subscription ($20), visit www.coloradoschoolguides.com.

The state of Colorado maintains lots of data about its public schools; it's available through the Department of Education's Communications Center at 201 East Colfax in Denver, (303) 866–6600, www.cde.state .co.us.

Colorado's colleges and universities in many ways stand among the nation's best. The state has one of the highest percentages of population with bachelor's degrees in the nation.

Higher education is available in a wide variety of forms in Greater Denver, the most obvious choices being the major institutions such as the University of Colorado at Boulder and Denver and the Metropolitan State College of Denver. Private colleges and universities are generally smaller but are numerous and diverse. In many ways the most important part of Greater Denver's higher-education establishment is the community college system. At any one time around 40,000 students are attending the area's five community colleges. These are public colleges so well distributed around Greater Denver that no resident is very far from one of them. They tend toward curricula that are career oriented and designed for accessibility by working students.

One handy reference to area colleges and universities is the *LEARN Directory*, produced by the Local Educational Adult Resource Network. Log on to www.learn denver.com for more information about resources available in this program.

Our list of colleges and universities is by no means a full account of local adult educational opportunities. There are more specialized business, technical, and other schools than you can shake your brain at. Colorado has nearly 200 private occupational schools, ranging from the A-Plus Real Estate School to the Xenon International School of Hair Design. The bulk of these are in the Greater Denver area. Contact the state of Colorado's Department of Higher Education, Division of Private Occupational Schools at (303) 894-2960 or visit www.state.co.us/cche for more information.

Whatever educational needs and interests you may have, Greater Denver has an abundance of opportunities to offer. We'll begin with the public school systems.

## PUBLIC SCHOOLS

### Adams County School District No. 1
**Mapleton Public Schools**
**591 East 80th Avenue**
**(303) 853-1000**
**www.mapleton.us/**
Adams County School District No. 1, more familiar to most as Mapleton Public Schools, lies just north of Denver and includes part of the city of Thornton and some of unincorporated Adams County. With the third-smallest total enrollment in Greater Denver, the system has an early learning center, a Montessori preschool/elementary school, three elementary schools, six combination elementary/middle schools, two combination middle/high schools, and four high schools. Although this system has Greater Denver's lowest percentage of teachers with post-graduate (master's or higher) degrees and one of the highest pupil-teacher ratios, it has one of the area's

lower high-school dropout rates.

The district provides a lot of special opportunities for its diverse student body, including programs in back-to-basics, learning enrichment, accelerated classes, bilingual and multicultural education, Native American education, and open enrollment for all schools based on availability.

### Adams County School District 14
**4720 East 69th Avenue, Commerce City**
**(303) 853-3333**
**www.acsd14.k12.co.us/**
One of Greater Denver's smaller school systems, District 14 has seven elementary schools, two middle schools, two high school, and one alternative high school. It also has a full-time preschool. This district pulls students from Commerce City and areas in Thornton and unincorporated Adams County. It's solidly in the midrange of Greater Denver school districts as far as the education and salaries of its teachers and its spending per pupil. Its high-school dropout rate is the highest, and it has Greater Denver's lowest graduation rate and lowest composite ACT scores in the most recent rankings.

At the same time, District 14 has a gung-ho attitude about the future, with a new commitment to improving its schools under a basic "Reading + Writing x Math" CSAP-driven base curriculum. Adams City Middle School has a personalized alternative instructional program for students at risk of dropping out. Since it was established in 1991, the program has grown to serve 6,870 students and families. With more than 77 percent of its students Hispanic, Adams 14 puts a lot of effort into bilingual education and accommodating cultural diversity.

### Adams County School District 50
**4476 West 68th Avenue, Westminster**
**(303) 428-3511**
School District 50 serves the city of Westminster and parts of Arvada and unincorporated Adams County with one early-childhood program, 15 elementary

schools, 4 middle schools, 3 high schools, and a career enrichment park. Its average teacher salary is competitive in the metro area and its revenue per pupil is the lowest. Its mission statement is "Push to excel; prepare to succeed."

In 1993 the district began the Graphics Communication Cluster, a prototype for a new method of integrating academic and technical education. Today there are four cluster programs: Graphics Communication, Business Cluster, Engineering Cluster, and Health Studies Cluster. Through these, students are afforded the opportunity to succeed in an applied setting, where they can see the relevance of academics in a real-world environment.

Adams County 50 pushes for technological innovation and offers such features as comprehensive networked computer labs and a computer in every classroom that provides the teacher with classroom management. There are more than 1,800 Pentium-class computers district-wide.

### Adams 12 Five Star Schools
**1500 East 128th Avenue, Thornton**
**(720) 972-4000**
**www.adams12.org**
The Five Star Schools, Adams County's largest school district and the seventh-largest in the state, includes more than 36,000 students attending 48 schools in a 62-square-mile area serving Northglenn, Federal Heights, and parts of Thornton, Broomfield, Westminster, and unincorporated Adams County. In addition to 29 elementary schools, it includes 9 middle

---

*Colorado high-school seniors have the opportunity to take college courses at community colleges and state universities and colleges. Not only does this provide a challenging academic experience, but it also reduces the duration and expense of college.*

---

schools and 6 high schools as well as the Bollman Technical Education Center, Vantage Point Alternative School, and four charter schools—Stargate, for the gifted and talented; the Academy of Charter Schools, a basic school; Colorado Virtual Academy; and the Pinnacle Learning Center.

Per-pupil spending at Five Star Schools is in the midrange in Greater Denver, as are the graduation and dropout rates. Principals work in conjunction with school improvement teams to further student achievement at each school. The district reviewed and approved a strategic plan that sets goals for improved graduation rate and a lower dropout rate. Another district goal is an increase in proficiencies for all students. The district honors the diversity of individuals and believes a student's success is linked to a "responsive school community."

### Aurora Public Schools
**1085 Peoria Street, Aurora**
**(303) 344-8060**
**www.aps.k12.co.us/**
Aurora Public Schools covers most of Aurora, which is Greater Denver's second-largest city. The district's mission is to develop its kids into "lifelong learners who value themselves, contribute to their community, and succeed in a changing world."

Strong emphasis is placed on student achievement in basic subjects. The district is committed to preparing students for life in the 21st century by helping them become self-directed learners, collaborative workers, complex thinkers, community contributors, and quality producers. Special services and classes are offered for gifted and talented students, special-education students, and non-English-speaking young parents, preschoolers, and adults.

The Aurora district has a total of 34 elementary schools, 7 middle schools, and 8 high schools, 3 of which are alternative high schools. There are also 3 charter schools, a vocational school, and several specialty alternative schools.

Special classes in 50 skill areas are offered within the district at the T. H. Pickens Technical Center, 500 Airport Boulevard, Aurora. Some programs offer credit toward an associate degree from the Community College of Aurora.

The district has been designated by School Match, an international business relocation firm, as one of 50 in Colorado to provide "what parents want."

### Brighton Public Schools
### 630 South Eighth Avenue, Brighton
### (303) 655-2900

The closest thing to a small-town, country-school district in Greater Denver, Brighton Public Schools (District 27J) serves about 240 square miles of farmland around the 21,000 population of Brighton, the Adams County seat. As a school district, Brighton's enrollment is the second-smallest in Greater Denver. The district has five elementary schools, two middle schools, one high school, one charter school, and one alternative school. Just about half of Brighton's teaching staff has master's degrees. The dropout rate is the Denver area's second highest. In accordance with state law, District 27J is developing content standards for all academic areas. Included in this effort toward Standards Based Education are the improvement of instructional techniques as well as the assessment of skills and knowledge learned. The average composite ACT score for Brighton students is 17.5. The district's schools offer enrichment programs including bilingual education, programs in basic skills, and accelerated education.

### Cherry Creek School District 5
### 4700 South Yosemite Street, Englewood
### (303) 773-1184
### www.ccsd.k12.co.us/index.htm

Covering Greater Denver's southeastern corner, District 5 encompasses Cherry Hills Village, Glendale, parts of Aurora, Englewood, Greenwood Village, and some of unincorporated Arapahoe County. It includes the rapidly growing and well-to-do communities along the northern edge

*Greater Denver's largest student populations are not in the city and county of Denver but in Arapahoe and Jefferson Counties.*

of Douglas County and wraps around the Denver Tech Center.

District 5 has some impressive statistics, including the state's highest average teacher salary. It has 39 elementary schools, 11 middle schools, 6 high schools, and 1 alternative high school. Thirteen Cherry Creek schools have received the John Irwin Award, given to the state's highest-performing schools. In 1996 West Middle School also became a Blue Ribbon School. Smoky Hill High has one of Colorado's International Baccalaureate programs, in which advanced studies give students a jump on college. Every elementary and middle school in the district makes special accommodations for gifted and talented students.

### Denver Public Schools
### 900 Grant Street
### (720) 426-3200
### www.dpsk12.org

The Denver Public Schools is the second-largest district in the state, serving 72,000 students. It is home to many high-performing schools and programs that serve a diverse population. The district routinely produces graduates bound for the country's top colleges and universities, and it boasts the 2006 Kinder Excellence in Teaching national award-winner, Linda Alston, a kindergarten teacher at Fairview Elementary. The no-strings-attached, $100,000 grant recognizes an outstanding public-school teacher who teaches in a low-income community.

The district's George Washington and East High Schools were ranked among the nation's top by *Newsweek* for promoting Advanced Placement and International Baccalaureate classes. They ranked 50th and 84th out of 450, respectively. The district is also home to an array of magnet schools,

## CLOSE-UP

# The Teacher of the Century and Her School of Unlimited Opportunity

Emily Griffith is still Denver's best-known educator, even though she died more than 70 years ago. As a Denver public-school teacher who taught 8th grade at the Twenty-Fourth Street School during the day, Griffith volunteered at night teaching adults, many of them immigrants, to read and write and acquire basic math skills. But her true goal was to start a school where the age limit was lifted and the hours were flexible, so that a working adult who could spare an hour could come for some job training or self-improvement.

In 1916 Denver Public Schools converted the Longfellow School at 13th and Welton Streets into the Opportunity School. (It didn't become Emily Griffith Opportunity School until 1934, a year after Emily's death.) Her eponymous school, which has touched more than 1.5 million lives since it opened, had a dream to help people help themselves. On the first day

Emily sat near the front door and personally greeted each student. By the end of the first week, 1,400 students had registered. School was open 13 hours a day, five days a week. Tuition was free. Emily's goal was to provide training wherever it was needed.

One day a man came to look at course offerings. When he started to leave without registering, Emily asked why he hadn't signed up. "There are no courses for sign painters," he told her. Shortly thereafter, the school offered a course in sign painting. Over the years the course offerings have continued to meet students'—and society's—needs. From radio communications and ambulance driving during World War I to victory gardening and defense work during World War II, the Opportunity School has stayed current with a changing marketplace.

A few years ago, local grocery stores, including King Soopers, Safeway, and Cub

including the Center for International Students, two high-school computer magnet programs, and the Denver School of the Arts, the only one of its kind in the region. With the assistance of Collaborative Decision-Making Teams (school staff, parents, and community representatives) at each school, the district's neighborhood schools are constantly adapting and reshaping themselves to meet the unique needs of the city's many neighborhoods.

**Douglas County School District**
**620 Wilcox Street, Castle Rock**
**(303) 387-0100**
**www.dcsdk12.org**
This district's 42 elementary schools, 4 charter schools, 7 middle schools, 8 high schools, and 3 alternative schools cover a far-flung area ranging from the southern edges of Jefferson and Arapahoe Counties much of the way to Colorado Springs. Douglas is one of the fastest-growing counties in the United States.

Foods, approached the school's administration with a request for a program designed to train workers for bakery and deli work, an area that would continue to grow as more people turned to prepared foods for their meals. Thus was born the food-services department, which operates a bistro and restaurant where students can practice their craft.

Though many courses lean heavily toward technology, the school still offers classes in areas such as cake decorating, creative sewing, floral design, dental anatomy—even aircraft-accident investigation. In fact, just scanning course offerings can be enjoyable in and of itself.

What has remained constant since 1916 are the high-school and continuing-education courses for adults who never finished high school and immigrants who wish to become citizens. Each year the school enrolls between 11,000 and 15,000 students and graduates over 8,000. While the list of graduates isn't exactly filled with household names, their stories are the stuff of the American dream: a college dropout who took transportation courses at EGOS, went back to college,

then law school, and is now a transportation lawyer; a man who took automotive mechanics classes and today owns his own transmission shop; a woman who took typing classes, which launched her into the business world, and eventually become a state senator; a former mayor's sister-in-law who dropped out of high school 24 years earlier and graduated with a GED from EGOS in June of 1997, armed with a certificate in Early Child Care Professions.

Today almost 15,000 students train in 350 classes. Students range from age 17 to 94. Though tuition is no longer free (it was until several years ago), it now costs $1.55 an hour—still a bargain by anyone's standards. Better yet, the school and its students provide a wide range of services to the community at discount prices. Want a filling, inexpensive lunch? Twelfth Street Deli, which trains the food-service students, offers meals for $4.00 to $6.25. Need a haircut? A barber student will cut your locks for $3.00. How about a manicure for $4.00? Having dinner guests but don't have a table decoration? Floral centerpieces are $8.00 to $15.00.

---

The district currently has 48,000 students.

The majority of the county's elementary students go to school on a four-track, year-round calendar, a rotation of nine weeks in school followed by a three-week break, throughout the year.

Douglas County has one of the highest graduation rates and the lowest dropout rate. How do they do it? The system overall places a high value on educational excellence. Cherokee Trail Elementary

School in Parker was named by *Child* magazine as one of the 10 best schools in the nation. Greater Denver's first charter school, Academy Charter School, is in Castle Rock. Beginning in the 1994–1995 school year, the county approved a teacher-compensation plan linked to performance rather than longevity.

Douglas County is one of four school districts partnering in the Renaissance Expeditionary Learning Outward Bound School, which is located in Parker. The

K through 12 school has won national grants and acclaim for its challenging learning program.

### Englewood Schools
**4101 South Bannock Street, Englewood**
**(303) 761-7050**
**www.englewoodschools.org**
Also known as Arapahoe County School District No. 1, this district educates approximately 4,300 students in 10 schools spanning pre-K through 12th grade.

Englewood was not shy about its educational ambitions when it adopted a student-created name for its only alternative high school: Colorado's Finest Alternative High School. The school was devised by the Englewood School District for kids at risk of dropping out. It received the John Irwin Excellence in Education Award the first six years it was given, and the school was twice named one of the top 50 in the United States by *Redbook* magazine.

The Board of Education recently adopted 10 core beliefs; among them are emphasizing high student achievement, honoring diversity, and valuing every student and family.

### Jefferson County Public Schools
**1829 Denver West Drive, Golden**
**(303) 982-6500**
**www.jeffcoweb.jeffco.k12.co.us/**
Jefferson County makes up Colorado's largest school district, with more than 84,000 students and a budget of $735 million. Many people seem to want to get their kids into Jefferson County schools.

What is it about Jeffco that makes it so desirable? Well, it's a nice place to live, right up against the mountains with a lot of upscale neighborhoods and light-industry, white-collar employment. Also, the school system has one of Greater Denver's highest percentages of teachers with master's degrees or higher and the second-highest average teacher salary.

Jeffco has a "least-restrictive environment" policy for special-education students that gives primary responsibility for a special-needs student's education to the neighborhood school. The school district also has a Multicultural Learning Center that provides multicultural resources for teachers across the district.

Jeffco pursues these lofty goals in neighborhood schools—93 elementary schools, 19 middle schools, and 17 high schools—as well as a wide range of educational-choice programs. These include open enrollment where space is available, schools within a school, alternative schools, and self-governing charter schools. A brochure called *Choices* is available from the district's Communications Services office, (303) 982-6500.

### Littleton Public Schools
**5776 South Crocker Street, Littleton**
**(303) 347-3300**
**www.littletonpublicschools.net**
Pulling students from the city of Littleton and the city of Centennial, Littleton Public Schools is another one of those districts that does a good job with its money. The district serves more than 16,000 students in Littleton and Centennial, including 15 elementary schools, 4 middle schools, 3 senior high schools, 3 alternative schools, 2 charter schools, and 3 pre-school programs.

LPS students consistently rank above state and national averages on standardized tests. Littleton has one of Greater Denver's highest composite ACT scores in recent rankings, the third-highest average teacher salaries, and the third-lowest high-school dropout rate. Of the district's more than 1,000 full-time teachers, more than 64 percent hold master's or doctorate degrees, and they average 12 years of teaching experience.

The district places a high value on small class sizes, which range from 17 to 23 for elementary and 28 to 32 for middle- and high-school classes. School choice is available to all district residents through an open enrollment/transfer policy.

LPS also enjoys a high level of community involvement and support.

**Sheridan School District No. 2**
**4000 South Lowell Boulevard**
**(720) 833-6991**
Greater Denver's smallest school district, Sheridan has a total enrollment of 1,750 in two elementary schools, one middle school, and one high school. It serves the city of Sheridan, which surrounds the Englewood Municipal Golf Course and pieces of Englewood. The district's graduation rate is the fourth highest in Denver. Not surprisingly, it also has the lowest student-teacher ratio.

## PRIVATE SCHOOLS

Not every private school in the area is included here, of course, but you will find the larger, as well as many smaller, schools that come to us by word-of-mouth recommendation. Some accept only one sex, and many of them are religion-based private schools. None of the religious schools profess to turn away students on the basis of their religion or lack of religious commitment. Actually, however, religious schools require students to take religious instruction, and lack of adequate preparation can in some cases disqualify a student. At Yeshiva Toras Chaim School, for example, students need to have a sufficient grounding in the Hebrew language, since the school focuses heavily in Talmud and Torah.

**Accelerated Schools**
**2160 South Cook Street**
**(303) 758-2003**
**www.acceleratedschools.org**
Students, including the gifted and the learning disabled, study independently through individually prescribed instructional and motivational systems. Heavy use of computer instructional programs increases time spent on prescribed learning tasks and gives immediate feedback with an emphasis on practical business applications. Students on six campuses in Denver and Kansas City can attend part-time or full-time in morning, afternoon, and evening classes. The school offers acceler-

ated reading and college classes for extra credit as well as field trips and other activities. Transportation to and from home is included in tuition. Housing is available for students who need it. The school serves 150 students in grades K through 12.

**Alexander Dawson School**
**10455 Dawson Drive, Lafayette**
**(303) 665-6679**
**www.dawsonschool.org**
This college-prep school is on a 135-acre campus 35 minutes north of Denver. The school has a need-based financial aid program with more than $600,000 in grants, which go to 20 percent of the students. Though the school has historically had boarding students, it has been strictly a day school since 1998. The rigorous academic program includes a keen interest in the arts. Alexander Dawson takes part in interscholastic athletic competitions, including canoeing, skiing, and horsemanship. Stables with horses are on campus. The school has a new library as well as a $3 million gym and a $2.7 million arts center. It offers grades K through 12.

**Beacon Country Day School**
**6100 East Belleview Avenue**
**Greenwood Village**
**(303) 771-3990**
**www.beaconcountrydayschool.com**
Beacon Country Day School is a private, nonprofit school on a large acreage in Greenwood Village. The programs use each child's interests to promote learning in classrooms designed for small learning groups. The grounds include a pond and wetlands area for eco-studies. This school also has ponies that the children learn to care for and ride. Offering pre-K through eighth grade, the school has 125 students and is coed.

**Bethlehem Lutheran School**
**2100 North Wadsworth Boulevard**
**Lakewood**
**(303) 233-0401**
**www.bethluth.net/school.htm**
Bethlehem Lutheran, a coed school, is

part of the national network of Lutheran schools, the largest Protestant school group in the country. It offers quality education in a Christian environment and has received National Lutheran School Accreditation. It has a good music program, computer lab instruction, and interscholastic athletics as well as an advanced reading program for students in 3rd through 6th grades. The school's 365 students are in grades pre-K through 8.

### Bishop Machebeuf Catholic High School
**458 Unita Way**
**(303) 344-0082**
**www.machebeuf.org**
Formerly Machebeuf Catholic High School, this school emphasizes the students' "responsibility as children of God in a democratic society" as well as preparing them for college. The school boasts that more than 95 percent of its graduates enrolled in college by graduation, and it employs a full-time college admissions counselor. More than 480 students are in grades 9 through 12.

### Christ the King Roman Catholic School
**860 Elm Street**
**(303) 321-2123**
**www.christthekingdenver.org**
This school, where boys and girls in grades K through 8 wear uniforms, places a high premium on top-quality academic skills along with developing a sense of responsibility all within the framework of the Catholic faith. Along with religion, students are exposed to a core curriculum enhanced by music and art. Extracurricular activities include Junior Great Books, volleyball, basketball, and baseball. The school's enrollment is 250.

### Colorado Academy
**3800 South Pierce Street**
**(303) 986-1501**
**www.coloacad.org**
Founded in 1906, Colorado Academy is in southwest Denver on a lovely 94-acre campus. It's a college-prep program emphasizing a well-rounded education in academics, fine arts, and athletics with a 10-to-1 ratio of students to teachers. Bus transportation is available. About 875 students are in grades pre-K through 12.

### Colorado Catholic Academy
**11180 West 44th Avenue, Wheat Ridge**
**(303) 422-9549**
**www.coloradocatholicacademy.com**
Near the western edge of Wheat Ridge, this coed academy offers a traditional curriculum and teaches the Catholic faith to 50 students in grades 1 through 12. Students attend weekly Latin mass and daily rosary.

### Denver Academy
**4400 East Iliff Avenue**
**(303) 777-5870**
**www.denveracademy.org**
The Denver Academy applies a structured, closely supervised, and highly personalized approach to educating students with learning differences. This school has a 7-to-1 student-teacher ratio. About 420 boys and girls fill grades 1 through 12. Extracurricular activities on this 22-acre campus include drama and sports.

### Denver Christian Schools (DCS)
**2135 South Pearl Street**
**(303) 733-2421**
**www.denver-christian.org**
Denver Christian Schools was established by a small group that settled here before World War I, many of whom were from the Netherlands and ill with tuberculosis. Since the first classes in 1917, DCS has grown to four schools at three Denver locations: Denver Christian High School at 2135 South Pearl Street; Van Dellen elementary/middle school at 4200 East Warren Avenue; and Highlands Ranch elementary/middle school and Denver Christian Preschool, both located at 1733 Dad Clark Drive. More than 1,000 students study in grades K through 12.

### Denver International School
**1101 South Race Street**
**(303) 756-0381**
**www.dischool.org**

Denver International School is a multicultural school that attracts students committed to studying in two languages, choosing between French, Spanish, and Mandarin Chinese. Founded in 1977, it offers grades pre-K through 5 and prepares its students to thrive in a global society. More than 200 students study the usual round of subjects in bilingual instruction. Child care is offered before and after school. Language courses and clubs are offered to nonstudents as well.

## Denver Lutheran High School
3201 West Arizona Avenue
(303) 934-2345
www.denverlhs.org
Owned by the Colorado Lutheran High School Association, Lutheran High has been operating since 1955 on a 12-acre campus in southwest Denver. It was named in 1991 as one of 222 national recipients (4 in the state) of the National Exemplary School award for exceptional educational services with outstanding staff in an atmosphere conducive to achieving excellence. There are 230 students in grades 9 through 12.

## The Denver Waldorf School
940 Tillmore Street
(303) 777-0531
www.denverwaldorf.org
The Waldorf movement emphasizes working with the whole child—teaching to the hands, the head, and the heart, according to the school's administration. Contrary to the popular belief that it is an arts program, the Waldorf curriculum is academically rigorous, and by 8th grade, most students have had exposure to chemistry, biology, geometry, and algebra. The arts, both visual and performance, are integral to the program as well and permeate every aspect of learning in this integrated curriculum.

The school seeks to meet the needs of the child at each developmental age and works to establish a balance and rhythm throughout each day, week, month, and year. The school offers pre-K through 12 and serves approximately 300 students.

## Faith Christian Academy
6210 Ward Road (Elementary/Middle School), Arvada
(303) 424-7310

4890 Carr Street (High School), Arvada
(303) 424-7310
www.fca-schools.org
A unique, charismatic Christian school, Faith is open to anyone interested in a Christian education. The curriculum includes the full range of traditional subjects. About 1,250 students study in grades K through 12. The Ward Road address is for grades K through 5, with grades 6, 7, and 8 just across the street. The Carr Street address is for grades 9 through 12.

## Foothills Academy
4725 Miller Street, Wheat Ridge
(303) 431-0920
www.foothillsacademy.com
Valued by alumni and children of alumni, this is one of those schools where word-of-mouth is the best advertising. The small and interactive classes expose 200 boys and girls to basic skills as well as art, music, foreign languages, physical education, and an extensive outdoor education program. Foothills emphasizes "experiential learning and exploration," with field trips and visiting artist programs, outdoor experiences, and community projects and services. The academy built new classrooms and science facilities in 2001. Once a month they conduct a "mini-society" in which students buy and sell homemade goods, act out the workings of government, and simulate success in the real world. The school offers grades K through 12.

## Good Shepherd Catholic School
620 Elizabeth Street
(303) 321-6231
www.goodshepherddenver.org
Good Shepherd is between Sixth Avenue and East Colfax Avenue, York Street and Colorado Boulevard. It offers a Catholic education along with a core educational curriculum. The enrichment program is a

before- and after-school program, between 6:30 A.M. and 6:00 P.M., that includes guided study time, structured play time, and extracurricular activities. A Montessori program is also available for age 3 through grade 3. The school offers grades pre-K through 8 to 280 boys and girls.

### Graland Country Day School
**30 Birch Street**
**(303) 399-0390**
**www.graland.org**
Among Denver's premier private schools, Graland has a history of fostering academic and personal growth. Its enrollment is limited to maintain small classes and close interaction between teachers and students. Graland is in a residential neighborhood 5 miles south of downtown Denver. About 600 boys and girls study in grades K through 9.

### Havern Center Inc.
**4000 South Wadsworth Boulevard**
**Littleton**
**(303) 986-4587**
**www.haverncenter.org**
This is one of the best and oldest schools in the area for students with average IQs who have been diagnosed as learning disabled. With a better than one-to-one student-teacher ratio, the school offers kids with learning disabilities individualized instruction and occupational, speech, and language therapy as well as self-esteem groups. The goal of Havern is to ultimately reintroduce the child into mainstream education. The school has 10 students in the elementary grades.

### Holy Family High School
**5195 West 144 Avenue, Broomfield**
**(303) 410-1411**
**www.holyfamilyhs.com**
Founded in 1922 as a parish high school, Holy Family's mission statement proclaims a Catholic-Christian learning environment that "stresses academic excellence, fosters mutual respect, demands responsibility, and encourages self-growth." Besides the standard high-school core curriculum,

there are also courses in subjects such as theology, journalism, advanced computer applications, law, and drama. About 480 students study in grades 9 through 12.

### Humanex Academy
**2700 South Zuni Street**
**(303) 783-0137**
**www.humanexedu.org**
This alternative high school is for students grades 9 through 12 who may not have been successful in other schools. Humanex is dedicated to the idea that every student can succeed in the proper environment. The school has a student-teacher ratio of 7 to 1, a closed campus, progress reports to parents every two weeks, and parent notification within 20 minutes after school starts if the student does not show up. It is oriented to pupils with ADD or ADHD who read at least at the 6th-grade level. Enrollment is at 60 students, male and female.

### J. K. Mullen High School
**3601 South Lowell Boulevard**
**(303) 761-1764**
**www.mullen.pvt.k12.co.us/**
One of Denver's more well-known Catholic private high schools, Mullen was founded in 1931 as a home for orphaned boys. In 1965 it became J. K. Mullen Prep, a college-prep school for boys. It has been coeducational since 1989. It's run by the Christian Brothers of St. John the Baptist de LaSalle, a religious teaching order. Today it has a population of more than 1,000 students.

### Kent Denver School
**4000 East Quincy Avenue, Englewood**
**(303) 770-7660**
**www.kentdenver.org**
Kent Denver has roots going back to the founding of the Kent School for girls in 1922 and the founding of the Denver Country Day School for boys. The two schools merged to create the present institution in 1974. Its challenging, college-preparatory curriculum produced an average SAT score of 1,246 and an average

SAT II score of 1,304 in the graduating class of 2004. Kent Denver has a campus of 200 acres with five academic buildings that include more than 40 classrooms and laboratories; 6 studios for music, dance, and art; 2 gymnasiums; 6 tennis courts; and 20 acres of playing fields. In grades 6 through 12, there are 655 students.

## The Logan School for Creative Learning
**1005 Yosemite Circle**
**(303) 340-2444**
**www.theloganschool.org**
A school for gifted and creative children grades K through 8, the Logan School boasts a stimulating academic program with hands-on learning experiences for its 190 boys and girls. To be considered for admission, students must complete educational-assessment and intelligence testing and make an observation visit to a Logan classroom.

## Maranatha Christian Center
**7180 Oak Street, Arvada**
**(303) 431-5653**
**www.maranathachristiancenter.org**
A Bible-believing, nondenominational educational center with Christ-centered academics taught by qualified, born-again staff, Maranatha was opened in 1980 on an agricultural piece of land that previously had been occupied by a house and barn. Now its 15 acres include more than 60,000 square feet of classrooms, offices, a gymnasium, locker rooms, a learning center, a library, and a computer lab for 860 students in grades pre-K through 12.

## Mile High Adventist Academy
**711 East Yale Avenue**
**(303) 744-1069**
**www.milehighacademy.org**
This school dates from a one-room school established by Seventh-Day Adventists in Denver in 1913. The themes here are academic excellence, individual resourcefulness and responsibility, Christian philosophy, and making the world a better place within the student's sphere of influence. About 250 students attend grades K through 12.

## Montessori School of Denver
**1460 South Holly Street**
**(303) 756-9441**
**www.montessoridenver.org**
The oldest Montessori in Denver (there are other independent Montessori schools in metro Denver), this school has about 275 boys and girls, ages 3 through 12. As with all Montessori schools, this one adheres to a philosophy that allows students "the opportunity to achieve individually, creatively, and successfully." The school has a wide parent volunteer base and offers a Montessori curriculum including botany, zoology, language, math, art, physical education, and Spanish.

## Montclair Academy
**212 Syracuse Street**
**(303) 366-7588**
**www.montclairacademy.org**
This pre-K through 8th-grade school serves 185 students. The curriculum has a strong liberal arts emphasis with a variety of enrichment programs, including field trips and special classes. The student-teacher ratio is 15 to 1. Enrichment programs are offered after school until about 5:00 P.M.

## Most Precious Blood Parish School
**3959 East Iliff Avenue**
**(303) 757-1279**
**www.mpbdenver.org**
Students get a standard curriculum here along with religious instruction, including morning prayer and mass once a month. The school also features geography and spelling bees, science and art fairs, speech meets, and a "super citizens" program in which grades 3 through 5 choose a supercitizen from their class each month to be honored by the Colorado Optimists Club. Grades pre-K through 8.

## Our Lady of Fatima
**10530 West 20th Avenue, Lakewood**
**(303) 233-2500**
**www.fatimalakewood.com**
At this Catholic school, religious instruction is offered in addition to the academic

courses. The school has an extensive athletic program as well as special features including a science lab, a reading lab, and a computer lab. About 305 students are in grades pre-K through 8.

### Regis Jesuit High School
**6400 South Lewiston Way, Aurora**
**(303) 269-8000 (boys division)**
**(303) 269-8100 (girls division)**
**www.regisjesuit.com**

Regis has the Jesuit-school mystique of quality education with a public-service mentality. It has earned a U.S. Department of Education School of Excellence designation. Special senior projects, volunteerism, student retreats, counseling, and peer tutoring are among the additions to regular curriculum here, as well as college credit earned from Regis University. Its population is currently at about 1,350, including 500 girls.

### Ricks Center for Gifted Children
**2040 South York Street**
**(303) 871-2982**
**www.du.edu/ricks**

As the name implies, Ricks Center is for children who've demonstrated "educational needs in the gifted range." A strong academic curriculum is enhanced with extracurricular activities such as chess, student council, yearbook, and Odyssey of the Mind. The school serves 300 students, grades pre-K through 8, and is part of the University of Denver.

### St. Francis De Sales School
**235 South Sherman Street**
**(303) 744-7231**

Since 1904 this Catholic school has been serving the same neighborhood south of downtown Denver, combining religious instruction and experiences with a strong basic curriculum and small classes for its 240 students in grades pre-K through 8.

### St. James Catholic School
**1250 Newport Street**
**(303) 333-8275**
**www.stjamesdenver.org**

On Denver's eastern side, just northwest of the former Lowry Air Force Base, St. James provides a values-based education that emphasizes academic excellence, self-direction, responsibility, a genuine love of learning, and the wherewithal to become solid Catholic citizens. The school teaches 175 boys and girls in preschool through 8th grade.

### St. Louis Catholic School
**3301 South Sherman, Englewood**
**(303) 762-8307**
**www.stlouiscatholicschool.org**

Mastery of the basics is the focus at St. Louis, along with art, music, computer training, and programs such as Junior Achievement, Great Books, and Community Resource. It's a Catholic-sponsored school, but non-Catholics are welcome. There's religious instruction, student-prepared masses, and special sacramental instruction for 175 students in grades K through 8. Extracurricular activities include spelling and geography bees, competitive speech, and competitive sports.

### St. Mary's Academy
**4545 South University Boulevard**
**Englewood**
**(303) 762-8300**
**www.smanet.org**

St. Mary's Academy is a Catholic, independent school founded in 1864 by the Sisters of Loretto. In 1875 it awarded the first high-school diploma in the Colorado Territory. Among its features are its Early Learning Center at the Denver Tech Center and the all-girls' high school. St. Mary's emphasizes values-based education, small classes, strong curriculum, personalized attention, and community service. Coed through 8th grade, girls only in high school, St. Mary's serves a total of 785 students.

### St. Therese School
**1200 Kenton Street, Aurora**
**(303) 364-7494**
**www.sttthereseschool.com**

St. Therese School includes Catholic teaching with its conventional curriculum. It's staffed by Sisters of Charity as well as lay teachers. It has a reading specialist and full-time teachers in physical education, computer science, and music education for 225 students in grades K through 8.

### St. Vincent de Paul School
**1164 South Josephine Street**
**(303) 777-3812**
**www.stvincentdepaul.41pi.com**
A Catholic parish school, St. Vincent was founded to instruct children in the Catholic faith while also providing them with all the standard core academic subjects. Special features include a technology program and full-time teachers for computer education, art, music, and physical education. The student-teacher ratio is 20 to 1. St. Vincent's starts at preschool and goes up through 8th grade. It serves 480 students.

### Sts. Peter and Paul
**Catholic Elementary School**
**3920 Pierce Street, Wheat Ridge**
**(303) 424-0402**
**www.sppscatholic.com**
One of the west side's better-known Catholic schools, Sts. Peter and Paul provides sound academics and Catholic values and traditions to 425 students from pre-K through 8th grade. Features of its integrated curriculum include a literature program, computers, art, music, speech and drama, math, and physical education.

### Shrine of St. Anne Catholic School
**7320 Grant Place, Arvada**
**(303) 422-1800**
**www.stannescatholic.com**
A high-quality, well-rounded curriculum in basic academics is accompanied by daily classes in religion. The school describes itself as a "Christian community witnessing to the gospel message of Jesus Christ." Special features include an education fair, a science fair, and a life education program, which tackles real-world issues that students face and will face in life. The

school offers a computer lab, science lab, and library to its 473 students in grades K through 8.

### Silver State Christian School
**875 South Sheridan Boulevard, Lakewood**
**(303) 922-8850**
**www.ssbaptist.net/silverstate**
Strong in music and orchestra, with daily Bible classes, Silver State has its own mix of standard educational curricula. The school also participates in interscholastic sports governed by the Colorado High School Sports Athletic Association. Silver State has 195 students in grades K through 12.

### Stanley British Primary School
**350 Quebec Street**
**(303) 360-0803**
**www.stanleybps.org**
Stanley British Primary School (or B.P.S. as it's called locally) teaches 340 students in grades K through 8. Its philosophy is that education should be experiential, and to that end, students study where they are developmentally, rather than strictly by age or grade. The curriculum revolves around core subjects, with the inclusion of study skills. This school relies heavily on parental involvement, both in the classroom and in fund-raising.

### University of Denver High School
**2306 East Evans Street**
**(303) 871-2636**
**www.du.edu/duhs/**
Founded in 1995, the University of Denver High School accommodates students from the gifted to the mildly learning disabled (there is no specialist on staff). The course of studies is rigorous, and students have the opportunity to attend some university classes. Teachers here "adopt the role of coach rather than dispenser of information." The school has 120 students and a student-teacher ratio of 8 to 1. The students have access to several extracurricular activities, including a literary magazine, basketball, Amnesty International, and drama.

### Westland Christian Academy
**430 South Kipling Street, Lakewood**
**(303) 986-5500**

"Academic excellence in Christian education" is the motto of this school maintained by Westland Baptist Church. The Christ-centered and Bible-based education has a traditional academic curriculum and daily chapel service. The school has three main classroom buildings on a 4.6-acre campus. Westland has about 150 students in grades K through 12.

### Yeshiva Toras Chaim School
**1555 Stuart Street**
**(303) 629-8200**

This private orthodox Jewish high school would be one of many in New York, but here in the Rocky Mountain area it has been unique since its founding in 1967. Half of each day is spent in studying Talmud and Torah, and the other half is spent in secular studies. About half of the 65 male students board at the school.

## COLLEGES AND UNIVERSITIES

### Colorado Christian University
**180 South Garrison Street, Lakewood**
**(303) 963-3000**
**www.ccu.edu**

As the only major evangelical Christian university in the Rocky Mountain region, Colorado Christian University offers fully accredited undergraduate and graduate courses with 21 undergraduate majors. CCU also offers programs designed to serve the social and spiritual needs of all students. The university has an enrollment of more than 2,000 students in all programs. The Adult Studies program offers accelerated evening, weekend, and on-site corporate classes (on-site training to company personnel) for adult learners, with centers at Lakewood's main campus and in Colorado Springs, Loveland, and Grand Junction. It offers undergraduate and graduate degrees and a teacher-recertification program, as well as an online MBA program.

CCU is a Division II member of the NCAA, competing in men's and women's basketball, soccer, cross-country, and tennis in addition to women's volleyball and men's golf.

### Colorado School of Mines
**1500 Illinois Street, Golden**
**(303) 273-3000**
**www.mines.edu**

"Mines," as it's called, is a school of engineering, energy, environment, and economics nationally known for academic rigor. It was founded in Golden in 1874 because that city was the gateway to Colorado's booming minerals mining industry. A public school, Mines now has about 3,900 students who focus on areas such as engineering, engineering systems, chemical engineering, petroleum engineering, mining engineering, economics, geology, and geological engineering. Degrees are also available in chemistry, geochemistry, petroleum engineering, and physics. Its metallurgical, materials science, environmental science, and engineering programs are among the best in the nation. Not surprisingly, Mines is strong in math and computer science.

Mines also has the benefit of a beautiful location. Golden is nestled against the foothills behind (from Denver) South Table Mountain and retains a small-town atmosphere. The school is a short walk from downtown. Golden is connected by Interstate 70 and U.S. Highway 6 directly into Denver, by I-70 into the mountains, and by US 6 West through scenic Clear Creek Canyon into the Gilpin County/Clear Creek County historic mining areas and mountain communities.

Golden claims a higher per-capita concentration of Ph.D's than Boulder, home of the University of Colorado.

### Colorado State University—Denver Center (CSU)
**410 17th Street, Suite 1400**
**(303) 573-6318**
**www.learn.colostate.edu/denver**

Colorado State University in Fort Collins is one of the state's most highly esteemed public schools. It offers a significant number of majors that are not available anywhere else in the state. It's nationally famous for its College of Natural Resources and its School of Veterinary Medicine. CSU is the state's only land-grant university; its Agricultural Experiment Station and Cooperative Extension form the education/research backbone of Colorado's agriculture industry.

CSU's Denver-area educational and technical services are found in a single location, the Colorado State University—Denver Center. Located downtown on Tremont Avenue between 16th and 17th Streets are services aimed heavily toward downtown Denver's working population. Among the degree programs offered are the executive MBA program, communication management, organizational performance and change, and construction management. Certification programs are offered in construction management, process management, and project management. Offerings include courses in education, vocational education, business and professional, and personal advancement. This campus specializes in customized training for businesses.

**Columbia College at Aurora**
**14707 East Second Avenue, Suite 100**
**Aurora**
**(303) 340–8050**
**www.ccis.edu/aurora**
This is actually one of 30 extension centers of the Columbia College campus in Columbia, Missouri, but it's a sizeable operation. Some 700 students attend evening and weekend classes here, working toward associate and baccalaureate degrees in the liberal arts, business administration, computer information systems, psychology, criminal justice, history, government, and other subjects. It's primarily adult education, with an average student age of 34.

*The Colorado Free University (which isn't really free, but nearly so) offers a vast array of fun, interesting, and informative classes for busy people. Whether it's computers, yoga, or wine tasting, CFU has something for everyone. Pick up class schedules at grocery and convenience stores.*

**The Metropolitan State College of Denver**
**1201 Fifth Street (mailing); 900 Auraria Parkway (physical address)**
**(303) 556–5300**
**www.mscd.edu**
Founded in 1965, Metro, Colorado's third-largest college with more than 20,000 students, is a cosmopolitan city college on a 175-acre oasis on the edge of Denver's downtown business district. Half of its student body is of traditional college age (18 to 25), and nearly half consists of nontraditional students—those older than age 25 who have already been in the work force. This, of course, can be a delight to professors who find they are dealing not only with students fresh out of high school but also with professional adults as well. And it's great for students because they can learn from their peers as well as their professors. Metro has a reputation as the working student's college, with an emphasis on applied education, and takes pains to accommodate that student with a lot of weekend and evening classes.

The main campus, the Auraria Higher Education Center, is unique. Metropolitan State College of Denver shares the campus with two other institutions, the Community College of Denver and the University of Colorado at Denver and Health Sciences Center. The three schools together offer a more potent education package than any one could alone because they allow students to cross-register for classes in all three schools and enjoy a combined menu of lectures, concerts, plays, and student programs.

Metro offers a full lineup of NCAA Division II intercollegiate athletic competitions in men's and women's sports. The teams use one of the region's best athletic facilities, the Auraria Events Center, which seats more than 2,300 and is used for a variety of campus-wide events. Metro's basketball team has gone to nine consecutive NCAA tournaments.

Metro has all the elements of a traditional university, such as extensive physical education facilities, one of Greater Denver's best libraries, and a quiet, tree-lined campus. The historic 19th-century Bavarian-style brewery, the Tivoli, which until recently was an independent shopping center, has been transformed into one of the country's most picturesque student unions. The Tivoli houses shops, the campus bookstore, restaurants, an arcade, recreation rooms, and nightclubs as well as student offices and services.

Although there are no on-campus dormitories, many students get assistance from the campus housing office to live on their own in surrounding apartments. Plus, Metro is an easy walk from downtown Denver, the Denver Center for the Performing Arts, Six Flags Elitch Gardens, Coors Field, the nightlife and restaurants of Lower Downtown, and INVESCO Field at Mile High.

Oh yes, and Metro has classes, too, 2,400 of them each fall and spring. The emphasis at Metro is on individual attention, with an average class size of just 22 students. Each class is taught by a master teacher; no student teaching assistants here. Summer offerings are also available.

Metro has 50 majors, in addition to the individual degree program. Degree offerings cover business, performing and visual arts, liberal arts, natural and social sciences, and specialty areas such as criminology, aerospace, journalism, and aviation and engineering technology.

Metro also operates two other campuses that offer degree programs and specialty classes. Metro South, in Greenwood Village, offers evening and weekend classes to more than 1,500 students from southeast Denver. Metro North, in Northglenn, serves the northern suburbs.

**National American University**
**1325 South Colorado Boulevard**
**(303) 758-6700**
**www.national.edu**
Aimed at the career interests of the non-traditional adult student, National's average student is age 32. The university offers bachelor's degrees in accounting, applied management, business administration, and computer information systems; associate degrees in accounting, applied management, business administration, and computer information systems.

**Regis University**
**3333 Regis Boulevard**
**(303) 458-4100**
**www.regis.edu**
Regis University got a nice big PR boost in the summer of 1993 when it was chosen as the spot where President Bill Clinton met with Pope John Paul II on the pope's historic visit to Denver. Secret Service helicopters buzzed like flies over the surrounding residential neighborhoods. Regis has been around for a long time, founded in 1877, and it has a pretty 90-acre main campus, about 11,000 students, and a sterling reputation as an educational institution. It's a Colorado Jesuit university, centered around the Ignatius Loyola philosophy of leaders in service of others. Regis pursues that philosophy in three colleges: Regis College, The School for Professional Studies, and The Rueckert-Hartman School for Health Care Professions. Regis College itself is a relatively small school, with about 1,400 undergraduate students studying liberal arts, sciences, business, and education. The student-faculty ratio is 16 to 1.

The School for Professional Studies has undergraduate and graduate programs in business, education, and computer sciences and offers classes in Denver, Colorado Springs, Fort Collins, Broomfield, and Boulder.

The Rueckert-Hartman School for

Health Care Professions is particularly well-known among the Greater Denver nursing community. Its graduate and undergraduate programs include nursing, physical therapy, and health-care administration and management.

## University of Colorado at Boulder
**Broadway between Baseline Road and Colorado Avenue, Boulder**
**(303) 492-1411**
**www.colorado.edu**

Known in the vernacular as CU, this flagship institution of higher education in Colorado was founded in 1876, the year in which Colorado became a state. Today it is a university of international prominence. The university's campus in Boulder has 29,000 students, 75 percent of whom are undergraduates.

The University of Colorado at Boulder, or CU–Boulder, is where the university started, and it's still the state's largest and most important campus. Placed in the beautiful setting of Boulder's University Hill, its 786 acres of rural Italian-style buildings and complexes of Colorado sandstone make it one of the nation's most aesthetically pleasing campuses. A 1991 book, *The Campus as a Work of Art* by Thomas Gaines, ranked CU–Boulder fourth among 50 of the "most artistically successful campuses in the country." Because of nearby skiing and the many outdoor activities available, and because it's often the campus of choice for wealthy students who want an excellent place in which to spend their campus years, some people think of CU as a "party school." But CU–Boulder is far more than the place where actor and director Robert Redford played on the baseball team and waited tables in a local bar.

CU–Boulder excels as both a teaching and a research university. In 2005 *U.S. News & World Report* ranked CU 34th among the nations top 50 public universities offering doctoral programs.

CU–Boulder's leading programs include telecommunications, aerospace engineering, and atmospheric and space physics. The department of molecular, cellular, and developmental biology is ranked among the top 10 national doctoral programs by the National Research Council. The chemistry and biochemistry department boasts 1989 Nobel Laureate Thomas Cech among its teaching faculty. Two CU professors won the Nobel Prize in Physics in 2001 for their work on Bose-Einstein condensate: Eric A. Cornell and Carl E. Wieman. And the 2005 Nobel Prize in Physics was awarded to John L. Hall, a fellow and senior research associate at JILA (a joint research institute of CU and the National Institute of Standards and Technology). CU–Boulder has a separate 147-acre research park nearby that is home to some of its many research institutes.

Programs include the schools of law, business and administration, education, journalism and mass communications, arts and sciences, music, and architecture and planning. The schools offer more than 3,400 courses in more than 170 fields of study to some 29,000 students.

Part of the Big 12, the school's sports program is impressive, too. Between 1988 and 1996 the football team went to bowl games all nine years, then skipped a few years before playing bowls in 2001 and 2002. Its women's basketball team has also made big news, making it as far as the regional semifinals in 2003 for the sixth time in eight years.

*The Auraria Campus—shared by the Metropolitan State College of Denver, the University of Colorado at Denver, and the Community College of Denver—is a jewel of the metro region not only for its outstanding educational offerings but also for its accessibility to nontraditional students. Night classes have long been a mainstay for working students, and online classes are increasingly popular.*

**University of Colorado at Denver and Health Sciences Center**
**1250 14th Street (physical address, no mail delivery)**
**(303) 556-5600**
**www.cudenver.edu**

**University of Colorado Health Sciences Center (UCHSC)**
**4200 East Ninth Avenue**
**(303) 372-0000**
**www.uchsc.edu**

On July 1, 2004, the University of Colorado at Denver consolidated with the CU Health Sciences Center to create a new university with three campuses. The main campus is at the 175-acre Auraria Higher Education Center, shared with the Metropolitan State College and the Community College of.Denver. The Health Sciences Center itself is located at Ninth Avenue and Colorado Boulevard and includes the University of Colorado Hospital and the Colorado Psychiatric Hospital, as well as eight research institutes. The third campus is located at the 217-acre decommissioned Fitzsimons Army Medical Center in Aurora. By 2010 the Health Sciences Center will have relocated to the Fitzsimons campus, now being redeveloped as a biotechnology research and development park.

CU–Denver, as it's commonly referred to, has more than 80 undergraduate and graduate programs, and students can cross-register at all three schools. The more than 12,000 undergraduate students at CU–Denver are therefore part of a much larger student body and enjoy more academic and extracurricular opportunities than those provided by CU–Denver alone.

A five-minute walk from downtown, CU–Denver makes the opportunities of a state university available to working students in an urban environment. Strong programs include liberal arts and sciences, business and administration, engineering and applied science, architecture and planning, arts and media, and education.

The Health Sciences Center is Colorado's only academic health center and

the seat of medical research in the region. The main 46-acre campus offers baccalaureate and graduate programs in medicine, nursing, dentistry, pharmacy, and health-related fields. The center is as prominent nationally in research as it is regionally in medical education and is renowned in numerous fields including transplants, cancer, neuroscience, molecular biology, prenatal care, and cardiovascular services.

A new 160-acre research park, Colorado Bioscience Park Aurora, is being developed directly adjacent to the Health Sciences Center's Fitzsimons campus, and after its relocation is completed in 2010, UCHSC will begin to develop 1.5 million square feet of its own new research space. The University of Colorado Hospital also will relocate and, with the help of a $25 million grant, open new specialty clinics and ambulatory and outpatient care facilities. Planners hope the end result will be a world-class academic health and research center.

**University of Denver**
**2199 South University Boulevard**
**(303) 871-2000**
**www.du.edu**

Founded in 1864, this is the oldest independent university in the Rocky Mountain region and the reason why one of Denver's main north-south thoroughfares is named University Boulevard. In a residential area 8 miles southeast of downtown, the University of Denver, called "DU" by locals, is a good combination of big-university experience and small-liberal-arts-college atmosphere. The campus includes 100 buildings on 125 acres. Its Lamont School of Music and its College of Law are on the university's Park Hill campus, formerly Colorado Women's College. The student body counts about 10,400 students. About 4,500 of those are graduate students, and plenty of faculty members are at the forefront of research in their fields. The student-faculty ratio is 16 to 1 for undergraduates. Class sizes average 20 students. Undergraduate degrees are available in arts, fine arts, music, music education, science, business administration, accounting, chemistry, electrical engineering, and mechanical engineering. Campus Connection, a mentoring program, joins each new freshman with a faculty adviser in his or her major area of study.

## University of Phoenix
**10004 Park Meadows Drive, Lone Tree**
**(303) 694-9093**
**www.phoenix.edu**
This is the Colorado Campus of the University of Phoenix, which is based, of course, in Phoenix, Arizona, but has more than 100 campuses in the United States and Puerto Rico. It has four in the greater Denver area, plus campuses in Fort Collins, Pueblo, and Colorado Springs. To attend you have to be a high-school graduate or GED certificate holder and be employed. This university focuses on degree programs and services for working adults. Degrees range from nursing and business administration to educational administration, computer information systems, and technology management. The University of Phoenix has about 4,000 students in Colorado.

## Webster University
**9250 East Costilla Avenue, Suite 310**
**Greenwood Village**
**(303) 708-8305**
**www.webster.edu**
Webster University is based in St. Louis, Missouri, and has about 15,000 students worldwide; about two-thirds of them are graduate students. The Denver campus in Aurora offers graduate courses in business administration, business, computer resources and information management, human resources development, and human resources management. All programs are designed for working adults and offered in the evening format. The university has two other Colorado locations in Colorado Springs, one of which is at Peterson Air Force Base.

# COMMUNITY COLLEGES

## Arapahoe Community College
**5900 South Santa Fe Drive, Littleton**
**(303) 797-4222**
**www.arapahoe.edu**
Arapahoe Community College's 7,500-plus students attend classes on a 51-acre campus adjacent to Littleton's downtown and just east of the South Platte River, which affords great mountain views to the west. It was established as Arapahoe Junior College in 1965, the first two-year college in Greater Denver. It joined the Colorado State System of Community Colleges in 1970 as Arapahoe Community College.

Arapahoe leans toward two-year associate degrees that help students enhance their careers with a degree or certificate, often while working. Some 50 percent of its students are working students. But courses can also transfer to a four-year college or university. The college has more than 70 degree and certificate programs in both academic and vocational areas, with more than 2,400 classes per year. ACC also offers community education classes for the lifelong learner. The average cost of education here is 10 to 50 percent less than most Colorado four-year schools.

The college also operates satellite classrooms at the Denver Tech Center and in Parker.

## Community College of Aurora
**16000 East Centre Tech Parkway, Aurora**
**(303) 360-4700**
**www.ccaurora.edu**
Community College of Aurora has been the community college of Greater Denver's east side since its founding in 1983. It moved to a new 35-acre campus just west of Buckley Air National Guard Base in 1991 and, with the closing of Lowry Air Force Base, opened a second campus there in the fall of 1994, the Higher Education and Advancement Technology Center. Residence halls are available on the Lowry campus. Like other community

colleges, it accommodates adult learners. About 60 percent of the students are older than age 25.

Community College of Aurora offers the full range of courses needed by students planning to transfer to four-year institutions with associate of arts and associate of science degrees. It has vocational programs that focus on an associate of applied science degree and training for employment certification. And it provides a menu of courses that serves a wide variety of interests. The college's faculty development program, which trains faculty in better methods of teaching, has won several national awards and has been used as a model for schools across the country.

### Community College of Denver
### 1111 West Colfax Avenue
### (303) 556-2600
### www.ccd.edu

With about 6,600 full-time and part-time students, this is Greater Denver's "inner-city" community college. It shares the Auraria Higher Education Center's 175-acre campus with the Metropolitan State College of Denver and the University of Colorado at Denver. About 37,000 students can cross-register in the courses of all three schools.

The college offers degree programs in the full range of college subjects, as well as transfer courses for the baccalaureate degree, occupational programs for job entry skills or upgrading, remedial instruction and GED prep, continuing education, community services, and cooperative programs with the other schools.

### Front Range Community College
### 3645 West 112th Avenue, Westminster
### (303) 404-5550
### www.frcc.cc.co.us

The community college of Greater Denver's north side, Front Range is Colorado's largest community college. It has about 13,000 students at its Fort Collins, Longmont, Brighton, and Westminster campuses. Front Range has more than 100

degree and certificate programs, including associate degrees in arts, sciences, and general studies as well as degrees and certificates in applied sciences.

Front Range offers classes for GED, English as a second language, and literacy and classes for students with learning disabilities. It is the leader among local community colleges in delivering courses at business and industry work sites, including companies such as AT&T in Westminster, Geneva Pharmaceuticals in Broomfield, and Rocky Flats in Jefferson County, where Front Range has 600 employee-students. It is also one of the few places in the West that teaches hearing people to interpret for the deaf. Its nursing program won acclaim as a 1994 program of excellence, and in addition to its vocational programs, it has 60 courses that transfer to four-year schools. Locals can also take a lot of fun lifelong-learning courses such as handwriting analysis and garden management.

### Red Rocks Community College
### 13300 West Sixth Avenue, Lakewood
### (303) 914-6600
### www.rrcc.edu

Red Rocks is among the fastest-growing institutions of higher learning in the state, and given its location, that's not hard to understand. Its 140-acre main campus perches on the western edge of Lakewood, in some of Jefferson County's most beautiful natural settings. Since 1969, when Red Rocks Community College was established, its annual student body has grown to 14,000 students on two campuses.

Red Rocks was founded in 1969 as a two-year institution. It also serves northwest metro suburbanites with an Arvada campus.

Its largest enrollments are in math, followed by the sciences, computer information systems, English, multimedia, fire science technology, and criminal justice. More than half of the students say they attend for job-related reasons. The college has special programs in construction technology, film and video technology, medical assisting, and biotechnology. The Red Rocks Institute does customized training for businesses. The Red Rocks OSHA Training Institute began in 1992 as one of four sites in the nation designated by the U.S. Department of Labor for OSHA training. A Computer Access Center trains individuals with disabilities to use adaptive computer technologies.

# HEALTH CARE Ⓗ

In the past few years, health care in Greater Denver has grown as fast as the area's population.

That might be a slight exaggeration, but certainly Denver's health-care scene—most notably hospital mergers—have kept local headline writers busy and consumers trying to figure out what's what.

Despite all the changes, Denver remains a regional center for high-quality medicine. Three Level I trauma centers serve the region, along with two emergency helicopter companies, AirLife and Flight for Life. (Level I is the highest, most technologically advanced level of trauma care available and includes the highest staffing levels.) The emergency room at Denver General Hospital sees so much gruesome action that it inspired a book called *The Knife and Gun Club*. A number of facilities, including Craig Hospital and National Jewish Medical and Research Center, have earned national and international acclaim for outstanding care and research developments.

In all, Greater Denver has 18 acute-care hospitals and three rehabilitation centers. Two operations, Centura Health and HealthONE, own and operate several facilities. The largest of Denver's hospitals, Presbyterian/St. Luke's, just east of downtown, has 680 licensed beds and nearly 1,600 employees. The smallest, Platte Valley Medical Center, north of Denver in Brighton, has 58 licensed beds and about 290 employees.

Because of the city's attractive setting, Denver is able to lure high-quality professionals to staff its facilities. Hospitals and physicians work with university researchers and high-technology companies. University Hospital, at the University of Colorado's Health Sciences Center in Denver, has been ranked as one of the 25 best hospitals in the country in *The Best of Medicine* by Herbert J. Dietrich, M.D., and Virginia H. Biddle.

Pulmonary medicine is one example of a field in which Greater Denver enjoys renown. Many of the city's major hospitals, including the National Jewish Medical and Research Center and the Swedish and Exempla Lutheran medical centers, originally began as tuberculosis treatment centers back in the days when tuberculosis patients came to Colorado for the healthy air. Not surprisingly Greater Denver is a leader in pulmonary research and technology. Research and expertise at institutions such as National Jewish and the Web-Waring Lung Institute are one of the main reasons why some of the world's most advanced pulmonary-technology manufacturers make their homes in the Denver area.

Denver's other research and medical advancement highlights include the Belle Bonfils Blood Center, the Eleanor Roosevelt Institute, the Barbara Davis Child Diabetes Center, and the C. Henry Kempe National Center for the Prevention and Treatment of Child Abuse.

To insure their health, Denverites, like others across the nation, have turned to managed-care companies. Changes in this area happen so fast that only the industry pros can keep it all straight. Managed-care companies appeal to Greater Denver residents' sense of health and outdoor living through advertisements and policies that stress preventive care and healthy lifestyles.

## PHYSICIAN AND HOSPITAL REFERRALS

Clearly, health-care choices abound in Denver. To find what's right for you, you can go to research extremes and get a desk directory of Colorado hospitals from the **Colorado Health and Hospital Association,** (720) 489–1630, for $95. The agency also maintains a free online directory of hospitals at www.cha.com. Other publications include issue papers on such topics as violence, teen pregnancy, and smoking. You also can check the phone book under "Hospitals" or "Physicians" for a number of free referral services. **Mile High United Way** is a great place to start when seeking all kinds of community-service information, and medical service is no exception. You can call their HelpLine at (303) 433–8900.

Among the referral services to start with:

**Answer Line at Exempla Health Care**
**(303) 425–2929**

**Centura Ask-A-Nurse**
**(303) 777–6877**

**Children's Hospital ParentSmart!**
**HealthLine**
**(303) 861–0123**

**HealthONE**
**(877) HealthONE**
**(877) 432–5846**

**Rose Medical Center**
**(303) 320–7673**

**Physician Referral Line**
**(800) Doctors**
**(800) 362–8677**

Greater Denver has more than 100 nursing homes and more than a dozen hospices, some operated in association with hospitals. A good number to keep on the telephone if you have kids is the **Rocky Mountain Poison Center,** (303) 739–1123.

# HOSPITALS

## Denver

**Centura Porter Adventist Hospital**
**2525 South Downing Street**
**(303) 778–1955**
**www.porterhospital.org**

Formerly Porter Memorial Hospital, this hospital on Denver's southern border is a 369-bed, acute-care hospital that boasts more than 1,200 physicians. A nonprofit organization, it's one of four—along with Parker Adventist in Parker, Centura Health Littleton Adventist Hospital, and Centura Health Avista Adventist Hospital in Boulder County—affiliated under Rocky Mountain Adventist Healthcare. It was founded in 1930 by Denver pioneer and businessman Henry M. Porter after he was impressed by his treatment at California hospitals that were owned by the Seventh-Day Adventist Church. He and his daughter gave the church $315,000 and 40 acres to start a hospital in Denver. The hospital's mission is "to serve as a continuation of the healing ministry of Christ." Its specialties include cancer care and cancer support, heart care and healthy heart programs, the Clyde G. Kissinger Center for Sight, the PorterCare Birthplace, Porter Breastcare, a center for treatment of substance abuse and eating disorders, transplant services, and education programs in areas such as stress management, weight control, nutrition counseling, smoking cessation, and alcohol education. Independence Square helps cardiac rehabilitation patients return to normal activities by simulating situations patients will encounter when discharged from the hospital.

**Centura St. Anthony Hospital Central**
**4231 West 16th Avenue**
**(303) 629–3511**
**www.stanthonycentral.org**
St. Anthony Hospital Central was built by the Sisters of St. Francis in 1893. It operates one of the area's three certified Level I trauma centers and is home base to Flight for Life, probably the best known of Greater Denver's helicopter emergency rescue services. St. Anthony is an innovator in cardiovascular surgery and services and was one of the first hospitals to provide a chest pain emergency center. It's also performed more than 2,300 operations using gamma-knife surgery, which entails the use of gamma rays to eliminate deep-seated

tumors and other malformations in the brain. St. Anthony Hospital Central has 593 licensed beds, and 18,500 inpatients and 34,000 outpatients per year.

### Children's Hospital
**1056 East 19th Avenue**
**(303) 861–8888**
**www.thechildrenshospital.org**
The name says it all. Kids. Children's Hospital is a health-care system caring for kids with the full spectrum of needs from wellness and prevention through the most complex care. Children's was named in 2000 by *U.S. News & World Report* as one of the top 10 hospitals nationwide in caring for kids, and it was the only hospital so recognized between Chicago and Los Angeles. Serving a 12-state region, Children's has been an innovator in medicine since it was founded in 1908, with firsts including the largest and most successful pediatric heart transplant program, the nation's first pediatric transport system, and the discovery of toxic shock syndrome. In 1997 it was designated as a Level I pediatric trauma center, the only one in the region devoted solely to children. Children's mission focuses on clinical care, research, education, and advocacy.

Beyond the walls of the hospital, Children's offers pediatric services throughout the metropolitan area, the state, and the twelve-state Rocky Mountain region through partnerships with other health-care institutions and clinics. Children's also operates three specialty physician satellite offices, four community-based urgent and emergency care sites, and three specialty care centers. The hospital itself handles more than 10,000 inpatient and almost 350,000 outpatient visits yearly. Children's is also affiliated with the University of Colorado Health Sciences Center to pool pediatrics expertise and enhance treatment and research.

### Denver Health Medical Center (DHMC)
**777 Bannock Street**
**(303) 436–6000**
**www.denverhealth.org**

This is Colorado's largest public hospital. It is operated by Denver Health, which also runs Community Health Services, the Rocky Mountain Poison Center, and Denver CARES Community Detoxification.

The medical center includes 398 staffed beds for a range of inpatient medical and behavioral health services. The center runs the Rocky Mountain Regional Trauma Center—the region's only Level I trauma center certified for both children and adults. It also operates Denver's 911 emergency system, paramedic services, and one of the nation's most competitive emergency medicine residency programs.

To a large extent, DHMC is the safety net for Denver residents regardless of their social or economic status. Nearly half of all charges for inpatient and outpatient services come from people without health insurance, and more than a third are from people covered by Medicaid and Medicare. DHMC also emphasizes adolescent and adult inpatient psychiatry and handles some 3,000 childbirths a year. DHMC's Rocky Mountain Regional Trauma Center serves the entire Rocky Mountain region. With more than 3,000 trauma patients annually, it is the busiest Level I trauma center in the area. Denver Health also operates 10 health centers throughout Denver and 10 student health clinics in Denver Public Schools. Denver Public Health monitors communicable diseases such as AIDS, tuberculosis, measles, and hepatitis. It operates several outpatient clinics for diagnosis and treatment of these and many other diseases. Through its Environmental Health Division, Public Health also provides a wide range of non-clinical services such as air and water pollution monitoring, restaurant inspections, licensing for day-care facilities and personal boarding-care homes, and operation of the Denver Municipal Animal Shelter.

### Denver VA Medical Center
**1055 Clermont Street**
**(303) 399–8020**
Through the VA Medical Center, the federal government delivers health services to peo-

ple who have previously served in the military. With 382 beds in use, it provides medical, surgical, neurological, rehabilitation, and psychiatric care. The center also has a 60-bed Nursing Home Care Unit and reaches out to other parts of Front Range Colorado through outlying clinics and a mobile MEDIVAN program. Among their special programs are care and treatment for aging veterans, female veterans, ex-POWs, and Vietnam-era veterans and issues relating to Agent Orange and the Persian Gulf. The center is also a major research site, the 14th largest in the Veterans Administration, with projects including a Schizophrenia Center, a VA Alcohol Research Center, and an AIDS Clinical Trial Unit.

### Exempla Saint Joseph Hospital
### 1835 Franklin Street
### (303) 837-7111
### www.saintjosephdenver.org
Denver's oldest private hospital, Saint Joseph was founded in 1873 by the Sisters of Charity of Leavenworth, Kansas, and they still sponsor it. It has been designated as one of the top 100 hospitals in the United States by the Solucient 100 Top Hospitals: Cardiovascular Benchmarks for Success survey, and it has a national reputation for the quality of its heart care. There are 565 licensed beds and 1,300 physicians. It's the busiest childbirth center in Colorado: With more than 5,000 births per year, Saint Joseph is the birthplace of 10 percent of Colorado's babies. The hospital's Maternal/Fetal Medicine program and Level III Neonatal Intensive Care Nursery ensure that babies needing extra help get the best care available before and after birth. Saint Joseph excels in other services including oncology, orthopedics, gastroenterology, and pulmonology. It also has average patient charges among the lowest of the metro area's hospitals.

### National Jewish Medical and
### Research Center
### 1400 Jackson Street
### (303) 388-4461
### www.njc.org

People with asthma and other chronic respiratory diseases come here from all over the world because National Jewish has an international reputation as a leading—if not the leading—medical center for the study and treatment of chronic respiratory diseases, allergic diseases, and immune system disorders.

National Jewish's pedigree is impressive. It is ranked among the top 10 independent biomedical research facilities in the world and is the No. 1 private institution in the world for immunology research.

One of those Denver medical centers that originated to serve tuberculosis patients, it started in 1899 with the opening of the National Jewish Hospital for Consumptives. Today this nonsectarian medical center's staff of 1,100 serves patients on a sort of modified outpatient basis, in which patients usually stay in hotels or in some cases at another hospital. One out of every five pediatric allergists in the United States was trained here.

National Jewish operates a free telephone information service, Lung Line, to answer questions and forward literature on such subjects as acute bronchitis, asthma, emphysema, and pneumonia. Call (303) 355–LUNG if you're in Colorado or·(800) 222–LUNG if you're not for the 8:00 A.M. to 4:30 P.M. service.

### Presbyterian/St. Luke's Medical Center
### 1719 East 19th Avenue
### (303) 839–6000
### www.pslmc.com
A division of HealthONE, this huge medical center has more than 1,000 affiliated physicians and more beds (680) and staff than any hospital in Greater Denver. You would be hard put to dispute its claim to being the most comprehensive health-care provider in the Rocky Mountain West, given its amazing range of services including virtually everything you would traditionally expect of a general hospital to things such as the Mother and Child Hospital, the Mothers' Milk Bank, the Sleep Disorders Center, the Colorado Gynecology and Continence Center, the Institute

for Limb Preservation, the Senior Citizen's Health Center, the Hyperbaric Medicine Center, psychiatric services, organ and tissue transplants, Addictions Recovery Centers, and a wide variety of women's and pediatric services. The list goes on and on.

The Family Birth Place has been named as one of the top 10 maternity units in the United States by *Child* magazine. Close to Pres/St. Luke's, as the locals call it, The Inn at Presbyterian, 2021 High Street, (303) 839–7150, offers convenient lodging at reasonable rates to people undergoing preadmission testing and to families of patients.

### Rose Medical Center
### 4567 East Ninth Avenue
### (303) 320–2121
### www.rosemed.com

Rose Medical Center is well-known to many Greater Denverites as the place where their children, grandchildren, nieces, and nephews were born. That's not surprising considering its emphasis on women's health services, parent education classes, infertility, and high-risk pregnancies. The Rose Breast Center performs more mammograms than any other facility in the Denver area. And the Rose Children's Center is strong on inpatient, ambulatory, and emergency services for infants, children, and adolescents. All this is not to say that Rose is just for women and children. Opened in 1949 and named after Denver World War II hero General Maurice Rose, the Medical Center provided the first comprehensive, primary-care-oriented health program designed especially for men. The special Suites at Rose continue to provide a distinctive level of care, including private chefs. Among the general list of hospital services provided by Rose's 1,100 affiliated physicians is advanced oncology research and Colorado's first coronary-care unit.

With 420 licensed beds, it was also the first adult acute-care metro medical center to formally affiliate with the nearby University of Colorado Health Sciences Center. Rose is also a teaching hospital. Other special features include a surgical treatment of emphysema program and sports medicine orthopedists, who provide care for professional and weekend athletes alike. In 1994 Rose created what it calls an orthopedic center of excellence, the Rose Institute for Joint Replacement, which is recognized for its model of full-service care. At the new Elaine and Melvin Wolf Ambulatory Surgery Building, Rose offers cosmetic and laser surgery services and a minimally invasive breast biopsy technology that is taught to physicians from around the world.

### Spalding Rehabilitation Hospital
### 900 Potomac Street
### (303) 367–1166
### www.spaldingrehab.com

Although Spalding is officially in Denver, it's actually located all over the place. The hospital's 169 licensed beds are, in fact, located at other hospitals. At each of these, Spalding operates as a wing or unit specializing in the treatment of stroke, brain injury, chronic pain, neck/back injuries, neurological disorders, multiple sclerosis, and orthopedic problems. Spalding was founded in 1965 as a stand-alone hospital but sold that facility in 1992 and went the "hospital-within-a-hospital" route to save on costs and also to bring care to people in their own communities. There is also a freestanding facility at the main Potomac location in Aurora where inpatient and outpatient specialty care is offered. Other locations include units at Presbyterian/St. Luke's Medical Center and Rose Medical Center. Spalding is a division of HealthONE.

**University of Colorado Hospital**
**4200 East Ninth Avenue**
**(303) 372-0000**
**www.uch.edu**
If the state of the medical art is what
you're looking for, it's said, a research hospital is a good place to go. University Hospital is part of the University of Colorado
Health Sciences Center. It is physically
connected with Colorado's major health-
research base, which pulls in $139 million
annually in research and training grants.
The University of Colorado, known around
here as CU, has its School of Medicine
here. The schools of nursing, pharmacy,
and dentistry are also on-site, as is the
Colorado Psychiatric Hospital. At any one
time, University Hospital provides 393
beds along with outpatient services. It
was founded in 1921, performed the
nation's first successful liver transplant,
and in 1998 was listed among top hospitals in *U.S. News & World Report.* Pushing
the medical frontiers, the hospital has
developed special expertise in areas ranging from heart surgery to cancer. Its
National Cancer Institute–designated Cancer Center, for example, does specialized
experimental cancer treatments in conjunction with its research.

Work is currently under way to move
the hospital and Health Sciences Center to
the decommissioned Fitzsimons Army Medical Center in Aurora. The first phase of the
Anschutz Inpatient Pavilion opened in
2004 as a family-focused community hospital. Subsequent phases will provide
highly specialized care, with the next due
to open in late 2006. In addition, the
Anschutz Outpatient Pavilion and the
Anschutz Cancer Pavilion are fully opera-
tional. By 2010 the UCH/UCHSC Fitzsimons
campus will consist of more than 3 million
square feet of educational, research, clinical,
and support space. The current student/fac-
ulty/staff population is expected to grow
from 8,000 to 10,000 to 15,000 by 2012.
Space at the current campus will be renovated and reallocated as the project proceeds to handle critical short-term needs.

# Adams County

**Centura St. Anthony North Hospital**
**2551 West 84th Avenue, Westminster**
**(303) 426-2151**
**www.stanthonycentral.org**
One of three major hospitals operated by
Centura Health (see St. Anthony Central,
in Denver), St. Anthony North was built in
1971 to serve the northern suburbs. This
198-bed hospital is oriented toward the
needs of young families in a growing community. The emergency room is one of the
state's busiest. Major medical specialties
include diabetes management, family
practice, pediatrics, cardiology, and
obstetrics, with advanced intermediate
and intensive-care nurseries. It also plays
an educational role, offering parent education classes, wellness seminars, obstetrics classes, sick child day care, and
health-promotion activities for businesses.

**North Suburban Medical Center**
**9191 Grant Street, Thornton**
**(303) 451-7800**
**www.northsuburban.com**
Since 1985 North Suburban has served
the north metro communities of Westminster, Northglenn, and Thornton. It now
has 157 beds, and it offers women's diagnostic and treatment services at its
Women's Center as well as diagnostic,
intervention, and rehab treatment
through its Cardiovascular Services
department. The 26-bed emergency
department is rated a Level IV trauma
center with heliport facilities and has six
beds dedicated to pediatric treatment.

**North Valley Rehabilitation Hospital**
**8451 Pearl Street, Thornton**
**(303) 288-3000**
**www.northvalleyrehab.com**
This is a comprehensive medical rehabilitation facility for adult inpatients and outpatients with traumatic brain injury, stroke,
amputation, orthopedic conditions, arthri-
tis, neurological disorders, pulmonary conditions, psychiatric disorders, or other

disabling conditions. It's a 117-bed facility near Interstate 25 just off the 84th Avenue exit. Comprehensive brain injury services include coma rehabilitation, acute brain injury rehabilitation, and neurobehavioral rehabilitation. Comprehensive rehab includes multiple trauma, neurologic, stroke, orthopedic, amputee, arthritic, and neuromuscular rehabilitation. Pulmonary rehab includes ventilator rehab, ventilator management, and pulmonary restoration. There's a substance-abuse program for people with disabilities.

### Platte Valley Medical Center
**1850 Egbert Street, Brighton**
**(303) 659-1531**
**www.pvmc.org**
Platte Valley stays busy because of its proximity to U.S. Highway 85 and Interstate 76. It's also the closest hospital to Denver International Airport. Founded as Brighton Community Hospital in 1960, it came under the management of Rocky Mountain Adventist Health Care in 1980. Although it's one of Greater Denver's smallest acute-care hospitals, it provides a solid spectrum of general hospital care ranging from coronary care and cardiac rehabilitation to perinatal and pediatric services, and it is in the process of building a completely new facility on a 50-acre campus in the Bromley Park planned community. The new hospital will be more than triple the size of the present one, with a planned build-out of three six-story buildings and more than 300 beds, transforming it into a full-scale regional medical center.

## Arapahoe County

### Centura Health Littleton
### Adventist Hospital
**7700 South Broadway, Littleton**
**(303) 730-8900**
**www.mylittletonhospital.org**
Centura Health Littleton (formerly Littleton Hospital–Porter) was opened in 1989 in response to growing development in south Greater Denver, from Littleton and Englewood to Highlands Ranch and Castle Rock. It's just north of C–470, near the intersection of Broadway and Mineral Avenue. Centura Health Littleton features services including obstetrics and gynecology, pediatrics, surgical, radiology, cardiopulmonary, rehabilitation, and 24-hour emergency care. All of its rooms are private. The hospital's Family Life Center offers a wide selection of classes and programs. This 139-licensed-bed hospital is owned by PorterCare Adventist Health System and represents an extension of the Adventist healing mission. In 2003 the hospital completed a $38 million expansion that added about 100,000 square feet to its original 210,000-square-foot structure, most in its emergency room area, but also adding a neonatal intensive care unit.

### Craig Hospital
**3425 South Clarkson Street, Englewood**
**(303) 789-8000**
**www.craighospital.org**
Craig Hospital dates from 1907, when it was started as a tuberculosis colony by Frank Craig, who himself suffered from the disease. Today Craig Hospital is dedicated exclusively to patients with spinal cord and brain injuries. It has been rated in the *U.S. News & World Report* compilation of top hospitals every year since the ratings began. Some 25,000 patients have been treated and rehabilitated since Craig converted to a rehabilitation facility in 1956. Another of those Greater Denver hospitals with an international reputation in a specialized niche, Craig pulls the majority of its patients from outside Colorado. It supports that widespread patient base with an air-transport team that flies an average of 200,000 miles a year in a specially equipped air-ambulance, a Lear jet, and other aircraft. About a mile south of the Denver border in Englewood, Craig tries to maintain a casual, home-away-from-home atmosphere because it's a long-stay hospital that encourages family involvement in a patient's progress. In 1996 Craig opened a

$10 million addition to the hospital known as the Transitional Care Facility. In 2002 it added a new outpatient and family housing facility, and in 2003 it built an in-house cell center for clinical research trials. In these apartment-like units, patients during the last phase of their inpatient stay can work on adjusting to independent life. The units are designed to hold the patient's family members as well, so family can help with the adjustment. Acute-care patients can be managed almost immediately after injury by Craig physicians and therapists in neurotrauma units at adjacent Swedish Medical Center and at St. Anthony Hospital Central in Denver. The hospital is licensed for 93 beds.

### The Medical Center of Aurora
### 1501 South Potomac Street, Aurora
### (303) 695-2600
### www.auroramed.com

Aurora's only full-service hospital, this facility consists of three campuses: the Main campus, the North campus, and the Centennial campus. The center as a whole employs nearly 1,200 people and is licensed for 346 beds.

The Main campus hosts among other things a Level II trauma center, the Women's Center, and the Colorado Spine Center. The North campus includes the Sleep Disorders Center and the Geriatric Psychiatry/Senior Care Center. The Centennial campus has day-surgery services, imaging and lab services, and the Broncos Sports Medicine and Rehabilitation Center.

### Sky Ridge Medical Center
### 10101 RidgeGate Parkway, Lone Tree
### (720) 225-1000
### www.skyridgemedcenter.com

Sky Ridge is metro Denver's newest campus, covering 57 acres and serving residents of Highlands Ranch, Lone Tree, Parker, Castle Rock, and Littleton. It opened in 2003, and staff delivered its first baby 52 minutes later. The facility has 156 beds and maintains a Level III trauma center, with 24-hour emergency care and orthopedic surgeons. It also provides cardiac services, has a cancer center and a sports medicine and rehabilitation center, and provides women's and children's services. Sky Ridge also advertises its sleep disorders, bariatric surgery, and complementary/alternative medicine services.

### Swedish Medical Center
### 501 East Hampden Avenue, Englewood
### (303) 788-5000
### www.swedishhospital.com

A division of HealthONE, Swedish serves as a regional center for the most complex trauma, neurological, and infertility cases. Swedish received the Consumer-Choice-Quality-Leader Award four years in a row between 1996 and 2000, and in 2002 it was ranked among Solucient's Top 100 Hospitals. Because it shares its campus with two major regional rehab hospitals, Craig Hospital and Spalding Hospital, it is well positioned to provide continuum care for victims of spinal cord injury, stroke, neurological disorders, and complex orthopedic problems. Critical health care includes cardiovascular and pulmonary services, oncology services, and emergency and trauma services. Special facilities include the Women's Center and the Oncology Center. The Laser Clinic has state-of-the-art treatment for removing port-wine stains, spider veins, birthmarks, moles, tattoos, etc.

## Jefferson County

### Exempla Lutheran Medical Center
### 8300 West 38th Avenue, Wheat Ridge
### (303) 425-4500
### www.exempla.org

This community-owned nonprofit health system was founded in 1905. In recent years it has rated among the top 100 hospitals in the nation. Lutheran offers a variety of outpatient and community outreach programs in addition to a 409-bed hospital, inpatient and outpatient psychiatric services, a rehabilitation center, a

skilled nursing unit, a residence for seniors, and a full-service home-care and
hospice division.

Lutheran has a long-standing reputation for providing high-quality, low-cost
health care and stressing preventive
medicine. It owns and operates a wide
spectrum of integrated health services.
Recently opened was the new Family
Birth Center that provides support and
education in all aspects of birthing and
family planning with a holistic approach.
Lutheran partners with Rocky Mountain
Radiologists, P.C. and Nordstrom department stores to operate a mammography
center at the Park Meadows shopping
center.

Lutheran offers a program called EZ
Care, a community-based health service
designed to meet the needs of the homeless and those with inadequate or no
insurance. Its Youth Education Alliance for
Health is a collaborative effort with the
public-school system to enhance science
curricula and improve health and wellness
behaviors.

## MENTAL HEALTH

**Adams County Mental Health Center**
**8931 Huron Street, Thornton**
**(303) 853-3500**
**www.adamsmentalhealth.org**
Founded in 1957 this center has been
serving Adams County residents with
emergency and outpatient mental-health
needs. About 4,000 people a year receive
treatment for such things as anxiety disorders, substance abuse, and family issues.
It also has five outpatient offices in the
Adams County area.

**Aurora Community Mental Health Center**
**14301 East Hampden Avenue, Aurora**
**(303) 617-2300**
**www.aumhc.org**
Thousands of people a year receive
help from Aurora Community Mental
Health's six counseling centers and
six residential facilities and through

the Aurora and Cherry Creek school
districts. Services include counseling
for depression, older adults, divorce,
parenting, drugs, and alcohol and group
therapies. Also offered are residential
services from overnight to long-term
adjustments.

**Colorado Mental Health Institute**
**at Fort Logan**
**3520 West Oxford Avenue**
**(303) 866-7066**
**www.cdhs.state.co.us/ohr/mhs/mif/**
**index.html**
This is the state psychiatric hospital,
charged with providing treatment and
services for the mentally ill. It was
founded in 1961 and has 410 staff members. Fort Logan houses the statewide
program for all deaf and hearing-impaired
clients with mental illness. Areas of
specialty fall in three treatment divisions:
children and adolescents, adult psychiatry,
and geriatrics. An inpatient-only facility
with 153 inpatient and 20 residential beds,
this hospital is based on a treatment team
approach—a patient's team consists of a
psychiatrist, a psychologist, a social
worker, psychiatric nurses, and mental-
health clinicians. The team also has special-
education teachers for children and
adolescents.

**Comitis Crisis Center**
**9840 East 17th Avenue, Aurora**
**(303) 343-9890**
This privately owned nonprofit has been
serving youth awaiting placement into
permanent residential homes since 1971.
Comitis is a short-term residential care
facility with a small emergency housing
area for homeless kids. It helps get people
off the streets and into low-income housing. Its main mission is to care for runaway
and throwaway kids.

**Denver Alcohol, Drug & Psychiatric Care**
**Emergency**
**777 Bannock Street**
**(303) 436-6266**
This is the emergency psychiatric facility

for Denver Health Medical Center. The center is open 24 hours to serve people who come to DHMC and are referred for a variety of mental health reasons, including drug and alcohol abuse and crisis situations.

## Devereux/Cleo Wallace Center
**8405 Church Ranch Boulevard**
**Westminster**
**(303) 466-7391**
**www.devereux.org**

Devereux/Cleo Wallace Center is Colorado's largest and most comprehensive behavioral health-care organization dedicated to the treatment of psychiatric, emotional, and behavioral problems in children and adolescents. Cleo Spurlock Wallace was a local schoolteacher who saw a need for special services for troubled youth, which was why she started the center in 1943. The center provides an inpatient hospital, residential facilities, day treatment, and outpatient services for children and adolescents with behavioral health concerns and for their families. In all, the center has 112 beds. It runs a school certified by the Colorado Department of Education, each classroom having both a teacher and a paraprofessional to integrate treatment into education. Devereux/Cleo Wallace is accredited by the Joint Commission on the Accreditation of Health Care Organizations. John Wayne used to come here for fundraising events; he was a member of the Sigma Chi fraternity, which selected Cleo's hospital and school as its special charity.

## Jefferson Center for Mental Health
**5265 Vance Street, Arvada**
**(303) 425-0300**
**www.jeffersonmentalhealth.org**

A wide variety of mental-health services are offered, including counselors in schools, an older adult program, several residential areas for inpatient services, and 24-hour emergency services. In all, Jefferson Center operates 16 satellite locations in Jefferson, Gilpin, and Clear Creek Counties.

# ALTERNATIVE AND HOLISTIC HEALTH

The alternative health scene is growing and gaining notice—and credibility—in Greater Denver. In fact, Denver has more professionals than most comparably sized cities. And nearby Boulder is well-known for its array of alternative healers.

Colorado's alternative health doctors got a boost in 1997 when the state legislature passed a law protecting the ability of M.D.'s to do business by prohibiting the state medical board from disciplining doctors merely for practicing alternative medicine. The stamp of credibility was seen as a sign from lawmakers that alternative medicine is a viable option for thousands of people across the state.

Alternative medicine is generally defined as anything outside the mainstream of Western medicine. Services generally include herbology, acupuncture, massage, counseling, hypnotherapy, nutrition, hydrotherapy, reflexology, homeopathy, and chiropractics. Holistic is an approach to healing that views the patient as a whole being with a diverse life and range of reasons for ill-health. Holistic practitioners look for the interconnections of a person's health—not just the source of one given problem.

Colorado doesn't have any central listing of alternative practitioners, nor is there a yellow pages listing under "Alternative." But there is a yellow pages section under "Holistic Practitioners" with several listings, and practitioners tend to be a close-knit group with knowledge of each other's expertise. People in search of recommendations can try the ones listed or can contact one of the seasoned pros at local Wild Oats and Whole Foods markets, grocery stores known for vast offerings of natural foods, vitamins, medicines, and friendly staffs who dispense advice on holistic health. The stores also are a good source of publications, from national magazines to local advertising supplements, on alternative healing.

As with many states, Colorado has varying requirements for alternative practi-

tioners. Depending on the specialty, one may be required to be licensed, certified, or registered. The following listings are recommended as organizations committed to professionalism and overall health.

**Bridges Integrative Health Services**
**8550 West 38th Avenue, Suite 200**
**Wheat Ridge**
**(303) 425–2262**
**www.bridgesforhealth.org**
Bridges is the only hospital-based center of its kind in the Denver metro area. It is a joint project of Exempla Healthcare and Lutheran Medical Center Community Foundation. Services range from massage and acupuncture to nutrition counseling, holistic counseling, and a wellness nurse consultation. Its mission is to offer complementary therapies that can be combined with traditional medicine, offering patients the best of both worlds and nourishing the mind, body, and soul. All

practitioners meet the professional credential standards for their specialties.

Bridges also offers classes and workshops to the public, including yoga and meditation, as well as lectures on complementary healing topics.

**East West Health Centers Inc.**
**8200 East Belleview, Suite 280**
**Greenwood Village**
**(303) 694–5757**
**www.east-west-health.com**
This center includes more than 20 practitioners, including an internist and family physician, with both Eastern and Western specialties. Western-services include family and sports medicine, preventive medicine, geriatric care, physical therapy, counseling, and OB-GYN. Eastern offerings include acupuncture, herbology, naturopathy, chiropractics, massage, Rolfing, nutrition education, exercise prescription, and stress management.

# RETIREMENT 🌴

Forget Wednesday-night bingo and mashed potatoes in a dingy dining room. Today's retirement homes are called communities for a reason: They offer residents a place to recreate, socialize, and thrive.

Denver's offerings are no exception to the standard that retirement communities should be enticing to those who call them home. Brochures are more likely to sound like a pitch for a vacation than a place to grow old. Auditoriums, fitness centers, restaurants, and swimming pools are only a few of the amenities. And with the older generation getting stronger and more prevalent—Denver's age-60-and-older population is expected to climb 13 percent by 2013—housing options are getting better.

Greater Denver isn't exactly a retirement mecca on par with Arizona or Florida. But its sunny, mild climate (belied by our rare but news-making blizzards) has lured thousands over the years, including seniors who want to be closer to relatives or who end their careers in colorful Colorado.

The city and county of Denver has by far the greatest number of independent and assisted-living facilities for seniors in the area, but when you seek word-of-mouth recommendations, Denver's outlying areas, and especially the suburban counties, tend to get the most praise. That may not be fair to Denver's senior communities. It may simply say more about life being more difficult for the elderly in an urban setting.

There are a variety of information sources to aid your decision. Referral agencies, such as **Community Housing Services,** (303) 831–4046, are a good place to start. Community Housing Services provides free housing referrals to use as a start in comparing costs, availability, and other factors. Another good one is

**Senior Housing Options,** (303) 595–4464, a nonprofit corporation that owns and manages assisted-living properties and HUD-subsidized properties.

You can do your own word-of-mouth research by asking other seniors you meet in groups, such as the **American Association of Retired Persons,** (303) 830–2277, and the **Association for Senior Citizens,** (303) 455–9642. The **Aging Services Division of the Denver Regional Council of Governments,** (303) 480–6734, offers information and referral services for seniors, as well as a Nursing Home Ombudsman Program. You can hobnob with seniors at any of Greater Denver's numerous senior centers. For other senior tips as well as just a lot of good ideas about enjoying the area, you might take a look at *Uniquely Denver: A Discovery Guide to the Mile High City for Those Over 50,* written by Virginia Brey and published by American Source Books, Lakewood, Colorado. You might also get a copy of *The Denver Business Journal Book of Lists,* an annual publication of the *Denver Business Journal,* (303) 837–3500. We've mentioned it before as a great resource for all kinds of area information. One of its lists ranks the top 25 retirement communities.

The *Seniors Blue Book* is another source of information for seniors in the Denver metro area. Call (303) 393–1971, or try their Web site at www.seniorsresource guide.com.

Once you know what part of Greater Denver you'd like to live in and have some communities in mind, call their sales offices for brochures and information packages. Then check them out in person. Arriving around meal time gives you a sense of the staff and how well it relates to residents. Of course, most communities have marketing representatives eager to give guided tours.

Vital to picking the right place is the surrounding neighborhood: whether it's clean, pleasant, and quiet; whether there are parks and shopping within walking distance; and whether the surroundings are congenial to the elderly. Greater Denver's four-lane traffic arteries such as Wadsworth Boulevard can be tough to negotiate, even for speed-walking teenagers. A more docile setting might be best for those with difficulties moving around.

The following entries represent the more-talked-about examples of retirement communities in Greater Denver. But by no means is the list comprehensive or meant to suggest other places aren't equally good. We have tended to look specifically at places with independent and assisted living in which seniors have their own homes or apartments. These are the midrange of a spectrum of senior living and care options ranging from nursing homes to prestigious single-family developments. Assisted living simply means that assistance is available for such needs as medication reminders; help with dressing, grooming, and bathing; close-by medical and health monitoring; laundry; in-apartment meal services; and rehabilitation programs. Typically, both independent and assisted-living units have call buttons at strategic locations so residents can summon help if needed.

Overall, these senior living communities resemble moderate to upscale apartments or condominiums. The difference is in the community feel, which places more emphasis on communal dining and gathering areas, shared activities, and services. Typically, at least one meal is included in rent, although this may vary. Housekeeping is a fairly standard service. Virtually every community listed here offers a calendar of social activities, many have their own newsletters, and all of them have their own transportation services to area shopping and other attractions. Residents are likely to have their own garage or carport space and storage lockers. Perhaps best of all, someone else cleans the bathroom and does the dishes!

## RETIREMENT COMMUNITIES

### Alterra Villas at Canterbury
**11265 East Mississippi Avenue, Aurora**
**(303) 341-1412**
**www.brookdaleliving.com/brookdale 2004**

Canterbury was the first independent- and assisted-living community for seniors in Aurora when it opened in the late 1970s, and some of the pioneer residents are still there. It consists of two-story structures built around two ponds in a landscaped courtyard with a gazebo. They have 200 unfurnished private or shared one- and two-bedroom apartments for seniors, with on-site meals. This community actually consists of two sections: Alterra Villas at Canterbury, the independent-living section, and Alterra Wynwood at Canterbury, which is assisted living.

Canterbury is owned and operated by Brookdale of Chicago, a company that specializes in developing and managing retirement communities. The community includes a fireside lounge, library, TV and movie living area, a beauty/barber shop, a full-service dining room with soup and salad bar, private dining, complimentary van service for scheduled trips, an ice-cream cart, guest apartments, and a hobby and crafts room.

### Cherry Creek Retirement Village
**14555 East Hampden Avenue, Aurora**
**(303) 693-0200**
**www.americanlifestyles.com/colorado_cherrycreek.htm**

Cherry Creek has a nice location in a residential neighborhood, across the street from Aurora's public Meadow Hills Golf Course. The village is in a three-story, buff-colored building with a large circular drive and two atriums for relaxing and entertaining.

Some apartments have patios or balconies. Every unit has a window over the kitchen sink that looks out into one of the halls. They have 30 assisted-living and 185 retirement apartments. Monthly rent covers amenities ranging from continental breakfast and weekly housekeeping to excursions. Meals and other amenities are available at a nominal charge. The village has card and game rooms, an exercise room, library, country store, billiards, an arts and crafts area, restaurant-style dining, and a private dining room. Independent and assisted living are provided. Cherry Creek Retirement Village is owned by American Lifestyles, Cleveland, Tennessee.

### The Courtyard at Lakewood
**7100 West 13th Avenue, Lakewood**
**(303) 239-0740**
**www.holidaytouch.com**
Three blocks east of Wadsworth Boulevard and a couple blocks south of Colfax Avenue in Lakewood, the Courtyard is in a quiet residential neighborhood. Every apartment in the three-story building has a view of the center courtyard, where there are flowers, rock gardens, and a pond. The Courtyard is managed by two husband-and-wife teams who live on the premises.

Beyond the living quarters, the Courtyard's amenities include a giant-screen TV room, large kitchen for group activities, beauty shop, library, billiards areas, and a spa. They have 122 apartments. The Courtyard is owned by Holiday Retirement Corporation.

### Dayton Place
**1950 South Dayton Street**
**(303) 751-5150**
**www.daytonplace.com**
Dayton Place is on the western edge of the city of Aurora's south side, just off Parker Road, a major thoroughfare that runs northwest to Denver and southeast past the Cherry Creek Reservoir State Recreation Area. It is a three-story complex with an open feel, in part due to its suburban location and perhaps in part due to its setback on large grounds with meandering walkways, gardens, and outdoor patios. Dayton has a general store, chapel, beauty and barber shop, TV lounges, a billiards room, and a cards and

*Check the fine print when looking for a retirement home. Some communities require long-term leases and large down payments, while others are month-to-month. Decide what's best for you, then take the time to ask good questions.*

activities room. The have 96 assisted-living and 104 independent-living units.

### Harvard Square Retirement Community
**10200 East Harvard Avenue**
**(303) 696-0622**
**www.leisurecare.com**
Harvard Square's interiors are bright and open yet reminiscent of the club spaces in an Ivy League university, with dark wood and formal, old world style. They maintain 189 private, unfurnished rooms. The exterior and grounds—overlooked by a second-story deck—also exude a country club air. Harvard Square is in the northwest corner of Denver's Hampden Heights neighborhood, just west of Aurora near the pleasant green spaces of Babi Yar Park and the private Los Verdes Golf Club. Although it's basically an independent-living community, it has a formal Assisted Living Program managed by a professional social worker with nursing support. Under the same roof, Harvard Square also includes a dining room, beauty and barber shop, game room, library, and multipurpose room.

### Heritage Club
**2020 South Monroe Street**
**(303) 756-0025**
**www.elderlivingsource.com/facilities/co/heritage.php**
Heritage Club has a good reputation for elegant living at affordable prices. The apartments are luxurious. The dining room looks like something in an upscale downtown restaurant with a menu to match, and there's a private dining room for special occasions. Heritage Club has a private library, exercise room with whirlpool and spa, country store and ice-cream parlor, billiards room, cards and games room, arts

and crafts studio, and a beauty and barber shop plus shuffleboard, a putting
green, and horseshoes pit. The bay windows and balconies are nice features, and
the community is in the University Park
neighborhood, a pleasant part of the city
southwest of Colorado Boulevard's intersection with Interstate 25.

**Meridian**
**10695 West 17th Avenue, Lakewood**
**(303) 232-7100**

**1805 South Balsam Street, Lakewood**
**(303) 980-5500**

**9555 West 59th Avenue, Arvada**
**(303) 425-1900**

**3455 South Corona Street, Englewood**
**(303) 761-0300**
**www.meridians.com**
Denver's western suburbs in Jefferson
County have the largest number of retirement communities. One of the most
extensive retirement-residence organizations that gets mentioned in a positive
light is Meridian, which has four retirement
communities in Greater Denver. All are
owned by LeGan Corporation, a Denver
company that also owns a Meridian in
Boulder. Each is managed independently,
but all are essentially the same: nicely
appointed buildings on campus-like settings, with elegant interiors and formal
furniture. The only major difference is that
the Lakewood Meridian and the Englewood Meridian have nursing-home sections, while the other two have
independent and assisted living only.

**Parkplace**
**111 Emerson Street**
**(303) 744-0400**
**www.arclp.com**
In the heart of Denver, this 18-story
independent- and assisted-living facility
resembles one of those quiet, elegant
hotels that get known by word-of-mouth.
Its elegance is immediately apparent in
the dark wood and rich upholstery of the
lobby, lounge, and formal dining room,

and the atmosphere is maintained
throughout. It's next to Hungarian Freedom Park on the south side of Speer
Boulevard, south of Denver's downtown
and not far from the Cherry Creek shopping area. The Cherry Creek greenbelt and
its pedestrian/bicycle path runs along
Speer Boulevard out front. Parkplace has
an indoor swimming pool with a hot tub,
exercise room, convenience store, beauty
and barber shop, library, card lounge,
patio dining area, and auditorium.

Parkplace is owned and managed by
American Retirement Corporation, Brent-
wood, Tennessee.

**Porter Place**
**1001 East Yale Avenue**
**(303) 765-6802**
**www.porterplace.org**
Porter Place is on the campus of Porter-
Care Hospital in Denver's University Park
neighborhood on the northernmost edge
of Englewood. In addition to independent
and assisted living (with studio, one-
bedroom, and two-bedroom apartments),
it offers small studio apartments for visiting family and friends of residents, and
the facility offers respite care. Porter Place
is affiliated with PorterCare Hospital, Centura Health, and PorterCare Hospital–
Littleton, but that doesn't mean it looks
like a medical facility. The interiors are
lovely, from the grand piano and high ceilings of the lobby to the pleasant tranquil-
ity of the library. There are flower gardens
and outdoor patios, activity rooms, a
chapel, gift shop, beauty and barber shop,
big-screen TV room, parlor, card room,
and craft room. Plus residents have access
to the hospital's Porter Health Club. A
recently completed addition provides
assisted living in a secure environment,
called Memory Care, in the Elizabeth Rose
Wing.

**Shalom Park Senior Residences**
**14800 East Bellevue Drive, Aurora**
**(303) 680-5000**
**www.shalompark.org**
One of Greater Denver's newest retire-

ment additions is Shalom Park Senior Residences. The 41-acre community offers residents lovely grounds to mill around on as well as an in-house activity department to keep them entertained. There are a total of 104 units, including 44 patio homes and 60 apartments. Any of the 104 units can be assisted or independent living, depending on the needs of the occupants.

### Springwood Retirement Campus
### 6550 Yank Way, Arvada
### (303) 424-6550
### www.springwoodretirement.com

The Springwood Retirement Campus is a "beautiful facility," and that's according to an administrator of a competing retirement community. It's just off Yankee Doodle Park in a nice residential section of Arvada. Facilities and services include a full-time social director, dining room, maid service, laundry and dry cleaning, general store, library, chapel, hair salon, game room, and exercise facility. Nightingale Lane, a new Alzheimer's ward with 28 beds, opened in 2003. Lutheran Medical Center provides input to Springwood's health-care and health-promoting activities.

Springwood offers a variety of one- and two-bedroom apartments, with two-way intercom and emergency buzzers; it also offers assisted living at its Nightingale Suites. The cottages at Springwood are 1,100-square-foot residences built on a private cul-de-sac. Each includes a foyer, liv-

*If you're in the market for a retirement community, start early. Allow yourself up to a year to compare and visit locations, especially if you need a large space. Many communities have waiting lists for two-bedroom units, which are tougher to come by.*

ing room, dining room, covered patio, master bedroom with its own bath and oversize walk-in closet, guest bedroom, second bathroom, laundry and utility room, and attached garage.

### Sunny Acres
### 2501 East 104th Avenue, Thornton
### (303) 452-4181
### www.centuraseniors.org

Perhaps the most oft-recommended retirement community by word-of-mouth, Sunny Acres is a large facility on a campuslike setting just south of Stonehocker Park in Thornton. The northern suburbs are quiet areas with good mountain views and a lot of remaining open space, and the landscaped grounds include two fishing lakes as well as gardening areas for residents. To that Sunny Acres adds amenities including home health care, 10 libraries, a 3,000-square-foot fitness center, a whirlpool, pool tables, a woodworking and carpentry shop, lounges, dining rooms including a restaurant, a convenience store, and beauty and barber shops.

# MEDIA

Greater Denver is not exactly a media center, at least not in the sense of New York or Los Angeles. It doesn't produce a lot of television programs or magazines, though it does occasionally show up in movies. Still, at least in part because Greater Denver is home to telecommunications industry giants Jones Intercable and Tele-Communications Inc., it may very well become a major stop on the information highway.

## NEWSPAPERS

Denver was among the last U.S. cities to have two independent newspapers. That changed in 2001 following the approval of a joint operating agreement between the *Denver Post* and the *Rocky Mountain News.* The agreement brought to an end the bitter circulation and advertising rivalry that had contributed to the *News* sustaining more than $100 million in losses in the 1990s. Under the agreement, circulation and advertising is handled by the newly formed Denver Newspaper Agency, of which each paper is 50 percent owner.

Both the *Post* and the *News* continue to publish their papers Monday through Friday. On Saturday the *News* is responsible for the editorial content of a joint edition, while on Sunday the *Post* is responsible for that content.

Hate it or love it, many Denverites pick up *Westword,* the city's weekly arts and entertainment paper. Why not?—it's free and has comprehensive lists of what's going on around town.

There are also many community

papers, too numerous to list here. Specialized publications are always coming into and going out of existence to serve a particular region (downtown) or interest (art).

## Dailies

### *The Denver Post*
**1560 Broadway**
**(303) 820–1010**
**www.denverpost.com**
The *Denver Post* has a long and colorful history. It was founded in 1895 by Harry Heye Tammen and Frederick Gilmer Bonfils. The early *Post* was a prime example of sensational journalism, relying on stunts and gossip to attract readership. In the 1920s Tammen and Bonfils got themselves entangled in one fine mess, the Teapot Dome scandal. Originally vehemently opposed to questionable oil leases in Wyoming, the *Post* dropped the issue when paid to do so. Tammen died of cancer in 1924, and Bonfils resigned in 1926.

After Bonfils died in 1933, ownership passed largely to his daughters. In the 1960s May Bonfils sold her stock to S. I. Newhouse, head of a chain of newspapers and magazines. Helen Bonfils contested the sale, and after years of litigation, Newhouse finally dropped his bid to gain control of the *Post* in 1973.

The *Post* was sold to the Times Mirror Company, owners of the *Los Angeles Times,* in 1980, and sold again to William Dean Singleton of the Denver-based MediaNews Group in 1987.

The *Post* switched from evening to morning distribution in 1982. Notable *Post* columnists include sportswriters Woody Paige and Jim Armstrong, news columnist Diane Carman, and society man-about-town Bill Husted. Daily circulation for the *Post* is about 265,000; Sunday circulation is 750,000.

i *Gardeners love the special "Grow" supplement in Friday's* **The Denver Post,** *published beginning in April and running through midsummer.*

## Rocky Mountain News
400 West Colfax Avenue
(303) 892-5000
www.rockymountainnews.com
The first issue of *Rocky Mountain News*—four pages, 500 copies—came out in 1859, published by William N. Byers. In 1901, the first year that accurate measurements could be made, the upstart *Denver Evening Post* surpassed *Rocky Mountain News* in circulation for the first time. Until their recent merger, the two papers battled for readership and advertising. The *News* was purchased in 1926 by Scripps-Howard during a decade of particularly acrimonious competition, and in 1928, having disposed of or incorporated their other competitors, the *Post* and the *News* called a truce. But in 1993, when the *News* temporarily dropped the price of its Sunday issue from 75 cents to 25 cents, Greater Denver saw the return of the kind of drastic price-cutting that characterized the 1920s. This price war finally ended in 2001 when the two papers came to a joint operating agreement, merging their advertising and circulation operations.

The *News* is generally more conservative in its editorial viewpoints than the *Post,* but this varies depending on the topic.

The Saturday *News* is best known for its "Spotlight" and "Home Front" sections. Popular columnists include city columnists Tina Griego and Mike Litwin, sports columnists Dave Krieger and Tracy Ringolsby, and movie reviewer Robert Denerstein. Daily circulation is about 265,000; Saturday's is about 600,000.

## Weeklies

In addition to the following non-dailies, weekly newspapers are published for residents of Englewood, Highlands Ranch, Littleton, Evergreen, Golden, Greenwood Village, and Westminster. If you live there or are interested in news about those communities, check for these papers at local newsstands.

## Broomfield Enterprise
1006 Depot Hill Road, Suite G
Broomfield
(303) 466-3636
www.dailycamera.com/bdc/broomfield
This community paper is owned by the Colorado Publishing Co., a partnership of the E. W. Scripps Company and MediaNews Group Inc., which publishes the *Daily Camera,* Boulder's daily newspaper. The *Enterprise* is delivered free to Broomfield residences and businesses and carries news of Broomfield, Greater Denver's most northwestern community. Regular offerings include news and feature stories, editorials, and classified ads. Coverage is strong on government, business, schools, and sports. The paper also publishes special sections ranging from homes and gardens to election issues.

## Denver Business Journal
1700 Broadway, #515
(303) 837-3500
www.bizjournals.com/denver
The weekly *Denver Business Journal* covers local business news in depth and includes a small-business strategy section, along with specialized sections that relate to a variety of topics from health care to personal finance. The paper comes out on Friday and is available by subscription or throughout metro Denver by single copy.

## Mile High Newspapers
1000 10th Sreet, Golden
(303) 279-5541
www.jeffconews.com
This company publishes weekly newspapers for residents of Arvada, Lakewood, Golden, and Wheat Ridge and an online edition. The papers focus on news relevant to these suburbs and include quarterly education sections and a yearly garden insert.

## Westword
969 Broadway
(303) 296-7744
www.westword.com

Owned by Village Voice Media, a national publisher of "alternative" papers, *Westword* is known for its muckraking investigative stories and is depended upon for its arts and entertainment coverage. Not everyone admires the weekly paper's zeal in pursuing stories, as is evidenced by heated letters to the editor. But at least a dozen of its articles, such as an investigation of the Rocky Flats grand jury proceedings that examined who should be held responsible for environmental crimes, have won awards and national media attention.

*Westword* is distributed free throughout Greater Denver and hits the streets late Wednesday afternoon. You can find it in boxes on street corners all over town. Its arts/dining/entertainment listings are superb.

## MAGAZINES AND SPECIAL-INTEREST PUBLICATIONS

### Colorado Expressions
**New West Publishing**
**3600 South Beeler Street, Suite 100**
**(303) 694-1289**
Poised somewhere in terms of longevity between *Colorado Homes & Lifestyles* and *5280* is *Colorado Expressions.* Every issue features a comprehensive "Dining Guide." And every issue celebrates the Colorado lifestyle—from winter activities to cultural outings.

### Colorado Homes & Lifestyles
### Colorado Business Magazine
**Wiesner Publishing**
**7009 South Potomac Street, Englewood**
**(303) 397-7600**
**www.coloradohomesmag.com**
Two magazines with long track records are *Colorado Homes & Lifestyles* and *Colorado Business Magazine,* both Wiesner publications. *Colorado Homes & Lifestyles,* published nine times a year, not only includes a wealth of information about home and garden design, but also person-

ality profiles of Colorado residents. The monthly *Colorado Business Magazine* surveys the movers and shakers in the state, with an emphasis on Denver.

### Colorado Parent Magazine
**5460 South Quebec Street, Suite 130**
**Greenwood Village**
**(303) 320-1000**
**www.colorado.parenthood.com**
This magazine includes a comprehensive calendar of events and lists classes of interest to parents in the Greater Denver area. The free paper comes out the first of each month and can be picked up in about 800 different locations around town, including libraries and bookstores. The folks at *Colorado Parent* also publish an annual A-to-Z directory of local resources for parents each January.

### 5280
**1514 Curtis Street, Suite 300**
**(303) 832-5280**
**www.5280.com**
Denver has seen its share of city magazines come and go. The new kid on the block, *5280,* "Denver's Mile-High Magazine," debuted in 1993. (For those who don't know, 5,280 feet equals a mile.) It's fresh and independent and has a lively design like any city magazine. It covers things of interest to locals—restaurants, getaways, and interesting people. *5280* is published bimonthly.

### High Country News
**119 Grand Avenue, Paonia**
**(970) 527-4898**
**www.hcn.org**
An environmentally oriented newspaper, *High Country News* is published in Paonia, Colorado. The much-praised paper focuses on issues intrinsic to the West, such as use of public lands and water and grazing rights. This sharp biweekly is highly recommended to Greater Denver newcomers who would like to know more about the region they now call home. It's available at the Tattered Cover Book Store

(see our Shopping chapter) and other locations throughout the city, or call for a subscription.

***Out Front Colorado***
**723 Sherman Street**
**(303) 778–7900**
**www.outfrontcolorado.com**
A gay and lesbian newspaper, *Out Front Colorado* is published every two weeks (with a break at Christmas). The paper is free and is available at local bars, restaurants, gay businesses, and bookstores. It's noted for its entertainment and nightlife listings. Mail subscription is available for a small charge.

# RADIO

Nothing but the Rocky Mountain weather changes as much as Denver radio stations. One day you're listening to jazz; the next day the station has gone country-western. Consider that caveat when tuning in to the stations listed below. For an up-to-date list, check the TV section in the Sunday *Denver Post*.

## ADULT CONTEMPORARY
KIMN 100.3 FM
KOSI 101.1 FM
KALC 105.9 FM

## CLASSICAL
KVOD 90.1 FM

## COUNTRY
KCKK 1600 AM
KYGO 98.5 FM
KCUV 102.3 FM (alt.)

## CHRISTIAN
KLTT 670 AM
KPOF 910 AM
KRKS 990 AM and 94.7 FM

## HIP-HOP
KQKS 107.5 FM

## JAZZ
KUVO 89.3 FM
KJCD 104.3 FM

## MEXICAN/SPANISH
KMXA 1090 AM
KBNO 1280 AM
KLVZ 1220 AM
KXPK 96.5 FM

## NATIONAL PUBLIC RADIO
KCFR 1340 AM
KGNU 88.5 FM

## NEWS/TALK/SPORTS
KHOW 630 AM
KNUS 710 AM
KKZN 760 AM
KOA 850 AM

## OLDIES
KEZW 1430 AM
KRFX 103.5 FM (classic rock)
KXKL 105.1 FM (1960s–1970s)

## ROCK AND PROGRESSIVE
KTCL 93.3 FM
KBCO 97.3 FM
KQMT 99.5 FM
KBPI 106.7 FM

## SPORTS ONLY
KLZ 560 AM (ESPN)
KKFN 950 AM

# TELEVISION

With all the recent mergers and acquisitions in the cable industry, Denver is down to one main cable TV supplier for most of the metropolitan area. Call Comcast at (303) 930–2001 for service information for your area. An alternative to cable is satellite TV. DirecTV operates its national direct-satellite service out of Castle Rock, about a half hour south of Denver. Call (800) 709–5333 for information. The area's other provider is Echo Star, in Englewood, (888) 825-2557

# Major Local TV Stations and Network Affiliates

KWGN Channel 2 (Independent/WB)
KCNC Channel 4 (CBS)
KRMA Channel 6 (PBS)
KMGH Channel 7 (ABC)
KUSA Channel 9 (NBC)
KBDI Channel 12 (PBS)
KTVD Channel 20 (Independent/UPN)

KDVR Channel 31 (Fox)
KRMT Channel 41 (Independent)
KCEC Channel 50 (Univision)
KWHD Channel 53 (Independent)
KTBN Channel 57 (Trinity)
KMAS Channels 63 and 67 (Telemundo)

# Religious Television Programming

The sermon from the Riverside Baptist Church, 2401 East Alcott Street, (303) 433-8665, is broadcast by KXPC-59 at 9:00 A.M. each Sunday. Check local listings for other religious programming.

# WORSHIP ●

Drive around town on Sunday and chances are you'll find church parking lots full. Denver is definitely a "church town," but in a most laid-back and casual way. Denverites are not only observant (our church attendance average is right up there with national numbers) but also open to new and different spiritual experiences. From traditional services to religious seminars, we fill our spiritual coffers in a variety of ways.

Denver offers every major denomination as well as most of the smaller ones. Catholics make up the largest denomination, though their presence is not a dominant force. Still, with the installation of Archbishop Charles Chaput in April 1997, the Denver Catholic community is likely to enjoy some national attention. Chaput, who is part Native American, is gregarious, a people person, and the kind of religious leader, Insiders say, who will establish himself as a mover and shaker in the national Catholic Church.

Every branch of Protestantism is also represented, and Denver has active Jewish, Buddhist, Muslim, and Mormon communities as well. Chances are, no matter what your beliefs, Denver will have a congregation to satisfy you.

This is truly an ecumenical city—one where a great deal of collegiality exists among different faiths. When graffiti on a synagogue made local news, Christians and Muslims took little time to publicly show their outrage. Denverites are church consumers. They shop around, looking for a good fit. And churches here have responded to that trend by being open and hospitable.

Denver's religious diversity dates from before Colorado was a state; by the time of statehood in 1876, 20 religious denominations had been organized in the city. St. Joseph Hospital, the first of Denver's many church-affiliated hospitals, was founded in 1873, and Jews and Catholics as well as many Protestants were conducting services in and around Denver at that time. Present-day Congregation Emanuel can trace its beginnings from its incorporation in 1874 and, even before that, to the establishment of the Hebrew Burial Society in 1859. Similarly, enough Catholics were in Colorado during the territorial period that the Rocky Mountains were removed from the authority of Santa Fe and recognized as a separate vicariate in 1868. The first bishop of Denver, Joseph Machebeuf, was consecrated in 1887.

Today that diversity still prevails, and Denver is a town fueled by religious energy. In addition to the much heralded 1993 visit by Pope John Paul II for World Youth Day, Denverites eagerly anticipated the visit of the Dalai Lama in the summer of 1997. Sponsored by the Colorado Friends of Tibet and the Naropa Institute in Boulder, the Dalai Lama took part in a four-day spirituality fest held in Denver and Boulder that featured other notables such as Joan Halifax and Huston Smith. The Dalai Lama gave two public talks—at Macky Auditorium in Boulder and at an interfaith ceremony at McNichols Arena.

Meanwhile, for your own immediate religious needs, plan to get out and visit some churches or synagogues. In addition to your hands-on research, read the column "How Coloradans Worship" in the Monday *Rocky Mountain News,* which features a different house of worship each week.

Also be sure to check out two of the area's more popular destinations: the Mother Cabrini Shrine and Red Rocks Park. The **Mother Cabrini Shrine,** 20189 Cabrini Boulevard in Golden, (303) 526-0758, is where pilgrims go for prayer and contemplation. The shrine is open to the public daily, and mass is celebrated each morning. Take Interstate 70 west to the

*The* Rocky Mountain News *publishes a good religion page on Saturday, listing upcoming events and special services.*

Morrison exit 259, then take U.S. Highway 40 (the frontage road) west about a mile. Also in Morrison, scenic **Red Rocks Park** is the site of an annual nondenominational Easter sunrise service that fills the 9,000-seat natural amphitheater to capacity in good weather. Take I-70 west to the Morrison exit 259, and turn south toward Morrison; watch for signs marking the entrance to Red Rocks on the right.

There are also several houses of worship worth a visit (see our Tours and Attractions chapter) for their historical and architectural value.

This brief chapter is merely an overview of the religious scene in the metro area. It would not be practical to list every place of worship in Denver, nor would it be appropriate for us to suggest one rather than another. To find a specific place of worship for yourself and your family, consult the following listing of religious organizations or the yellow pages.

## RESOURCES

Catholic Archdiocese of Denver
1300 South Steele Street
(303) 722-4687 (weekdays)

Church of Jesus Christ of
Latter-Day Saints
Denver North Mission
100 Malley Drive, Northglenn
(303) 252-7192

Denver South Mission
2001 East Easter Avenue, Littleton
(303) 794-6457

Colorado Council of Churches
3690 Cherry Creek South Drive
(303) 825-4910

Colorado Muslim Society
2071 South Parker Road, Aurora
(303) 696-9800

Denver Buddhist Temple
Tri-State Buddhist Headquarters
1947 Lawrence Street
(303) 295-1844

Episcopal Church Center of Colorado
1300 Washington Street
(303) 837-1173

Fifth District of the African Methodist
Episcopal Churches of Colorado/
Shorter Church
3100 Richard Allen Court
(303) 320-1712

The Greek Orthodox Cathedral
of the Assumption
4610 East Alameda Avenue
(303) 388-9314

Mt. Gilead Baptist Church
195 South Monaco Parkway
(303) 355-0297

Presbytery of Denver
(Presbyterian Church U.S.A.)
1710 South Grant Street
(303) 777-2453

Reorganized Church of Jesus Christ of
Latter-Day Saints
Denver Stake & Regional Office
9501 Lou Drive, Thornton
(303) 426-5900

Rocky Mountain Conference United
Church of Christ
1140 West Fifth Avenue
(303) 984-9118

Rocky Mountain Synod/Evangelical
Lutheran Church in America
455 Sherman Street
(303) 777-6700

CLOSE-UP

# Quiet Time

One of the most peaceful and powerful services in Denver is Taize (pronounced TEZZ-ay), a communal meditation hour for people of almost any faith. Held on the second Sunday of the month at Calvary Baptist Church, 6500 East Girard Avenue, (303) 757-8421, the service has no liturgy, no sermon, no apparent plan. It is held by candlelight and involves meditation and music. A how-to sheet helps first-timers with breathing and meditation. People drive from across town to attend this monthly service.

*People of all faiths walk the labyrinth during Taize.* THE DENVER POST/MATTHEW STAVER

Rocky Mountain United Methodist Conference
**2200 South University Boulevard**
(303) 733-3736

**Synagogue Council of Greater Denver**
P.O. Box 102732, Denver, CO 80250
(303) 759-8485

## ADDITIONAL RESOURCES

*Faith on the Frontier,* a book compiled by the Colorado Council of Churches in 1976, was used as the source for much of the historical data in this chapter. *Denver: The City Beautiful* by Thomas J. Noel and Barbara S. Norgren (Historic Denver Inc.) contains a brief section on Greater Denver church architecture and is a wonderful resource for anyone interested in Denver's architectural history.

# INDEX

# ABOUT THE AUTHORS

Linda Castrone is a Colorado native, and although she has lived on both coasts and several places in between, she can't escape the lure of its mountains and prairies. Her first newspaper job (at age 4) was selling display ads door-to-door for her father's four-page southwestern Colorado weekly, the *Dove Creek Press*. She graduated from the University of Colorado's journalism school and never looked back, working as a reporter and editor in Boulder, Denver, and Charlotte, North Carolina. She now works as an assistant business editor at the *Denver Post* and lives in a suburb of Denver with her husband, Jim.

Jim Castrone came to Colorado with his family in 1965 when he was 14 years old. He spent his first three years here swearing that when he turned 18 he was going back east, going "home." Forty-one years later Colorado is an irremovable part of his life and spirit. He has explored all four corners of the state—from traveling the backstreets and cosmopolitan nightlife of Denver to driving over the wide-open eastern plains; from experiencing the one-horse, one-stoplight towns of the central western slope to elk hunting in the majestic and humbling expanse of the San Juan Mountains. One of his greatest pleasures is telling strangers in other states that he is from Colorado and watching their eyes light up.

He has been married to the coauthor of this book, Linda, since 1973, the year after he met her in a mixed-doubles bowling league. They share a home just north of Denver, two extraordinary daughters, a manic miniature schnauzer, a lifelong love of the state, and back-to-back desks in the office where this book was put together.

ABOUT THE AUTHOR

## HELP US KEEP THIS GUIDE UP TO DATE

Every effort has been made by the authors and editors to make this guide as accurate and useful as possible. However, many things can change after a guide is published—phone numbers change, facilities come under new management, etc.

We would love to hear from you concerning your experiences with this guide and how you feel it could be improved and be kept up to date. While we may not be able to respond to all comments and suggestions, we'll take them to heart and we'll also make certain to share them with the authors. Please send your comments and suggestions to the following address:

The Globe Pequot Press
Reader Response/Editorial Department
P.O. Box 480
Guilford, CT 06437

Or you may e-mail us at:

editorial@GlobePequot.com

Thanks for your input, and happy travels!